Learning iPhone Game Development with Cocos2D 3.0

Harness the power of Cocos2D to create your own stunning and engaging games for iOS

Kirill Muzykov

BIRMINGHAM - MUMBAI

Learning iPhone Game Development with Cocos2D 3.0

First published: June 2014

Production reference: 1190614

Published by Packt Publishing Ltd.
Livery Place
35 Livery Street
Birmingham B3 2PB, UK.

ISBN 978-1-78216-014-4

www.packtpub.com

Cover image by Svetlana Muzykova (svetlana.muzykova@gmail.com)

Credits

Author
Kirill Muzykov

Reviewers
Saeed Afshari
Nader Eloshaiker
Muhammad Lukman Nasaruddin
Kazuki Sakamoto
Sergio De Simone
Marcio Valenzuela

Acquisition Editor
Rebecca Youé

Content Development Editor
Azharuddin Sheikh

Technical Editors
Indrajit A. Das
Shashank Desai

Copy Editors
Sarang Chari
Janbal Dharmaraj
Deepa Nambiar
Karuna Narayanan
Alfida Paiva

Project Coordinator
Binny K. Babu

Proofreaders
Maria Gould
Ameesha Green

Game Artwork
Svetlana Muzykova

Indexer
Tejal Soni

Production Coordinator
Kyle Albuquerque

Cover Work
Kyle Albuquerque

About the Author

Kirill Muzykov has been passionate about programming since the age of six, when he wrote his first line of code in BASIC. After graduating from university, he worked for a couple of years in a software development company, but then decided he wanted to be in charge and founded a new company with two of his colleagues.

It took several years to grow the company from a small team consisting of cofounders to one of the leading companies in the region. However, after almost six years and dozens of completed projects for clients, he tried game development and fell in love with it. A few years ago, he made a big turn in his career and started working as an independent game developer.

In his free time, he loves to play games and watch Simpsons and Futurama. You can find his blog and forum for this book at `www.kirillmuzykov.com`.

I would like to thank my wife, Svetlana, who always believed in me. With her support, it was much easier to write this book. Also, she created all the art for this book and saved you from the nightmares that you would definitely have had if you would have seen my drawings.

I would like to thank both our families for their constant support and patience. Thanks to all my friends; without them I wouldn't become the person I am.

Also, thanks to the reviewers of this book. The issues you found, as well as your ideas and suggestions, definitely made this book better.

Finally, I want to thank all the people who contributed to Cocos2D. Without them, writing this book simply wouldn't be possible. Special thanks to Ricardo Quesada for creating Cocos2D for iPhone and to Lars Birkemose for leading it forward!

About the Reviewers

Saeed Afshari is an independent game developer based in Luxembourg. He is focused on developing mobile games for the iOS and Android platforms under the brand Neat Games. Previously, he created the open source XNA-based Neat Game Engine, which is a library on top of the XNA framework that contains features such as console and scripting, geometry helpers and polygon collision detection, menus and UI, Kinect for Windows support, and so on. He also created the 2.5D graphics engine, Sectors, as well as several other open source XNA-based projects.

Apart from independent game development, he works as the game developer on the European Commission project, LiveCity, which deals with long distance multiplayer gaming on multitouch tables. Currently employed by the University of Luxembourg, his research projects deal with interaction with mobile games, virtual-reality head mounted displays, and behavior change through serious gaming.

In 2013, he became interested in Cocos2D due to the fact that it is a robust, free, multiplatform game engine. Since then he has been actively using Cocos2d-x in his mobile projects and has published several games using Cocos2d-x on the iTunes App Store and Google Play Store.

Nader Eloshaiker is an electrical engineer in computer systems. His first involvement with technology was at the beginning of high school when he built and sold 8-bit audio digitizers connected via parallel ports for the Commodore Amiga 500.

He became deeply involved in the home upgrade consumer market, always finding employment relating to computers and electronics.

At the advent of web-hosted databases for retail websites, he worked with Mark Cavallo of AEON Graphics developing high-end e-commerce websites. Since then he has been involved in a number of creative and advanced web projects with Mark.

For most of Nader's professional career, he has worked at one of the largest automotive manufactures in the world, based in Australia, managing a global engineering design releasing system.

During this time, he was also a part-time lecturer at Swinburne University of Technology. His subjects included Object-oriented Software Design, Java Development, Web Development, Server Side Web Development, and User Interface Design. He also taught and was the convener for a Master's subject in Internet Networking Infrastructure.

Nader has open source applications hosted with GitHub titled Teamcenter Engineering Admin View, used to manage system security and workflow configuration for Siemens data management software. He has also developed BigZip; a free Java-based WinZip equivalent with an intuitive user interface that was ahead of its time.

Nader's current project is developing an original iPhone game with Mark Cavallo. The last five years have seen him develop a vast wealth of knowledge with Cocos2D and the Apple iOS. This is an exciting direction for Nader and one he will continue to expand upon with his new company, Rotate Gears.

I would like to personally thank my loving and incredibly smart wife Hanaa as well as my adorable one-year old son Zain, both of whom have been very patient with me while I spend a lot of time researching Cocos2D and Apple's API so that I can develop my game. I would like to also acknowledge Mark Cavallo who is my partner at Rotate Gears; his expertise as an artist and intuitive knowledge in game design has injected some amazing creativity into the game. Finally, I would like to thank my beautiful five-year old daughter, Raya, who has been the source of my inspiration to develop a game. I hope that when this game is released, I will be able to spend more time at home and watch her grow into a woman.

Kazuki Sakamoto is a software engineer, quite experienced in embedded systems, UNIX kernel, device drivers, game consoles, web applications, and iOS/Android mobile game applications; including Cocos2D. Actually, he is one of the contributors of Cocos2D for iPhone and Cocos2d-x.

His expertise is also further confirmed through his book, *Pro Multithreading and Memory Management for iOS and OS X: with ARC, Grand Central Dispatch, and Blocks (Professional Apress)*.

You can follow him on Twitter `@splhack`.

Sergio De Simone has been working as a software engineer for over fifteen years across a range of different technologies and companies, including different work environments such as Siemens, HP, and also small startups. Currently, his focus is on development for mobile platforms and related technologies. He tries to be a successful iOS independent developer and is always on the lookout for challenging and new endeavors as a consultant. He is also a part of the InfoQ editorial team.

He is based in Barcelona and can be reached at `labs@freescapes.org`. You can have a look at his work at `http://labs.freescapes.org`.

Marcio Valenzuela is a biochemist who has studied programming as a hobby for over 12 years. He is perseverant, autodidactic, and is always looking into the latest technologies. Marcio started by picking up ASP back in the early 90s as a chief web developer for a consulting firm that developed web applications for private companies. He also delved into PHP applications with a MySQL database backend. Then in 2008, he started his path down iOS and has had experience developing applications and games for the platform. His experience is mostly in business applications where there exists a cloud-based web service to interact with, and more recently in games created in Cocos2D.

Marcio is the cofounder of `activasolutions.com` and currently runs a small iOS project called `santiapps.com`, which programs for companies wishing to enter the iOS platform. He is also a forum moderator at `raywenderlich.com`.

I would like to acknowledge the time I have taken from raising my son, Santiago, to dedicate to this book. I just hope someday he follows in the programming tradition as it fosters critical skills such as problem solving and innovation, which is something we share.

---

www.PacktPub.com

Support files, eBooks, discount offers, and more

You might want to visit www.PacktPub.com for support files and downloads related to your book.

Did you know that Packt offers eBook versions of every book published, with PDF and ePub files available? You can upgrade to the eBook version at www.PacktPub.com and as a print book customer, you are entitled to a discount on the eBook copy. Get in touch with us at service@packtpub.com for more details.

At www.PacktPub.com, you can also read a collection of free technical articles, sign up for a range of free newsletters and receive exclusive discounts and offers on Packt books and eBooks.

http://PacktLib.PacktPub.com

Do you need instant solutions to your IT questions? PacktLib is Packt's online digital book library. Here, you can access, read and search across Packt's entire library of books.

Why subscribe?

- Fully searchable across every book published by Packt
- Copy and paste, print and bookmark content
- On demand and accessible via web browser

Free access for Packt account holders

If you have an account with Packt at www.PacktPub.com, you can use this to access PacktLib today and view nine entirely free books. Simply use your login credentials for immediate access.

Table of Contents

Preface

Cocos2D Swift is a popular and robust framework used to develop 2D games and applications. It is fast, easy to use, open source, and has a big and friendly community. It is free, and you can use it for commercial purposes with no restrictions.

Cocos2D can be used to create games and applications for iOS, OS X, and even Android (via Apportable). There are thousands of games in the AppStore created with this Cocos2D framework, including many bestsellers.

Cocos2D Swift is written in Objective-C and was previously named Cocos2D for iPhone. Renaming the project simply shows that Cocos2D developers are looking into the future and will continue improving the project to support all the latest Apple's innovations.

At the time of writing this book, you can only use Objective-C to create games using Cocos2D Swift, but in future, both languages will be supported. This book covers the Cocos2D API and Cocos2D concepts that will remain unchanged, independent of the language you use to write your code.

There are several ways to learn a new topic, but I think the best way to learn game development is by actually making games. In this book, we're going to take a practical approach and complete many common tasks that arise when creating games. We will work on rendering and animating sprites and text, handling user input and controlling the game, implementing game logic, adding sound effects and music, building user interface, using physics, and so on.

At the end of this book, you will know all the basics and will have some practical experience to start creating games.

What this book covers

Chapter 1, All About Cocos2D, provides basic information about game engines, additional information about Cocos2D, as well as examples of great games created with Cocos2D.

Chapter 2, Hello Cocos2D, guides you through the installation process and reviews the contents of the Cocos2D distribution package and demo projects that come with it.

Chapter 3, Cocos2D – Under the Hood, describes the architecture of the framework and its main classes. In the second part of this chapter, we will review several Cocos2D configuration options.

Chapter 4, Rendering Sprites, begins to unveil the process of game creation. In this chapter, we will add a game scene, background image, player, and enemy characters. We will review some of the main properties of Cocos2D nodes and will make them move, rotate, flip, and so on.

Chapter 5, Starting the Action, covers the process of controlling the game using states, handling touches, or using a gyroscope to get player input. At the end of this chapter, we will have a skeleton of a playable game.

Chapter 6, Rendering Text, shows you how to display score, lives, earned points, and winning and losing labels. In this chapter, we will use both True Type and Bitmap font-based labels of Cocos2D and will discuss benefits and performance considerations.

Chapter 7, Animations and Particle Systems, demonstrates the use of different animation types and shows how to use particle systems to get really cool effects such as explosion and fire.

Chapter 8, Adding Sound Effects and Music, shows how to easily add sound effects and music, switch between music tracks, and adjust audio properties.

Chapter 9, User Interface and Navigation, concentrates on creating a convenient user interface using Cocos2D controls such as buttons, the scroll view, table view, and so on. In this chapter, we will see how to create scenes that exist in most games, such as the menu scene, about scene, and so on, and how to navigate between them.

Chapter 10, Physics, shows how to use the physics engine in your game. In this chapter, we will create a playable level using the physics engine; we will review how to create physics objects, adjust their properties, detect and filter collisions, use joints, and so on.

Chapter 11, Working with Tile Maps, explains tile maps and shows the complete process of creating and using a tile map in the game.

Chapter 12, Standing Out – Integrating Game Center and In-App Purchases, covers integrating Game Center and adding In-App purchases to the game. This is a downloadable chapter and you can download this chapter from `https://www.packtpub.com/sites/default/files/downloads/0144OS_Chapter_12.pdf`.

What you need for this book

To run the code listed in this book, you will need the following:

- A Mac computer running OS X 10.8.4 (Mountain Lion) or a higher version
- Xcode 5.1 or a higher version

To test the code on your device, you must be enrolled as an iPhone developer on the Apple iOS Developer program. However, you can test all the code in the book on the simulator, except the small part where we use gyroscope to control the game in *Chapter 5, Starting the Action*, and to test In-App purchases covered in *Chapter 12, Standing Out – Integrating Game Center and In-App Purchases*.

Sample game art, sound, music, and all the other required assets are included in the book's supporting files, which you can download for free at the Packt website.

Who this book is for

This book is for anyone who wants to start making games. No previous experience in game development or working with previous versions of Cocos2D or any other game engine is required.

You should have at least basic Objective-C knowledge, as all the code in this book as well as the Cocos2D-iPhone framework itself is written in Objective-C. You don't have to be an Objective-C expert, but you should at least know how to create class, add an instance variable and property, call a method, and be familiar with classes such as `NSString` or `NSArray`.

Sections

In this book, you will find several headings that appear frequently.

To give clear instructions of how to complete a procedure or task, we use:

Time for action – heading

1. Action 1
2. Action 2
3. Action 3

Instructions often need some extra explanation so that they make sense, so they are followed with:

What just happened?

This heading explains the working of tasks or instructions that you have just completed.

You will also find some other learning aids in the book, including:

Pop quiz – heading

These are short multiple-choice questions intended to help you test your own understanding.

Have a go hero – heading

These practical challenges give you ideas for experimenting with what you have learned.

You will also find a number of styles of text that distinguish between different kinds of information. Here are some examples of these styles and an explanation of their meaning.

Code words in text, database table names, folder names, filenames, file extensions, pathnames, dummy URLs, user input, and Twitter handles are shown as follows: "Name this class `Bird` and make it a subclass of `CCSprite`."

A block of code is set as follows:

```
#import "CCSprite.h"

typedef enum BirdType
{
    BirdTypeBig,
    BirdTypeMedium,
    BirdTypeSmall
} BirdType;

@interface Bird : CCSprite

@property (nonatomic, assign) BirdType birdType;

-(instancetype)initWithBirdType:(BirdType)typeOfBird;

@end
```

When we wish to draw your attention to a particular part of a code block, the relevant lines or items are set in bold as follows:

```
@implementation GameScene
{
   Hunter *_hunter;
}
```

New terms and **important words** are shown in bold. Words that you see on the screen, in menus or dialog boxes for example, appear in the text like this: "After filling out all the fields, click on the **Next** button."

Warnings or important notes appear in a box like this.

Tips and tricks appear like this.

Reader feedback

Feedback from our readers is always welcome. Let us know what you think about this book—what you liked or may have disliked. Reader feedback is important for us to develop titles that you really get the most out of.

To send us general feedback, simply send an e-mail to `feedback@packtpub.com`, and mention the book title through the subject of your message.

If there is a topic that you have expertise in and you are interested in either writing or contributing to a book, see our author guide on `www.packtpub.com/authors`.

Customer support

Now that you are the proud owner of a Packt book, we have a number of things to help you to get the most from your purchase.

Downloading the example code

You can download the example code files for all Packt books you have purchased from your account at `http://www.packtpub.com`. If you purchased this book elsewhere, you can visit `http://www.packtpub.com/support` and register to have the files e-mailed directly to you.

Downloading the color images of this book

We also provide you a PDF file that has color images of the screenshots/diagrams used in this book. The color images will help you better understand the changes in the output. You can download this file from:

`https://www.packtpub.com/sites/default/files/downloads/0144OS_ColoredImages.pdf`

Errata

Although we have taken every care to ensure the accuracy of our content, mistakes do happen. If you find a mistake in one of our books—maybe a mistake in the text or the code—we would be grateful if you would report this to us. By doing so, you can save other readers from frustration and help us improve subsequent versions of this book. If you find any errata, please report them by visiting `http://www.packtpub.com/submit-errata`, selecting your book, clicking on the **errata submission form** link, and entering the details of your errata. Once your errata are verified, your submission will be accepted and the errata will be uploaded to our website, or added to any list of existing errata, under the Errata section of that title.

Piracy

Piracy of copyright material on the Internet is an ongoing problem across all media. At Packt, we take the protection of our copyright and licenses very seriously. If you come across any illegal copies of our works, in any form, on the Internet, please provide us with the location address or website name immediately so that we can pursue a remedy.

Please contact us at `copyright@packtpub.com` with a link to the suspected pirated material.

We appreciate your help in protecting our authors, and our ability to bring you valuable content.

Questions

You can contact us at `questions@packtpub.com` if you are having a problem with any aspect of the book, and we will do our best to address it.

1
All About Cocos2D

Before diving deep into the fun world of game development, we will spend some time (but only a little) understanding what Cocos2D is, how it can help you develop games, and why you should use it.

In this chapter, we're going to review the following points:

- What a game engine is and why you should use it
- Why you should choose Cocos2D as a game engine
- A list of games created with Cocos2D

> There are several versions of Cocos2D. The original Cocos2D is written in Python and was first released in 2008. There is also a C++ version called cocos2d-x, HTML5 version called cocos2d-HTML5, and several other versions.
>
> In this book, we're going to review the currently most popular version of Cocos2D, that is, Cocos2D Swift (previously named Cocos2D-iPhone). However, for brevity, I will just call it Cocos2D.
>
> If in future you will want to learn some other version, it will be quite easy, because all versions share the same architecture, main concepts, and a majority of functions.

Game engines

Long before the mobile-games era or even PC-gaming era, each game was created for a specific hardware. This means that if you wanted to create a game, you had to spend some time learning low-level details of hardware specification and take into account all of its characteristics, constraints, and sometimes, issues.

Then, when the game was completed and you wanted to create a different game, there was very little you could reuse from the previous games you created. We're not even speaking about porting your existing game to another platform. In this case, you just had to rewrite it almost from scratch.

But hey! We're very lucky to live in a different time. A game developer's life is much easier these days. In our time, we have a lot of different game engines at our disposal; these make our lives much easier.

So what is a game engine?

A game engine is a software framework that adds a level of abstraction between hardware, video drivers, sound drivers, and your code. Typical game engines provide the following functionalities:

- **Rendering**: This is the main function of the majority of game engines. This function helps you actually draw something on the screen without the need to write any low-level code. In addition, a game engine sets up a lot of features for you, such as initializing graphics and loading textures. For example, using a modern game engine, you can draw a player character on screen with 2-3 lines of code compared to 30-50 lines of code if you're using OpenGL ES 2.0 directly. In addition to static drawing, game engines provide the ability to animate, scale, rotate, and do many other useful things just by changing an object property.
- **User input**: There might be a few great games I don't know about, where you don't have to do anything and don't control the game flow in any way. You just watch what happens on the screen and enjoy (if you know of such games, let me know!). All the recent popular games take some kind of user input (cutting the rope with a finger swipe, touching to activate jetpack, and so on). A game engine lets you get that user input in a convenient manner and respond to it in the game.

- **Sound**: Games with sound are so much better! Adding the right sound effects and music can turn a mediocre game into a real gem. Again, game engines come to the rescue and let you play sound effects and background music with only a few lines of code.

Some game engines provide additional functionalities such as physics engine, collision detection, scripting, artificial intelligence, networking and multiplayer support, and localization support. However, many great games were created only using the three functionalities mentioned earlier.

So what is this all about?

First, it is nice to know that you're lucky to live in a time when you can take a game engine and concentrate on making great games instead of spending time on learning hardware specification. So, you have no excuses to not start creating games right now!

Second, Cocos2D is a game engine, so it is a good idea to get a basic understanding of a game engine, its purpose, and its main functions.

Third, many developers including myself love to reinvent the wheel. If you're just beginning game development and considering whether you should invest your time in learning a game engine and using it, or learning low-level features such as OpenGL and possibly creating your own game engine with blackjack, I strongly advise you to start with a game engine such as Cocos2D.

You will learn a lot of game development concepts, and more importantly, you will be able to actually make games. After releasing your first game, you will get invaluable experience, and later, if you decide to dive deeper into low-level details, you will find it much easier after working with a game engine.

Also, it is nice to know that Cocos2D is based on OpenGL ES 2.0 and won't constrain you in any way. You will be able to write low-level code where you think it is required, but still leave all the routine work to Cocos2D.

Why Cocos2D?

Now that we have discussed why game engines are good for you, let's have a look why you should use Cocos2D.

Cocos2D is easy

You can start creating your first game in no time. A few chapters later, you will see this yourself. Cocos2D has a very beginner-friendly learning curve, and although there is a lot you can learn about Cocos2D, you can actually start making games and learn as you go.

This is very important, as making games is not about learning advanced tools; it is about creating a fun and exciting experience for your players. You don't have to master Cocos2D to create your first game that might reach the top of the AppStore.

Cocos2D is free

Yes, Cocos2D is completely free for commercial use. You will never have to pay anything for it, and there are a bunch of extensions, utilities, tools, and frameworks that work with Cocos2D. Of course, there are other free game engines, but some of them just don't reach the required quality level, and some of them are free only until you start to earn some real money, and I'm sure you're planning to do that.

I know it is tempting to buy the new, shiny game engine, because you think that if it costs money, it is better. Well, it is not always true. It is hard to believe, but Cocos2D's quality can be compared to top-level commercial products, and you still get it for free! Even more, big companies are not only using Cocos2D, but also contributing to it!

Cocos2D is popular

Cocos2D has a huge and very responsive community. You will almost never be left alone, struggling to solve some complicated tasks. A task is either already solved and maybe even integrated in Cocos2D, or there is a third-party framework or class implementing the required functionality.

Cocos2D is open source

You can have any opinion about open source projects, but I can assure that you will be very glad to have access to full source code when things go wrong. When you just start learning Cocos2D, you will mostly make errors that are easy to spot and fix; we've all done them. However, later, when you start doing some advanced stuff, having access to the under-the-hood internals of game engine is just great!

Regarding the source code, it is well written, well-structured, and commented. You can learn a lot just from reading it. In fact, I would suggest every beginner game developer read it at some point.

Want more?

In addition to all the preceding goodies, you will get the following too:

- Physics simulation with the Chipmunk physics engine
- Visual tools for building interfaces and levels
- Porting to Android with only a few steps
- Lots of ready-to-use controls
- A lot of other features

Porting to Android has become possible due to efforts of the Apportable company (`www.apportable.com`), which is a sponsor of Cocos2D project.

They are also providing a great free tool called **SpriteBuilder**, which definitely stands out from the rest. High chances that after some time this will be the only tool you need to develop games for Cocos2D. With SpriteBuilder, you can design your scenes using GUI editor, create animations, edit physics shapes, and many more.

However, using SpriteBuilder doesn't eliminate the need to write the code and understand how Cocos2D works. This is why, I strongly believe that first you need to learn pure Cocos2D and after that it will be very easy to start using SpriteBuilder and make your life even easier.

Both SpriteBuilder and porting to Android are not covered in this book.

Games created with Cocos2D

I'm sure you are wondering if there are any great games created with Cocos2D. The answer is that there are plenty! Let's have look at some of them right now.

This is only the tip of the iceberg. We physically cannot list all the great games made using Cocos2D, as it will take up a significant part of the book.

BADLAND

BADLAND is a very atmospheric side-scroller action game with great gameplay and graphics. *BADLAND* received a lot of awards (including an award from Apple) and reached the number one place in more than 80 countries.

The game makes good use of physics and has an amazing design. *BADLAND* was developed by a two-man game studio called Frogmind. A screenshot of the game is as follows:

Feed Me Oil 2

Feed Me Oil 2 is a great mind-bending puzzle game, where you need to deliver oil to the target zone using many different devices. The game reached the top of the AppStore and was featured in many countries. Its predecessor, *Feed Me Oil*, was also a great success!

The game was developed by an independent game developer, Alexander Ilin. A screenshot of the game is as follows:

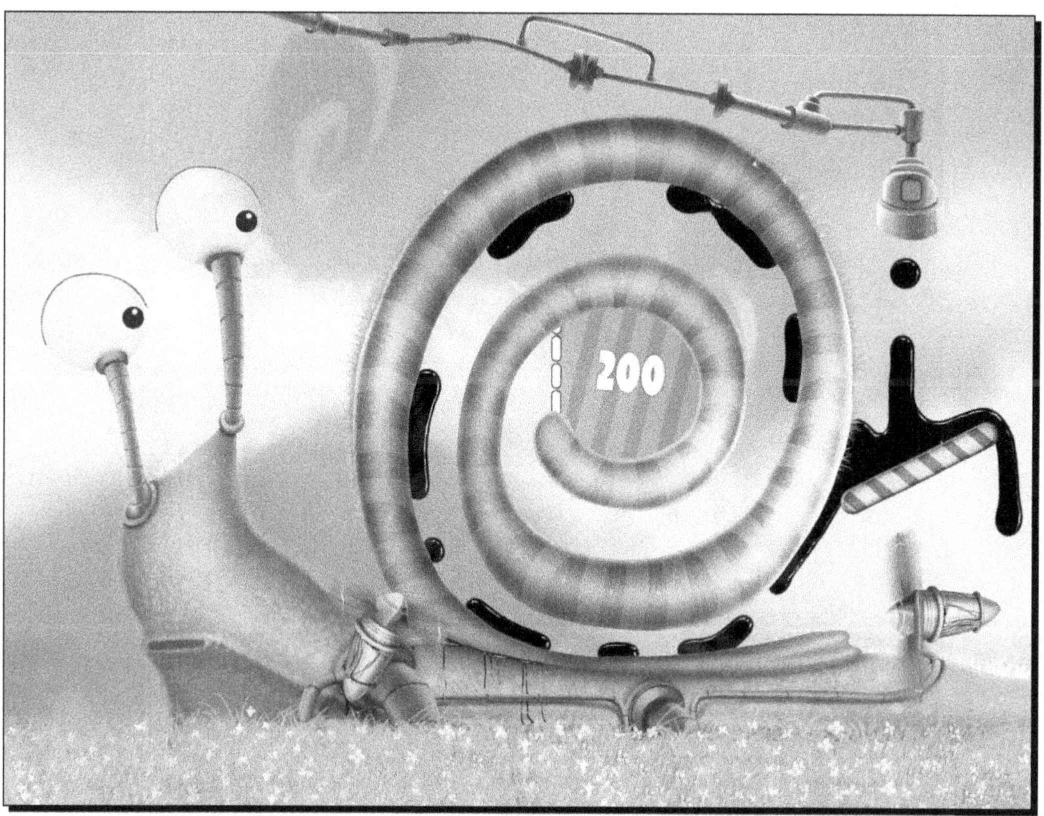

Lep's World 2

Lep's World 2 is a really cool and fun platformer game with more than 60 million downloads. The game reached the number one place in several countries and still is very popular. I think you won't be surprised to know that it was created using Cocos2D. A screenshot of the game is as follows:

Other games

The listed games here are just a small set of all the games created using Cocos2D. The games listed earlier were picked because of their quality, high ratings, and to be honest, because I like them. There are thousands of games created with Cocos2D.

If you don't believe me and want to see a huge list of Cocos2D games, please visit `http://www.cocos2d-iphone.org/games`. However, note that this is also not a full list of games, as it contains only the manually submitted games.

Summary

In this chapter, we've learned some general information about game engines and Cocos2D in particular. Don't worry if this part seems too abstract; it serves several very important purposes.

First, you should understand what benefits you get from using game engines, that is, a higher level of abstraction and faster development at the cost of less control. Don't worry; this cost is minimal with Cocos2D and in fact, is close to zero as Cocos2D is an open source project.

Also, if you were still deciding whether Cocos2D is the right way to go, this chapter should have dispelled all doubts. You've seen some examples of great and successful games developed using Cocos2D. I believe they will inspire you to create your own great and successful game.

In the next chapter, we're going to use a more practical approach. We will download and install Cocos2D and will create and run our first Cocos2D project.

2

Hello Cocos2D

We learned a bit about Cocos2D in the previous chapter, but it is now time to get our hands dirty and try it out in action. This chapter covers all the steps from installing Cocos2D to seeing your first Cocos2D game running. In addition to this, we're going to review Cocos2D distribution and will see some sample Cocos2D code in action.

In this chapter, we will complete the following tasks:

- Downloading and installing Cocos2D
- Creating and modifying our first Cocos2D project
- Reviewing the contents of Cocos2D distribution
- Running sample projects that come with Cocos2D

Starting with Xcode

Xcode is an **Integrated Development Environment** (**IDE**) created by Apple. It provides everything you need to create apps and games for iOS. In fact, you can even use Cocos2D to create apps and games for Mac OS X, but this is not covered in this book as we're going to concentrate on making games only for iOS.

We will use Xcode throughout this book for all of our projects, so if you don't have it installed yet, you should go and install it now. Downloading and installing Xcode will take some time, as it is about 2 GB; so, don't delay this and start installing it right away.

Don't worry, it won't cost you a dime. Yes, this great IDE from Apple is completely free and you can get it easily from the Mac App Store. To install Xcode, go to the Mac App Store (don't get confused with the iTunes App Store) and search for **Xcode**, or alternatively, you can just visit `https://developer.apple.com/xcode/downloads/` and click on **View on the Mac App Store**.

If you have an Xcode version prior to Xcode 5, you should update to the latest version. All samples in this book are written and tested in Xcode 5, and although you shouldn't have problems completing them using later versions of Xcode 4, it is better to update just to be on the safe side.

Integrating Cocos2D with Xcode

We'll have to perform a small setup before we can use Cocos2D in our games. This won't require much of our time or a lot of complicated actions. We only need to download the Cocos2D installer from the official website and run it. The installer will integrate Cocos2D with Xcode and add new project templates and documentation.

Time for action – downloading and installing Cocos2D

We're going to install Cocos2D in three easy steps, which are as follows:

1. Head over to `http://www.cocos2d-iphone.org/download/` and download the installer of the latest stable version of Cocos2D.

At the time of writing this book, Cocos2D Version 3.0.0 was the latest stable version and Version 3.1 was shortly to be released. However, most of the changes will not affect the code presented. They are mostly feature enhancements and performance optimizations. Also, the Cocos2D team stated that they will focus on the backwards compatibility with next releases, so you should be fine with any later version.

However, keep in mind that even with all the developers' efforts trying to maintain the backwards compatibility, it is really hard to guarantee that the next versions will be fully backwards compatible. If you have any issues with the latest version, you can use the `Chapter_02/Cocos2D+Installer+3.0.0.zip` installer that comes with this book's supporting files (which can be downloaded from `www.packtpub.com/support`). Don't worry, switching to the latest version will be easy as soon as you know all the basics, but it is better to ensure that there are no differences that cause problems when you're still learning.

2. After the download is complete, unpack the archive and you should see the `Cocos2D Installer 3.0.0.app` installer application. Run the installer by double-clicking on the file.

> At this point, you should already have Xcode installed on your computer. We're going to run the installer in the next step, and this installer will copy files to the `Xcode templates` folder as well as the document set to the library, which is kind of difficult if you don't have Xcode.

3. The installer will do everything automatically, so all you need to do is sit and wait until it completes. At the end, you should see something similar to what is shown in the following screenshot and can close the dialog by pressing the **Quit** button:

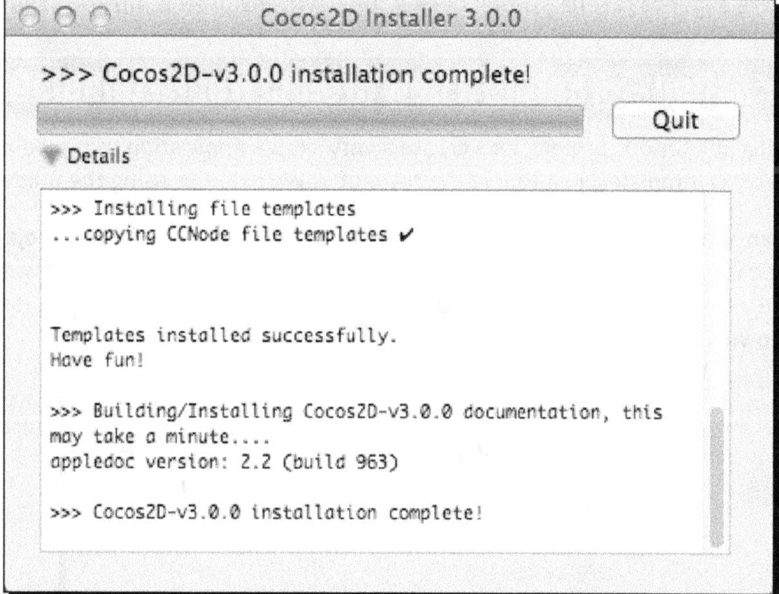

Congratulations, now we have Cocos2D installed and ready to use!

What just happened?

We now have everything we need to create Cocos2D games. Mostly this is source code of Cocos2D and source code of the libraries used by Cocos2D internally. However, the installer took care of everything, and we didn't have to copy everything manually or create Xcode templates.

If you had any issues installing Cocos2D, a good place to search for help is the Cocos2D forum, which can be found at `http://forum.cocos2d-iphone.org/`.

Creating a Hello World project

I'm sure you're eager to create a project using the newly installed templates. Let's do this!

Time for action – creating a new project from a template

Before starting any serious project, let's create a very simple application using the newly installed Cocos2D templates, just to feel the taste of it. We'll do this using the following steps:

1. Open Xcode and create a new project by navigating to **File** | **New** | **Project**. This will open the project creation dialog. In this dialog, you should see the new **cocos2d v3.x** category by navigating to **iOS** | **cocos2d v3.x** on the left of the screen. Refer to the following screenshot:

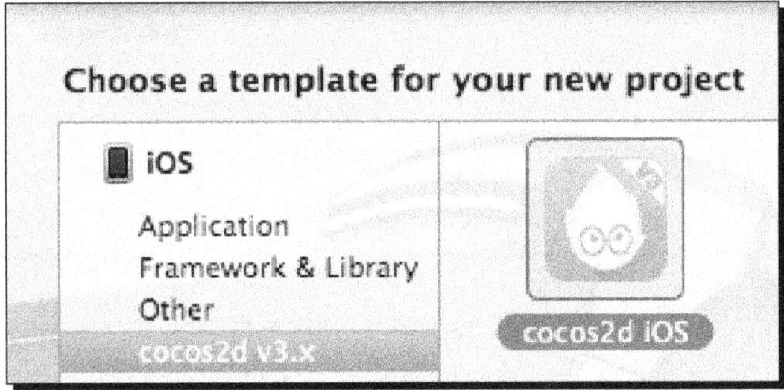

2. Go ahead and select the **cocos2d iOS** template. After this, click on the **Next** button.

3. Let's fill out the required information. Enter `HelloWorld` for the **Product Name** and fill out the **Organization Name** and the **Company Identifier** fields as you like. The following is how I filled out the information in this dialog:

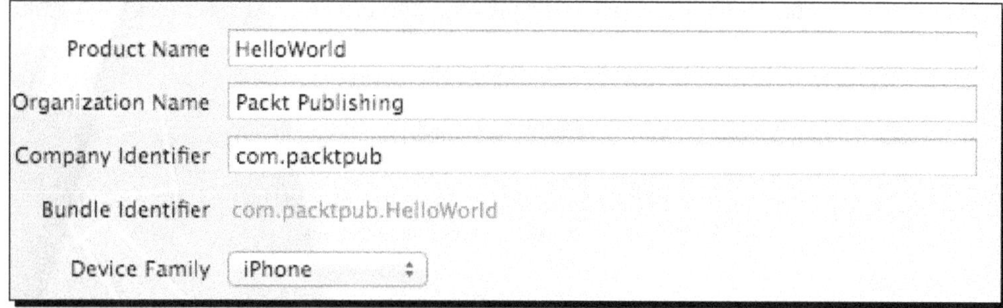

Filling out the project options

[Right now, you can enter anything in these fields, just to keep Xcode happy. However, when you want to actually publish your game in the App Store, you will need to make sure that **Bundle Identifier** is a combination of **Company Identifier** and **Product Name** is unique across the App Store.]

4. After filling out all the fields, click on the **Next** button. Save the project anywhere you like.

[It is a good idea to create a folder in `Documents` or on your desktop where you will place all your sample projects for this book. This way, you can easily find them later.]

That's it! Xcode will do the rest of the job.

What just happened?

You've just created your first project using the Cocos2D template. Using the template provided by Cocos2D is very convenient. Without this template, we'd have to create an empty iOS application, add all the required files, frameworks, and libraries, and then write the Cocos2D initialization code manually each time we want to create a new project.

We will review the contents and structure of the project created via this template later in *Chapter 3, Cocos2D – Under the Hood*. Right now, we're going to modify it a little because I'm sure you're very eager to actually write some code.

However, before writing the code, let's make sure we can run the project.

Testing your projects on a device and simulator

It is a good idea to build and run the project as often as you can, especially while you're learning. If you've just changed one line of the code and the project doesn't build anymore, crashes, or there is some kind of a new bug that you didn't notice before, most likely, there is an error in the line of code you just wrote.

Note that typical real-life projects are quite complicated and the bug you've just noticed may have been there for some time. Nevertheless, the earlier you spot it, the less code you will have to review to find the bug. A good way to spot a bug is to run the project as often as possible.

We're going to follow this tradition and run the project we've just created a few paragraphs later. Before this, let's review what options we have.

When developing for iOS, you can test your game on a simulator or on an actual device. Testing on an actual device all the time can be time consuming, as it takes time to install on the device and copy all resources. However, it is highly recommended to test your game on an actual device at least from time to time, as it is as close as you can get to the actual user's device.

Note that there are some bugs that you can catch only when running on a device. For example, if your game uses a lot of memory, it can run fine on the simulator but will crash on the device.

On the other hand, your game may run slow on the simulator, as there is no hardware acceleration, but will run smoothly on the device. So, before optimizing your game, try running it on a device. There are cases when you simply cannot make it run smoothly on the simulator while it runs great on all the supported devices.

In addition to this, there are some other restrictions when you run your game on the simulator. For example, there is no convenient way to simulate the accelerometer and gyroscope or complex multi-touch gestures on the simulator. Although there are some workarounds using third-party software, it cannot be compared to testing on the actual device, especially in dynamic games.

You can find more information about the simulator's limitations at `https://developer.apple.com/library/ios/documentation/IDEs/Conceptual/iOS_Simulator_Guide/TestingontheiOSSimulator/TestingontheiOSSimulator.html`. (short link: `http://bit.ly/1hsORkY`).

Despite all limitations, the simulator is a convenient way to test your game, especially in the early stages.

Don't worry if you don't have an iOS device or an Apple iOS Developer Program membership right now. Almost all the code in this book can be tested on the simulator. However, if you plan to actually submit your games to the App Store, it is highly recommended that you have at least one device to test everything.

> To run your projects on devices such as iPhone and iPad, you should be a member of the Apple iOS Developer Program. At the time of writing this book, it will cost you $99 a year and will also let you submit your apps to the App Store and sell your games. You can read more about the program and enroll at `https://developer.apple.com/programs/ios/`.

Time for action – running the project on the simulator

The project generated using Cocos2D already contains some code that we can see in action, so let's make sure that Xcode is targeting the simulator and run the project, before making any changes. To do this, perform the following steps:

1. Switch to Xcode and take a look at the top-left corner of the Xcode window, as shown in the following screenshot:

2. Click on the **iPhone** label marked with the black square as shown in the previous screenshot. It will open a drop-down list similar to what is shown in the following screenshot:

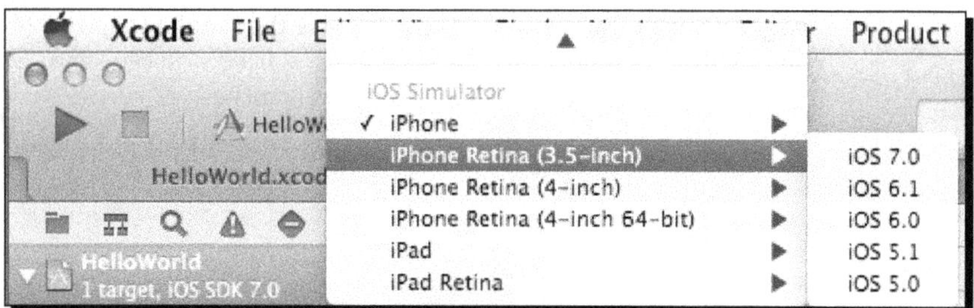

3. Here, we can see the different simulators we can run our project on. Let's select **iOS 7.1** by navigating to **iPhone Retina (4-inch)** | **iOS 7.1** and click on the **Run** button (*command* + *R*).

[If you don't see some of the simulator versions in this drop-down list, you just don't have them installed. To install additional simulators, navigate to **Xcode** | **Preferences** and select the **Downloads** tab in the opened dialog.]

It will take some time to build a project for the first time and launch the simulator. After about half a minute, depending on your hardware, you should see the Cocos2D splash screen followed by the Hello World application generated by the Cocos2D template, as shown in the following screenshot:

[The good thing is that you don't have to close the simulator and relaunch it every time. Once the simulator is started, you can keep it running and save a lot of time for the next launches.]

Personally, I find iPhone Retina, especially iPad Retina simulators screens, too big. This shouldn't be surprising as iPad with Retina display has a screen with a higher resolution than most of the modern displays, unless you're a lucky owner of the Retina monitor. To make it more convenient to work with, you can set up the scale of the simulator window. You can do this by switching to the simulator window and selecting different options by navigating to **Window** | **Scale**. You can also find many useful options in the simulator menu at the top. For example, you may need to simulate the home button press, the shake gesture, or simply rotate the simulator window to test the game in different orientations.

What just happened?

Congratulations, you've just run your first Cocos2D game. Don't worry if it feels like magic right now and you don't feel you are in control, as too much is happening behind the scenes. After all, we haven't written a single line of code yet.

However, this generated project already does a lot of useful things. We'll see this ourselves when we review the structure of the Cocos2D project in the next chapter.

I'm sure it feels great to see something on display of the simulator, but you know what, it can be even better when you make some changes to the project!

Modifying the project

We're going to create a new view from scratch and will display it instead of the view with the **Hello World** label generated by the Cocos2D template.

Time for action – creating a new scene

We will create an empty scene and display it on the screen using the following steps:

1. Switch to Xcode and create a new Objective-C class. To do this, open the Xcode menu and navigate to **File** | **New** | **File** and select **Cocoa Touch** by navigating to **iOS** | **Cocoa Touch** on the left of the screen. Then, in the list of templates, select the **Objective-C class** item and click on the **Next** button. Refer to the following screenshot:

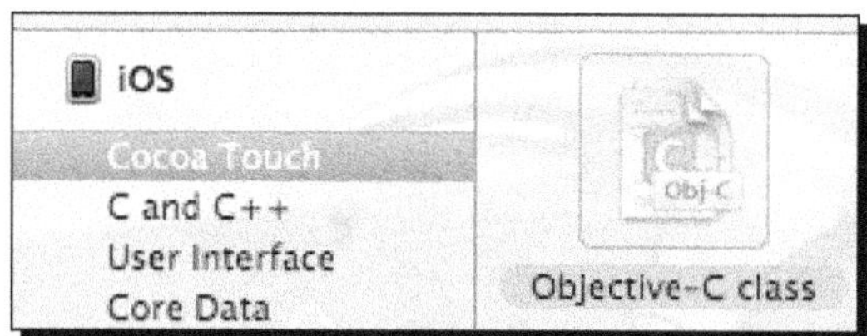

2. In the next dialog, name our new scene class `FirstScene` and make it a subclass of `CCScene`. After filling out fields in this dialog, as shown in the following screenshot, click on the **Next** button:

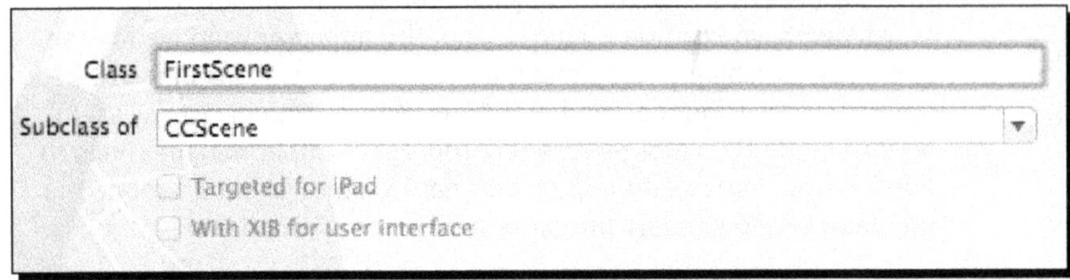

3. Click on **Create** and save the files somewhere inside the project folder.

> In this book, we will not concentrate too much on organizing the files that are stored on the disk, and for simplicity, we will store them in the root of the project folder. If you prefer organizing files using physical folders, you can create subfolders within the project folder and save files there.

4. Now that we have the scene, we need to display it. Open the `AppDelegate.m` file (it is in the `HelloWorld\Classes` group) and import the `FirstScene.h` header, at the top of the file and just below other `#import`, as follows:

```
#import "FirstScene.h"
```

5. After importing the header file, search for the `startScene` method and replace it with the following:

```
-(CCScene *)startScene
{
  return [[FirstScene alloc] init];
}
```

6. Build and run the project. You should see the Cocos2D splash screen displayed for a few seconds just like before, but then you should see a black screen instead of the default view generated by the Cocos2D template as follows:

The empty FirstScene on the screen

What just happened?

We created a new blank scene and displayed it on the screen. We'll discuss scenes and scene management in detail in the next chapter. For now, just remember that you need to place your objects in the scene to display them, as you can only pass a scene for Cocos2D to display. This is exactly what we've done in the `AppDelegate.m` file. We changed the code in the `startScene` method to display our `FirstScene` scene instead of the `IntroScene` scene generated by Cocos2D.

The black screen is exactly what we expected to see. We didn't add anything to our `FirstScene` scene, and thus, we only displayed an empty scene that is completely transparent and all we see is the black background.

As you can see, the screen is not entirely black; there are some numbers displayed at the bottom-left corner of the screen and we didn't add them. This is the debug information displayed by Cocos2D globally (not a part of any scene). We will discuss what these numbers mean later and I will show how to turn them off.

By the way, Malevich got famous for a similar painting! Of course, we're not going to rest on its laurels, and in a moment, we're going to add some objects to our layer to see them on the screen.

Time for action – displaying the world

Making a video game implies drawing on the screen. Everybody knows that! So, let's go ahead and finally draw something on the screen. We're not going to step aside from the tradition of saying hello to the world, but we're going to make it more visual.

In this part, we will display an image of the earth, and in the next part, we will welcome it using some text. Refer to the following steps:

1. First of all, we'll need an actual image to display on the screen. It is not some kind of a special image; we could use any, but I've prepared an earth image that works best for this sample. To display images in the game, we should first add them to the project so that they are packed and distributed with the game or application.

> If you haven't downloaded the supporting files for the book, it is time to do so. Visit `http://www.packtpub.com/support/`, select the title of this book from the drop-down list, and then follow the download instructions.

Go ahead and open the folder with the supporting files for the book. Find the `Chapter_02\Assets` folder. Here, you will find the following two files that we'll use:

- `earth.png`
- `earth-hd.png`

There are several ways we can add these files to our Xcode project. The simplest way is to drag-and-drop them right into Xcode. Select both files in `Finder` (hold the *command* key when clicking to select multiple files) and then drag them over to the `Resources` group in the Xcode project.

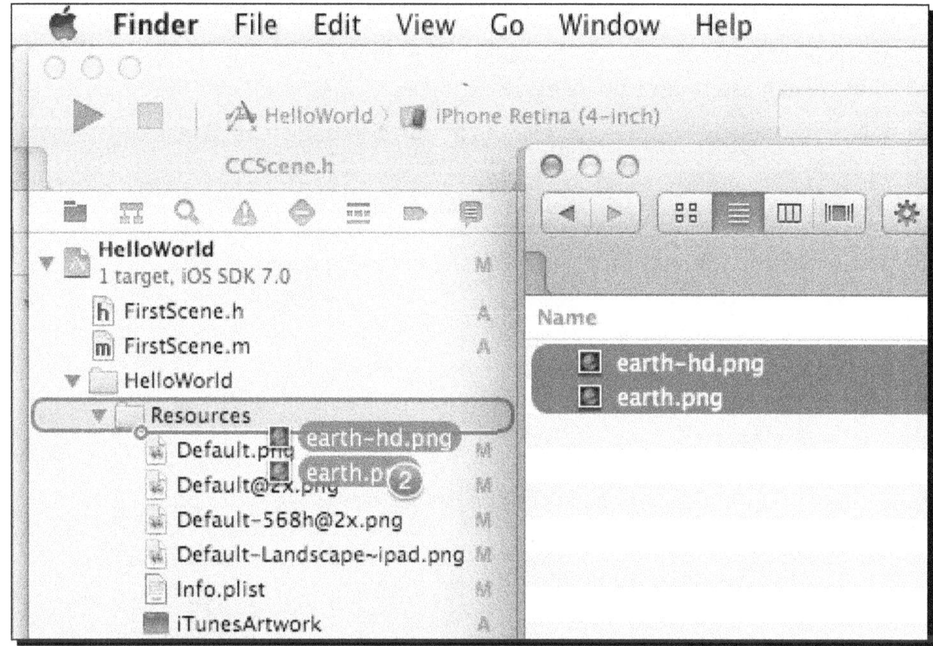

Adding images to the project by dragging them over the Resources group in Xcode

2. When you release the mouse button, Xcode will ask you a few questions about how you want to add those files to the project. Make sure that you set the options, as shown in the following screenshot, and then click on **Finish**:

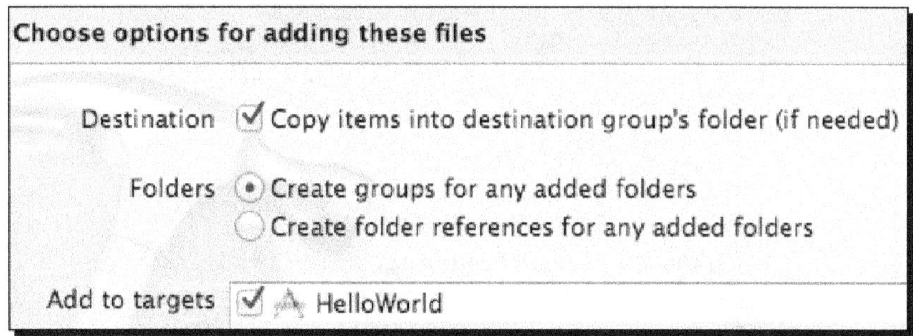

You can find information about the options to add files by visiting the following link:

`https://developer.apple.com/library/mac/recipes/xcode_help-structure_navigator/articles/Adding_an_Existing_File_or_Folder.html` (short link: `http://bit.ly/1fdJp6u`).

3. Now, when the files are added to the project, they will be bundled with the rest of the project contents and will be available on the simulator and the actual devices so that we can use them from the code.

4. Switch to the `FirstScene.m` file and import the `cocos2d.h` header file at the top, as follows:

```
#import "cocos2d.h"
```

5. After this, add the `init` method with the following code:

```
-(instancetype)init
{
    if (self = [super init])
    {
        //1
        CCSprite* earth =
          [CCSprite spriteWithImageNamed:@"earth.png"];

        //2
        CGSize winSize = [CCDirector sharedDirector].viewSize;

        //3
        earth.position = ccp(winSize.width / 2.0f,
        winSize.height / 2.0f);

        //4
        [self addChild:earth];
    }

    return self;
}
```

Downloading the example code

You can download the example code files for all Packt books you have purchased from your account at `http://www.packtpub.com`. If you purchased this book elsewhere, you can visit `http://www.packtpub.com/support` and register to have the files e-mailed directly to you.

6. Build and run the project (*command* + *R*) and you should see a lonely earth in space, as shown in the following screenshot:

What just happened?

We implemented the `init` method for our scene. It will be called when we create our scene in the `AppDelegate` class and return as a start scene in the `startScene` method.

It is a common technique of adding objects to the scene in its `init` method, this way all objects will already be in the scene before it shows up on the screen.

In our `init` method, we created a sprite with an `earth.png` image that we've added to the project before. After creating the sprite, we added it to the scene, making it appear on the screen.

Think of a sprite as another way of saying 2D image.

Now, let's analyze each line marked by comments with numbers in the `init` method using the following steps:

1. To draw sprites, Cocos2D provides a special class called `CCSprite`. In this line, we created an instance of `CCSprite` using the earth image. The `CCSprite` class loads the image from the disk into memory and prepares to draw it.
2. The `CCDirector` class is one of the cornerstone classes in Cocos2D. We will discuss it in detail in the next chapter. This time, we used it to get the size of the game view in points, which we'll discuss below. As most games are fullscreen, the size of the view is equal to the size of the screen.
3. We set the position of the sprite on the screen using the `position` property, which also uses points. The `ccp` macro is just a shorthand for `CGPointMake`, which creates a point taking the (*x*, *y*) components. We didn't hardcode coordinates; instead, we used half of the values of the width and height of the screen to position our sprite at the center of the screen. This will put it at the center of the screen on any device (iPhone 4, iPhone 5, or even iPad if we were creating a universal app).

By default, setting the sprite position will set the center of the sprite to this position. Later, we will see how you can change this using the `anchorPoint` property.

4. Finally, we add the sprite to the scene. Before this point, the sprite was just an instance of the `CCSprite` class in memory. Adding the sprite to the scene is what makes it visible, as the scene will draw all of its children.

There are a few interesting things that you might have noticed:

1. We added two image files: `earth.png` and `earth-hd.png`, but there is only one earth displayed.
2. The size of the screen is returned in some points instead of good old pixels; also, the `position` property uses points to position the sprite on the screen.

Using points and providing two images is required to support devices with different displays. If you simply take a 100 x 100 pixel image and display it on iPhone 3GS and then on iPhone 4 without scaling, it will look twice as small on iPhone 4.

This happens because iPhone 4 has the same physical size of the screen as iPhone 3GS, but has twice the resolution to that of iPhone 3GS. This means that 100 pixels on iPhone 4 take two times less physical space on the screen, just to fit double the amount of pixels in the same physical screen.

In other words, if we place the two iPhones side by side, the image on iPhone 4 will look two times smaller to our eye. Also, if we specify a position in pixels, let's say (`240, 160`), it will be at the center of iPhone 3GS, but it will be at the left-bottom corner on iPhone 4.

This is not what you usually want. To solve this, we need to provide a picture that is two times bigger to display on Retina displays and use points instead of pixels to set coordinates. Refer to the following screenshot:

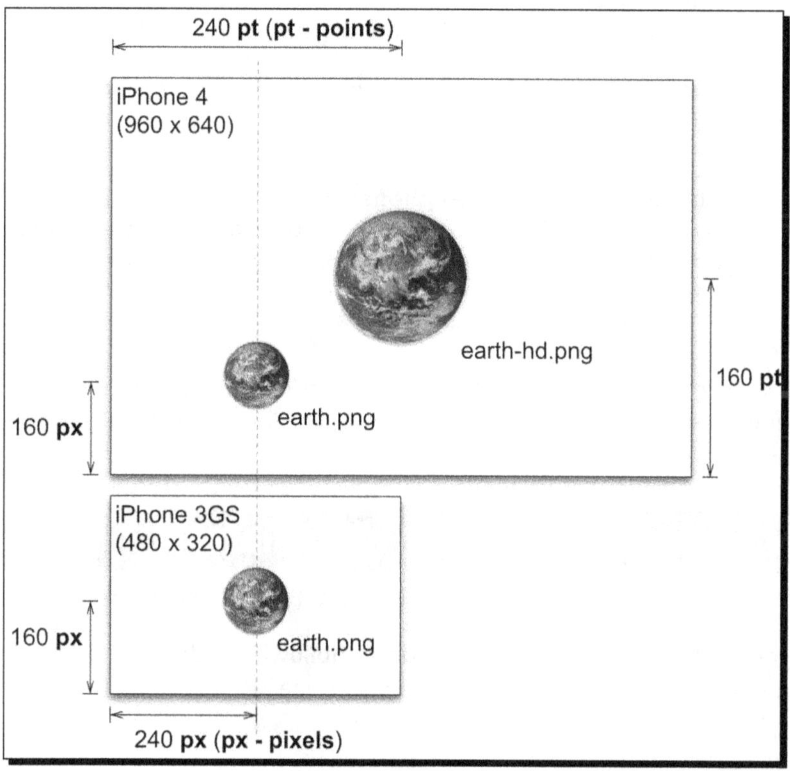

Points are logical measurement units used to unify coordinates on Retina and non-Retina displays. On old devices like iPhone 3GS, 1 point equals 1 pixel, but on new devices with Retina display like iPhone 4 or newer, 1 point equals 2 pixels. This way, you can set the coordinates and size of the object in points and it will be displayed at the same position on both Retina and non-Retina displays.

To provide separate images for Retina and non-Retina displays, Cocos2D provides several options. The first option is by using suffixes, just as we did, and the second way is by using different folders for each resolution.

With any approach, you can specify only one name of the file in the code (for example, `@"earth.png"`) and Cocos2D will automatically choose an image for the current screen type, so you don't have to detect the screen type at runtime and provide a corresponding image. However, there are differences on how you should set up your project to use one mode or another.

To separate different images using the folders approach, you have to create a folder for each screen type and place images in different folders. You should also adjust some Cocos2D configuration settings to switch to the folders mode (suffixes are used by default).

To separate different images using the suffixes approach, you have to add corresponding suffixes to all images (for example, `-hd` for Retina display).

You can also provide `earth-iphone5hd.png` if you need a specific image to be displayed on iPhone 5 or `earth-ipad.png` and `earth-ipadhd.png` to support iPad and iPad Retina. Irrespective of how many different images you specify, you can always write `earth.png` in the code and Cocos2D will automatically load the corresponding file.

As Xcode is not very "folder friendly" and previous versions of Cocos2D used only the suffixes mode (the folders mode was introduced in Cocos2D Version 3.0); we'll be using the suffixes mode in this book.

Time for action – displaying the welcome label

Now that we have a world displayed, let's welcome it! Refer to the following steps:

1. Open the `FirstScene.m` file and add the following code in the `init` method, right after the `[self addChild:earth];` line.

```
//1
CCLabelTTF* welcome =
  [CCLabelTTF labelWithString:@"Hello!"
  fontName:@"Helvetica"
  fontSize:32];

//2
welcome.position = ccp(winSize.width  / 2.0f,
  winSize.height * 0.9f);

//3
[self addChild:welcome];
```

2. Build and run the project.

You should see the **Hello!** label at the top half of the screen. Refer to the following screenshot:

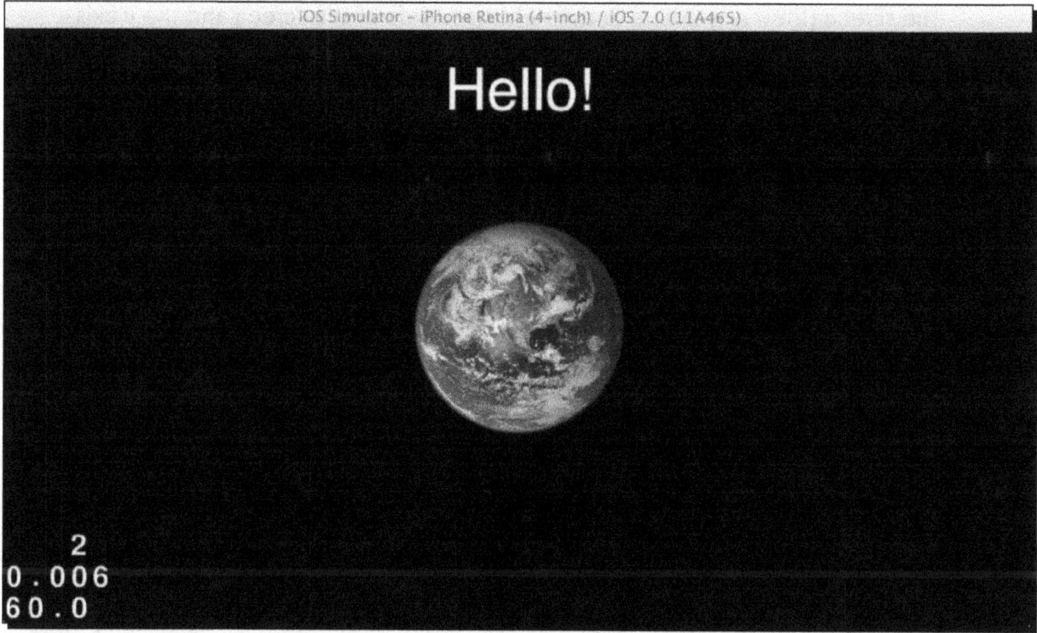

Displaying the Hello! label and the earth sprite

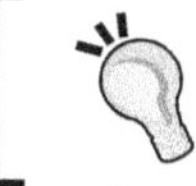

If you have any trouble with the project, you can always compare your project with the completed project in the book's supporting files. You can view the HelloWorld project in the `Chapter_02/HelloWorld` folder.

What just happened?

This is our **Hello** part from the **Hello World!**. The following is a step-by-step description of what we've done:

1. We created a label object using the `CCLabelTTF` class. It takes the text to display, the name of the font to use, and the font size in points as parameters. You can specify the system font, such as Helvetica, or add your own True Type font to the project and use it.

You can review available fonts at `http://iosfonts.com/`.

2. We positioned the label at the top of the screen. Cocos2D uses the coordinate system where the origin (**0,0**) by default is situated at the left-bottom corner of the screen (the *x* axis points to the right-hand side of the screen and the *y* axis points to the top of the screen).

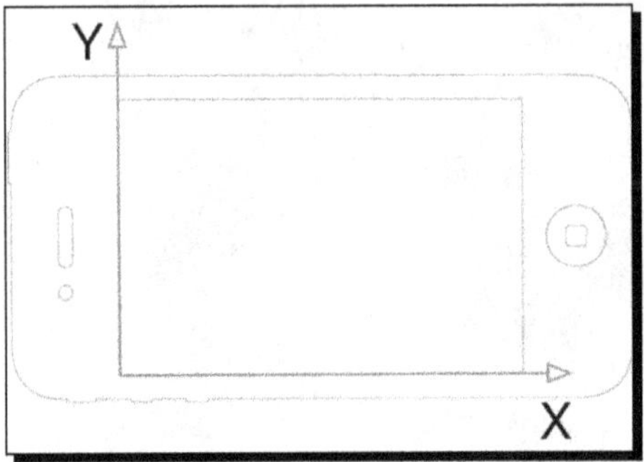

Cocos2D coordinates system

Again, we used values relative to the screen size instead of hardcoding coordinates so that the label is positioned well on all devices. This time we placed it at `0.9` height of the screen.

You've probably noticed that all numbers are explicitly specified as floats (for example, `2.0f`, `0.9f`). This is a good habit that will allow you to avoid some hard detectable errors. For example, consider the following:

```
float half = 1 / 2;
NSLog(@"%f",half);
```

If you write this, then, the output will be `0.0` and this is not what you expected. However, if you write the following code, you get an expected output of `0.5`:

```
float half = 1.0f / 2.0f;
NSLog(@"%f",half);
```

In fact, to make it work, you can just write `1.0` and `2.0` without `f` in the end, but this will make the compiler parse them as the `double` type and then convert to `float`.

3. We added a label to our scene to display it on the screen.

Have a go hero

This looks nice! We can draw images and text. In fact, some of the games consist of only this. I encourage you to play with positions of elements, font, and font size. The following is a list of things you can try:

1. Place the image of the earth at the bottom-left corner of the screen, then in the right-bottom corner.
2. Place the label at the center of the screen.
3. Change the label's font and font size.
4. Try to place them at the same position and see what is displayed on top (the image of the earth or the label).
5. In addition to changing positions, change the number of the objects on the screen. Add another earth or another label, or add more of both of them!
6. Remove the `earth-hd.png` image from the project and see what happens when you run the game on the iPhone simulator (non-Retina version), and then on the iPhone Retina simulator. This will help you to understand why you need two images for Retina and non-Retina displays.

In order to see changes, you will need to remove the application from the simulator (by clicking and holding the mouse button over the icon) and executing the **Clean** command in Xcode by navigating to **Product** | **Clean** or by pressing *shift* + *command* + *K*. If you don't do this, you might not see any changes after removing the `earth-hd.png` image. This happens because removing the file from the project doesn't remove it from the simulator, as it only copies or overwrites files. This way, without removing the app from the simulator and doing a cleanup, the `earth-hd.png` file might still be present on the simulator and will be used just as before.

Reviewing Cocos2D distribution

Previous versions of Cocos2D were distributed only in the form of archive, which you needed to download, unpack, and run the install script from the console. Now, there is an installer and this is much more convenient, especially if you have never worked with a console.

However, although the installer is convenient, it makes it impossible to review the contents of Cocos2D distribution, which previously was automatically at your disposal when you unpacked the archive.

Of course, there is still a way to review it. You can download it on the same page where you downloaded the installer (`http://www.cocos2d-iphone.org/download`), but select **Cocos2D zip archive 3.0.0** this time, or if you downloaded the book's supporting files, you can find it in the `Chapter_02/cocos2d-iphone-v3.0-distribution` folder.

Most of the items in the Cocos2D distribution are self-explanatory, but the following are a few items I should mention separately:

- `AUTHORS`: This is a list of people who contributed to the Cocos2D-iPhone project. These are the people you should thank after you make your first million on a Cocos2D game.
- `Cocos2D`: This is the Cocos2D source code. I encourage you to review it after you become familiar with Cocos2D. You don't need to keep distribution for that, as you can find this folder in any project created with the Cocos2D template (in the `Libraries/cocos2d` group).
- `cocos2d-ui`: These are the Cocos2D user interface controls. We will review them in *Chapter 9, User Interface and Navigation*. The source code is also definitely worth reviewing.
- `externals`: These are the several external libraries used by Cocos2D or with Cocos2D.
- `tests`: This folder contains code to demonstrate usage of some of the Cocos2D features and test them. It is quite useful when you want to see the usage example of some Cocos2D features.

Let's review the tests more carefully.

Time for action – running tests

There are several Xcode projects in the distribution folder and one is particularly interesting to us. It is called `cocos2d-tests-ios.xcodeproj`. We're going to open this project and run it. Refer to the following steps:

1. Go ahead and open the `cocos2d-tests-ios.xcodeproj` project in Xcode.
2. After the project is loaded, open a list of its targets, as shown in the following screenshot:

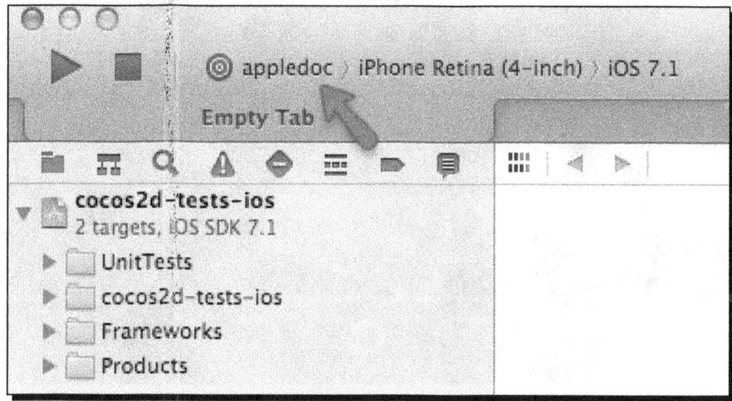

3. Select the **cocos2d-tests-ios** target to run on **iPhone Retina (4-inch)** using **iOS 7.1** (or any other simulator or even your device), as shown in the following screenshot:

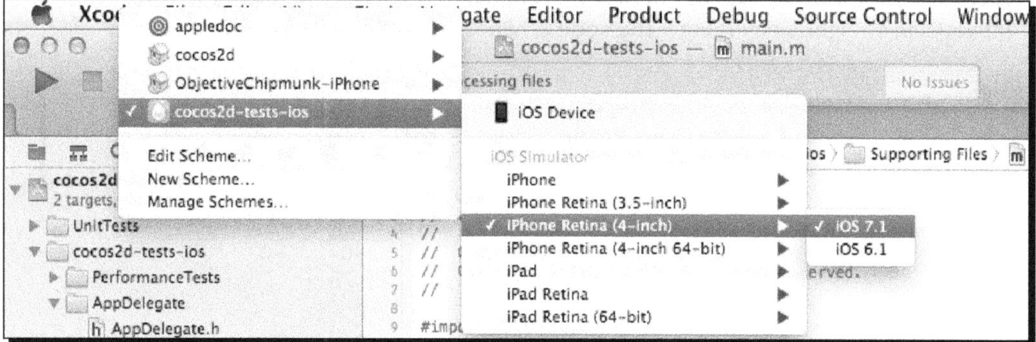

4. Now run the project. You should see a list of tests you can run. Select different tests and use arrows in the bottom corners to review different test variations.

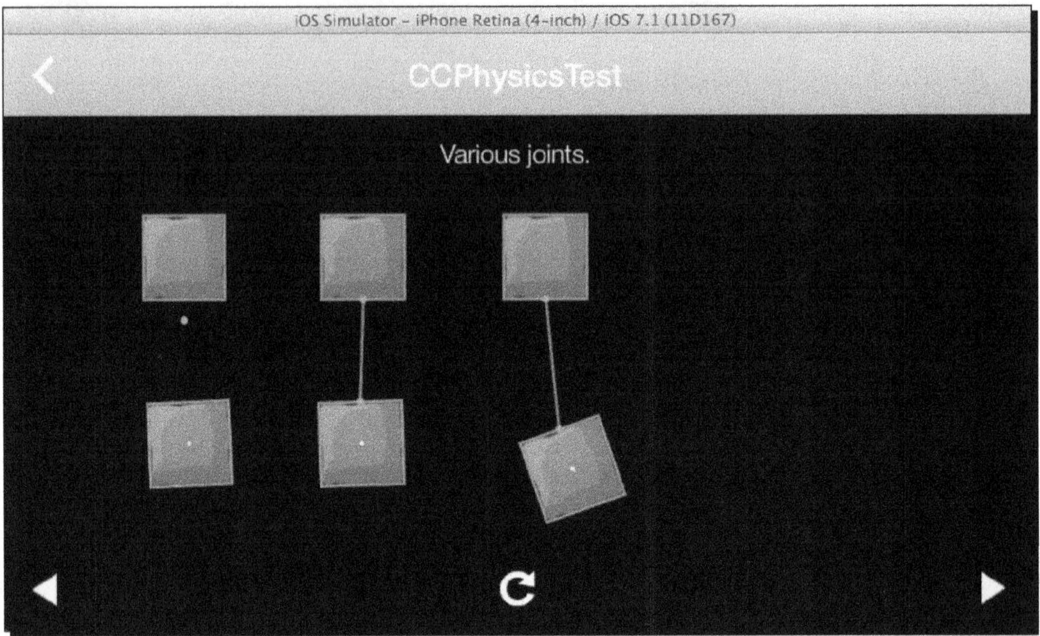

What just happened?

We just found a great source of Cocos2D sample code as well as seeing some of Cocos2D in action. You can review all tests and find something interesting. The most important part is that you can straight away review the code of what you see on the screen.

> Note that understanding the code right now might be quite hard, but after you become familiar with the basics of Cocos2D, you can return and learn some new tricks from the code of the tests.

Pop quiz – hello quiz

Q1. Which class will you use to display an image on the screen?

1. `CCLabelTTF`
2. `CCSprite`
3. `CCScene`
4. `CCDirector`

Q2. In which corner of the screen is the `ccp(0,0)` point?

1. Bottom-left
2. Bottom-right
3. Top-left
4. Top-right

Summary

In this chapter, we took a more practical approach to learning Cocos2D. We've done a few very important things: installed Cocos2D and learned how to create a simple project and then modify it to the point where you can actually write the code, experiment with it, and immediately see results.

We've learned to use two main things used in most games: sprites and text.

In the next chapter, we are going to analyze the structure of the typical Cocos2D project, learn more Cocos2D classes, and their hierarchy.

3

Cocos2D – Under the Hood

At this point, you should be a little familiar with Cocos2D. We've set everything up and even created a basic project. Before we can move to some actual game making, we have to review a few basic concepts and review how Cocos2D works under the hood. This is required so that we can concentrate on writing code in the future without huge side notes about each line of the code. After this chapter, you will have a general top-level understanding of Cocos2D concepts, main classes, and techniques and will be able to concentrate on actually using Cocos2D to solve real-world tasks.

In this chapter, we will cover the following topics:

- An overview of the Cocos2D architecture
- The main Cocos2D classes `CCNode`, `CCScene`, and `CCDirector`
- The Cocos2D initialization code and configuration options

Reviewing Cocos2D

I know that you want to start writing the code and creating games as soon as possible. If you just can't fight this feeling, then skip to *Chapter 4, Rendering Sprites*, and continue reading the book from that point. The rest of the book uses a purely practical approach.

Then, after some time or even after completing the whole book, you can return and read this skipped chapter. However, I believe that spending some time now and not skipping this chapter will help you to get the ideology of Cocos2D, understand some under-the-hood concepts and get a deeper understanding of the practical material in the rest of the book.

If you decided not to skip, then let's move on.

It is hard to review a seasoned framework, library, or a project's source code. Even if you have decades of experience in software development, when you take a first glance at a project that has evolved over several years, you don't quite understand why things are done the way they are. The answer is pretty simple—evolution.

When any project starts, its initial architecture is pretty simple and easy to understand. In most cases, when the architecture is complicated right from the start, it is a sign of a bad design. However, you then start to evolve the project, you add more and more code to support more use cases and more hardware, sometimes you have to write unclear code to fix some operating system bug, and if the person reviewing the code doesn't know about this bug, the code solving the issue might look like buggy code itself. After couple of years of iterations, your code won't be easy to understand although the main concepts and ideology can still be very clear.

Cocos2D might seem complicated at first glance, but it is only a bit complicated compared to some other open source projects out there. The code of Cocos2D is structured and maintained very well.

We're going to use an unusual approach and will spend some time imagining how we would have implemented Cocos2D from scratch if we were developing it and then the main concepts of the real Cocos2D will become crystal clear. So here we go.

Have Cocos2D your way

So, what would we do if we wanted to make a game engine like Cocos2D? Let's pretend that we're developing Cocos2D from scratch and see how we would evolve our code.

This is only an illustration of how things could happen, not a history of Cocos2D development. Many things are omitted or simplified just to show the idea behind the main Cocos2D classes. Of course, I don't know what exactly the developers had in mind while designing Cocos2D, so I'm guessing that they might have thought something similar.

Rendering on the screen and the birth of CCNode

First of all, we want to render things on the screen. After all, this is the main part of any video game.

The main elements to render are images (sprites) and text. As we want to follow an object-oriented programming pattern (after all, we're writing in Objective-C), we're going to create two classes to solve this task.

- `CCSprite`
- `CCLabelTTF`

We're not going to actually write the code of the following classes, let's just pretend that we've created these classes in some magical way, which do what we need.

> You're probably asking why did we name the class `CCLabelTTF` instead of just `CCLabel`? The reason is that there are different implementations of labels in Cocos2D, and `CCLabelTTF` is one of them. As we still want to use actual class names and don't want to introduce other kind of labels at this point to keep everything simple, we're taking the `CCLabelTTF` class that we used earlier as an example.

Nice! Now we can render sprites and labels on the screen. You've seen both of the classes in action in the previous chapter.

Both classes have common code, similar properties (position, rotation, scale, and so on), and methods (draw, add on screen, remove, and so on). Of course, we want to follow the **Don't Repeat Yourself** (**DRY**) principle.

So, it might seem a good idea to create a base class that will contain all the common code, implement all of the common methods and properties, and then inherit both sprite and label classes from that base class.

This will be a very generic class, so let's give it a suitable name and call it a **Node**. Also, as we're using the `CC` prefix for all our classes, let's name the class `CCNode`. This class will contain the common code for `CCSprite` and `CCLabelTTF`.

Looking good! Now, we can draw sprites and text on the screen and we've even done a little refactoring. What is our next step?

Organizing the game with CCScene

Most games consist of different game views. A game starts with a splash screen, then opens a menu, and then the player can start playing by opening the `GameScene` scene or visit the screens that show the high scores or about the game, and other parts of the game.

Just refresh any recently played real game in your mind; there are different views that you can open and each contains a different set of elements (sprites, text, buttons, and so on).

Our game is no different, we also want to have a menu. We want to tell players about our cool game studio in the About us screen and of course we need a game view where players can actually play our game. How can we do this with only a sprite and label objects?

Well, we can add all objects from all parts of the game to one view and then show only the elements that correspond to the current view or a game state. This will work, but it would lead us to a total mess in the code. Just imagine how many elements we will have to juggle. Also, think about the size of the source file with the code to handle every possible aspect of the game—it will be enormous and totally unmaintainable.

In most cases, each game part can be easily separated. For example, the menu doesn't need to know anything about the About us screen and vice versa. Why don't we separate them?

To do this, we'll create a `Scene` class that will contain all objects specific to the current view. Let's name it `CCScene`. We will split the game into scenes and will be able to switch between them. This way, we can better organize our code and avoid one huge unmaintainable file replacing it with several scene files, each responsible only for a part of the game.

Now, when each object is contained in the corresponding scene, we might think what if we want to move all objects in one scene at once, rotate them, or zoom in/out (scale)? Just imagine if we want a special effect, such as a scene sliding from the top, popping out from the bottom, or something even cooler. To avoid manipulating all sprites and labels one by one, we could move, rotate, or scale the scene itself and all the transformations would simply propagate to the contained sprites and labels.

It looks like the scene would benefit from inheriting from our `CCNode` class that has all of this implemented. As we're in control in our imaginary game engine, let's just do this and inherit the `CCScene` class from `CCNode`.

Children of CCNode

Our `CCScene` is a container class. It contains all those sprites and labels in the current scene. A good way to implement this in the code is to create a `children` array in the `CCScene` class where we'll hold all of the objects contained in the current scene.

Our decision to inherit `CCScene` from `CCNode` brings an interesting question. Should we move the `children` property to the parent `CCNode` class and allow `CCNode` and all of its descendant classes to have children just as the `CCScene` can? Will we benefit from it? Yes we will!

We will be able to use the `CCNode` class to create groups of objects in the scene and organize everything even better. We will be able to add child objects to sprites and labels. For example, we can add a health bar or a label with the character name as a child of a sprite. Then, when we move the sprite, the health bar and label will automatically move as they position themselves relative to the parent node, which is our sprite. We can also scale, rotate, or change other properties of the parent class and they can be propagated to the children node.

We will see many scenarios later in the book where the decision of moving the `children` array to the `CCNode` base class serves us well.

Back to real Cocos2D

I think it is becoming a bit too complicated to build our game engine in our minds, so we'll stop here. We will have to add many more classes to catch up with the real Cocos2D project anyway. However, at this point, we can already do a lot with our imaginary game engine.

Before we return to the real Cocos2D, let's take a look at our classes' diagram. The following is what we've ended up in our imaginary engine:

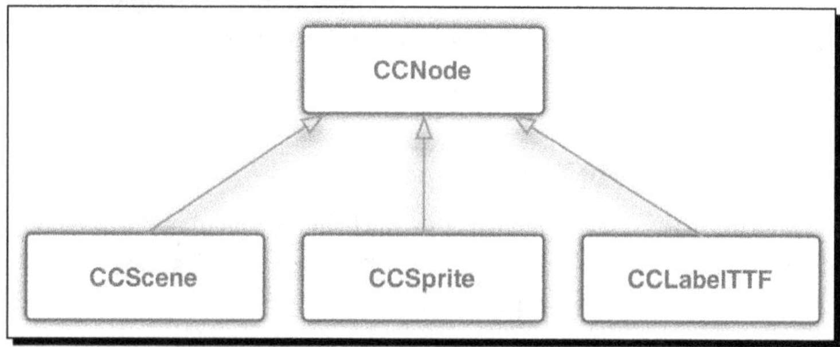

The imaginary basic version of Cocos2D

Looks pretty simple, but this is an oversimplified model of how the part of Cocos2D related to rendering and scene management can be implemented. I hope it will help you to understand how things work in the actual Cocos2D game engine.

[If you want to take a look at the list of classes in the real Cocos2D, just visit `http://www.cocos2d-iphone.org/docs/api/index.html`.]

If you open the preceding link, you will see that Cocos2D has more classes than we had in our imaginary game engine, but trust me the main concept is similar.

If we continue to improve our imaginary game engine, we'll end up with something like this. Of course, it would take a lot of time and effort. It is also much easier to understand the idea behind any framework or a library if you review its minimal implementation rather than the latest version.

I hope you've got the big picture of the Cocos2D architecture, and how everything works when it comes to actually rendering elements on the screen. There are also animations, user input handling, scene management, startup code, and many other things that we'll review later. But when you ask yourself why you need `CCScene` or why every object is inherited from `CCNode` you should have answers for those questions after reading this part of the chapter.

Cocos2D game life cycle

Now that we know more about Cocos2D, let's have a look at how this is all glued into an iOS application. After all, for an iOS operating system, our game is just a usual application, just like a clock or a calculator app.

> This part of the chapter might be hard to grasp, but don't worry if you don't understand every piece of it, just keep reading. You don't have to fully understand everything right now, but try to continue reading the book. Later, you might want to return to this part of the book and reread everything.

Reviewing the AppDelegate class

This is the starting point for all iOS applications, and this is the place where you enter the Cocos2D world. To review the contents of the `AppDelegate` class, open the `HelloWorld` Xcode project from the previous chapter.

> If you don't have the `HelloWorld` project from the previous chapter, you can find it in the book's supporting files under the `Chapter_02/HelloWorld` folder.

After the project loads, open the `AppDelegate.m` file and find the `application:didFinishLaunchingWithOptions:` method.

> If you're new to iOS development, don't worry, just think of `AppDelegate` as an entry point of the iOS application. Of course, there is a standard `main` function, which you might be looking for if you know languages such as C++, but in most cases, you never have to touch anything outside the `AppDelegate` class for an app startup code. Even the `Empty iOS application` template generates an `AppDelegate` class for you.

Let's review how a usual iOS application becomes a Cocos2D game in this method. In fact, there is not much to see, as Cocos2D takes care of everything with a single call to the `setupCocos2dWithOptions:` method.

Right now, this method has only one option passed, the `CCSetupShowDebugStats` option, and many options that have been commented out to show you. Refer to the following screenshot:

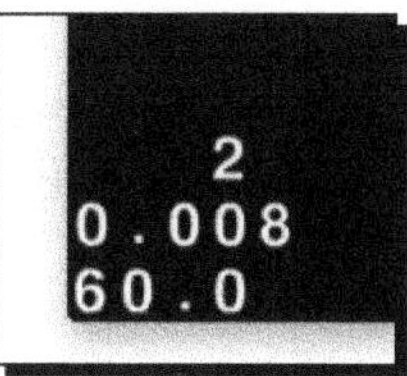

By the way, setting `CCSetupShowDebugStats` to `YES` makes Cocos2D display the debug numbers in the left-bottom corner. So, if you want to hide them, simply change it to `NO`.

There is a lot happening in that function, but there are a bunch of configuration options that we need to focus on.

Cocos2D does a lot of work under the hood and passing parameters to the `setupCocos2dWithOptions:` method is one of the places where you can configure how it does its work.

We're not going to review all the low-level details, but the following is a list of actions that take place inside the `setupCocos2dWithOptions:` method.

1. A `UIWindow` view is created just as in any iOS application.
2. Then, a `CCGLView` view is created using the options passed to the `setupCocos2dWithOptions:` method. The `CCGLView` view takes care of many things that we need to set up manually if we were using pure OpenGL ES, such as setting up the CoreAnimation layer, handling iOS touches and dispatching them to the Cocos2D responder manager for a more convenient touch handling, and so on.

We can say that Cocos2D is a single-view application; as Cocos2D applications don't use the standard view management, there is only one `UIView` and the whole game is drawn in this `UIView`. Switching between scenes is done internally by Cocos2D, by simply drawing the currently running scenes into this view.

3. Then, a `CCDirector` class is created and configured. The `CCDirector` class will be the root view controller of the application and will take care of many other tasks. It is one of the most important classes in Cocos2D and we will discuss the `CCDirector` class later.

4. The rest of the configuration options passed to the `setupCocos2dWithOptions:` method are processed. The code of the method sets up the update intervals, scaling, texture pixel format, file utils mode (suffixes versus folders), and other OpenGL-related configuration options.
5. The audio framework is initialized.
6. Finally, everything is configured and set up, added to `UIWindow` and is displayed on the screen. After this, Cocos2D takes the scene you return from the `startScene` method and displays it on the screen.

You can find the full source code of the `setupCocos2dWithOptions:` method in the `CCAppDelegate` class in the `CCAppDelegate.m` file. You can review any other method, class, or any piece of Cocos2D, as you always have its source code in your `Libraries/cocos2d` group in Xcode.

In many cases, the easiest way of finding the required file, class, or method is just pressing the *command* + *shift* + *O* combination and just typing the class name, method name, and so on. So, if you want take a quick look at the `CCAppDelegate` class, simply press this combination and type `CCAppDeleagate`.

As you can see, there are lots of things going on behind the scene. It is a good thing that you don't have to dive deep in it and try to understand all the complicated code or adjust it. Cocos2D provides several configuration options that you can simply pass to the `setupCocos2dWithOptions:` method.

Cocos2D configuration options

Let's review some of the configuration options. You won't have to change any of them for quite some time, at least during this book, but it is better to know about them. Maybe later, when you will actually need them, you will get the so-called "aha" moment and will remember that you can change these parameters. Refer to the following points:

- `CCSetupShowDebugStats` – This will enable or disable debug stats in the left-bottom corner. We'll speak about what these numbers mean in the next chapter.
- `CCSetupPixelFormat` – This is the format for the OpenGL render buffer.

Don't confuse it with the texture format (that is, the images you use in the game). Think of the `CCSetupPixelFormat` format as the format of the final rendered image, displayed on each frame on the screen.

The more bits per color component you have, the better the color precision is. The default is **RGBA8 (kEAGLColorFormatRGBA8)** that gives 8 bits per color component. The alternative is **RGB565 (kEAGLColorFormatRGB565)**, which provides five bits per red and blue, and six for green. It is faster but has a lower color precision, which can badly affect things like gradients.

RGBA8 also has an alpha channel, which can be useful in some advanced scenarios.

- `CCSetupScreenMode` – This is the mode of the screen, which can either be `CCScreenModeFlexible` or `CCScreenModeFixed`. The `CCScreenModeFlexible` mode is the default mode. In this mode, the screen size will vary in size (for example, 480 in width on iPhone 4 and 568 on iPhone 5 in the landscape mode). In the `CCScreenModeFixed` mode, the dimensions of the screen are always 568 x 384; this means that the edges of the screen might be cropped on some devices. In other words, in the `CCScreenModeFlexible` mode, the scene fills the device screen, while in `CCScreenModeFixed`, it always stays the same. This, for example, will lead to a different behavior, if you express the size or position of your elements in percentage of the screen size.
- `CCSetupScreenOrientation` – This is the screen orientation of your game. The default is landscape (`CCScreenOrientationLandscape`) if you want the game to run in the portrait mode, set it to `CCScreenOrientationPortrait`.
- `CCSetupAnimationInterval` – This is the desired framerate of your game. In most cases, you should leave this untouched, which defaults to 60 FPS.

You should always try to get your game running near 60 FPS, but setting a desired FPS to this value doesn't guarantee you that. If you make heavy calculations or many draw calls per frame, your FPS can easily drop far below 60 FPS. We will discuss framerate later in the book.

- `CCSetupFixedUpdateInterval` – This sets the fixed timestep. We will discuss this in *Chapter 10, Physics*.
- `CCSetupTabletScale2X` – This will make the iPad work in the 2x scale mode (4x for iPad Retina).
- `CCSetupDepthFormat` – This sets the depth buffer and stencil parameters. The default is zero, which means you don't use a depth buffer. Most of the time, you don't need to change this option. A few cases where you need to specify the non-zero depth format is when you're using 3D effects, drawing 3D objects, or using `CCClippingNode`.

- `CCSetupPreserveBackbuffer` – This parameter controls whether a back buffer should be retained. In most cases, you should leave this option to its default value of `NO`. Setting it to `YES` can be only useful if you need to preserve the contents of the color render buffer between frames, and even in this case, there are some other options. If you don't understand what this means, it is totally fine. There is very little chance that you will ever need to change this option.
- `CCSetupMultiSampling` – The multisampling is one of the techniques used to achieve antialiasing, which means removing jagged edges and not letting your edges turn into staircases. The following is an illustration of antialiasing:

  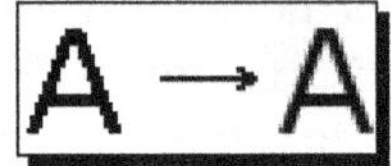

  This is done by sampling each pixel at the edge several times, each time with a slight offset (smaller than a pixel) and then using an averaged value of all samples. Of course, this comes at a price of performance, so you should only enable multisampling when you know you need it.
- `CCSetupNumberOfSamples` – This parameter is used only when multisampling is enabled. It specifies a desired number of samples to take.

Understanding all these options is quite hard, mostly because there are so many new options introduced such as multisampling, pixel format, depth format, and so on. All of these new concepts can be quite overwhelming for someone with little or no OpenGL experience.

As I've mentioned before, don't worry, you don't have to understand all of the options to make great games, but you need to know where you can configure the options in case you need it.

Further life of the game

After the code in the `AppDelegate` class, you're on your own. Cocos2D is running one of your scenes and it is up to you to decide what will happen next.

With any project, you will spend most of the time starting from this point creating the game, but it is important to know how you got here.

Before we write some code to consolidate the knowledge, let's discuss one more Cocos2D classes that we've already used but haven't discussed in detail.

Reviewing the CCDirector class

The `CCDirector` class is one of the cornerstones of Cocos2D classes. The following are some of its responsibilities:

- Initializing the OpenGL ES context
- Configuring OpenGL properties such as pixel format, depth buffer, and projection
- Managing scenes such as running, replacing, pausing, and resuming scenes
- Converting the UIKit coordinates to Cocos2D and vice versa

The difference between UIKit and Cocos2D (which uses OpenGL) coordinate systems is that in UIKit, the origin is at the top-left corner and the *y* axis extends downwards whereas in Cocos2D, the origin is at the bottom-left and the *y* axis extends upwards.

- Providing access to the current configuration, such as the current view size
- Displaying FPS stats at the left-bottom corner

There is more; the whole scene drawing is started in `CCDirector` class's `drawScene` method, so believe me that `CCDirector` is a significant part of Cocos2D.

We're not going to review every aspect of the `CCDirector` class right now. I think you're already overwhelmed with the details in this chapter and I'm sure you want to get to the code as soon as possible. However, we're going to quickly review the scene management aspect of the `CCDirector` class.

First of all, you need to know something about `CCDirector`. It is a singleton class; this means there is only one instance of it and you can access it from anywhere in the code using the class method to get an instance of `CCDirector`. You simply write `[CCDirector sharedDirector]` and then you can use any of its methods.

Singleton is a design pattern that restricts creation of more than one instance of the class. You can access it globally using a class method of the class. The Singleton pattern is quite useful when you want to have a globally accessible object. There are ongoing debates about the Singleton pattern; some consider it an antipattern and provide some arguments that have a right to live, but personally I find the Singleton pattern quite useful. The Singleton pattern is widely used in the Cocos2D source code, and we are also going to use this pattern in our code later in the book.

Now that we know how to access `CCDirector`, let's have a look at some of the methods it provides for scene management, which are as follows:

- `runWithScene:` – This method is only used to feed the first scene to `CCDirector` at the start and shouldn't be used after that. In Cocos2D v3.0, you don't even need to use it anymore, as you simply return the first scene from the `startScene` method of the `AppDelegate` class.
- `replaceScene:` – This method is used to replace the currently running scene, in other words, to switch to a different scene. The currently running scene will be deallocated.
- `pushScene:` – This is used when you don't want to remove the current scene. Instead of removing it, it will be suspended and pushed on the stack, and a new scene will be displayed. The Cocos2D documentation advises you to avoid having a big stack of pushed scenes (that is, pushing many scenes without popping). I would recommend that you avoid using the `pushScene:` method at all if you can use the `replaceScene:` method instead.
- `popScene`: This is a counterpart of the `pushScene:` method. It removes the currently running scene, pops the previously pushed scene from the stack and makes it run again.
- `popToRootScene`: This is a handy method that pops all the pushed scenes, leaving only the root scene. It is handy if you don't know or don't care how many scenes are pushed using `pushScene:` and want to close all of them to return to the root scene.

This is actually all we need to manage the scenes for now. In *Chapter 9, User Interface and Navigation*, we're going to return to this topic and review everything in more detail, but right now, this will be enough to display different scenes that we'll create shortly.

We will meet the other `CCDirector` properties later in the book.

Pop quiz – under the hood

Q1. Which is the base class for all objects displayed by Cocos2D?

1. `CCScene`
2. `CCNode`
3. `CCLabelTTF`
4. `CCSprite`

Q2. Which configuration option would you use to toggle the debug information in the bottom-left corner?

1. `CCSetupShowDebugStats`
2. `CCSetupScreenMode`
3. `CCSetupFixedUpdateInterval`
4. `CCSetupPixelFormat`

Q3. How do you specify which scene to run first in your game?

1. Use the `replaceScene:` method of the `CCDirector` class
2. Use the `pushScene:` method of the `CCDirector` class
3. Use the `popScene` method of the `CCDirector` class
4. Return this scene from the `startScene` method of the `AppDelegate` class

Summary

After reading this chapter, you should now have a general understanding of the Cocos2D architecture and some of its main classes. Also, thinking how to create a game engine like Cocos2D should give you some ideas about why things in Cocos2D might work the way they do.

I believe that it is always important to understand the idea that stands behind some technology rather than just mindlessly memorizing names of the classes and their properties. This knowledge should help you grasp more advanced concepts of Cocos2D with ease in the rest of the book and even beyond it.

Don't worry if you don't fully understand right now what happens in `AppDelegate` or some of the configuration options. It will get clearer when you will actually need to adjust something. The same can be said about the `CCDirector` class. Don't worry, you will be shown how to use it and you will fully understand its significance during the course of this book.

This is the final theoretical chapter of this book. In the next chapter, we'll start creating a game and you will see the first results on the screen of your simulator or device in no time.

4

Rendering Sprites

In this chapter, we'll start building our sample game called Cocohunt. We'll start by creating the Xcode project skeleton and adding the `GameScene` *class to the project. Then, we'll start filling the empty* `GameScene` *scene with the actual game objects. We will add the most common type of objects used in games—sprites. We'll learn their main properties, such as position and anchor point. We will make them move and will even add an animation.*

The goal of this chapter is to learn how to work with sprites and get to know their main properties. After reading this chapter, you will be able to add sprites to your games.

In this chapter, we will cover the following topics:

- Setting up the initial project
- Sprites and their main properties
- Adding sprites to the scene
- Adding sprites as a child node of another sprite
- Manipulating sprites (moving, flipping, and so on)
- Performance considerations when working with many sprites
- Creating spritesheets and using the sprite batch node to optimize performance
- Using basic animation

Creating the game project

In the next few chapters of the book, we're going to practice every new thing we learn straight away. We could create many separate mini projects, each demonstrating a single Cocos2D aspect, but this way we won't learn how to make a complete game. Instead, we're going to create a game that will demonstrate every aspect of Cocos2D that we learn.

The game we're going to make will be about hunting. Not that I'm a fan of hunting, but taking into account the material we need to cover and practically use in the game's code, a hunting game looks like the perfect candidate.

The following is a screenshot from the game we're going to develop. It will have several levels demonstrating several different aspects of Cocos2D in action:

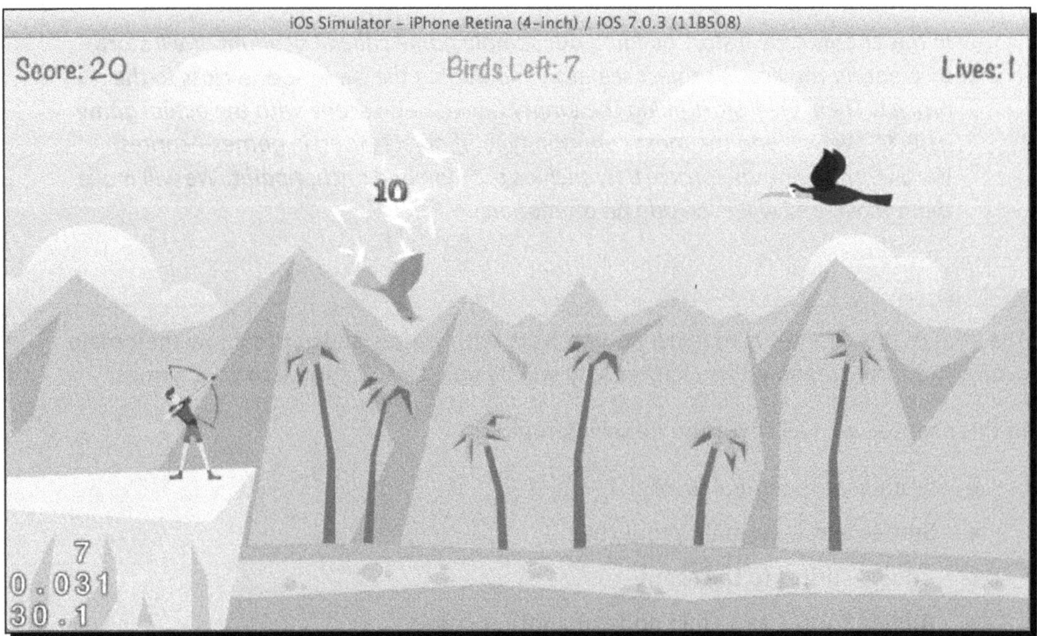

Time for action – creating the Cocohunt Xcode project

Let's start creating this game by creating a new Xcode project using the Cocos2D template, just as we did with `HelloWorld` project, using the following steps:

1. Start Xcode and navigate to **File** | **New** | **Project...** to open the project creation dialog.
2. Navigate to the **iOS** | **cocos2d v3.x** category on the left of the screen and select the **cocos2d iOS** template on the right. Click on the **Next** button.

3. In the next dialog, fill out the form as follows:
   - **Product Name**: `Cocohunt`
   - **Organization Name**: `Packt Publishing`
   - **Company Identifier**: `com.packtpub`
   - **Device Family**: `iPhone`
4. Click on the **Next** button and pick a folder where you'd like to save this project. Then, click on the **Create** button.
5. Build and run the project to make sure that everything works. After running the project, you should see the already familiar Hello World screen, so we won't show it here.

> Make sure that you select the correct simulator version to use. This project will support iPhone, iPhone Retina (3.5-inch), iPhone Retina (4-inch), and iPhone Retina (4-inch, 64-bit) simulators, or an actual iPhone 3GS or newer device running iOS 5.0 or higher.

What just happened?

Now, we have a project that we'll be working on.

The project creation part should be very similar to the process of creating the `HelloWorld` project, so let's keep the tempo and move on.

Time for action – creating GameScene

As we're going to work on this project for some time, let's keep everything clean and tidy by performing the following steps:

1. First of all, let's remove the following files as we won't need them:
   - `HelloWorldScene.h`
   - `HelloWorldScene.m`
   - `IntroScene.h`
   - `IntroScene.m`

2. We'll use groups to separate our classes. This will allow us to keep things organized. To create a group in Xcode, you should right-click on the root project folder in Xcode, `Cocohunt` in our case, and select the **New Group** menu option (*command* + *alt* + *N*). Refer to the following sceenshot:

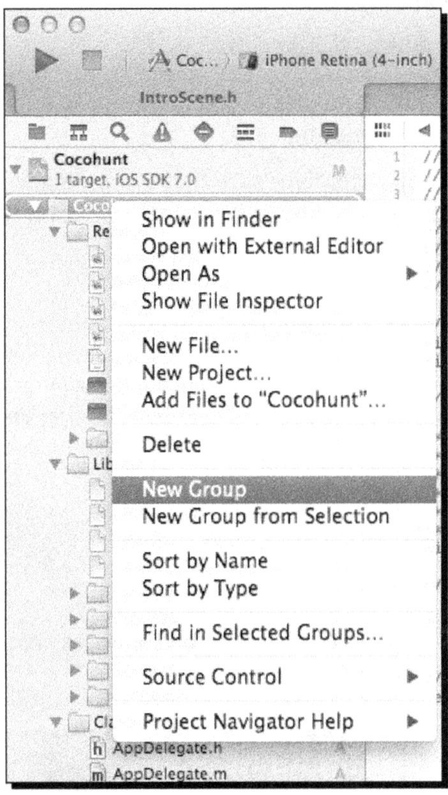

Creating a new group

3. Go ahead and create a new group and name it `Scenes`. After the group is created, let's place our first scene in it.
4. We're going to create a new **Objective-C class** called `GameScene` and make it a subclass of `CCScene`. Right-click on the `Scenes` group that we've just created and select the **New File** option.

> Right-clicking on the group and selecting **New File** instead of using **File** | **New** | **File** will place our new file in the selected group after creation.

5. Select **Cocoa Touch** category on the left of the screen and the **Objective-C class** on the right. Then click on the **Next** button.

6. In the next dialog, name the the class as `GameScene` and make it a subclass of the `CCScene` class. Then click on the **Next** button.

7. Make sure that you're in the `Cocohunt` project folder to save the file and click on the **Create** button.

You can create the `Scenes` folder while in the save dialog using **New Folder** button and save the `GameScene` class there. This way, the hierarchy of groups in Xcode will match the physical folders hierarchy on the disk. This is the way I'm going to do this so that you can easily find any file in the book's supporting file's projects.

Take this into account that if you compare your code with the source code of project that comes with the book, they might have different physical layout for the files. However, the groups and files organization within groups will be identical, so you can always just open the `Cocohunt.xcodeproj` project and review the code in Xcode.

8. This should create the `GameScene.h` and `GameScene.m` files in the `Scenes` group, as you can see in the following screenshot:

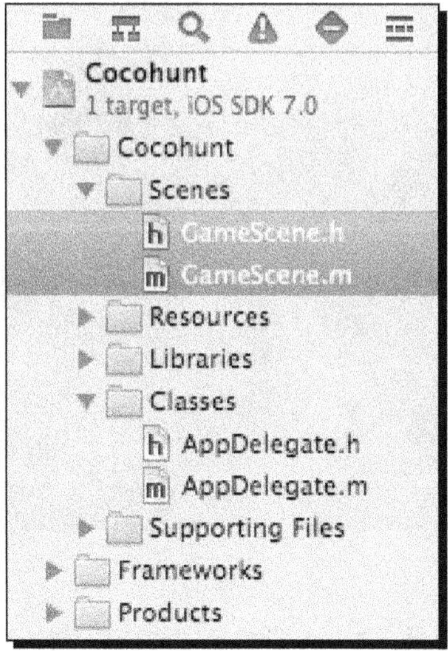

9. Now, switch to the `AppDelegate.m` file and remove the following header imports at the top:

```
#import "IntroScene.h"
#import "HelloWorldScene.h"
```

It is important to remove these `#import` directives or we will get errors as we removed the files they are referencing.

10. Import the `GameScene.h` header as follows:

```
#import "GameScene.h"
```

11. Then find the `startScene:` method and replace it with following:

```
-(CCScene *)startScene
{
  return [[GameScene alloc] init];
}
```

12. Build and run the game. After the splash screen, you should see the already familiar black screen as follows:

You can find a snapshot of the project at this point in the book's supporting files in `Chapter_04/Cocohunt_Creating_GameScene`. You can download book's supporting files from the Packt website; just visit `http://www.packtpub.com/support` and follow the instructions.

What just happened?

We've just created another project using the Cocos2D template. Most of the steps should be familiar as we have already done them in the past.

After creating the project, we removed the unneeded files generated by the Cocos2D template, just as you will do most of the time when creating a new project, since most of the time you don't need those example scenes in your project.

We're going to work on this project for some time and it is best to start organizing things well right away. This is why we've created a new group to contain our game scene files. We'll add more groups to the project later.

As a final step, we've created our `GameScene` scene and displayed it on the screen at the start of the game. This is very similar to what we did in our `HelloWorld` project, so you shouldn't have any difficulties with it.

If you do have difficulties, just compare your project with the one that comes with the book's supporting files. I will provide several snapshots of the project during each chapter so that you can compare it with yours in case of any issues.

Adding sprites to your game

A sprite is just a two-dimensional image used in the game. A sprite can represent a player character, an enemy, or even a background image. The following is a sample of a sprite:

The player character sprite

A sprite can represent a tiny player character that is moved and animated, but at the same time, a sprite can be just a static image that we use to cover the whole background. The following is an example of this:

A background sprite

As you can see, sprites can come in different shapes and sizes depending on what they represent on the screen.

In Cocos2D, a sprite is represented by the `CCSprite` class that we already used in the past when we displayed the earth image on the screen in the `HelloWorld` project. The `CCSprite` class has everything you need to load the sprite image from the disk, position it, and draw it on the screen.

Let's start by adding a background image to our game scene.

Time for action – adding the background sprite

We will start by adding a good-looking background image instead of a boring black screen by performing the following steps:

1. Open the `Cocohunt` project in Xcode if you've closed it.
2. Before we can add background sprite to our game scene, we need to add an image file with the background to our project.
3. Right-click on the `Resources` group in the Xcode Project Navigator on the left of the screen and choose the **New Group** option in the menu to create a subgroup. Call this group `Backgrounds`.

4. Open the `Chapter_04/Assets/Backgrounds` folder and drag the following files (all files in the folder) over to the `Backgrounds` group that you just created:

    - `game_scene_bg.png`
    - `game_scene_bg-hd.png`
    - `game_scene_bg-iphone5hd.png`

    Refer to the following screenshot:

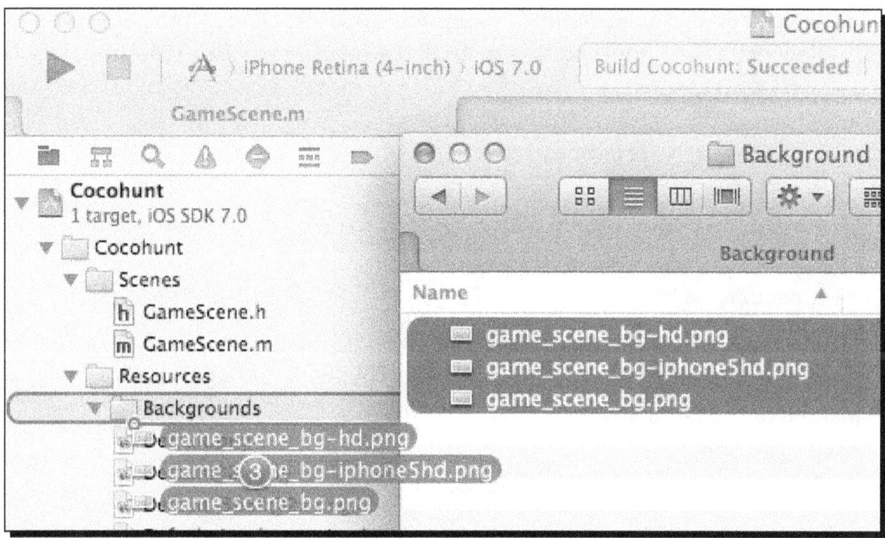

5. In the **Choose options for adding these files** dialog that appears after you release the mouse button, make sure that **Copy items into destination group's folder (if needed)** is checked and in **Add to targets** list the **Cocohunt** target is selected. Then, click on the **Finish** button. You should see all three files nicely added into `Backgrounds` group.

6. Now open the `GameScene.m` file and import the `cocos2d.h` header file at the top, right below the `#import "GameScene.h"` line as follows:

```
#import "cocos2d.h"
```

7. After this, add the following `addBackground` method between the `@implementation` and `@end` parts in the `GameScene.m` file as follows:

```
-(void)addBackground
{
    //1
    CGSize viewSize = [CCDirector sharedDirector].viewSize;

    //2
    CCSprite *background =
```

```
        [CCSprite spriteWithImageNamed:@"game_scene_bg.png"];

    //3
    background.position = ccp(viewSize.width  * 0.5f,
                              viewSize.height * 0.5f);


    //4
    [self addChild:background];
}
```

8. However, adding the `addBackground` method is not enough to get it executed. Add the following `init` method that will call the `addBackground` method:

```
-(instancetype)init
{
    if (self = [super init])
    {
        [self addBackground];
    }

    return self;
}
```

9. Build and run the game. You should see the following nice background image instead of the black screen:

GameScene with the background sprite

Looks better than the black screen, doesn't it? This clearly shows how significant sprites are in any modern game. Most of the objects on the screen are sprites!

What just happened?

As you can see, displaying a big background image wasn't any different from displaying an image of the earth in the `HelloWorld` project. All we did was add a background image to the Xcode project and then add a background sprite to the `GameScene` scene.

Let's review each step in detail.

Adding the background image to the Xcode project

You should already know how to add image files to the project and how to create groups in Xcode. We've combined both of these actions and added images into the `Resources` subgroup. In real games, you have dozens or even hundreds of sprites, so keeping all of them in one `Resources` group will lead to a total mess.

The interesting part is that this time we've added three versions of the same image. Let's briefly review each one as follows:

- The `game_scene_bg.png` file: This is the basic background image used on older devices; in our case, it is used when a game is running on the iPhone 3GS device or the iPhone simulator (non-Retina). Several years ago, before the iPhone 4 (Retina) was introduced, the `game_scene_bg.png` file would be the only file that we need to add. This is why it comes without any suffix.
- The `game_scene_bg-hd.png` file: This image is designated to iPhones with the Retina display, this means the image can be used on iPhone 4 or newer versions, including iPhones with 4-inch displays (for example, iPhone 5S).
- The `game_scene_bg-iphone5hd.png` file: This image is intended only for iPhones with 4-inch Retina display, such as iPhone 5 or newer.

Note that there is no such suffix as `-iphone5shd` or `-iphone5chd` for iPhone 5S or iPhone 5C. Instead, for all 4-inch displays, you should use the `-iphone5hd` suffix.

If you remember, we had only the `earth.png` and `earth-hd.png` images when we created the `HelloWorld` project. You are probably wondering how our `HelloWorld` project worked on iPhone Retina (4-inch) simulator without the `earth-iphone5hd.png` image?

The answer is in the way Cocos2D searches for the images. Let's review what happens when you write `[CCSprite spriteWithImageNamed:@"earth.png"]` and then execute this code on an iPhone 5 device or an iPhone Retina (4 inch) simulator in the following steps:

1. Cocos2D detects that the game is currently running on an iPhone device with 4-inch display and the corresponding suffix for that device is `-iphone5hd`. So, it adds this suffix to the original file name that you've provided and the file name becomes `earth-iphone5hd.png`.
2. Then, Cocos2D searches for this file, and if the file is found, it uses it. If the file is not found, Cocos2D tries the next most appropriate suffix, which is `-hd`, as this is still a Retina device suffix.
3. Cocos2D searches for the file named `earth-hd.png` and if it finds the file, it uses this file, even though we're running on an iPhone device with a 4-inch display.

This was the case in our `HelloWorld` project, and it is often used to provide one set of images for 3.5-inch and 4-inch displays. We'll discuss this later in the chapter.

4. If the file is not found, Cocos2D searches for the original file name that we've specified, which is `earth.png`, and if it can find this file, it uses the file with no suffix. After all, it is better than nothing.
5. If the original file with no suffix is also not found, then an error occurs and an exception is thrown.

If you're not handling this error in your code, it will mean that the game will crash at this point.

This is a simplified version of what is happening internally in Cocos2D, but it describes everything close enough to understand how images are searched.

Here is a little explanation of why it is done this way. If you're developing a game that supports both iPhone 4 (with 3.5-inch display) and iPhone 5 or a newer version (4-inch display), in most cases, you will still use the same set of sprites for both. Using separate sprites will make your game heavier (as you include two versions of each image) and you will also have to adjust your game logic and layout to support slightly different sizes of the images (for example, when you are checking collisions between them or positioning them on the screen).

Knowing that Cocos2D will fall back to the `-hd` suffix allows us to save some traffic and space on the player's disk and use the same images for the 3.5- and 4-inch displays, when appropriate, by specifying the `-hd` suffix. We will see this in action very soon, but first let's review the rest of changes we've made to the project.

Adding a background sprite to the GameScene

The only difference from the `HelloWorld` project aside using another image is that we've added the `addBackground` method and called it from the `init` method, instead of just adding the code to create a sprite straight into the `init` method.

This is done simply because adding all the code to the `init` method makes it harder to update the method in the future, and we're going to do a few more things in the `init` method.

I assume the code in the `addBackground` method looks familiar, but let's review it line by line as follows:

1. This line of code gets the size of the current view.
2. A background sprite is created using one of the `game_scene_bg*.png` images, depending on the screen size of the device or the simulator as described earlier.
3. Then the created sprite is positioned at the center of the screen.

> Don't forget that setting the sprite `position` property sets the position of the center of the sprite by default. It is easy to forget this at first.

4. Finally, the sprite is added to the scene. The scene now owns (retains) the sprite, so it won't be deallocated.

This is a typical list of actions required to add a sprite: create the sprite, set its properties, and finally add it to the scene. We'll be doing this sequence a lot of times.

Time for action – adding the player character

Now that we have added the background image, let's add our hunter character. There will be two images, as we're going to split our character in the following two halves:

- Torso
- Legs

This will allow us to rotate the torso (the upper body) when aiming. It will get clearer in a moment.

It is a good idea to group these two images into one Cocos2D node to have the ability to operate with both of them as a single game object. Also, we're going to add some code to implement the properties and behavior of our hunter character game object, so we'll need a class for it anyway.

To add the hunter to our game, we need to do the following:

1. Create a new group for our game objects so that we can separate game object classes from the rest of the classes in the project. Go ahead and create a group called `GameObjects` next to the `Scenes` group.
2. Then, right-click on the `GameObjects` group and click on the **New File...** option.
3. Create a new **Objective-C class**. Name the class `Hunter` and make it a subclass of `CCSprite`.
4. Save the file in the Xcode project folder.
5. Before we can use the images in our code, we need to add the image files of the hunter to the project. Create a subgroup in the `Resources` group and name it `Hunter`, just as we created the `Backgrounds` group earlier.
6. Open the book's supporting files available in `Chapter_04\Assets\Hunter` and drag all of the files from this folder into the `Hunter` group that we've just created.
7. Make sure that the **Copy items to destination group's folder (if needed)** option and the **Cocohunt** target in the **Add to targets** list are checked.

> All of the options mentioned above should be selected by default, but it is always a good idea to check them just to be on the safe side. Bugs that appear due to incorrect settings are hard to detect and often appear only after some time, making you wonder what recent changes lead to the bug you're experiencing right now.

8. After you've performed all the actions, you should see something like the following screenshot in your **Project Navigator** panel on the left.

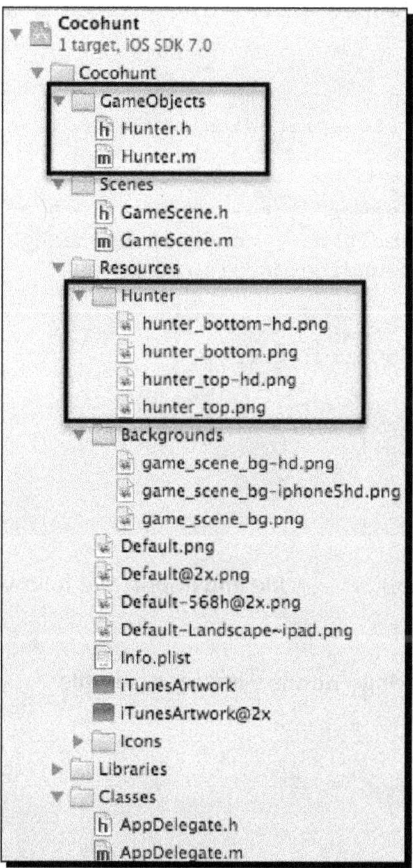

The Hunter class and images inside their corresponding groups

9. Finally, it is time to display the character on the screen. Open the `Hunter.m` file and replace its contents with the following:

```
#import "Hunter.h"

//1
#import "cocos2d.h"

@implementation Hunter
{
    //2
    CCSprite *_torso;
}

-(instancetype)init
{
    //3
```

```
        if (self = [super initWithImageNamed:@"hunter_bottom.png"])
        {
            //4
            _torso =
              [CCSprite spriteWithImageNamed:@"hunter_top.png"];

            //5
            _torso.anchorPoint = ccp(0.5f, 10.0f/44.0f);
            _torso.position = ccp(self.boundingBox.size.width/2.0f,
              self.boundingBox.size.height);

            //6
            [self addChild:_torso];
        }

      return self;
    }

    @end
```

10. Now, open the `GameScene.m` file and import the following `Hunter.h` header:

```
#import "Hunter.h"
```

11. Then, add the following `_hunter` instance variable:

```
@implementation GameScene
{
  Hunter *_hunter;
}
```

12. After this, add the following `addHunter` method below the `addBackground` method:

```
-(void)addHunter
{
    CGSize viewSize = [CCDirector sharedDirector].viewSize;

    //1
    _hunter = [[Hunter alloc] init];

    //2
    float hunterPositionX =
      viewSize.width * 0.5f - 180.0f;

    float hunterPositionY =
      viewSize.height * 0.3f;

    _hunter.position = ccp(hunterPositionX,
```

```
                                            hunterPositionY);

    //3
    [self addChild:_hunter];
}
```

13. Add a call to the `addHunter` method inside the `init` method as follows:

```
-(instancetype)init
{
    if (self = [super init])
    {
       [self addBackground];

       [self addHunter];

    }

    return self;
}

@end
```

14. Build and run the project. You should see our hunter standing on the cliff, as shown in the following screenshot:

You can find a snapshot of the project at this point in the book's supporting files in the `Chapter_04/Cocohunt_Adding_Player_Character` folder.

What just happened?

We've performed one more step towards a complete game and added the hunter character to our game scene. So that you understand it better, we will split everything that we did into several steps.

Preparations step

In this step, we created a stub class for our hunter character and added images of the hunter into the Xcode project. A separate class will allow us to gather the code related to the character in that class, implement the behavior of the hunter, and allow `GameScene` to work with our hunter as an object. Also, if you have several similar game scenes or levels, you can reuse the `Hunter` class in all of them.

Creating a class and adding resources should be something that we've done several times in the past, so we'll review different and interesting topics. Why did we split our character image into two images?

A picture is worth a thousand words they say. Well, the following is a screenshot demonstrating the benefits of having the torso separated from the legs:

Different poses of the hunter by rotating its torso

As you can see, applying a slight rotation to the torso part will allow us to show where the hunter is aiming. This will make shooting from a bow at a different angle look much more realistic compared to the hunter just standing still, aiming straight forward. However, when he shoots, the arrow will fly in a different direction.

Another thing worth mentioning is that we don't have the special images for 4-inch iPhone devices and the simulator (the `-iphone5hd` suffix). This demonstrates the technique I've mentioned before when we can have the same resource for 4 and 3.5-inch displays and thus save some space.

In most cases, you can have the same images for non-fullscreen sprites on the screen (for example, player character, enemies, buttons, and so on); you will just show a bit more of the world on wider screens.

Adding images to the hunter character

The fact that our character consists of two images isn't all that good. It makes our life a bit harder, as this means that we need two `CCSprite` objects to display both images. As this is one character after all, we'll have to write the code to make it behave like one character so that we don't end up with the situation where the legs are separated from the body.

We can create two separate `CCSprite` objects in the `GameScene` scene and manage them separately, but it is more convenient to group them into one object. This way we can work with the hunter as with one object; for example, we can set its position, add, or remove it from the scene.

A common way to group objects in Cocos2D is to add a node as a child node of the other node. For example, you can add a hand as a child sprite of the body sprite, or in our case, we can add a torso as a child node of the legs' sprite, as it sits on top of the legs, or in other words, it grows out from the legs if we can say it this way.

The reason why we put the torso as the child of the legs and not vice versa is that when we're rotating a parent node, it rotates all of the children contained in it as well and we don't want the legs to be rotated when we rotate the torso.

In many cases, you may want to group several objects into one. For example, you might want your character to have different hats, weapons, or even body parts. Of course, you can do this by drawing several different characters, but there can be many combinations, which can lead to a lot of work for the designer and will take a lot of space to store. We will discuss this in more detail in *Chapter 7, Animations and Particle Systems*.

Since we're not only grouping the objects but are also going to write some code to manage these objects (hunter's methods and properties), it is a good idea to make our class inherit from `CCSprite` and put all the code into this class. This is exactly what we've done in our code. We've inherited our class from `CCSprite` to extend it and make it a more specific `Hunter` class.

Let's review each code block marked by the comment with the number in the `Hunter.m` file as follows:

1. The first thing we did was import the `cocos2d.h` header file so we can use the different Cocos2D classes.
2. Next, we added an instance variable to hold the reference to the torso sprite, as we're going to manipulate it later.
3. The `init` method uses the `super` class's `initWithImageNamed:` method to initialize itself with the legs' image. This current sprite will be the parent to the torso sprite, but as we've inherited the `CCSprite` class, we can also use it to display the legs' image. This way the `Hunter` class itself will be a container for the torso and will display the legs. Two birds with one rock!
4. A separate sprite for the torso was created and stored in the `_torso` instance variable.
5. After the sprite was created, its anchor point and position are changed.

When we set the position of the child node, such as the torso, we set the position relative to its parent node. There is a good figure demonstrating the coordinates system a few pages later.

6. Finally, the torso was added as the child to the current legs' sprite.

There is a tricky point in the code block marked with the number `5`. Here, we calculated the position and the anchor point. Let's review it more carefully starting with the anchor point part.

An anchor point is the point around which all transformations and positioning manipulations are made. When we set the position of the sprite and any other node, we actually move the sprite using the anchor point as the pivot for the sprite. When we rotate the object, it rotates around the anchor point. Remember I mentioned that when we set the position for the sprite, we actually set where the center of the sprite will be by default. This is because the anchor point is set to the center of the sprite by default.

This is only true for sprites and shouldn't be assumed for scenes and nodes.

Imagine a sheet of paper that you pierced with a needle. When you move this needle, a sheet of paper follows. When you pin this needle on the board, you pin the whole sheet of paper in the position of the needle, although it might not be at the center of the sheet of paper. When you rotate this sheet of paper, it rotates around the needle. This is what an anchor point is.

In Cocos2D, the anchor point is normalized; this means that it goes from **0** to **1** for each side of the image and **(0,0)** is the left-bottom corner whereas **(1,1)** is the top-right corner. It doesn't depend on the actual size of the image; it is always **0** to **1**.

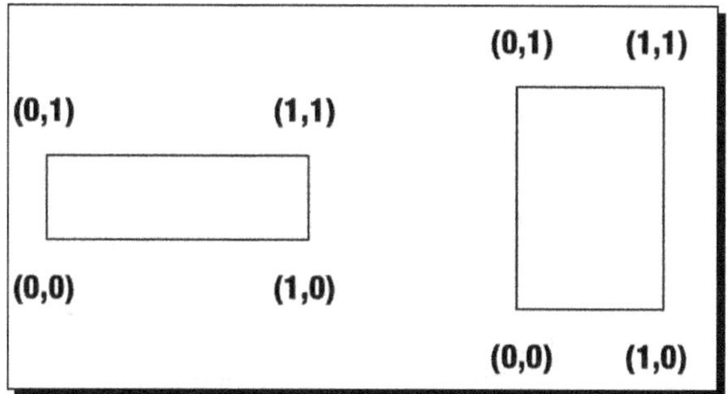

Anchor point values independent of the image size

Another important note is that you can set an anchor point out of the **(0,0)** – **(1,1)** range; for example, you can set it to (-1,-1), which is outside the sprite rectangle. This will make the sprite rotate around that point outside itself. It might be quite useful when you want to rotate one object around another object; you just set the anchor point of the object to be rotated to the center of the object it should rotate around and then it will rotate around this object.

> If you do this, don't forget that the anchor point is still in the local sprite coordinates, and you should first find the position of other node in the local coordinates of current sprite.

Back to our hunter. We're going to change its default anchor point, as we don't want to rotate around the center of the torso. We want to rotate around the point that is situated around the waist as is demonstrated in the following screenshot:

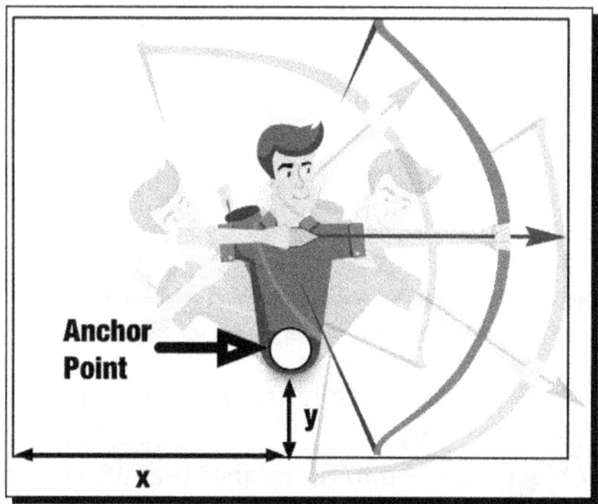

Rotating torso around an anchor point instead of the center of the image

You can clearly see that `x=0.5` (as it is the center of the image's width) and `y` is about `10` points from the bottom edge of the image, while the whole image is about `44` points high, which gives us `y=10/44`. Now this line of code that we added to the `init` method of the `Hunter` class should be much clearer:

```
_torso.anchorPoint = ccp(0.5f, 10.0f/44.0f);
```

The remaining changes that we've made to the `Hunter.m` file set the position of the torso. This should be quite simple when we remember that we set the position using the anchor point. We want our hunter's anchor point (which is in the middle of the waist, as shown earlier) to be at the middle of the top edge of the legs' image.

Instead of hardcoding the coordinates, we used the `boundingBox` property. This property gives us the size of the legs' sprite rectangle. We can use it to calculate the position of the middle point of the top edge of the legs' image.

Don't forget that we set the position relative to the legs' image sprite because the torso is the child node of the legs. And as you remember, each node is positioned relatively to its parent and not relative to the global origin. This means that from the torso's point of view, the bottom-left corner of the legs' image is **(0,0)**, and we want our anchor point to be positioned at (width / 2.0, height). Refer to the following screenshot:

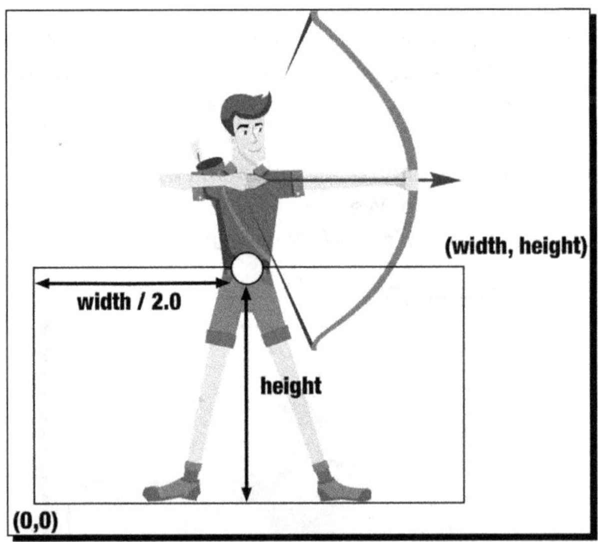

Placing the torso image relative to the parent sprite using an anchor point

It might seem strange that we placed our child sprite outside of the parent, but this is totally normal in the Cocos2D world. The only downside of this approach is that when we want to move the whole hunter object, we need to remember that we should position the center of the legs' sprite, not the center of the whole hunter.

> This can be fixed if we change the anchor point of the legs to (0.5, 1). The anchor points (legs and torso) will then be at one point. But since we won't move the hunter after placing it we can leave everything as is.

Adding the hunter object to our game scene

As the final step, let's review the updated code in the game scene. The only thing we've done here is add our hunter object to the scene.

To do this, we imported the `Hunter.h` header file, added the `addHunter` method, and called it from the `init` method. Let's review the code in the `addHunter` method as follows:

1. We created the instance of the hunter and stored it in our instance variable.
2. We calculated the position of the hunter by calculating the *x* component relative to the screen center, instead of the left part of the screen. More on this will be explained later.
3. Finally, we added the hunter to the scene.

Again, there is a small tricky part with the *x* component of the hunter's node position. We need to calculate the position relative to the center of the screen. This allows us to place our hunter's node at the same position relative to the background on the 4-inch display as well as on older devices. If you have tested the game on different simulators, you've probably noticed that the background image differs on a 4-inch simulator and it has extra space on the sides. These outer edges of the image are cropped on 3.5-inch displays, and the central part of the background image stays the same on all devices. Refer to the following screenshot:

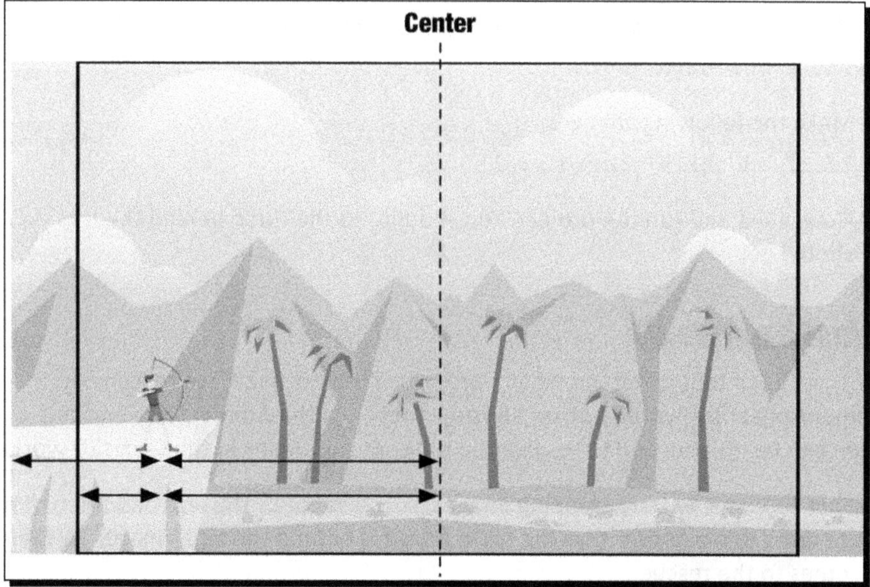

Distance from the center and left side of the screen on a 4-inch display and older devices

In the preceding image, you can see that because new 4-inch display screens are wider than older devices. We need to provide a wider background image (a little extra beyond the rectangle), but we still want to position our character on the same place in the world. So, we're calculating the distance from the center and not from the left edge of the screen.

A set of such tricks that allow you to avoid hardcoding positions and use relative values will help you position your objects on the screen much easier and avoid using a lot of `switch` and `if` conditions to calculate the position depending on the current screen size.

Time for action – fixing z-order

If you were highly attentive and have a sharp eye, you might have noticed a little issue with our hunter's legs and torso. The issue is that the torso is displayed above the belt part of the pants.

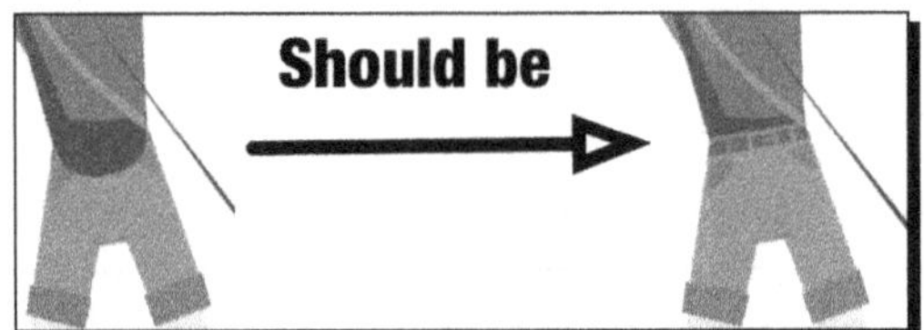

The current z-order and the correct z-order

It is hard to notice since the character is pretty small, but if you zoom in (*Ctrl* + mouse wheel,) you will be able to see the issue. Let's fix this using the following steps, and then I'll explain why this is happening:

1. Open the `Hunter.m` file to find the following line in the `init` method:

   ```
   [self addChild:_torso];
   ```

2. Make the following change:

   ```
   [self addChild:_torso z:-1];
   ```

3. Now, build and run the project. You should see the torso behind the legs, as it should be.

What just happened?

First of all, we need to understand what z-order is. With Cocos2D, we're living in a two-dimensional (2D) world, but we all know there is a third dimension, and this dimension can be quite useful to resolve the order of the things in the Cocos2D world.

Imagine that you have two overlapping images, such as that of the legs and torso of our hunter. We want to make sure that the torso image is behind the legs' image. This is when z-order comes to the rescue.

> You might wonder why the torso should be curved and behind the legs. The answer is simple. If we just cut the hunter body into two halves by a straight line and then rotate the torso part around its anchor point, we will get a gap on one side of the waist. This happens because the real body stretches, while our image does not.

Each node has an integer property called `zOrder`, which is defined all the way up the hierarchy in the `CCNode` class. Cocos2D sorts the nodes using this property and then renders them. This way all nodes (sprites, labels, and so on) with low z-order values are rendered first and those with high z-order values are rendered last, and overwrite everything that is drawn before.

Imagine you're drawing in some kind of painting program. You draw a red rectangle and then draw a blue rectangle that overlaps the red one. The overlap of two rectangles will be blue because you've drawn the blue rectangle last. This is exactly how z-order works if the red rectangle has a lower z-order than the blue one.

You might wonder how the hunter is displayed over the background when we didn't set any z-order in our `GameScene`.

Here is how. If you don't specify a value for z-order, it will be set by default to `0`, so all of our elements had the same z-order set to zero. Then, if there are two nodes with the same z-order, their order on the screen is determined by the order in which they were added. In our case, we first added the background and then the hunter; this way the hunter was on top of the background.

The z-order only works within the current parent node. It means you can only order nodes that are at the same level. That is why setting z-order of the torso to `-1` only puts it behind the parent legs' sprite and not behind the background image, which has z-order set to a default value of `0` because the background image is on another level.

> At the time of writing this chapter, there are plans to change this behavior and switch to global z-order of nodes and their child nodes. In this case, setting z-order for the torso to `-1` will put it under the background that has z-order of `0`, even though the torso sprite is a child of the legs sprite, which is on top of background. If Cocos2D switches to global z-order to make things work, you will need to assign the correct value of z-order to all nodes. For example, set background to `0`, legs to `2`, and torso to `1`.

It will get clearer when we'll use `zOrder` later in the book to order other elements.

Adding more sprites and moving them

Now that we have our hunter standing with the tense bow, we need to add some targets.

Time for action – adding birds

In this game, the hunter will hunt birds, so let's create a bird object by performing the following steps:

1. Open Xcode and create a new subgroup in the `Resources` group, next to the `Hunter` and the `Backgrounds` groups. Call this new group `Birds`.
2. Open the `Chapter_04/Assets/Birds` folder and drag all images into the new `Birds` group in Xcode. Make sure that **copy** option is checked.
3. Create a new **Objective-C class** in the `GameObjects` group. Name this class `Bird` and make it a subclass of `CCSprite`.
4. Open the `Bird.h` file and replace its contents with the following code:

```
#import "CCSprite.h"

typedef enum BirdType
{
    BirdTypeBig,
    BirdTypeMedium,
    BirdTypeSmall
} BirdType;


@interface Bird : CCSprite


@property (nonatomic, assign) BirdType birdType;

-(instancetype)initWithBirdType:(BirdType)typeOfBird;

@end
```

5. Open the `Bird.m` file and add the following implementation of the `initWithBirdType:` method listed:

```
-(instancetype)initWithBirdType:(BirdType)typeOfBird
{
    //1
    NSString *birdImageName;

    switch (typeOfBird) {
        case BirdTypeBig:
            birdImageName = @"bird_big.png";
```

```
            break;
        case BirdTypeMedium:
            birdImageName = @"bird_middle.png";
            break;
        case BirdTypeSmall:
            birdImageName = @"bird_small.png";
            break;
        default:
            CCLOG(@"Unknown bird type, using small bird!");
            birdImageName = @"bird_small.png";
            break;
    }

    //2
    if (self = [super initWithImageNamed:birdImageName])
    {
        //3
        self.birdType = typeOfBird;
    }

    return self;
}
```

6. Open the `GameScene.m` file and import the `Bird.h` header file at the top, as shown in the following code:

```
#import "Bird.h"
```

7. Add the following `_bird` instance variable to hold our `bird` object, next to the `_hunter` instance variable that we added earlier:

```
@implementation GameScene
{
    Hunter  *_hunter;
    Bird    *_bird;
}
```

8. Then, add the following `addBird` method:

```
-(void)addBird
{
    CGSize viewSize = [CCDirector sharedDirector].viewSize;

    _bird = [[Bird alloc]
                    initWithBirdType:BirdTypeSmall];

    _bird.position = ccp(viewSize.width * 0.5f,
                         viewSize.height * 0.9f);
    [self addChild:_bird];
}
```

9. Add a call to the following `addBird` method in the `init` method, after calling the methods that add the background and the hunter:

```
-(instancetype)init
{
    if (self = [super init])
    {
        //…skipped…

        [self addBird];
    }

    return self;
}
```

Note that some part of the code that it is already there is skipped. I will mark the skipped parts of the methods with `//..skipped..` comment, so that you don't have to guess if you need to delete everything that is not shown in the listing.

10. Now build and run the game. You should see a bird in the top center of the screen.

What just happened?

We've just added one more game object to our game scene. In fact, we wrote the code that allows us to add birds of three different types. Let's review step-by-step how we did so much with so little code.

Just as with the hunter and the background sprites, we started by adding images of the birds to our Xcode project.

Then, after creating the empty `Bird` class, we defined the `BirdType` enum type that will allow us to use one single class for three different bird types. This is quite convenient, as the behavior of all the birds will be almost identical and they will only differ by their image and maybe by a few other properties.

After adding a property, which we'll use later, we created a special `init` method named `initWithBirdType:`. This method expects a type of bird we want to create as a parameter and picks the corresponding image. Let's review the implementation of this method in the following points:

1. Depending on the `typeOfBird` parameter, a corresponding image is selected.

> Note that we added a `default:` case to our `switch` statement, which logs a warning that this is an unknown type of bird, but still uses a small bird image. You might change the code to throw an exception and crash the game so that you surely don't miss the log message.

2. As the `Bird` class is a subclass of the `CCSprite`, it uses the parent `initWithImageNamed:` method to initialize itself with the selected image based on the bird type.
3. The type of the bird parameter is saved in the property. This is required if we need to know which bird type this is.

Finally, we created the bird object and added it to the scene in the `GameScene` scene so that we could see it.

Time for action – making the bird move

It is nice to have a cute bird on the screen, but our hunter can't shoot an unmoving bird, as this is simply not sportsman-like. So, before we give our hunter the ability to shoot, we're going to make the bird fly.

1. Open the `GameScene.m` file and add the following `update:` method below all other methods:

```
-(void)update:(CCTime)dt
{
    //1
    CGSize viewSize = [CCDirector sharedDirector].viewSize;

    //2
    if (_bird.position.x < 0)
        _bird.flipX = YES;

    //3
    if (_bird.position.x > viewSize.width)
        _bird.flipX = NO;

    //4
    float birdSpeed = 50;
    float distanceToMove = birdSpeed * dt;

    //5
    float direction = _bird.flipX ? 1 : -1;

    //6
    float newX = _bird.position.x + direction * distanceToMove;
    float newY = _bird.position.y;

    //7
    _bird.position = ccp(newX, newY);
}
```

2. Now build and run the game. You should see the bird moving from the left edge of the screen to the right edge and then back.

You can find the snapshot of the project at this point in the book's supporting files in the `Chapter_04/Cocohunt_Making_Bird_Move` folder.

What just happened?

This was a small bit of code, but the changes we see are quite significant. Our static image on the screen is starting to become an actual game. We'll review the code shortly, but before we review the body of the `update:` method line by line, let's get to know what this `update:` method is all about.

Meeting the update: method

In the real world, we have no frames or update intervals. When we see a bird flying, we don't think of it as a set of position points, instead we see its trajectory as an absolutely continuous line. Refer to the following screenshot:

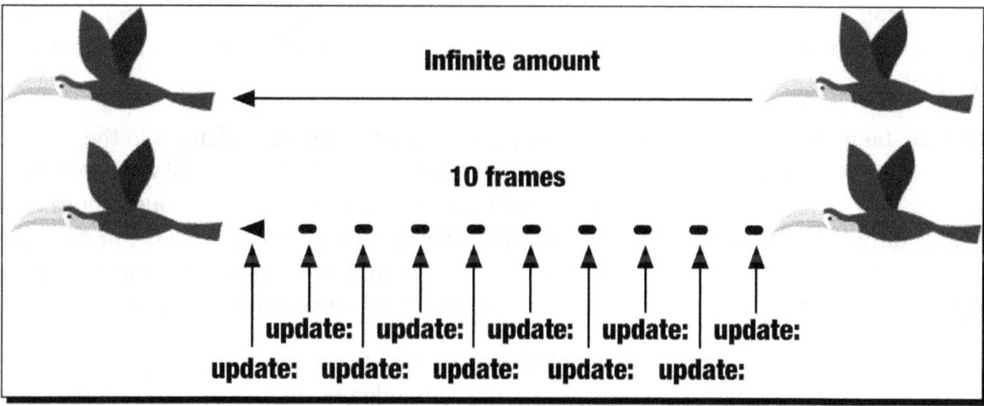

The issue with the real-life trajectory is that it is infinitely subdividable. This means that there is an infinite number of positions between the start and finish positions of the bird. Of course, we cannot provide an infinite number of positions for a finite time interval in our game. Just like how a one-hour movie cannot have an infinite number of frames.

However, while the movie is just a finite set of frames; when we watch the movie, we see movements just like in real life. This happens because if we supply a sufficient amount of frames per second, our brain does the rest of the job.

Video games work in a similar way. We just update our objects and render the scene to the current frame. Then, we update them once again and render another frame. The goal is to simulate the seamless action on the screen by providing a sufficient amount of frames per second.

This is where the `update:` method comes on stage. This method is called once per frame, and we have the ability to update objects on the screen, just like an animator who draws the frames of a cartoon one-by-one. Then, after we run the `update:` method, Cocos2D draws everything on screen for us.

When we reviewed the code in `AppDelegate`, there was the `CCSetupAnimationInterval` configuration option, which defaults to `1.0/60.0`. I've said that this is the desired amount of frames per second. The value of `1.0/60` means that we want to run 60 **frames per second** (**FPS**), and in an ideal world, this would mean that the `update:` method will be called 60 times per second.

This way, we would know for sure that 1/60th of the second has passed since the last `update:` call. However, we should get back to the cruel real world where we cannot guarantee that the game will run at 60 FPS and the `update:` method will be called once each 1/60th of a second.

There can be many reasons for this. We can perform many heavy calculations in the `update:` method that take more than 1/60th of a second, and Cocos2D will wait until the previous call to `update:` method completes before it calls it again. So, obviously more time will pass between calls. There can be some other background processes in iOS (for example, SMS or push notifications) that will eat up some of the processor time and our game will have to wait a little extra before the `update:` method will be called the next time.

It might seem that there is no issue with this, but that's not entirely true. Imagine that we want our bird to spend 10 seconds flying from one edge of the screen to another. Calculations are quite simple in this case. We take the width of the screen (let's take the 3.5-inch screen width of 480 points for this sample) and divide it with the number of seconds and we get that the bird should fly `480/10=48` points per second.

Given that `update:` is called 60 times per second, we can think that each time `update:` is called, the bird should move `48/60=0.8` points. Now, imagine that in addition to moving the bird, we perform some actions in `update:` that take a lot of time and our game actually runs only about 30 frames per second. This means that the `update:` method is called only 30 times per second, and our bird only moves `0.8*30=24` points per second, or 240 points per 10 seconds. Thus, instead of moving completely from one side of the screen to another, the bird only flies half of the way due to the lower frame rate. Refer to the following screenshot:

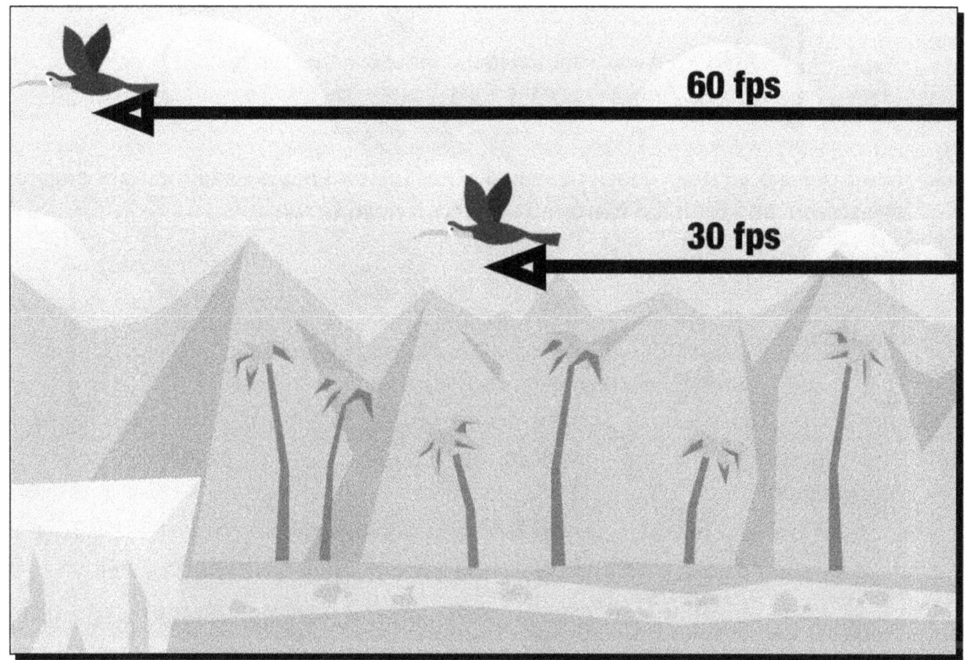

Frame dependence

To solve this frame dependence issue, the following is the extra parameter in the `update:` method:

```
-(void)update:(CCTime)dt
```

The `dt` parameter means delta time. Basically, it is just a `float` parameter that holds the amount of time passed since the last update call. If in the preceding bird example, we'd used this `dt` parameter instead of a constant value, we would've had no frame dependence issues.

Let's see how we used it and review the full code of our `update:` method.

Reviewing bird movement in the update: method

Let's review each code block marked by comment in the following points:

1. We get the size of the screen. We then use this size to detect when the bird reaches the screen bounds.
2. This code block checks whether the bird has passed the left edge of the screen and flips the bird around if the condition is `true`. We've used a property of the sprite called `flipX`. This property allows us to mirror the sprite image over the *x* axis. The bird image is designed in a way that it looks to the left, so setting `flipX` to `YES` will make it look to the right. This is exactly what we want as the bird is about to move to the right and we don't want it to fly backwards.

> If you want to flip the sprite over the *y* axis, you can use the `flipY` property.

3. Next, there is another check to see whether the bird has passed the right edge of the screen, and then flip it around to make it head to the left.

> Remember that, by default, the sprite's `position` property is where the center of the sprite is, because the anchor point is set to the center. This is why our bird flies with half of its body outside the screen before turning around.

4. The distance that the bird flew since the last `update:` call is calculated. Refer to the following points:
   - The `birdSpeed` parameter: This is the distance in points that the bird should fly in 1 second. We could use any value but `50` works well.
   - The `dt` parameter: This is the time passed since the last `update:` call.
5. When we multiply the distance per second with the number of seconds passed, we get the actual distance. As we use `dt` instead of a constant value, we get a frame independent movement of the bird.

> Note that `distanceToMove` contains the absolute distance. This means that it contains the length of the flight, but not the direction.

After the absolute distance is calculated, we need to understand where to move, to the left or to the right. If `flipX` is set to `YES`, then the bird moves to the right. In this case, we should add the traveled distance to the current position *x* coordinate, as the *x* axis extends to the right. If `flipX` is set to `NO`, then the bird moves to the left and we should subtract the traveled distance from the current position's *x* coordinate.

6. Finally, the bird's new position is calculated.
7. Then, this new position is assigned to the bird and the bird moves on the screen. As this process is repeated for each frame, the bird moves a little in each frame. This way we're simulating seamless movement of the bird.

That's all we have to do to make the bird move.

> Although we've made our code frame independent by using the `dt` parameter instead of the fixed position delta, it is still very important to try to keep the frame rate high. If the frame rate drops below 30-40 FPS, the game might look jerky, even if you're using the `dt` parameter, just because the changes between the frames will be too significant and our brain will notice this.

Understanding debug FPS labels

Now, when we know that the frame rate is important, let's have a look once again at those debug labels that are displayed in the left bottom corner. Refer to the following screenshot:

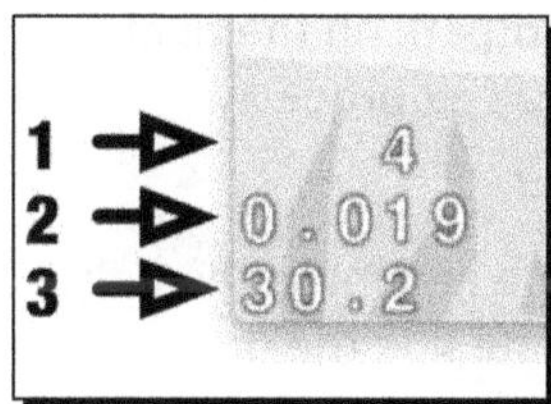

The following explains each numbered line shown in the preceding screenshot:

1. The number of OpenGL draw calls per frame: Each call to the OpenGL draw function has a performance cost. We have four objects in our scene: background, bird, hunter's torso, and his legs. This gives us four OpenGL draw calls. If you add one more bird to the scene, this number will increase to five and so on. Soon, I will show you how to draw several objects in one call and increase performance.
2. Time required to render one frame.
3. The average framerate (FPS) the game is currently running.

> You should try to keep the FPS around 60.0 when testing on actual device. Don't worry if you get a lower FPS when running on the simulator; this might only mean that you should test on an actual device, as the simulator doesn't have hardware acceleration. This is why you need an actual device to test the performance.

Knowing the meaning of each number will let you monitor the basic performance of your game. Of course, if you want more information about your game performance, it is better to use special tools such as the **Instruments** tool that comes with Xcode.

If you want to disable debug labels, simply change the `CCSetupShowDebugStats` configuration option to `NO` while calling the `setupCocos2dWithOptions:` method in the `AppDelegate.m` file.

Have a go hero

Before we move to our next topic, you have a chance to experiment with the current project. I encourage you to copy the project somewhere, to keep the original project safe and untouched as we're going to build on it, and try to do the following:

1. Try changing the position of the hunter and the bird.
2. Place the hunter on the footpath on the right side of the background and make him look to the left using the `flipX` property.
3. Change the type of the bird.
4. Add more birds to the scene and make them fly. You might want to add an array to store all birds and enumerate it in the `update:` method.
5. Change the bird's fly trajectory by applying a function to the *x* and *y* coordinates calculation in the `update:` method. For example, you can try changing the `newx` and `newy` calculation formula to the following:

```
float newX = _bird.position.x + direction * distanceToMove;
float newY = viewSize.height * 0.9f +
             10 * sinf(_bird.position.x / 20.0f);
```

Spritesheets and animation

We've learnt that Cocos2D provides a convenient way to display sprites on the screen using the `CCSprite` class. However, we must understand that no matter what wrapper classes are provided by the game engine for rendering, they are just hiding all the technical details from us and making our life easier. In the end, it all comes down to interacting with the graphics drivers. In the case of iOS and many other mobile platforms, this means using the OpenGL ES API internally, because this is as close as you can get to the metal.

OpenGL ES is a topic for a separate book, and you don't need to know it to start making games, but there is one aspect that is worth mentioning. When we render sprites using Cocos2D, it is like saying to OpenGL, "hey, we have an image, please draw this whole image in this rectangle area on the screen". Refer to the following screenshot:

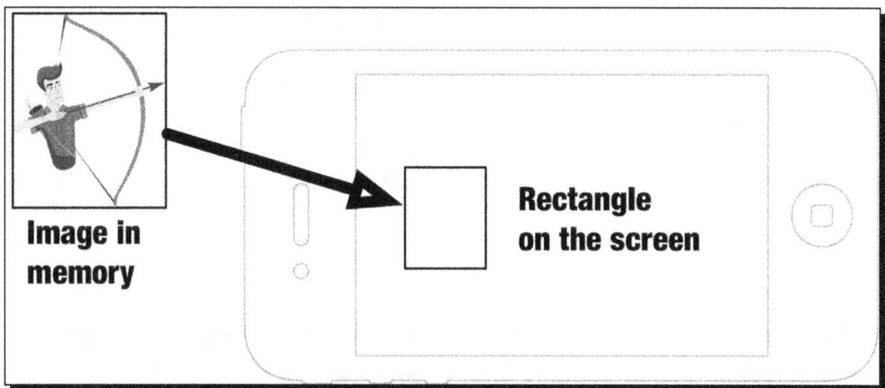

Rendering an image to the rectangle area on the screen

Each render of the image takes one call to the OpenGL ES function, and each such call has a performance cost. So, if you have to render 100 images, it will mean 100 calls per frame and the frame rate might drop making the game slow and jerky.

There is a technique to avoid this. Instead of making one OpenGL call per image, we can make one call per several images by gathering them into one big image. This way, instead of rendering the whole image into the rectangular area on the screen, we can ask OpenGL to render the part of the image in one rectangle, then another part of the image into another rectangle and so on. The following image illustrates this technique:

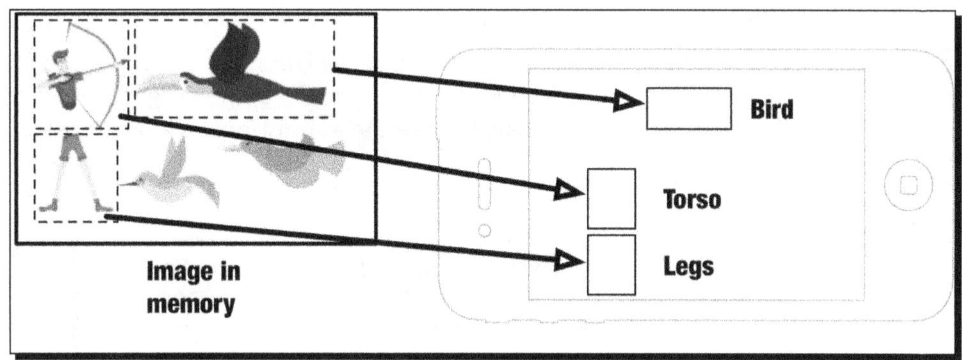

Rendering parts of the big image into the different rectangle areas on the screen

You might ask why this is faster than rendering each image separately. Well, this is quite hard to explain without getting into the details of OpenGL, so for now we can just think that switching between images is an expensive operation.

The preceding image is called a **spritesheet** or **texture atlas**. Using spritesheets is a very common practice in game development on any platform as well as in other software development areas. A good thing to know is that there are many tools that will allow you to use spritesheets in your Cocos2D game almost effortlessly.

We're going to use the TexturePacker tool as I find it the most user friendly for beginner developers. Also, you can use the basic functionality of TexturePacker for free, and this basic functionality is more than enough for a good start.

Time for action – creating a spritesheet

Let's create our first spritesheet that will contain all of the images that we've used before and the new images that we'll be using very soon as follows:

1. Of course, before we create spritesheet, we need to install TexturePacker. Visit `http://www.codeandweb.com/texturepacker/download` and download the latest version of TexturePacker.
2. When the download completes, open the downloaded `.dmg` file and it will mount a new drive called `TexturePacker`. It should open in `Finder` straight away.
3. Drag the `TexturePacker.app` in the `Applications` shortcut and you have TexturePacker installed. Now, we're ready to create the spritesheet itself.
4. Open the TexturePacker application (by navigating to **Applications** | **TexturePacker.app**). It will create a blank project at the start.
5. Open the book's supporting files at the `Chapter_04/Assets/Spritesheet/hd` folder in `Finder`. This folder contains the Retina version of the images that we're going to use in our game. We're going to generate a spritesheet containing all of these images.

As we're supporting both Retina and non-Retina displays, we'll need to create two spritesheets; this is why there are two sets of images. The `hd` folder inside the `Chapter_04/Assets/Spritesheet/` folder contains Retina images and the `sd` folder the non-Retina ones. We'll start by creating the spritesheet for Retina, and then you'll repeat the process to create the non-Retina spritesheet.

6. Select all images in the `Chapter_04/Assets/Spritesheet/hd` folder and drag them into the TexturePacker application's right panel called **Sprites**. They should appear in this panel list on the right as it is shown in the following screenshot:

A Texture Packer project with images added on the right

7. After adding the images, we need to set some TexturePacker options on the left in the **TextureSettings** panel, which are as follows:
   - Make sure **Data Format** is set to `cocos2d`
   - Change **Algorithm** in **Layout** section to `Basic`
   - Change **Trim mode** also in **Layout** section to `None`

8. Navigate to **File** | **Save** or press *command* + *S* shortcut and save the project anywhere you like. Name the project file `Cocohunt-hd.tps`.

9. After we've saved the project, we can publish it and get the big image and the `.plist` file with technical information. Navigate to **File** | **Publish** or use the *command* + *P* shortcut and name the published file `Cocohunt-hd.plist`. Save this file near the `.tps` file we saved previously. This will also create a PNG image, named in the same way as `.plist`, except that it has the `.png` extension.

10. At this point, you should have these files: `Cocohunt-hd.tps`, `Cocohunt-hd.plist`, `Cocohunt-hd.png`. Now we need to repeat this process to create the non-Retina version of the spritesheet.

11. Create a new TexturePacker project and repeat steps 4 to 9, but this time, take the images from the `Chapter_04/Assets/Spritesheet/sd` folder.
12. Save the TexturePacker project as `Cocohunt.tps` (without the `-hd` suffix) and publish the spritesheet as `Cocohunt.plist` (also without the `-hd` suffix).
13. At the end, you should have six files, three for the Retina display and three for the non-Retina display.

You can find all the resulting files in the `Chapter_04/Assets/Spritesheet/result` folder.

What just happened?

It might seem hard to follow all these steps, but believe me, once you do them a couple of times, it will be quite easy. All we had to do is create a TexturePacker project, add images that we want to put in our spritesheet, set some options and publish the spritesheet.

As we are using a free version of TexturePacker, we had to repeat this for the non-Retina image. If we used the TexturePacker Pro version, then we could have used the **AutoSD** option and got two spritesheets from the set of images for the Retina display.

Let's review the files that we got in the result. Open the folder where you saved the project file and published the spritesheet. Check whether you have following files:

Name	Date Modified
Cocohunt-hd.plist	Today 16:51
Cocohunt-hd.png	Today 16:51
Cocohunt-hd.tps	Today 16:51
Cocohunt.plist	Today 16:51
Cocohunt.png	Today 16:51
Cocohunt.tps	Today 16:51

The Spritesheet projects and published files

First of all, the `Cocohunt.tps` and `Cocohunt-hd.tps` files are the project files of the TexturePacker application. Each file contains the settings, list of the images used, and other internal information used by TexturePacker. This file is only used to create a spritesheet and later to modify this spritesheet if we need to. We don't need to add it to the Xcode project.

Next are the two pairs of `.plist` and `.png` files. Each pair describes one spritesheet. This is because each spritesheet consists of two files: `.plist` and `.png`.

The `.plist` file contains coordinates of the images that we've used to create the spritesheet within the generated spritesheet's PNG image. Without this file, Cocos2D won't be able to separate sprites from that big image.

The `.png` file is the resulting big image for Retina or non-Retina that contains all of the images we've packed. You can open it using the Preview application or your any favorite image viewer and see it yourself.

I encourage you to actually take a look at the image files and open the `.plist` files in some text editor to understand what they contain.

We need to add both the `.plist` and `.png` files to the Xcode project so that Cocos2D can use the spritesheet. It is important to understand that without the `.plist` file, the `.png` file is just one big image.

Ok, we have two files per spritesheet and we have two spritesheets, one for the Retina display defined by the `Cocohunt-hd.plist` and `Cocohunt-hd.png` files and the other for the non-Retina display defined by the `Cocohunt.plist` and `Cocohunt.png` files. This is why we have four files to add to the project in total.

The few settings that we had to change were the **Algorithm** and **Trim mode** in the **Layout** section. This is the restriction in the free version of TexturePacker. We can only use the basic algorithm and can't trim the whitespace around images, but it will do the work in many cases!

Using the `MaxRect` algorithm and enabling trimming can decrease the size of the final image. A better algorithm can save some space by positioning sprites better, while trimming will remove the whitespace around the sprites and pack them tighter. Later when the sprites will be loaded into Cocos2D, that whitespace will be restored, so the size of the sprites won't change. This is important, especially if you store animation frames. We will discuss this in *Chapter 7, Animations and Particle Systems*.

Time for action – modifying the game to use spritesheets

Now that we've generated the spritesheet, let's modify our Cocohunt game to use it instead of the single sprites by performing the following steps:

1. Let's remove the `Birds` and the `Hunter` groups with all their contents from the `Resources` group in Xcode.

[You can either right-click on the group and select **Delete** or just select the group(s) and press the *delete* key on the keyboard.]

2. In the remove dialog, you can select **Move to Trash**, as we're not going to use those images anymore.
3. After removing the images, let's add our spritesheet. Create a new group inside the `Resources` group and call it `Spritesheets`.
4. Open the folder with the files that you've published from TexturePacker and add the following files to the `Spritesheets` group by dragging them into this group as usual. You'll need to add the following files:
   - `Cocohunt.plist`
   - `Cocohunt.png`
   - `Cocohunt-hd.plist`
   - `Cocohunt-hd.png`

[If, for some reason, you don't have the files generated in TexturePacker, you can take the files from the `Chapter_04/Assets/Spritesheet/result` folder.]

5. Open the `GameScene.m` file and add an instance variable for the spritesheet batch node as follows:

```
@implementation GameScene
{
    CCSpriteBatchNode *_batchNode;

    Hunter  *_hunter;
    Bird    *_bird;
}
```

6. In the `GameScene.m` file, add the `createBatchNode` method as follows:

```
-(void)addBird
{
    CGSize viewSize = [CCDirector sharedDirector].viewSize;
    _bird = [[Bird alloc]
             initWithBirdType:BirdTypeSmall];
    _bird.position = ccp(viewSize.width * 0.5f,
                         viewSize.height * 0.9f);

    [_batchNode addChild:_bird];
}
```

7. Then, add a call to it in the `init` method, before the hunter and the bird are added to the scene, as follows:

```
-(instancetype)init
{
    if (self = [super init])
    {
        [self createBatchNode];

        [self addBackground];
        [self addHunter];
        [self addBird];
    }

    return self;
}
```

8. Then, change the code at the end of the `addHunter` method to add the hunter to the batch node instead of the scene as follows:

```
-(void)addHunter
{
    //..skipped..

    [_batchNode addChild:_hunter];
}
```

9. Do the same at the end of the `addBird` method. Also, add it to the batch node instead of the scene, as shown in the following code:

```
-(void)addBird
{
    CGSize viewSize = [CCDirector sharedDirector].viewSize;

    _bird = [[Bird alloc]
      initWithBirdType:BirdTypeSmall];

    _bird.position = ccp(viewSize.width * 0.5f,
                         viewSize.height * 0.9f);

    [_batchNode addChild:_bird];
}
```

10. Open the `Hunter.m` file and find the following line:

```
_torso = [CCSprite spriteWithImageNamed:@"hunter_top.png"];
```

Change the previous line of code to the following:

```
_torso = [CCSprite
          spriteWithImageNamed:@"hunter_top_0.png"];
```

11. Then, open the `Bird.m` file and make the following changes in the `initWithBirdType:` method:

```
-(instancetype)initWithBirdType:(BirdType)typeOfBird
{
    NSString *birdImageName;

    switch (typeOfBird) {
        case BirdTypeBig:
            birdImageName = @"bird_big_0.png";
            break;
        case BirdTypeMedium:
            birdImageName = @"bird_middle_0.png";
            break;
        case BirdTypeSmall:
            birdImageName = @"bird_small_0.png";
            break;
        default:
            CCLOG(@"Unknown bird type, using small bird!");
            birdImageName = @"bird_small_0.png";
            break;
    }

    if (self = [super initWithImageNamed:birdImageName])
```

```
        {
            self.birdType = typeOfBird;
        }

        return self;
    }
```

12. Build and run the project. You should see the exact same result as you saw earlier.

You can find a snapshot of the project at this point in the book's supporting files in the `Chapter_04/Cocohunt_Using_Spritesheet` folder.

What just happened?

You should see no visible changes, a hunter standing on the cliff and the bird moving from one side of the screen to another. However, you might notice that the number of the draw calls in the left-bottom corner has decreased to only two although we're still drawing the background, hunter's torso and legs, and bird.

What we've done is combined the hunter's torso and his legs and the bird into one image and drawing them using one call. If we add more birds or hunters, we won't increase the number of calls.

Let's review the changes that we've made. As I've mentioned before, we need both the `.plist` and `.png` files to use a spritesheet in our game, and we also have Retina (with the `-hd` suffix) and non-Retina versions. So, the first thing we did is add these files to our Xcode project and remove the old separate images as we don't need them. After adding spritesheets, we needed to modify the code to use them.

Changes in GameScene

Let's start reviewing from the changes in the `GameScene.m` file. We've added the `_batchNode` instance variable and the `createBatchNode` method to initialize the batch node and add it to the scene.

Let's review the code of the method in the following points:

1. The first thing we did is load the frames' information into the `CCSpriteFrameCache` class. Cocos2D uses this class to load and cache sprite frames. In our case, it loads the information about the sprites from the `.plist` file of the spritesheet files pair.

2. Then, we created a special node called `CCSpriteBatchNode`. This is the node that will draw all of our sprites from the spritesheet in one call. It won't require us to make a lot of changes. The only thing we need to do is add all of the sprites that use the spritesheet as child nodes of this batch node, instead of adding them to the scene directly.
3. The batch node itself is added to the scene so that it could draw. The important thing to note is that we add the batch node with z-order set to `1`. Refer to the following code:

```
[self addChild:_batchNode z:1];
```

This way we make sure that it is displayed above the background, which has z-order set to `0` by default.

Then, we need to call the `createBatchNode` method in the `init` method before we create the hunter and the bird. The reason for this is that all sprites that use the spritesheet must be added as children of the batch node. Only then will the batch node be able to draw all of them in one draw call.

As the batch node renders all of its children with one draw call, you can only add sprites from the spritesheet used to create this batch node as child nodes.

In other words, if you have a sprite from another spritesheet or a sprite that uses a separate image, you will get the following error if you try to add it to the batch node:

CCSprite is not using the same texture id.

Before the changes, the hunter and the bird were added directly to the scene in the `addHunter` and the `addBird`, respectively. We modified these methods, and now we add the hunter and the bird to the batch node instead of the scene directly.

Note that the batch node can only have sprites as its children, and children of its children, and so on. If you try to add any object other than `CCSprite` or its descendants, you will get the following error:

CCSpriteBatchNode only supports CCSprites as children.

Adding the `Bird` and `Hunter` classes works fine as they inherit from the `CCSprite` class.

The following is a small to-do list on how to use the batch node in your game:

1. Create a spritesheet files pair (`.plist` and `.png`) in TexturePacker or any other tool.
2. Add these files to the Xcode project.

3. Load the `.plist` information into `CCSpriteFrameCache`. It is important to do this before adding any sprites from that spritesheet.
4. Create a `CCSpriteBatchNode` node and add all sprites within one spritesheet into this `batch` node instead of the scene directly. Don't forget to add the `batch` node itself to the scene.

Changes in the Hunter and Bird classes

Changes in the `Hunter` and `Bird` classes are mostly not related to our migration to spritesheets. If you open the TexturePacker project, or just take a look at the filenames of the images that we've packed in the spritesheet, you will see that there are no such files as `hunter_top.png`, `bird_small.png`, `bird_medium.png`, and `bird_big.png`.

Instead, there are several numbered files for the hunter's torso and different bird types, such as `bird_small_0.png`, `bird_small_1.png`, and so on. These are the animation frames that we're going to use very soon.

We will talk about animation in the next section. For now, we just need to understand that there is no reason to have a separate image for the hunter's torso and the birds if it is the same image as one of the frames of the animation. For example, the following is the animation of our hunter shooting:

Hunter shooting animation

As you can see, the first frame of the animation is exactly what we had in the `hunter_top.png` image that we've used before (just a hunter standing still and aiming). So, there is no reason to have a separate identical image in the spritesheet.

However, since the frames have slightly different names with numbers in them, we needed to update the code. This is what we've done in the `Hunter.m` and `Bird.m` files.

If we use the same image names in the spritesheet as we've used before when they were separate images, we will not make any changes at all in the `Bird` and `Hunter` classes, just as how we didn't change this line in the `Hunter.m` file. Refer to the following code:

```
if (self = [super initWithImageNamed:@"hunter_bottom.png"])
```

The image used for the hunter's legs is called the same way in the spritesheet as it was called when it was a separate image. This is because we won't animate the hunter's legs and have only one sprite for them.

Understanding spritesheet's limitations

With all the great things about spritesheets, there are some limitations. The two main limitations you should know about spritesheets are the maximum texture size limit and the z-order issue.

The size of the spritesheet image is limited by the maximum size of the texture that can be loaded by the device's graphics chip. For example, you can only have a 2048 x 2048 texture size on the devices such as iPhone 3GS, iPhone 4, and iPad (1st generation). More recent devices support 4096 x 4096 texture.

Although these are quite big images, when developing a complicated game, it is really easy to get more images than one spritesheet can contain. So unfortunately, putting all of your images in one spritesheet often is not an option.

This is why backgrounds are not usually packed within a spritesheet.

Of course, we can organize the images into several spritesheets, but this gives us another issue. In the current implementation of Cocos2D, z-order only works within one node level. This means that you cannot place sprite A to be under sprite B if the spritesheet with the sprite A is above the spritesheet with sprite B.

This z-order issue will be solved if Cocos2D starts using global z-order. This, as I've mentioned earlier, is currently being discussed and probably will be implemented in one of the upcoming Cocos2D versions.

Automatic batching

While making final changes to this chapter, the Cocos2D team revealed a few new features that are planned to be added in Cocos2D v3.1. One of the features is automatic batching. This means that you can use separate images just as we used before, and the spritesheet will be created and configured by Cocos2D on the fly.

This will be a really great feature and theoretically you won't need to generate spritesheets manually anymore. However, I decided not to remove this part of the chapter because understanding how spritesheets work is important even if it is generated automatically. Also, automatic batching might not always work in an optimal way, as in many cases you know best how your sprites are used in the game.

Time for action – animating the birds

Now that we have animation frames ready, we can animate our game objects. We're not going to make a hunter shoot in this chapter, so let's start with the bird.

1. Open the `Bird.m` file and import the following headers at the top:

```
#import "cocos2d.h"
#import "CCAnimation.h"
```

2. Then, add the `animateFly` method, below the `initWithBirdType:` method as follows:

```
-(void)animateFly
{
    //1
    NSString *animFrameNameFormat;

    switch (self.birdType) {
        case BirdTypeBig:
            animFrameNameFormat = @"bird_big_%d.png";
            break;
        case BirdTypeMedium:
            animFrameNameFormat = @"bird_middle_%d.png";
            break;
        case BirdTypeSmall:
            animFrameNameFormat = @"bird_small_%d.png";
            break;
        default:
            CCLOG(@"Unknown bird type, using small bird anim.!");
            animFrameNameFormat = @"bird_small_%d.png";
            break;
    }

    //2
    NSMutableArray *animFrames =
      [NSMutableArray arrayWithCapacity:7];

    //3
    for (int i = 0; i < 7 ; i++)
    {
        //4
        NSString *currentFrameName  =
          [NSString stringWithFormat:animFrameNameFormat, i];

        //5
```

```
            CCSpriteFrame *animationFrame =
              [CCSpriteFrame frameWithImageNamed:currentFrameName];

            //6
            [animFrames addObject:animationFrame];
        }

        //7
        CCAnimation* flyAnimation =
          [CCAnimation animationWithSpriteFrames:animFrames
                                           delay:0.1f];

        //8
        CCActionAnimate *flyAnimateAction =
          [CCActionAnimate actionWithAnimation:flyAnimation];

        //9
        CCActionRepeatForever *flyForever =
         [CCActionRepeatForever actionWithAction:flyAnimateAction];

        //10
        [self runAction:flyForever];
    }
```

3. Add a call to this method inside the `initWithBirdType:` method as follows:

```
-(instancetype)initWithBirdType:(BirdType)typeOfBird
{
    //..skipped..

    if (self = [super initWithImageNamed:birdImageName])
    {
        self.birdType = typeOfBird;

        [self animateFly];
    }

    return self;
}
```

4. Build and run the game. Now, the bird will not just move from one side of the screen to another like a static image, but it should flitter.

> You can find the final project for this chapter in the book's supporting files in the `Chapter_04/Cocohunt_04_Final` folder.

What just happened?

The most interesting part is the `animateFly` method. Apart from this method, we only imported the required headers so that we can use all animation and actions in the `animateFly` method. Also, we added the code to call the `animateFly` method in the `initWithBirdType:` method to start the animation right when the bird is created.

So, we will spend our time reviewing this method in a very detailed manner in the following points:

1. All of the bird's fly animations have seven frames each, but the name of the animation depends on the bird type, as each bird has its own fly animation. In the block of code under the first bullet point of the Time for action section, we detected the current bird type and the corresponding format of animation frame names.

> We've hardcoded the amount of frames (seven) for simplicity so that we could review the entire code at once. However, normally you should have created a constant or `#define` with the number of frames somewhere in your game instead of hardcoding this "magic-number".

2. This `animFrames` array is created to store all animation frames for the current bird type.
3. This code is used to get all animation frames, which differ only by a number in their name.
4. We've used the `NSString`'s `stringWithFormat:` method to get the actual frame name by substituting the `%d` parameter in `animFrameNameFormat` with the current `i` value (for example, `@"bird_big_0.png"`, `@"bird_big_1.png"`, `@"bird_big_2.png"`).
5. After we got the name of the animation frame, we created `CCSpriteFrame` using it. Note that you should add the spritesheet information into `CCSpriteFrameCache` before you use `frameWithImageNamed:` as in the other case, it won't be able to find this frame and will just search for the image with that name. We are doing this in the `createBatchNode` method of the `GameScene` class that is executed before the bird is created.

> In fact, you can create animation without spritesheets. In this case, you actually have to have separate images called `bird_big_0.png`, `bird_big_1.png`, `bird_big_2.png`, and so on, but this will be inefficient. With the use of a spritesheet, we will render all the birds in one draw call.

6. After we created the frame object, we added it to the array with the rest of the frames.
7. When all frames were created and stored in the array, we created the `flyAnimation` animation. The `CCAnimation` class is used to create animations in Cocos2D. This class takes an array of animation frames and delay time between each frame. We used `0.1` seconds delay between the frames to get a smooth animation. Decreasing the delay will make our bird flitter faster. Increasing the delay will make it flitter slower.

> You should carefully increase or decrease the animation delay in the code. Most often, you should think upfront about how fast the animation is, how many frames per second you want, and draw the required number of frame images. If you increase the delay too much, you will get a "slide-show" instead of the animation. If you decrease the delay too much, you might get a situation where the game's overall FPS is slower than your animation FPS. However, the latter case happens much less often than the "slide-show" case.

8. In Cocos2D, you cannot just say to the sprite that it should run some animation, instead you command the sprites using actions. There are different actions for almost any kind of task. You can command the sprite to move over time to some position, to show or hide gradually, and so on. We will speak about actions later. For now, we just need to remember that there is a special action called `CCActionAnimate` that commands the sprite to play the given animation.
9. The next good thing about actions is that you can group and stack them. You can create a sequence of actions and command a sprite to execute this sequence or you can command a sprite to repeat some action forever. However, as I've mentioned before, you can only pass an action to the sprite. So, there is a special action called `CCActionRepeatForever` and everything that it does it just waits for the given action to complete and then starts it again. As we want our bird to keep flying, this action is exactly what we need.
10. Finally, we commanded our sprite to execute the animation action and repeat itself forever.

We will use animations more through the book and will discuss them in detail in *Chapter 7, Animations and Particle Systems*, but at this point it should be clear that animating an object is quite easy.

Pop quiz – sprites

Q1. What will happen if you run the following code on iPhone 5S without adding `image-iphone5hd.png` to the Xcode project, but will add the `image.png` and `image-hd.png` images?

```
CCSprite *sprite = [CCSprite spriteWithImageNamed:@"image.png"];
```

1. The game will crash as iPhone 5S requires the `image-iphone5hd.png` image
2. The `image.png` file will be used as no `image-iphone5hd.png` image is provided
3. The `image-hd.png` file will be used as no `image-iphone5hd.png` image is provided
4. The game won't crash, but nothing will be displayed on the screen

Q2. What is the maximum spritesheet image size you can use on iPhone 5?

1. 2048 x 2048
2. 1024 x 1024
3. 4096 x 4096
4. 512 x 512

Q3. You have a scene with three sprites, **Sprite A**, **Sprite B**, and **Sprite C**, which is a child of **Sprite A**. **Sprite A** has **zOrder** set to **10** and **Sprite B** has **zOrder** set to **20**.

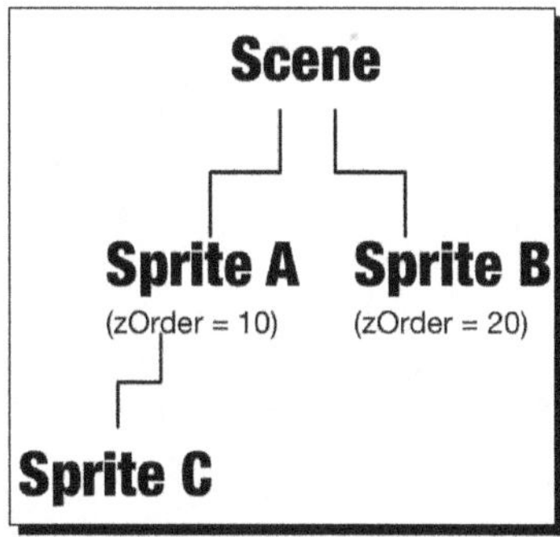

Can you make **Sprite C** be displayed on top of **Sprite B** by setting its **zOrder** property?

1. Yes, by setting its **zOrder** to **21**
2. Yes, by setting its **zOrder** to **1337**
3. Yes, by setting its **zOrder** to **-21**
4. No, because z-order only works within the parent node and **Sprite A** is always under **Sprite B**

Summary

Wow, we've done a lot in this chapter. We've learned how to use sprites and change their basic properties such as position, anchor point, and z-order. These properties are crucial to understand if we want to make video games.

We created our main game objects, the hunter and the bird, and added them to the scene. We made the bird move and even animated its flight in the end. Our game now uses spritesheets and we know how to track the performance using debug labels.

In fact, we've done a good portion of a real game. In the next chapter, we're going to learn how to add some action to our game, and we'll learn how to aim, shoot, and score points. We'll add more birds and will get really close to completing the first playable level of the game.

5
Starting the Action

In this chapter, we're going to add some action in the game and at the end of the chapter, we will be able to finally play the game. We will make our hunter aim for the bird using a finger and gyroscope, shoot the arrow from the bow, and make the arrow fly and hit the bird. Then we'll add more birds to the game as well as the winning and losing conditions.

In this chapter, we will learn the following topics:

- Detecting when the player touches the screen, moves, and lifts the finger
- Rotating the hunter's torso to aim at the desired point
- Detecting collisions between two sprites using bounding boxes
- Using states to control objects and the game life cycle
- Detecting winning and losing
- Using device orientation to control the game

Making the hunter aim and shoot

We'll make the hunter shoot in several steps. Some people may just close their eyes and shoot based on luck, but not our hunter; he will carefully aim first. We're going to use our finger to direct him, so the first thing we need to do is to learn how to handle touch.

Time for action – handling touches

Let's add the code that will allow us to handle touches:

> In this and the subsequent chapters, we're going to build on top of the **Cocohunt** project we started in the previous chapter. If you've completed the code of the previous chapter, simply continue from the point where you left.
>
> If you skipped some part of the book or don't have the code for some reason, you can take the final project of the previous chapter from the book supporting files. For this chapter, you can take the code from the `Chapter_04/Cocohunt_04_Final` folder.
>
> You can download the book's supporting files at `http://www.packtpub.com/support` and follow the instructions.

Perform the following steps:

1. Open the Xcode project at the point where we left it at the end of the previous chapter. After opening the project, open the `GameScene.m` file and add the following methods below the `update:` method:

```
-(void)touchBegan:(UITouch *)touch withEvent:(UIEvent *)event
{
    CCLOG(@"finger down at : (%f, %f)",
          touch.locationInWorld.x,
          touch.locationInWorld.y);
}

-(void)touchMoved:(UITouch *)touch withEvent:(UIEvent *)event
{
    CCLOG(@"finger moving at : (%f, %f)",
          touch.locationInWorld.x,
          touch.locationInWorld.y);
}

-(void)touchEnded:(UITouch *)touch withEvent:(UIEvent *)event
{
    CCLOG(@"finger up at : (%f, %f)",
          touch.locationInWorld.x,
          touch.locationInWorld.y);
}
```

2. Then, scroll at the top of the `GameScene.m` file and add the following line at the beginning of the `init` method:

```
-(instancetype)init
{
    if (self = [super init])
    {
        self.userInteractionEnabled = YES;

        //..skipped..
    }

    return self;
}
```

3. Build and run the game. You won't see any visual changes right now. However, if you click inside the simulator window or touch your device screen with a finger, move it a little, and then release it, you should see an output in the Xcode console. This output should be similar to what is shown in the following screenshot:

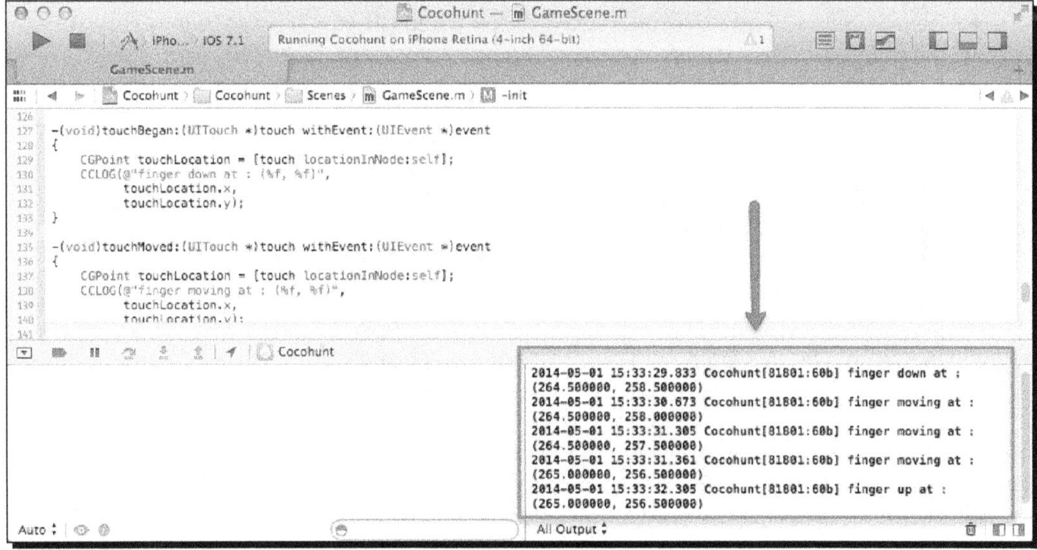

The Xcode console output after touching and moving the finger

What just happened?

Any CCNode or CCNode descendant can handle touches. In our case, we want to handle touches not on some specific node, but anywhere on the screen, so we added touch handling code to the scene itself.

To handle touches, we needed to enable user interaction by setting the userInteractionEnabled property of the scene to YES. We did this in the init method of the GameScene class.

After this, we added the following methods to the node to receive different touch notifications:

- touchBegan:: This method is called when you put your finger on the screen. If you want to handle touches, you must add this method, even if it will be empty. If you don't add this method, none of the following methods will be called.
- touchMoved:: This method is called when the finger moves. You can use this method to track the movement of the finger.
- touchEnded:: This method is called when you lift your finger from the screen. At this point, you can consider the touch life cycle completed.
- touchCancelled:: This method is called when the touch is cancelled. This can happen when something interrupts the normal flow of touch life cycle.

There can be several reasons for the touchCancelled: method to be called. The simplest one is if you touch the node and move the finger outside of it without lifting it. A more exotic example is if you touch the node and someone calls your iPhone causing your game to go into the background so that you can answer the call.

Right now, we are simply logging the touch coordinates using the CCLOG macro, but in the next section, we're going to make the hunter aim at this point.

The CCLOG macro is a wrapper around the standard NSLog function and is very useful when you need to output some debug values, as you cannot always use breakpoints and inspect variables without breaking the flow of the game.

The CCLOG macro works similar to the stringWithFormat: function of the NSString class, but instead of creating a new string and returning it, CCLOG prints it into the debug console.

Time for action – aiming at the touch position

Now that we can point where to shoot, let's make the hunter to aim at this point.

1. Open the `Hunter.h` file and add the `aimAtPoint:` method declaration:

```
#import "CCSprite.h"

@interface Hunter : CCSprite

-(void)aimAtPoint:(CGPoint)point;

@end
```

2. Then, open the `Hunter.m` file and add the following methods below the `init` method:

```
-(CGPoint)torsoCenterInWorldCoordinates
{
  //1
  CGPoint torsoCenterLocal =
    ccp(_torso.contentSize.width / 2.0f,
        _torso.contentSize.height / 2.0f);

  //2
  CGPoint torsoCenterWorld =
    [_torso convertToWorldSpace:torsoCenterLocal];
  return torsoCenterWorld;
}

-(float)calculateTorsoRotationToLookAtPoint:
   (CGPoint)targetPoint
{
  //1
  CGPoint torsoCenterWorld =
    [self torsoCenterInWorldCoordinates];
  //2
  CGPoint pointStraightAhead =
    ccp(torsoCenterWorld.x + 1.0f,
        torsoCenterWorld.y);
  //3
  CGPoint forwardVector =
    ccpSub(pointStraightAhead, torsoCenterWorld);

  //4
  CGPoint targetVector =
    ccpSub(targetPoint, torsoCenterWorld);
  //5
  float angleRadians =
    ccpAngleSigned(forwardVector, targetVector);
  //6
```

```
    float angleDegrees =
      -1 * CC_RADIANS_TO_DEGREES(angleRadians);
    //7
    angleDegrees = clampf(angleDegrees, -60, 25);
    return angleDegrees;
}

-(void)aimAtPoint:(CGPoint)point
{
    _torso.rotation =
      [self calculateTorsoRotationToLookAtPoint:point];
}
```

3. Finally, open the `GameScene.m` file and replace the `touchBegan:` and `touchMoved:` methods with the following code:

```
-(void)touchBegan:(UITouch *)touch withEvent:(UIEvent *)event
{
    CGPoint touchLocation = [touch locationInNode:self];
    [_hunter aimAtPoint:touchLocation];
}

-(void)touchMoved:(UITouch *)touch withEvent:(UIEvent *)event
{
    CGPoint touchLocation = [touch locationInNode:self];
    [_hunter aimAtPoint:touchLocation];
}
```

4. Build and run the game. Touch the screen and move the finger or mouse to see whether the hunter is aiming at the point you're pointing to. Refer to the following screenshot:

You can find a snapshot of the project at this point in the `Chapter_05/Cocohunt_05_Aiming` folder.

What just happened?

Although we've added only one public method to the `Hunter` class interface, we've also created several methods that we're using internally, and as it happens, they contain most of the code. Let's review each method separately.

Start with the `torsoCenterInWorldCoordinates` method. We've used this method to get the center point of the torso sprite in the world space coordinates.

We first encountered a difference between world space and node space when we positioned the torso inside the legs sprite and had to set the torso position relative to its parent.

Sometimes, grasping world space versus node space can be difficult, so here is a real-world example. Imagine a cup of tea placed right in the center of the table. Then, you take the table and carefully move it. When you finish moving the table, the cup of tea still will be at the center of the table. Well, at least if you moved the table carefully enough.

The cup's local position relative to the table (node space) will not change. However, its global (world space) position will change (relative to the room, earth, and so on).

A position in node space can match its position in world space. If the node (for example, scene) is positioned at (0, 0) in world space, then all of its child nodes have the same position in node space and world space.

Moreover, there can be several levels of nested node spaces (imagine a spoon in that cup of tea, which changed position while you were moving the table). The following is a figure to demonstrate some of the node spaces we have:

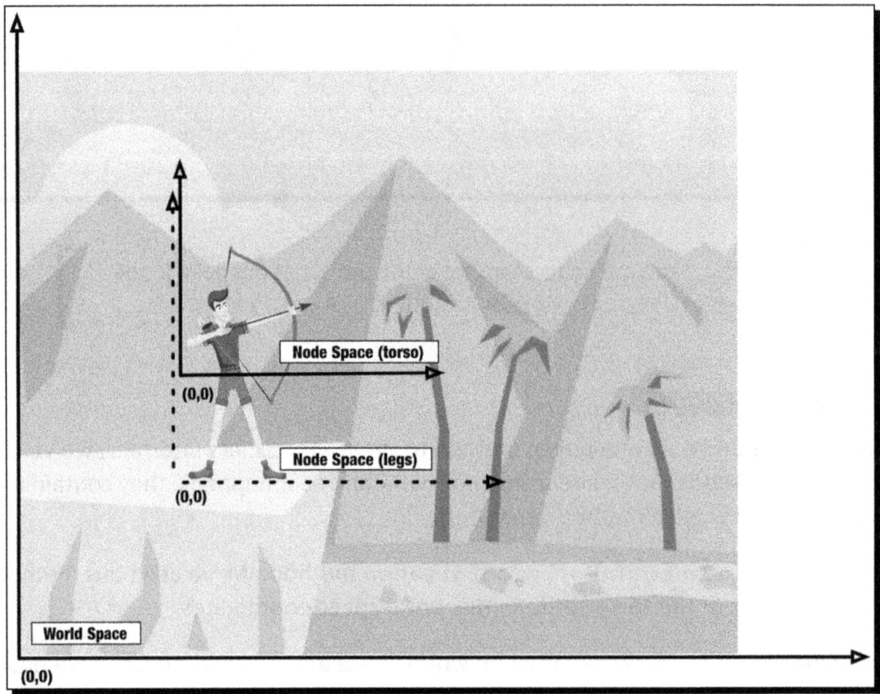

World space and node space

In the preceding figure, our scene is positioned at (0, 0), which is why scene node space matches world space.

However, to work with two points from different node spaces, we need to convert them into one space.

In most cases, we want to convert both points to world space. However, in some cases, you might want to convert one point to another point's node space.

This is why we need the center of the torso in world space, and this is what the `torsoCenterInWorldCoordinates` method does. Refer to the following steps:

1. The torso image was specially drawn in a way so that the hand and the tail of the arrow are at the center of the image for easy calculation. The designer had added some extra whitespace on the left for this. Refer to the following figure:

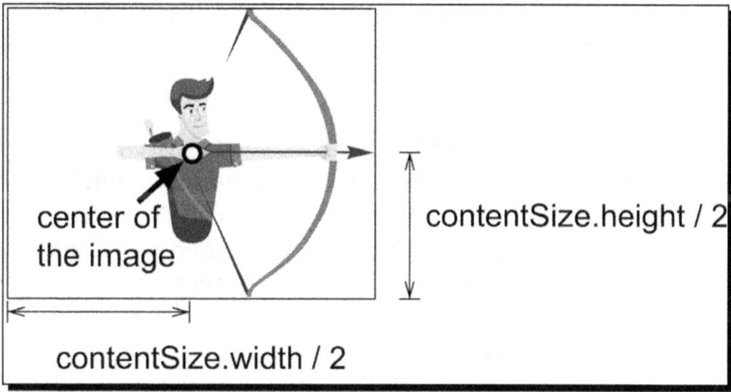

   This is why we took only half of the height and width of the image, as this is the center in the torso's node space.

2. Then, we used the `convertToWorldSpace:` method of the torso sprite to convert this point into world space.

There is a reverse method called `convertToNodeSpace` to convert a point in world space to node space.

This way, we got the center of the torso image, which as I've mentioned is the tail end of the arrow. Let's review the `calculateTorsoRotationToLookAtPoint:` method to understand why we needed this coordinate anyway.

1. We took the coordinate point of the tail of the arrow using the `torsoCenterInWorldCoordinates` method described earlier.
2. Then, we added `+1` to the *x* coordinate of this point and got the `pointStraightAhead` point, which is a straight line to the right from the torso's center. There is an illustration at the end of this list.

> The next few steps assume that you're familiar with the basics of vector algebra. If you feel uncomfortable with adding, subtracting, and rotating vectors, you should refresh your knowledge. To do this, you can watch this free course at **Khan Academy**, `https://www.khanacademy.org/math/linear-algebra/vectors_and_spaces`.

3. If we draw a line through `torsoCenterWorld` and `pointStraightAhead`, we'll get a line that is parallel to the *x* axis, and the arrow lies on this line when the torso is not rotated. Then, we used the `ccpSub` Cocos2D function that subtracts `torsoCenterWorld` from the `pointStraightAhead` point, and we get the vector pointed just like our arrow before any rotations (straight forward).

> There are a lot of useful functions such as `ccpSub`, `ccpAdd`, and `ccpMult` to subtract, add, or multiply vectors, respectively. Also, there are dot and cross products, distance, and many other useful functions that come with Cocos2D. You can find a full list of functions and their description in the `CGPointExtension.h` file in the Cocos2D distribution or Cocos2D documentation.

4. Using the same `ccpSub` function, we created a vector that points from the tail of the arrow to the target point. This is where we want our arrow to point when we rotate the torso.
5. To rotate the torso, we calculated the angle between the vectors using the `ccpAngleSigned` Cocos2D helper function, which returns the angle in radians.
6. As the sprite `rotation` property is in degrees, we needed to convert our radians to degrees. Also, as rotations in Cocos2D are clockwise positive, and normally rotation angles are counter-clockwise positive, we needed to change the sign of the angle.

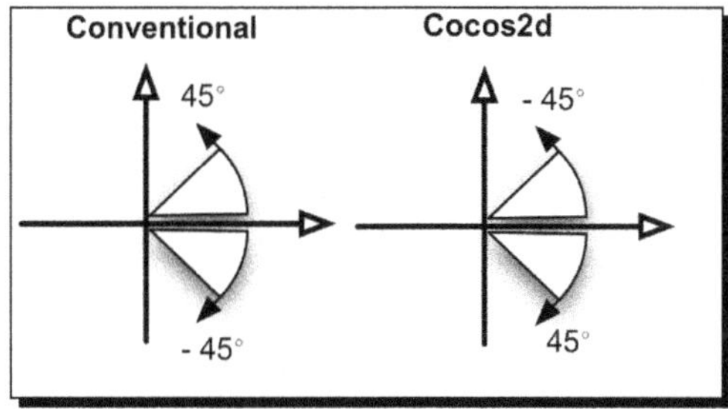

7. Our hunter is a human, so his waist cannot rotate 360 degrees. This is why we used the `clampf` function to limit our rotation degrees. This function simply checks whether the value is lower than the given minimum or higher than the given maximum values and sets it to the minimum or the maximum value, respectively. If the value is within given the minimum and maximum interval, then it is returned unchanged. I believe the following figure will clarify the idea a bit more:

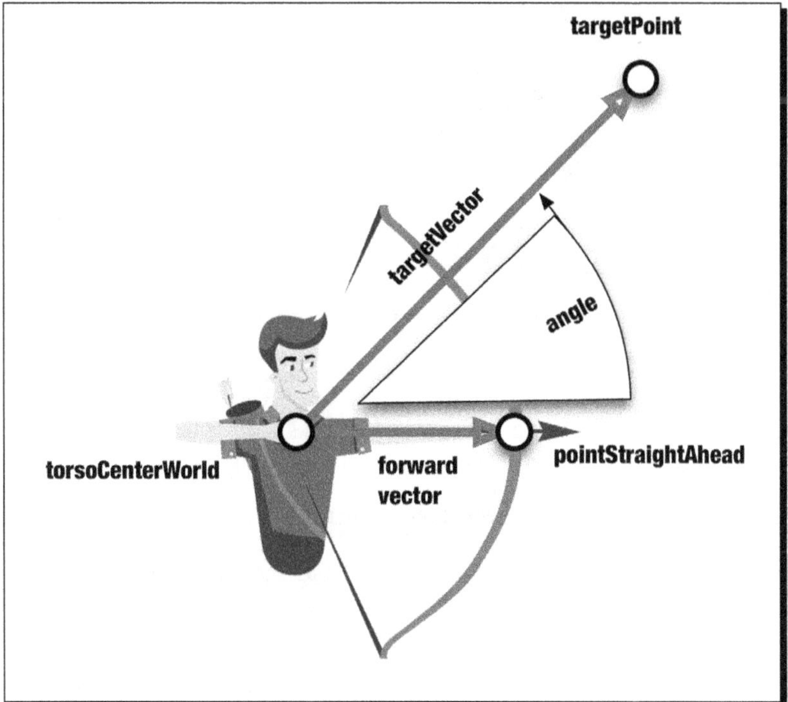

Calculating the torso rotation angle

Then, when we had the rotation angle, the only thing we needed to do was to assign it to the torso `rotation` property in the `aimAtPoint` method. This way, we used another cool property to transform sprites and other Cocos2D nodes.

Finally, to make the hunter aim at the position of our finger, we needed to call the `aimAtPoint:` method and specify the target point. We did this in both the `touchBegan:` and `touchMoved:` methods, as we want the hunter to start aiming when we touch the screen, but we also want the hunter to follow our finger while we move it.

The new method that we used in both the `touchBegan:` and `touchMoved:` methods is the `locationInNode:` of `UITouch`. This method converts the touch location from world space to the given node space.

Right now, our scene's node space is equal to world space, but this is not always the case. As we want the hunter to target at a point in the scene even if we move it, we need to convert the touch to the scene's node space.

To understand this, let's review what happens if we move the scene by 160 points to the right, as shown in the following figure:

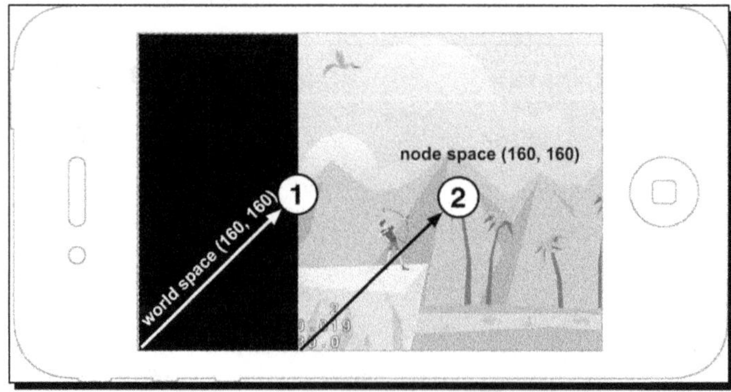

Consider that we want to spawn a bird at a position where the player touches the screen.

The player touches the screen at point **1**, so we should spawn a bird to the left of the hunter, that is, on the left edge of the scene. We would write the following code:

```
spawnedBird.position = touch.locationInWorld;
```

The bird's position will be `(160, 160)`, as `touch.locationInWorld` will return coordinates of point **1** in world space.

> Don't be confused that the *y* component of the point is also `160`. This is just the half the height of the screen, which by coincidence matched the *x* coordinate in my example.

However, as the bird is a child of the scene, setting its position to `(160, 160)` will place the bird at point **2**.

To avoid this, with our hunter target, we've used the `locationInNode` method of the `UITouch` class, which converts coordinates of point **1** to scene's node space and gives as a point at `(0, 160)`.

The `locationInNode` method is added to the `UITouch` class by Cocos2D using the extension category. So, you won't find this method if you're developing an iOS application without Cocos2D.

I hope you're not too tired from all that vector algebra. I know it is boring and doesn't feel like you're making games when you're calculating all those angles and adding or subtracting vectors. However, I must encourage you to refresh your knowledge of it. You don't have to be a vector algebra or trigonometry expert to make cool and fun games, but you will definitely benefit from it.

Time for action – shooting the arrow

Here is the fun part. We're going to shoot the arrow:

1. Open the `Hunter.h` header file and add the following method declaration after the `aimAtPoint:` method declaration:

```
-(CCSprite*)shootAtPoint:(CGPoint)point;
```

2. Then, open the `Hunter.m` file and add the following implementation part of this method:

```
-(CCSprite*)shootAtPoint:(CGPoint)point
{
    //1
    [self aimAtPoint:point];

    //2
    CCSprite *arrow =
      [CCSprite spriteWithImageNamed:@"arrow.png"];

    //3
    arrow.anchorPoint = ccp(0, 0.5f);

    //4
    CGPoint torsoCenterGlobal =
      [self torsoCenterInWorldCoordinates];
    arrow.position = torsoCenterGlobal;
    arrow.rotation = _torso.rotation;

    //5
```

```
    [self.parent addChild:arrow];

    //6
    CGSize viewSize = [CCDirector sharedDirector].viewSize;
    CGPoint forwardVector = ccp(1.0f, 0);

    float angleRadians =
      -1 * CC_DEGREES_TO_RADIANS(_torso.rotation);
    CGPoint arrowMovementVector =
      ccpRotateByAngle(forwardVector,
                       CGPointZero,
                       angleRadians);
    arrowMovementVector = ccpNormalize(arrowMovementVector);
    arrowMovementVector = ccpMult(arrowMovementVector,
                                  viewSize.width * 2.0f);
    //7
    CCActionMoveBy *moveAction =
      [CCActionMoveBy  actionWithDuration:2.0f
                                 position:arrowMovementVector];
    [arrow runAction:moveAction];

    //8
    return arrow;
}
```

3. Finally, open the `GameScene.m` file and make the following changes in the `touchEnded:` method:

```
-(void)touchEnded:(UITouch *)touch withEvent:(UIEvent *)event
{
    CGPoint touchLocation =
      [touch locationInNode:self];

    [_hunter shootAtPoint:touchLocation];
}
```

4. Build and run the game. Wow, now we can shoot arrows!

> You can find the project completed until this point in the `Chapter_05/Cocohunt_05_Shooting`.

What just happened?

Let's review the `shootAtPoint:` method in detail:

1. First of all, we're making sure our hunter is aiming at the point we're going to shoot. This also calculates the up-to-date rotation of the torso, which we'll use later in this method.
2. Then, we created the arrow sprite.

> I'm sure you are wondering when we added this arrow image to the project. We added the arrow image with the rest of the images when we created the spritesheet. You can open the `TexturePacker` project and review the list of the images currently in the spritesheet (and this means you can use them in your project) if you haven't done this already, or alternatively, you can take a look at images in the `Chapter_04/Assets/Spritesheet/hd` folder. All of them are packed in the spritesheet we're using.

3. Set the arrow's anchor point to the tail of the arrow. We need to rotate it around the tail and set the position of the arrow's tail to the center of the torso image, where the hunter's hand is. This is why we set the anchor point to the arrow's tail so that all transformations were made around that point.

> We discussed the `anchorPoint` property in detail in *Chapter 4, Rendering Sprites*.

4. Set the arrow's position to the center of the torso and set the rotation to the same angle as the torso. This made the arrow to be directed at the point where the hunter is currently aiming.
5. Then, we added the arrow to the parent of the current sprite. Don't be confused and don't forget that the current sprite (`self`) is the legs sprite and not the torso. The parent of the legs is `CCSpriteBatchNode` in the scene. This way, adding the arrow to the parent node will put it in the batch node.
6. This block of code might seem hard to understand, but all we did is calculate the trajectory for the arrow. We took a unit vector that is collinear to the *x* axis, and then we rotated this vector to the same angle as the arrow and multiplied it with the value equal to the double width of the screen to set its length. This way, we made sure its endpoint is off the screen and that our arrow will definitely leave the screen when following along that vector.

7. Here, we used another Cocos2D action called `CCActionMoveBy`. It takes the distance it should move the sprite by and the time it should take to travel to the endpoint. This will make our arrow fly off screen in two seconds, which sets a good speed for the arrow, that is not too fast, but fast enough.
8. At the end of this method, we returned the arrow sprite as the return value. The `GameScene` class that calls this method does not use it just yet, but it will be used soon.

Apart from the `shootAtPoint:` method itself, we've only added a small portion of the code to the `GameScene` class, to trigger this method the moment we lift the finger from the screen. The code in the `touchEnded:` method should be pretty straightforward, so we're not going to stop and review it.

Adding more birds to the GameScene class

Soon, we will write the code to hit the bird with the arrow, but it won't be very interesting if there is only one bird flying around, so we'll add more birds before shooting them.

Time for action – adding more birds

We are going to add more `Bird` objects to fly around. To do this, we're going to replace our `_bird` variable with an array and write some code to spawn the birds:

1. Open the `GameScene.m` file and remove the `_bird` variable. Instead, add two new instance variables to the `GameScene` class, as shown in the following code:

```
@implementation GameScene
{
    CCSpriteBatchNode *_batchNode;

    Hunter  *_hunter;

    float _timeUntilNextBird;
    NSMutableArray *_birds;
}
```

2. Add following method somewhere below the `update:` method:

```
-(void)spawnBird
{
    //1
    CGSize viewSize = [CCDirector sharedDirector].viewSize;

    //2
    int maxY = viewSize.height * 0.9f;
```

```
    int minY = viewSize.height * 0.6f;
    int birdY = minY + arc4random_uniform(maxY - minY);
    int birdX = viewSize.width * 1.3f;
    CGPoint birdStart = ccp(birdX, birdY);

    //3
    BirdType birdType = (BirdType)(arc4random_uniform(3));

    //4
    Bird* bird = [[Bird alloc] initWithBirdType:birdType];
    bird.position = birdStart;

    //5
    [_batchNode addChild:bird];

    //6
    [_birds addObject:bird];

    //7
    int maxTime = 20;
    int minTime = 10;
    int birdTime =
          minTime + (arc4random() % (maxTime - minTime));
    CGPoint screenLeft = ccp(0, birdY);

    //8
    CCActionMoveTo *moveToLeftEdge =
      [CCActionMoveTo actionWithDuration:birdTime
                               position:screenLeft];
    CCActionFlipX  *turnaround =
      [CCActionFlipX actionWithFlipX:YES];
    CCActionMoveTo *moveBackOffScreen =
      [CCActionMoveTo actionWithDuration:birdTime
                               position:birdStart];

    //9
    CCActionSequence *moveLeftThenBack =
      [CCActionSequence actions: moveToLeftEdge,
                                 turnaround,
                                 moveBackOffScreen,
                                 nil];
    //10
    [bird runAction:moveLeftThenBack];
}
```

3. Replace the contents of the `update:` method with the following code:

```
-(void)update:(CCTime)dt
{
    //1
    _timeUntilNextBird -= dt;

    //2
    if (_timeUntilNextBird <= 0)
    {
        //3
        [self spawnBird];

        //4
        int nextBirdTimeMax = 5;
        int nextBirdTimeMin = 2;
        int nextBirdTime = nextBirdTimeMin +
         arc4random_uniform(nextBirdTimeMax - nextBirdTimeMin);

        _timeUntilNextBird = nextBirdTime;
    }
}
```

4. Scroll to the `init` method and add the following code at the start:

```
-(instancetype)init
{
    if (self = [super init])
    {
        _timeUntilNextBird = 0;
        _birds = [NSMutableArray array];

        //..skipped..
    }

    return self;
}
```

5. Remove the `addBird` method and the call to it from the `init` method, as we're now going to spawn birds in the `update:` method.

6. Build and run the game. We should now have plenty of birds on the screen, as shown in the following screenshot:

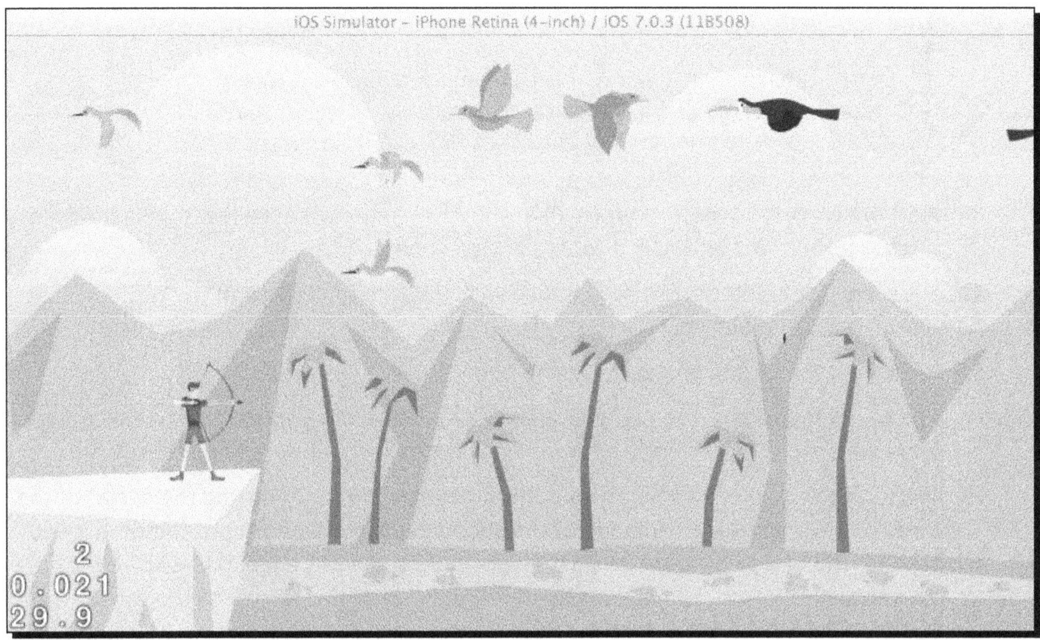

What just happened?

We've made several big changes at once. First of all, we've replaced our single `_bird` instance variable with the `_birds` array, as we're going to have many birds and not just one.

Then, we created a method to spawn a bird at a random altitude and make it fly to the left-hand side of the screen and then back. This time, instead of updating the bird position for each frame in the `update:` method, we used an action in the `spawnBird` method to set the bird's movement, so we don't need the code in the `update:` method anymore.

Instead of that old code, we've added the code to spawn the birds at some interval of time, this is why we need the `_timeUntilNextBird` instance variable.

Let's review the code for each method. We'll start with `spawnBird`:

1. We need the size of the screen to set the initial position of the bird off screen. This way, we can create it off screen and then make it fly from the left edge of the screen instead of it just magically appearing on the screen.
2. Instead of constant altitude for all of our birds, we added some variation by setting values for the minimum and maximum starting height. This code block just randomizes the initial *y* coordinate and sets the starting position for the bird off screen.

To randomize values, we use the `arc4random_uniform(N)` function that returns a value from `0` to `N` (excluding `N`).
In places where we need a value from `M` to `N`, we use the `M + arc4random_uniform(N - M)` code.

3. Also, we want random bird types. Our `enum` has `3` items, so we just took a random integer from `0` to `2` and cast it to `BirdType` enum.
4. Here, we just created the bird instance with the random type and the position that we've generated before.
5. We added the bird to the scene batch node.
6. We added the bird to the `_birds` array. This is also very important as we're going to work with those birds a little later, so we want to keep a reference of them.
7. We want to make our game as random as possible, so randomizing the speed of the birds is also a good idea. Instead of the speed itself, we randomized the time it will take for the bird to fly from its starting position to the left edge of the screen. Also, we calculated the coordinates of the left-hand side of the screen as the same height as the initial height of the bird.
8. We created a set of actions: move to the left edge of the screen, flip the bird sprite horizontally, and then fly back to the initial position off screen.
9. We used a special action called `CCActionSequence` that takes a list of actions and runs them one by one.
10. Finally, we commanded the sprite to run the sequence of the actions we created before.

Before we review the new code of the `update:` method, let's stop for a second to discuss the `CCActionSequence` action.

What any action does is simply allow you to write less code. Most actions change some property of the node over time or instantly. For example, the `CCActionMoveTo` action moves a node to a given point within given interval.

You could simply add some code in the `update:` method and move the node yourself, just as we did with our bird before. However, it is much easier to create the action and order the bird to run it, especially taking into account that you can stack, group, or create the sequence of actions.

To get a full list of possible actions, simply read the Cocos2D API documentation and search for classes starting with `CCAction`, available at `http://www.cocos2d-iphone.org/docs/api/index.html`.

Some of you might wonder why we should create a `CCActionSequence` action and how it is different from running each action one by one using the following code:

```
[bird runAction:moveToLeftEdge];
[bird runAction:turnaround];
[bird runAction:moveBackOffScreen];
```

The reason to use the `CCActionSequence` action is that the `runAction:` method doesn't wait for the action to complete. It returns immediately, simply scheduling what a sprite should do over some time or right away if we're using some instant action such as `CCActionFlipX`. This way, we will try to execute three actions at the same time. You can try this and see what happens, but I can assure you that this will be far from what we wanted to do.

Using the `CCActionSequence` action and adding actions into it makes the sprite run each action only after the previous action completes. This way, the bird flies all the way to the left, and only after this does it flip horizontally, and after flipping, it flies all the way back.

As I've said before, actions are quite convenient and there is an action almost for any kind of task.

You can run the action and forget about it. However, if you need to, you can stop all actions that are currently running using the `stopAllActions` method of the `CCNode` class, or you can stop individual action using the `stopAction:` or `stopActionByTag:` methods. In the first case, you need to save the action in some variable and pass it as parameter; and in the second case, you need to set the action's tag property to be able to stop it from using its tag. This is especially useful with actions such as `CCActionRepeatForever`, which we'll use later, as you don't need to know the number of repeats and can schedule an action to repeat forever and stop it at the required moment.

However, we should go back to reviewing the code, and the final thing we need to review for this part is the code of the `update:` method:

1. Here, we decreased the amount of time until we need to spawn a new bird by the delta time passed since the last call. When the time runs out, we'll spawn a new bird and reset this variable.
2. We checked whether it is time to spawn a new bird.
3. We spawned the bird using the `spawnBird` method we've reviewed before.
4. We then added a bit of randomness here and calculated the time until the next bird should be spawned.

Now, we're ready to detect whether the arrow will hit the bird.

Time for action – detecting if the arrow hits the bird

To make the arrow hit the bird, we need to check that the arrow and the bird are intersecting. After we have found an intersection, we need to remove the bird and the arrow. Let's add the code to perform this:

1. Open the `Bird.h` file and add the following method declaration:

```
-(void)removeBird:(BOOL)hitByArrow;
```

2. Then, open the `Bird.m` file and add its implementation:

```
-(void)removeBird:(BOOL)hitByArrow
{
    if (hitByArrow)
    {
        CCLOG(@"Bird hit by arrow");
    }
    else
    {
        CCLOG(@"Bird flew away");
    }

    [self removeFromParentAndCleanup:YES];
}
```

3. Open the `GameScene.m` file and add the `_arrows` array instance variable as follows:

```
@implementation GameScene
{
    //..skipped..
    NSMutableArray *_arrows;
}
```

4. Scroll to the `init` method and add the following array initialization code at the top:

```
-(instancetype)init
{
    if (self = [super init])
    {
        _arrows = [NSMutableArray array];

        //..skipped..
    }

    return self;
}
```

5. Find the `touchEnded:` method and update its contents as follows:

```
-(void)touchEnded:(UITouch *)touch withEvent:(UIEvent *)event
{
    CGPoint touchLocation = [touch locationInNode:self];

    CCSprite *arrow =
        [_hunter shootAtPoint:touchLocation];

    [_arrows addObject:arrow];
}
```

6. Add following code to the end of the `update:` method:

```
//1
CGSize viewSize = [CCDirector sharedDirector].viewSize;
CGRect viewBounds = CGRectMake(0,0,
                         viewSize.width, viewSize.height);

//2
for (int i = _birds.count - 1; i >= 0; i--)
{
    Bird *bird = _birds[i];

    //3
    BOOL birdFlewOffScreen =
      (bird.position.x + (bird.contentSize.width * 0.5f)) >
        viewSize.width;

    //4
    if (bird.flipX == YES && birdFlewOffScreen)
    {
        [_birds removeObject:bird];
        [bird removeBird:NO];

        continue;
    }

    //5
    for (int j = _arrows.count - 1; j >= 0; j--)
    {
        CCSprite* arrow = _arrows[j];

        //6
        if (!CGRectContainsPoint(viewBounds,
                                 arrow.position))
        {
            [arrow removeFromParentAndCleanup:YES];
            [_arrows removeObject:arrow];
```

```
                continue;
            }

            //7
            if (CGRectIntersectsRect(arrow.boundingBox,
                                     bird.boundingBox))
            {
                [arrow removeFromParentAndCleanup:YES];
                [_arrows removeObject:arrow];

                [_birds removeObject:bird];
                [bird removeBird:YES];

                break;
            }
        }
    }
```

7. Build and run the game. Now, when you hit the bird with the arrow, the bird disappears from the screen and you get an output in the console similar to the following:

```
Cocohunt[75440:70b] Bird hit by arrow
```

8. Also, when you let the bird fly away from the screen, you get an output in the console similar to this:

```
Cocohunt[75440:70b] Bird flew away
```

You can spend some time shooting the birds, and then we'll review the code that we've added to make this work.

> You can find a snapshot of the project at this point in the `Chapter_05/Cocohunt_05_Hitting_Birds` folder.

What just happened?

If you spent some time shooting the birds, you must have noticed that it feels unnatural. This is because sometimes the bird is hit before the arrow image actually touches the bird image. The reason for this is that we're checking the intersection of the bounding boxes, instead of actual bird and arrow.

All of our images are just rectangles with transparency areas from Cocos2D point of view, so all we can check with default sprites is that their bounding boxes intersect. Refer to the following figure:

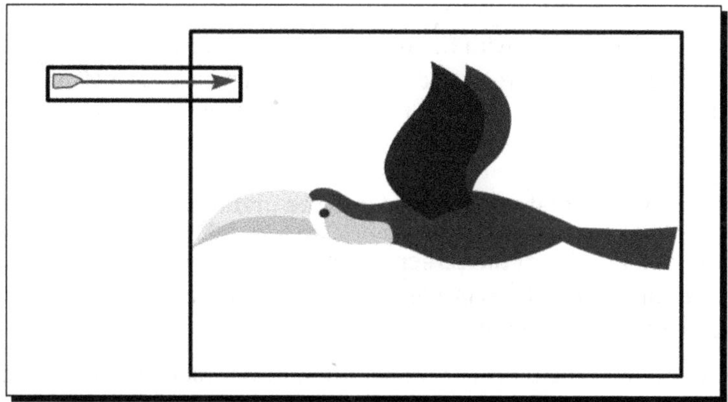

Bounding boxes intersect while images don't

As you can see in the preceding image, bounding boxes intersect, but the arrow didn't hit the bird just yet. This is why it feels unnatural.

There are different techniques that can help you to get more realistic collision detection; we will review them later in the book when we review physics engines.

> There are ways to create pixel-perfect collision detection without a physics engine. However, they require deeper knowledge and are not very beginner friendly. Also, they don't always perform well. I would suggest use bounding boxes for simple collision detection; if this is not enough, use a physics engine just for collision detection, especially as it is very easy to with new Cocos2D v3.0 integrated physics.

Now back to the code. We've added the `removeBird:` method to our `Bird` class so that we can remove the bird. It is called in two cases: when the bird is hit by the arrow and when the bird flies away from the screen.

For now, in both cases, we're just removing the bird sprite from the scene using the `removeFromParentAndCleanup:` method, which removes the node from its parent node.

> You can add sprites to the parent node using `addChild:`. Then, when you want to remove sprites, you use `removeFromParentAndCleanup:` or simply `removeFromParent`, which is equal to calling `removeFromParentAndCleanup:` and passing `YES`.

Then, we're modifying the `touchEnded:` method, and this time, we get the arrow sprite returned by the `shootAtPoint:` method. We store it in the `_arrows` array that we've just added and initialized.

At this point, we have two arrays: `_birds` and `_arrows`. It is time to check whether any arrow that is in the air intersects with the bird. In addition to this, we need to check whether the arrow or the bird is off the screen and remove it in that case, as it is not going to participate in the game anymore. We don't want to waste our resources on objects we are not going to use anymore.

Let's review the code block that we've added into the `update:` method in more detail:

1. First, we took the size of the screen and created a rectangle representing the bounds of the screen. If the point is inside this rectangle, then it is on screen, and if it is not, then it is outside the screen.
2. Then, we iterated the birds in reverse order, as we might need to remove the birds from the array as we go, which will change the size of the array.

> It is a common technique to iterate the array in the reverse order if there is a chance that you will remove elements as you go. As an alternative, you can iterate a copy of the array and remove its elements from the original array.

3. We checked whether the bird is beyond the screen bounds.
4. If the bird is off screen and also if it is flying to the right, we need to remove this bird as it flew away without being shot. It is important to check both conditions (off screen and `flipX`), otherwise we'll remove a spawned bird that just didn't fly onto the screen yet.

> Note the `continue;` operator, as we don't want to process the bird that we've already removed. By calling `continue`, we are moving to the next `for` iteration without processing the remaining code. Also, note the fact that we're passing `NO` to the `removeBird:` method, as the bird wasn't hit by an arrow.

5. At this point, we know that the bird is still on the screen, so we need to check whether any arrow is hitting the bird at the moment.
6. While we are iterating through arrows, we can also check whether the arrow is still on the screen, and if it is, we should remove it. We don't allow the arrow to hit the bird beyond the screen edge.
7. If the arrow's bounding box intersects the bird's bounding box, we remove both the arrow and the bird. However, this time, we pass `YES` to the `removeBird:` method, as the bird did not just fly away, but was hit by an arrow. This will allow us to perform some additional actions later.

It was easier than it looked, wasn't it? There is one more thing that we need to know about this approach. Currently, we're using a discrete collision detection algorithm to check whether the arrow and the bird are currently intersecting at each frame. This can lead to a situation when there is no intersection at the current frame and no intersection at the next frame although the arrow has clearly passed through the bird. This can happen because the arrow moves so fast that it travels each frame a distance bigger than the object it should collide with.

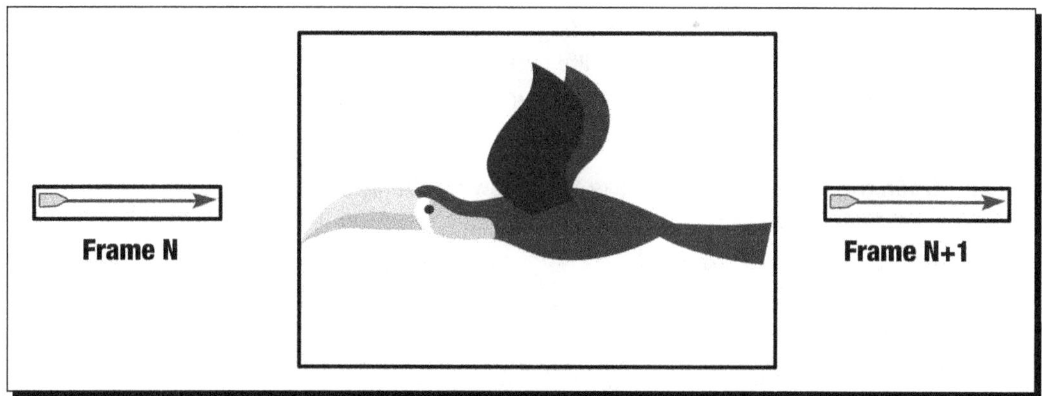

Tunneling effect

This effect is often called the **tunneling effect**. Due to this effect, not only can an arrow or a bullet fly through the object without hitting it, but also your character can be stuck to the wall or in the ground because it passes the surface edge in one frame.

After learning the last fact about this basic collision detection, you might think that you're doomed if you're going to use it. Well, it is not that bad, and this basic algorithm can serve you well in many cases.

Winning, losing, and other states

Shooting birds infinitely will get you bored at some point. You have to be able to win or lose the game to make it interesting. Also, our hunter shoots the arrows too fast. We should fix these issues before we can call our game minimally playable.

A good way to fix all of our issues is by introducing states. It is very common in game development to think about game objects or even the whole game itself as state machines.

To use states, you need to think upfront what states can your object be in and write the code to transition from one state to another. Then, you can check the current state of the object and understand what it can or should do in its current state. It will get clearer when we do this for our game objects.

Time for action – using states for the bird's life cycle

We're going to give our hunter several tries to hit the bird. This means that the bird will fly on the screen, then fly away, and then return. This sequence will repeat several times. This means we won't be able to use the `flipX` property to understand whether our bird is flying away completely or just making another pass.

Instead of using the `flipX` property as a flag, we're going to introduce a state's `enum` and change the bird's state during the bird's life cycle. Then, when we'll apply some action to the bird. We're going to check whether the bird is in the correct state for this action. Perform the following steps:

1. Open the `Bird.h` file and make the following changes to add the new `BirdState` enum, new `birdState` property, and a `turnaround` method declaration:

```
#import "CCSprite.h"

typedef enum BirdType
{
    BirdTypeBig,
    BirdTypeMedium,
    BirdTypeSmall
} BirdType;

typedef enum BirdState
{
    BirdStateFlyingIn,
    BirdStateFlyingOut,
    BirdStateFlewOut,
    BirdStateDead
} BirdState;

@interface Bird : CCSprite

@property (nonatomic, assign) BirdType birdType;

@property (nonatomic, assign) BirdState birdState;

-(instancetype)initWithBirdType:(BirdType)typeOfBird;

-(void)removeBird:(BOOL)hitByArrow;

-(void)turnaround;

@end
```

2. Then, switch to the `Bird.m` file and add a new instance variable called `_timesToVisit` as follows:

```
@implementation Bird
{
    int _timesToVisit;
}
```

3. Add the following lines at the start of the `if` block in the `initWithBirdType:` method:

```
-(instancetype)initWithBirdType:(BirdType)typeOfBird
{
    //..skipped..

    if (self = [super initWithImageNamed:birdImageName])
    {
        _timesToVisit = 3;
        self.birdState = BirdStateFlyingIn;

       //..skipped..
    }

    return self;
}
```

4. Find the `removeBird:` method and replace it with following code:

```
-(void)removeBird:(BOOL)hitByArrow
{
    [self removeFromParentAndCleanup:YES];

    if (hitByArrow)
    {
        self.birdState = BirdStateDead;
    }
    else
    {
        self.birdState = BirdStateFlewOut;
    }
}
```

5. While still in the `Bird.m` file, add the `turnaround` method implementation as shown in the following code:

```
-(void)turnaround
{
    self.flipX = !self.flipX;

    if (self.flipX)
      _timesToVisit--;

    if (_timesToVisit <= 0)
      self.birdState = BirdStateFlyingOut;
}
```

6. Open the `GameScene.m` file and in the `update:` method, inside the `for` cycle where we check that the bird is off screen, find the following condition:

```
if (bird.flipX == YES && birdFlewOffScreen)
```

7. Replace this condition with the following code:

```
if (bird.birdState == BirdStateFlyingOut && birdFlewOffScreen)
```

8. Then, scroll to the `spawnBird` method and replace the part where we create and run the actions, which is after the line where we calculate the `screenLeft` position, with the following:

```
-(void)spawnBird
{
    //..skipped..

    CGPoint screenLeft = ccp(0, birdY); //<-- after this line

    CCActionMoveTo *moveToLeftEdge =
      [CCActionMoveTo actionWithDuration:birdTime
                                position:screenLeft];

    //1
    CCActionCallFunc *turnaround =
              [CCActionCallFunc actionWithTarget:bird
                            selector:@selector(turnaround)];

    CCActionMoveTo *moveBackOffScreen =
      [CCActionMoveTo actionWithDuration:birdTime
                                 position:birdStart];

    //2
    CCActionSequence *moveLeftThenBack =
      [CCActionSequence actions: moveToLeftEdge,
                                 turnaround,
                                 moveBackOffScreen,
```

```
                                   turnaround,
                                         nil];

    //3
    CCActionRepeatForever *flyForever =
      [CCActionRepeatForever
         actionWithAction:moveLeftThenBack];

    [bird runAction:flyForever];
}
```

9. Build and run the game. Wow, that's a lot of birds!

Maybe, even too many to test the changes that we've made. To make it easier to test everything, it is better to limit the bird to one.

To do this, open the `GameScene.m` file and find the following line inside the `update:` method:

```
_timeUntilNextBird = nextBirdTime;
```

Change this to the following one:

```
_timeUntilNextBird = 10000; //nextBirdTime;
```

You should see one bird visiting the screen three times (because we set the `_timesToVisit` variable to `3`).

Don't forget to revert the temporary change and change the line back to have many birds.

[You can find a snapshot of the project at this point in the `Chapter_05/Cocohunt_05_Bird_States` folder.]

What just happened?

As we can see now, our bird can leave the screen several times and come back later. We cannot rely on just testing the `flipX` property and the fact that the bird is off screen. Instead we've introduced states of the bird.

Our bird can be in four states as follows:

- `BirdStateFlyingIn`: This is the state when the bird flies onto the screen area and it doesn't matter if the bird is doing this for the first time or returning.
- `BirdStateFlyingOut`: This is the state when the bird has already completed the required number of tries and it is going to fly away from the screen for good.

- BirdStateFlewOut: This is the state when the bird made it and left the game field unharmed.
- BirdStateDead: This is the state when the bird didn't make it and was hit by an arrow.

To store the current state, we've added the birdState property. In addition to this, we've added a counter for the number of times the bird should visit the screen called _timesToVisit and the turnaround method that updates this counter and changes the state to BirdStateFlyingOut when the bird visited the screen the required number of times.

Later, we'll use the counter to determine the number of points scored when the hunter hits the bird. If the hunter hits the bird on its first visit, he gets more points than if the bird is visiting for the second or the third time.

Irrespective of whether the bird was hit by the arrow or flew away, it ends its life in the removeBird: method. Then, we remove it from the scene using the removeFromParentAndCleanup: method, which stops all running actions and removes the bird.

We've made several changes to the GameScene.m file. We've changed the condition inside the update: method to check the correct state of the bird when it is leaving the screen and not just the flipX property.

Finally, we've made changes to the spawnBird method, which we'll review in detail:

1. First of all, we've changed the CCActionFlipX action to the CCActionCallFunc action, as we need to do more than just flip the sprite horizontally. This action calls the given method on a given target.
2. Then, we've added one more turnaround at the end of the sequence so that the bird turns around again when it is about to enter the screen for the second time. This way the sequence will be: move to the left edge, call the turnaround method, move to the starting point, and call the turnaround method.
3. Finally, we've wrapped the sequence into the CCActionRepeatForever action, as we don't know the number of repeats just yet. Instead of specifying the exact number of repeats, the bird will be removed after _timesToVisit becomes 0 in the update: method.

It might seem overcomplicated to have states on such a simple object as a bird. We can just add a property called isFlyingOut and use it instead of the states. However, the goal was to demonstrate how to use states. Also, as it often happens, when you start with one flag property, then add another one, and another. In the end, you've got a total mess where you should check several combinations of these properties to understand the state of the object. States allow you to control your game much better.

Time for action – animating the shooting and limiting the shooting rate

We will continue to add states to the game objects, and this time, we will update the `Hunter` class. We're going to animate the process of reloading the arrow and will limit the shooting rate. Let's do this using the following steps:

1. Open the `Hunter.h` file and add `HunterState enum` right after the last `#import` directive:

```
typedef enum HunterState
{
    HunterStateIdle,
    HunterStateAiming,
    HunterStateReloading
} HunterState;
```

2. Then, add a property called `hunterState` to the `Hunter` class as follows:

```
@property (nonatomic, assign) HunterState hunterState;
```

3. Add a declaration of the method called `getReadyToShootAgain` using the following line of code:

```
-(void)getReadyToShootAgain;
```

4. Switch to the `Hunter.m` file and import the `CCAnimation.h` header as follows:

```
#import "CCAnimation.h"
```

5. Then, initialize the hunter state to the `HunterStateIdle` state inside the `if` block in the `init` method as follows:

```
self.hunterState = HunterStateIdle;
```

6. Scroll down and add the implementation of the `getReadyToShootAgain` method as shown in the following code:

```
-(void)getReadyToShootAgain
{
    self.hunterState = HunterStateIdle;
}
```

7. Then, directly below this method, add the `reloadArrow` method as shown in the following code:

```
-(void)reloadArrow
{
    //1
    self.hunterState = HunterStateReloading;

    //2
    NSString *frameNameFormat = @"hunter_top_%d.png";
    NSMutableArray* frames = [NSMutableArray array];
    for (int i = 0; i < 6; i++)
    {
        NSString *frameName =
          [NSString stringWithFormat:frameNameFormat, i];
        CCSpriteFrame *frame =
          [CCSpriteFrame frameWithImageNamed:frameName];
        [frames addObject:frame];
    }

    //3
    CCAnimation *reloadAnimation =
      [CCAnimation animationWithSpriteFrames:frames
                                       delay:0.05f];
    reloadAnimation.restoreOriginalFrame = YES;
    CCActionAnimate *reloadAnimAction =
      [CCActionAnimate actionWithAnimation:reloadAnimation];

    //4
    CCActionCallFunc *readyToShootAgain =
      [CCActionCallFunc actionWithTarget:self
               selector:@selector(getReadyToShootAgain)];

    //5
    CCActionDelay *delay =
      [CCActionDelay actionWithDuration:0.25f];

    //6
    CCActionSequence *reloadAndGetReady =
      [CCActionSequence actions:reloadAnimAction,
                                delay,
                                readyToShootAgain,
                                nil];
    //7
    [_torso runAction:reloadAndGetReady];
}
```

8. Add the call to the `reloadArrow:` method at the end of the `shootAtPoint:` method as shown in the following code:

```
-(CCSprite*)shootAtPoint:(CGPoint)point
{
    //..skipped..
    [self reloadArrow];

    return arrow;
}
```

9. Then, switch to the `GameScene.m` file and add the following method somewhere below the `touchEnded:`

```
-(void)touchCancelled:(UITouch *)touch
              withEvent:(UIEvent *)event
{
    [_hunter getReadyToShootAgain];
}
```

10. Also, add the following code to the beginning of the `touchBegan:` method:

```
-(void)touchBegan:(UITouch *)touch withEvent:(UIEvent *)event
{
    if (_hunter.hunterState != HunterStateIdle)
    {
        [super touchBegan:touch withEvent:event];
        return;
    }

    CGPoint touchLocation = [touch locationInNode:self];
    [_hunter aimAtPoint:touchLocation];
}
```

11. Build and run the game. The good part is that our hunter is nicely animated while reloading the arrow, but it looks like he cannot shoot very fast anymore. This will make playing the game more interesting, as the player will need to aim more carefully rather than just shooting the bow as if it is a tommy gun.

If you've limited the number of birds to one, by setting a big time interval in the `update:` method, don't forget to change the line `_timeUntilNextBird = nextBirdTime;` back.

> You can find a snapshot of the project at this point in the `Chapter_05/Cocohunt_05_Hunter_States` folder.

What just happened?

Our hunter is a bit different from the bird. He has different states and the goals that we pursue when we add these states are different. What we wanted to do is separate three different states of the hunter and make sure that he can only shoot while idle.

This solves several important issues. We've added animation of hunter reloading the arrow and don't want to allow our hunter to shoot while he reloads the arrow. It would be strange if he could shoot while reloading. Also, now we can limit the rate of fire using `CCActionDelay`, to make the game more competitive.

Let's review all changes that we've made. I will omit the part where we added the `enum` and the `hunterState` properties, as this should be clear by now.

The `getReadyToShootAgain` method just resets the hunter. It is used after the animation and delay actions complete and is used in the `touchCancelled:` method. Without the call to this method, if touches are cancelled (for example, someone calls the player and the game goes to the background), we can get stuck in the aiming state forever.

The code that we've added into the `touchBegan:` method ignores all touches if we're not in the idle mode. This means that if the player touches the screen while reloading, we simply ignore that touch. Note the following line of code:

```
[super touchBegan:touch withEvent:event];
```

This line tells Cocos2D that we don't want to process this touch and should pass it to the underlying node. After the call to this method, the `touchMoved:` and `touchEnded:` methods won't get called for this particular touch. This is why we don't check the hunter state in these methods, as we only get to them when in the correct state.

> The unprocessed touch is passed to the underlying node. All touches are processed in the reverse render order, are regulated by z-order, and the order in which they were added. So, if our node is on top of some other node (that is rendered after it), it first has a chance to handle the touch, but if we pass the touch to the `super` class, it means we don't want to process this touch and it can be passed to underlying node. In our case, we don't have any underlying nodes that handle touches and we don't process this touch either, so it is simply left unhandled.

Finally, let's have a closer look at the most interesting part, that is, the `reloadArrow:` method that we call at the end of the `shootAtPoint:` method, right after we shoot the arrow:

1. Set the hunter state to the reloading state. This disables shooting until the reloading completes.
2. Here we loaded the animation frames. If you have a look at our spritesheet, you will find that we've added images called `hunter_top_0.png` and `hunter_top_1.png`. These are the frames of reload animation. We are using the same technique with the `stringWithFormat:` method to form an actual frame name as we did with the flying bird animation.
3. We created the animation and corresponding action. Note the following line of code:

   ```
   reloadAnimation.restoreOriginalFrame = YES;
   ```

   Without setting `restoreOriginalFrame` to `YES`, the animation action just leaves our sprite displaying the last frame of the animation. This works just fine for our birds, as animation is repeated forever. However, with our hunter, we don't want to leave it at the last frame; we want to reset the image back to the first frame where the hunter is aiming. You can comment out this line and see the difference.
4. We created the action that will call the `getReadyToShootAgain` method and will reset our hunter state to idle when he finishes reloading the arrow.
5. We created a special action called `CCActionDelay`. This action is very useful when used in sequence with other actions. It allows you to pause between two actions in a sequence or add a delay at the beginning of the sequence, before the first action that actually does something. The action itself does absolutely nothing; it just wastes some time.
6. We created the sequence of actions that we want the hunter to do to reload the arrow. We want to play animation, and then make a small delay to decrease the rate of fire, and finally reset the hunter and allow making the next shot.
7. Run the sequence on a torso sprite. It is important to remember that we run most actions on the torso sprite, not the whole hunter.

Now, when we have the behavior of the hunter and bird's objects close to what we want, we can concentrate on the winning and losing conditions of the game.

Time for action – winning or losing the game

In most games, we can win or lose. This makes the game interesting. In our game, we will win the game if we avoid losing. To be more specific, we will lose if we allow some number of the birds to fly away, for example, 3 birds out of 20. If we'll hit more than 17 birds, then we'll win.

Let's add the code to win and lose the game:

1. Open the `GameScene.h` file and add `enum` with game states and a property to hold the current state, as shown in the following code:

```
#import "CCScene.h"

typedef enum GameState
{
    GameStateUninitialized,
    GameStatePlaying,
    GameStatePaused,
    GameStateWon,
    GameStateLost

} GameState;

@interface GameScene : CCScene

@property (nonatomic, assign) GameState gameState;

@end
```

2. Switch to the `GameScene.m` file and add the following instance variables:

```
@implementation GameScene
{
    //..skipped..
    int _birdsToSpawn;
    int _birdsToLose;
}
```

3. Initialize the state property and the variables that we've added before in the `init` method as follows:

```
-(instancetype)init
{
    if (self = [super init])
    {

        self.gameState = GameStateUninitialized;

        _birdsToSpawn = 20;
```

```
        _birdsToLose = 3;

        //..skipped..
    }

    return self;
}
```

4. Add the following method below the `init` method:

```
-(void)onEnter
{
    [super onEnter];
    self.gameState = GameStatePlaying;
}
```

5. Add the three following methods below the `update:` method:

```
-(void)checkWonLost
{
    if (_birdsToLose <= 0)
    {
        [self lost];
    }
    else if (_birdsToSpawn <= 0 && _birds.count <= 0)
    {
        [self won];
    }
}

-(void)lost
{
    self.gameState = GameStateLost;
    CCLOG(@"YOU LOST!");
}

-(void)won
{
    self.gameState = GameStateWon;
    CCLOG(@"YOU WON!");
}
```

6. Make the following changes in the `update:` method:

```
-(void)update:(CCTime)dt
{
    if (self.gameState != GameStatePlaying)
        return;

    _timeUntilNextBird -= dt;
    if (_timeUntilNextBird <= 0 && _birdsToSpawn > 0)
```

```
    {
        [self spawnBird];
        _birdsToSpawn--;

        //..skipped..
    }

    //..skipped..

    for (int i = _birds.count - 1; i >= 0; i--)
    {
        //..skipped..

        if (bird.birdState == BirdStateFlyingOut &&
            birdFlewOffScreen)
        {
            _birdsToLose--;

            [bird removeBird:NO];
            [_birds removeObject:bird];
            continue;
        }

        //..skipped..

    }

    [self checkWonLost];
}
```

7. Scroll down to the part where we handle touches and make the following changes to the `touchBegan:` method:

```
-(void)touchBegan:(UITouch *)touch withEvent:(UIEvent *)event
{
    if (_hunter.hunterState != HunterStateIdle
        ||  self.gameState != GameStatePlaying)
    {
        [super touchBegan:touch withEvent:event];
        return;
    }

    //..skipped..
}
```

8. Then, make a similar change to the `touchEnded:` method as follows:

```
-(void)touchEnded:(UITouch *)touch withEvent:(UIEvent *)event
{
    if (self.gameState != GameStatePlaying)
        return;

    //..skipped..
}
```

9. Build and run the game. Play a little, and win and lose the game to check whether everything works correctly. For now, you should only get the console output when you win or lose, we will improve this in the next chapters.

[You can find a snapshot of the project at this point in the `Chapter_05/Cocohunt_05_Wining_and_Losing` folder.]

What just happened?

We finally got something completely playable. Of course, the game would benefit from a few improvements, which we'll do in the rest of this chapter and in the next few chapters, but you can already play around right now. Here is an explanation of what we just did; we started adding states to our `GameScene` class. Let's review each state:

- `GameStateUninitialized`: This is a special state that we use as an initial value. It is required so that the game doesn't start earlier than we want.
- `GameStatePlaying`: This is the main state of the game. In this state, all the action happens. We have several checks that the game must be in this state to make some actions. For example, we spawn birds and allow shooting only in this state.
- `GameStatePaused`: This state is not used yet, but later when we add a pause button to our game, this state will mean that the game is temporarily paused.
- `GameStateWon`: This is the final state of the game if we win.
- `GameStateLost`: This is the final state of the game if we lose.

In addition to states, we've added two counter variables, `_birdsToSpawn` and `_birdsToLose`, that we use to count the number of the birds we've already spawned and the birds that we didn't hit and flew away. We've set them to some test values, but you can tweak them as you like, as long as `_birdsToLose` is less than `_birdsToSpawn`; otherwise the player will always win.

We use the `onEnter` method to start the game. This will start the game as soon as our game scene will be displayed on the screen. The `onEnter` method is called when the scene is already displayed on the screen in contrast to the `init` method, which is called when we create the scene. We will discuss the `onEnter` method in more detail in *Chapter 9, User Interface and Navigation*.

We can do without this method and add some kind of a **Play** button to start the game, but starting the game straight away works just fine.

The `checkWonLost`, lost, and won methods are used to handle win and lose scenarios in the game. In the `checkWonLost` method, we check whether we've missed more birds than allowed and lost the game. In addition to this, we check whether we've spawned all the birds and there are no birds on screen. In the latter case, we can assume that we won the game. The lost and won methods are very simple for now; they are mostly stubs for the code that we'll add later.

The changes in the `update:` method are quite straightforward. We added a check that we're in the `GameStatePlaying` state, and if not, we just exit the `update:` method straight away, as everything that we do in the `update:` method assumes that the game is running.

Then, we added the code to decrease the number of birds to spawn when we spawn one. Finally, after we check the intersections of birds and arrows and remove all the birds hit by an arrow or those that flew away from the screen, we can check if we won or lost the game at the very end of the `update:` method.

Then, as a finishing touch, we updated our touch handling methods so that we don't shoot the birds when the game is not in the `GameStatePlaying` state. We don't want to waste arrows in despair when we've lost, neither do we want to waste arrows to celebrate winning, and more importantly, we don't want to allow shooting when the game has not yet started or is paused.

Improving the gameplay

At this point, we can play the game, but is it competitive enough? Let's add a few more changes that will make our game better.

Time for action – limiting the aiming range

Currently, we can just tap on the bird and the hunter will hit it. This is not very competitive; it would be harder to hit the bird if we needed to touch the screen closer to the hunter. We're going to limit the distance from the hunter where you can tap to aim.

At the end of the previous chapter, we added a bunch of images that we're going to use. There is one special image called `power_meter.png`, which we will use to show the aiming range.

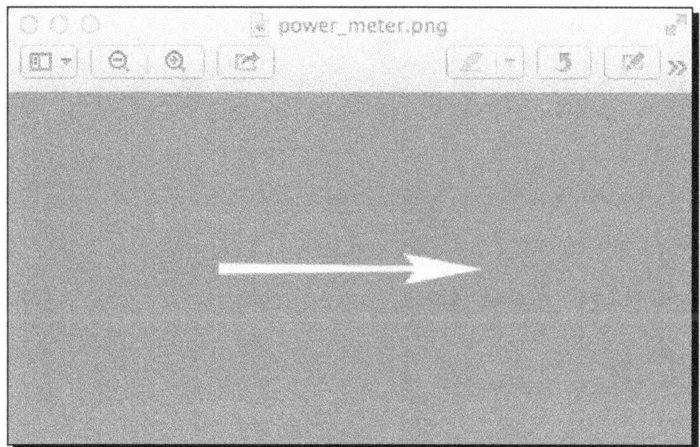

The `power_meter.png` image represents an arrow colored in white. Don't worry if you can't see it in the finder thumbnails or in preview, as you just can't see white image on a white background. If you want to see the image, you can open `power_meter.png` from the `Chapter_04/Assets/Spritesheet/hd` folder in the preview application. Later, it will become clear why we've used the white color.

Now, we're going to use this image in the code. Follow these steps to display the aiming indicator and limit the aiming range:

1. Open the `GameScene.m` file and add following instance variables:

```
@implementation GameScene
{
    //..skipped..

    int _maxAimingRadius;
    CCSprite *_aimingIndicator;
}
```

2. Now, add the `setupAimingIndicator` method:

```
-(void)setupAimingIndicator
{
    //1
    _maxAimingRadius = 100;

    //2
    _aimingIndicator =
      [CCSprite spriteWithImageNamed:@"power_meter.png"];
    _aimingIndicator.opacity = 0.3f;
    _aimingIndicator.anchorPoint = ccp(0,0.5f);
    _aimingIndicator.visible = NO;

    //3
    [_batchNode addChild:_aimingIndicator];
}
```

3. Call this method from the `init` method as follows:

```
-(instancetype)init
{
    if (self = [super init])
    {

        //..skipped..

        [self setupAimingIndicator];
    }

    return self;
}
```

4. Add the following method somewhere near the end of the `GameScene.m` file:

```
-(BOOL)checkAimingIndicatorForPoint:(CGPoint)point
{
    //1
    _aimingIndicator.position =
      [_hunter torsoCenterInWorldCoordinates];
    _aimingIndicator.rotation = [_hunter torsoRotation];

    //2
    float distance =
      ccpDistance(_aimingIndicator.position, point);
    BOOL isInRange = distance < _maxAimingRadius;

    //3
    float scale =
      distance/_aimingIndicator.contentSize.width;
```

```
    _aimingIndicator.scale = scale;

    //4
    _aimingIndicator.color =
      isInRange ? [CCColor greenColor] : [CCColor redColor];

    //5
    return isInRange;
}
```

5. Add the following code in the `touchBegan:` and `touchMoved:` methods:

```
-(void)touchBegan:(UITouch *)touch withEvent:(UIEvent *)event
{
    //..skipped..

    _aimingIndicator.visible = YES;
    [self checkAimingIndicatorForPoint:touchLocation];
}

-(void)touchMoved:(UITouch *)touch withEvent:(UIEvent *)event
{
    //..skipped..

    [self checkAimingIndicatorForPoint:touchLocation];
}
```

6. Replace the `touchEnded:` method with following code:

```
-(void)touchEnded:(UITouch *)touch withEvent:(UIEvent *)event
{
    if (self.gameState != GameStatePlaying)
      return;

    CGPoint touchLocation = [touch locationInNode:self];

    BOOL canShoot =
     [self checkAimingIndicatorForPoint:touchLocation];
    if (canShoot)
    {
        CCSprite* arrow =
          [_hunter shootAtPoint:touchLocation];
        [_arrows addObject:arrow];
    }
    else
    {
        [_hunter getReadyToShootAgain];
    }

    _aimingIndicator.visible = NO;
}
```

7. Open the `Hunter.h` file and add the following method declarations:

```
-(CGPoint)torsoCenterInWorldCoordinates;
-(float)torsoRotation;
```

8. Then, switch to the `Hunter.m` file and add the implementation of the `torsoRotation` method below the `torsoCenterInWorldCoordinates:` method (that already exists, and we've only made public by adding declaration in the header) as follows:

```
-(float)torsoRotation
{
    return _torso.rotation;
}
```

9. Build and run the game. Now, you can only shoot at the birds when the arrow is green, and it is green only if it is close enough to the hunter character. If the arrow is red, then you're too far from the hunter and you should tap/click closer to the hunter. Refer to the following screenshot:

The red aiming arrow indicates that we're tapping too far from the hunter

I'm sure the birds are happy with the last change, as it will be harder to hit the birds now.

> You can find a snapshot of the project at this point in the `Chapter_05/Cocohunt_05_Limiting_Aiming_Range` folder.

What just happened?

Let's start our review from the `GameScene` class. As you've probably guessed, two variables that we added are the maximum aiming range and the aiming indicator (arrow) sprite.

Let's review the code of the `setupAimingIndicator` method:

1. Set the maximum aiming radius to `100` points. It should be hard enough to hit the bird if we can only tap closer than `100` points to the hunter. As we're using this variable later in the code, we can always adjust this value here.
2. We created the aiming indicator sprite using the white arrow image. The following are a few interesting properties we set:
   - Setting the `opacity` property to `0.3f` makes our aiming indicator semitransparent. The `opacity` property takes values from `0` to `1`, where `0` means completely transparent and `1` means completely opaque.
   - Setting the `anchorPoint` property to `(0, 0.5)` moves the anchor point to the middle of the left edge of the sprite rectangle. This has several interesting effects. First of all, when we set the position of the aiming indicator, we set the position of the tail, just like we did when we added the arrow that we shoot from the bow. Second, when we rotate the aiming indicator, it rotates around the anchor point, similar to what we've seen before with the arrow. Finally, the aiming indicator scales relative to the anchor point; we'll see this in a moment.
   - Setting `visible` to `NO` makes our aiming indicator invisible. As we don't want to show it always, but we only show it when we're aiming with our finger.
3. Added the aiming indicator sprite to the batch node, as it is also a part of our spritesheet.

Now it is time to review the most interesting method, `checkAimingIndicatorForPoint:`. This method checks whether we tapped close enough to the hunter and decides whether we can shoot or are too far away. In addition to this, it changes the color of the aiming indicator to red or green depending on whether we can make this shot:

1. We started by setting the aiming indicator to the same position where the hunter is. It is required in case we move our hunter sprite. Also, when the torso rotates, its center moves a bit. In addition to this, we also set the rotation of the aiming indicator to the same rotation value as the torso, as this way it will point to the target point.
2. Now, we calculated the distance from the torso to the target point (the point we're currently clicking by mouse or touching finger) and checked whether it is closer than the maximum allowed distance.

3. We calculated the scale value that we need to set our aiming indicator image to so that it touches the target point with its tip.

> The `scale` property is used to make nodes bigger or smaller. To make the node bigger, you set it to the value higher than `1.0`; to make it smaller, you set it to a value lower than `1.0`. Setting the scale to values close to `0` will make the node so small that you won't see it. If you need to scale the object only horizontally or vertically, you can use the `scaleX` or `scaleY` property.

   An important point to note is that scaling is relative to the anchor point. As our anchor point is set to one side of the aiming indicator image, it scales from that anchor point, making the aiming indicator grow in the direction of our target point without moving the tail. If we left the anchor point in the center (`ccp(0.5, 0.5)`), it would move both the tail and the tip away from the center where the anchor point is, as it scaled up. We don't want that.

4. Here, we used a little trick that allows us to have one white image instead of two images for the green and red states of the aiming indicator. The color property sets the tint color. What it actually means is that it multiplies this color on the color of the each pixel of the sprite texture. The aiming indicator image is completely white, and the white color is represented by `1` in each color component of RGB (that is, `(1,1,1)`). This means that multiplying it with green (that is, `(0,1,0)`) will give us `(1*0, 1*1, 1*0) = (0,1,0)`), which is green and multiplying with red (that is, `(1,0,0)`) also gives plain red as a result. In other words, any color multiplied on a white color just gives the original color.
5. We returned the result of the distance check so that we could decide whether the hunter can shoot in the `touchEnded:` method.

The rest of the changes are simply showing and hiding the aiming indicator and checking whether we can shoot in the touch-handling methods.

Time for action – alternative control using a gyroscope

It will be even more fun to control our hunter using a gyroscope.

> A Gyroscope is a device that measures an iPhone's orientation. Using a gyroscope, you can tell how your iPhone is positioned in the world. This way, if you track the gyroscope information, you can track when the user tilts or rotates a device in hands. A gyroscope is often used in racing games, where you can use your iPhone as a steering wheel. We'll use it to control the hunter's aim.

Unfortunately, only happy owners of the iOS devices and participants of the Apple iOS Developer Program can test the code in this part of the chapter, as you cannot test a gyroscope on the simulator.

> You can still follow this chapter to learn information on how to use the gyroscope. If you decide to skip this chapter, take the final project for this chapter from the `Chapter_05/Cocohunt_05_Final` folder as a starter project for the next chapter as we're going to build on it.

To get information about the device's orientation, we need to use the `CoreMotion` framework. We can just add it to the project, but let's use the new `@import` feature through the following steps:

1. Open the **Cocohunt** project properties by clicking on the **Cocohunt** project in the **Project Navigator** pane on the left.
2. Switch to **Build Settings** tab and type `enable modules` in the search box. You should see only one option named **Enable Modules (C and Objective-C)** under **Apple LLVM 5.0 – Language – Modules section.**
3. Set **Enable Modules (C and Objective-C)** to `YES`. Take a look at the following screenshot if you have any difficulties finding this option:

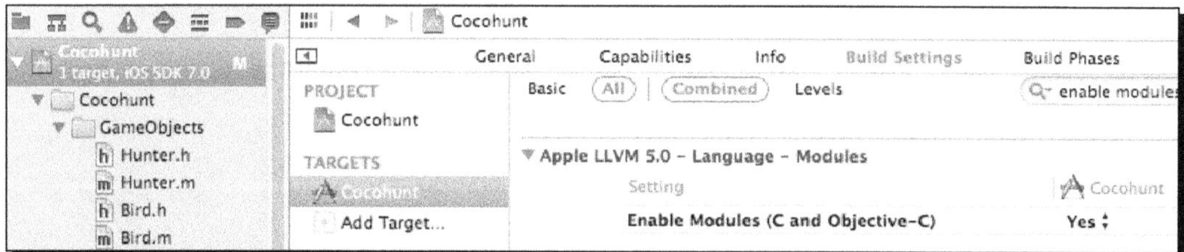

Enabling modules in Xcode's project settings

4. After enabling modules, let's use them and write the code to use the gyroscope to control the hunter. Open the `GameScene.m` file and import the `CoreMotion` framework. Below all `#import` directives, write the following line of code (make sure that you use `@import` and not `#import`):

```
@import CoreMotion;
```

5. Add two new instance variables as follows:

```
@implementation GameScene
{
    //..skipped..
    BOOL _useGyroToAim;
    CMMotionManager *_motionManager;
}
```

6. Add the `initializeControls` method below the `init` method as follows:

```
-(void)initializeControls
{
    if (_useGyroToAim)
    {
        _motionManager = [[CMMotionManager alloc] init];
        _motionManager.deviceMotionUpdateInterval = 1.0/60;
        [_motionManager startDeviceMotionUpdates];
    }

    self.userInteractionEnabled = YES;
}
```

7. Set `_useGyroToAim` to `YES` inside the `init` method as shown in the following code:

```
-(instancetype)init
{
    if (self = [super init])
    {
        _useGyroToAim = YES;

        //..skipped..
    }

    return self;
}
```

8. Add a call to the `initializeControls` method at the end of the `onEnter` method:

```
-(void)onEnter
{
    [super onEnter];
    self.gameState = GameStatePlaying;

    [self initializeControls];
}
```

9. Add the following two methods:

```
-(CGPoint)getGyroTargetPoint
{
    //1
    CMDeviceMotion *motion = _motionManager.deviceMotion;
    CMAttitude *attitude = motion.attitude;

    //2
    float pitch = attitude.pitch;

    //3
    float roll = attitude.roll;
    if (roll > 0)
```

```
            pitch = -1 * pitch;

        //4
        CCLOG(@"Pitch: %f", pitch);

        //5
        CGPoint forward = ccp(1.0, 0);
        CGPoint rot =
          ccpRotateByAngle(forward, CGPointZero, pitch);
        CGPoint targetPoint =
          ccpAdd([_hunter torsoCenterInWorldCoordinates], rot);
        return targetPoint;
    }

    -(void)updateGyroAim
    {
        if (!_useGyroToAim)
            return;

        CGPoint targetPoint = [self getGyroTargetPoint];
        [_hunter aimAtPoint:targetPoint];
    }
```

10. Add a call to the `updateGyroAim` method in the `update:` method:

```
-(void)update:(CCTime)dt
{
    if (self.gameState != GameStatePlaying)
        return;

    [self updateGyroAim];
    //..skipped..
}
```

11. Changes in the `touchBegan:` method are quite significant; it is easier to replace the whole `touchBegan:` method with the following code:

```
-(void)touchBegan:(UITouch *)touch withEvent:(UIEvent *)event
{
    if (self.gameState != GameStatePlaying)
    {
        [super touchBegan:touch withEvent:event];
        return;
    }

    if (_useGyroToAim)
    {
        if (_hunter.hunterState != HunterStateReloading)
        {
            CGPoint targetPoint =
              [self getGyroTargetPoint];
```

```
            CCSprite* arrow =
              [_hunter shootAtPoint:targetPoint];
            [_arrows addObject:arrow];
        }

        [super touchBegan:touch withEvent:event];
    }
    else
    {
        if (_hunter.hunterState != HunterStateIdle)
        {
            [super touchBegan:touch withEvent:event];
            return;
        }

        CGPoint touchLocation = [touch locationInNode:self];
        [_hunter aimAtPoint:touchLocation];

        _aimingIndicator.visible = YES;
        [self checkAimingIndicatorForPoint:touchLocation];
    }
}
```

12. Open the `Hunter.m` file and make the following changes to the `aimAtPoint:` method:

```
-(void)aimAtPoint:(CGPoint)point
{
    if (self.hunterState != HunterStateReloading)
        self.hunterState = HunterStateAiming;

    _torso.rotation =
       [self calculateTorsoRotationToLookAtPoint:point];
}
```

13. Select your iPhone as a target in the Xcode project instead of the simulator and run the game. Tilt your iPhone to aim and touch the screen to shoot the arrow.

You can find the final project for this chapter in the `Chapter_05/Cocohunt_05_Final` folder. As this project can be used as a starter project for the next chapter by readers who don't have access to a device and can't test aiming using gyroscope, I've set the `_useGyroToAim` to `NO`; change it to `YES` if you want to test aiming functionality using gyro.

What just happened

It might seem strange to control the hunter's aim by tilting the phone, although I find it pretty fun and more competitive than aiming with touches, but in some games, using orientation of the device as a controller is almost a standard way to go. As I've mentioned before, most racing games allow you to steer your wheel by tilting the iPhone.

When getting device orientation from a gyroscope, you should understand the meaning of **pitch**, **roll**, and **yaw** values, which define the device rotation and come from aviation terms. The following is a figure to demonstrate their original meanings:

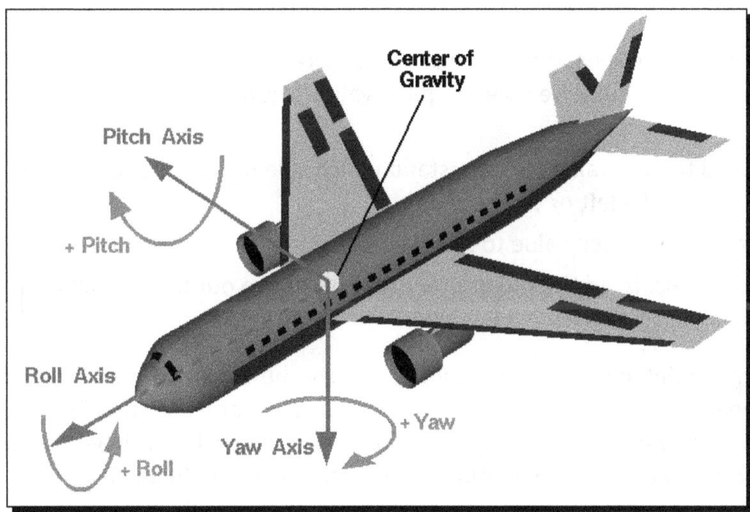

It is quite hard to imagine these when you look at your iPhone. To see them in action to better understand them, you can install a free app from the App Store called Gyroscope (`http://appstore.com/gyroscope`). With the help of this app, you can see how roll, pitch, and yaw change when you rotate your iPhone in your hands.

Before we could use the information about device orientation, we had to include the `CoreMotion` framework. This is not a Cocos2D-specific framework, and you can use it in any iOS application. We need it to be able to use `CMMotionManager`.

After importing the framework, we've added two instance variables. The `_useGyroToAim` flag will allow us to switch easily between the touch and the tilt controls, and we'll use `_motionManager` to get the device's orientation.

In the `initializeControls` method, we initialized our `_motionManager` instance, set the refresh rate to 1/60th of a second, which should be enough even if we ran our game at 60 FPS and started tracking the device motion.

We won't rewrite the `Hunter` class behavior, except for one small change in the `aimAtPoint:` method that is required, as when we use gyro, the hunter's torso rotation is updated every frame. This is because we constantly update its aim to the gyro values and not just when we touch and move the finger.

As we're not going to change the interface of the `Hunter` class, we still need a target point to aim. This is why we need the `getGyroTargetPoint` method.

Here's how it works:

1. We started by taking the information on the device orientation. We're interested in the pitch and roll values.
2. The pitch value is used for aiming. If you installed the gyroscope app I mentioned, it should be clear why we take the pitch value. It is already in radians, so we can use it without conversion.
3. We used the roll value to understand which side of the iPhone is up (the home button is on the left or on the right).
4. We logged the pitch value to see that everything works.
5. We then calculated the target point that will make our hunter aim at the given pitch angle.

To get the target point in the last code block, we take the vector pointed straight from the hunter (collinear to the *x* axis) and then we rotate this vector using the pitch angle. After rotating this vector, we take the point at the tip of this vector. This will be our target point, just as if we touched this point with our finger, as shown in the following figure:

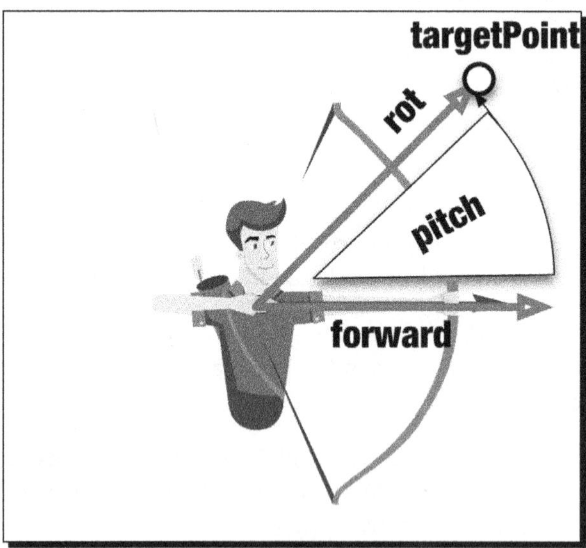

Getting a target point using pitch

In other words, we're simulating a touch at the point that lies on the line rotated by the pitch angle. This is done to minimize changes in the `Hunter` class.

After this, we only need to add a method to update the hunter's aim for each frame. This is what the `updateGyroAim` method does when called from the `update:` method. We wrote different code in the touch handling method to shoot when we touch the screen instead of when we release the finger.

Have a go hero

There are many things to tweak in our Cocohunt game at this point. The following is a list of things to try:

- Change the number of birds spawned, their speed, and the initial altitude range (the *y* coordinate)
- Change the number of times each bird visits the screen. Make it a random value between 1 and 5
- Change the value of the hunter's maximum aiming range and make it smaller and bigger
- Change the `color` property of hunter and the birds to some color
- Change the delay in the hunter's reload animation between frames
- Change the `getGyroTargetPoint` method to use `roll` or `yaw` to aim

As always, it is better to copy the project before making any experiments to have the original project untouched.

Pop quiz – geometry and actions

Q1. Which function will you use to check whether two sprites collide with their bounding boxes?

1. `CGRectContainsPoint`
2. `CGRectIntersectsRect`
3. `CGRectContainsRect`

Q2. You have three actions. How will you make a sprite run these actions one after another?

1. Call the sprite's `runAction:` method three times with each action
2. Gather all actions in the `CCActionSequence` and run the sequence action

Q3. You have `CGPoint point = ccp(100,100)` in node space, what coordinates will it have in world space?

1. `(100,100)`
2. `(0,0)`
3. `(200,200)`
4. It depends on where the node is in world space

Summary

This was one of the cornerstone chapters of the book. Making the objects move and interact with each other and allowing users to control the game is an essential part of any game.

Right now, the game might look like a simple tutorial demo, but even with just what we have now and tweaking the number of birds, their spawn time and speed, the hunter's shooting characteristics, and other parameters can turn this game into a fun and competitive one.

Of course, there are parts that beg for improvement. Logging into the console whether we've won or lost, and not displaying the number of points that we have definitely won't do compared to other games. Also, the collision detection is pretty rough, we have no sound, and the birds just disappear when we hit them.

We'll learn how to fix all these in the next chapters, but for now, make sure that you've learned how to add and remove sprites from the scene, how to store them in arrays, and make them interact. It is also very important to understand the difference between the world space and node space coordinates.

Handling user input (touches or device orientation) is also one of the main tasks you will work on when creating games. Using actions to command sprites, grouping actions into other actions to make sequences, and repeating them is what you're going to use very often.

Finally, using states to control the game flow will allow you to make complicated games without losing yourself in a mess of code.

It is very important to understand all of these before we continue. I wouldn't be lying if I told you that these topics are the main things you need to understand from this whole book.

In the next chapter, you're going to learn how to render text. We will display the current score, number of lives left, and a better indication of winning and losing.

6
Rendering Text

Displaying text in games is almost as important as displaying images and animations. In fact, some time ago many games were purely text-based. We're not going to go hardcore and make the player type "shoot 30 degrees" and get the "you've missed the bird" message as a result, but the game will definitely benefit from adding some text.

In this chapter, we are going to review the following topics:

- Adding text to the game using True Type font labels
- Updating labels, text, and performance considerations
- Creating and using bitmap fonts
- Using actions to create text effects

The easy way – CCLabelTTF

We've already used the `CCLabelTTF` class to display the text on the screen. It was pretty easy, wasn't it? We only specified the font name, the size, and the text itself, and here it was displayed on the screen. But there is a price for that simplicity.

Unfortunately, it is not that simple to draw text using OpenGL (which is used by Cocos2D internally). There is simply no built-in functionality that takes the text and renders it on the screen. We have to render the text manually by drawing each letter separately in its place using primitives (lines and triangles), and doing this for every frame badly affects performance.

To optimize this, Cocos2D renders the text only once, places the result into the texture, and then displays this texture. In other words, it creates an image in memory with this text on the fly, and then it easily renders this image using OpenGL.

This helps to optimize performance, but if we change any property of the label (font size, alignment, color, and so on) and of course the text itself, Cocos2D has to regenerate this texture. So if we plan to change the text often, we shouldn't use `CCLabelTTF` but use `CCLabelBMFont`, which we'll discuss in the second part of this chapter.

Taking the preceding points into consideration, you shouldn't think that the `CCLabelTTF` class is useless. It has several benefits, and the most important one is that we can easily use it. If we don't change the text displaying each frame, then we won't notice a performance hit.

Time for action – adding labels

It would be nice to know how many birds we've spawned, how many birds we've hit, and more importantly how many birds we've missed.

If you completed all code from the previous chapter, simply continue building on top of your project. If you've skipped a part or don't have the code for some reason, just take the final code of the project from the previous chapter in the `Chapter_05/Cocohunt_05_Final` folder and use it as a starter project.

You can download the book's supporting files by visiting `www.packtpub.com/support` and following the instructions.

Let's display those labels on the screen:

1. Open the **Cocohunt** project at the point where we left it in the previous chapter.
2. Right-click on the `Scenes` group, click on **New File**, and then select the **Objective-C class**. Name the class `HUDLayer` and make it a subclass of `CCNode`. Save the file.
3. Open the `HUDLayer.m` file and add the following code at the top of the file before the `@implementation` part:

```
#import "cocos2d.h"

#define kFontName @"Noteworthy-Bold"
#define kFontSize 14
```

4. Add three instance variables as follows—one for each label that we'll add to the code:

```
@implementation HUDLayer
{
    CCLabelTTF *_score;
    CCLabelTTF *_birdsLeft;
    CCLabelTTF *_lives;
}
```

5. After that, add the `init` method to create and position labels:

```
-(instancetype)init
{
    if (self = [super init])
    {
        //1
        _score = [CCLabelTTF
                    labelWithString:@"Score: 99999"
                    fontName:kFontName
                    fontSize:kFontSize];
        _birdsLeft = [CCLabelTTF
                        labelWithString:@"Birds Left: 99"
                        fontName:kFontName
                        fontSize:kFontSize];
        _lives = [CCLabelTTF
                    labelWithString:@"Lives: 99"
                    fontName:kFontName
                    fontSize:kFontSize];

        //2
        _score.color =
          [CCColor colorWithRed:0 green:0.42f blue:0.03f];
        _birdsLeft.color =
          [CCColor colorWithRed:0.84f green:0.49f blue:0.08f];
        _lives.color =
          [CCColor colorWithRed:0.64f green:0.06f blue:0.06f];

        //3
        CGSize viewSize = [CCDirector sharedDirector].viewSize;
        float labelsY = viewSize.height * 0.95f;
        float labelsPaddingX = viewSize.width * 0.01f;

        //4
        _score.anchorPoint = ccp(0, 0.5f);
        _score.position = ccp(labelsPaddingX, labelsY);

        //5
        _birdsLeft.anchorPoint = ccp(0.5f, 0.5f);
```

```
        _birdsLeft.position = ccp(viewSize.width * 0.5f,
                                        labelsY);

        //6
        _lives.anchorPoint = ccp(1, 0.5f);
        _lives.position =
          ccp(viewSize.width - labelsPaddingX, labelsY);

        //7
        [self addChild:_score];
        [self addChild:_birdsLeft];
        [self addChild:_lives];
    }

    return self;
}
```

6. Open the `GameScene.m` file and add the following code at the top of the file before the `@implementation` part:

```
#import "HUDLayer.h"

typedef NS_ENUM(NSUInteger, Z_ORDER)
{
    Z_BACKGROUND,
    Z_BATCH_NODE,
    Z_HUD
};
```

7. Scroll down to the `addBackground` method and change the final line, where we add the background to the scene to this:

```
[self addChild:background z:Z_BACKGROUND];
```

8. Make a similar change in the `createBatchNode` method as follows:

```
[self addChild:_batchNode z:Z_BATCH_NODE];
```

9. Add the `_hud` instance variable:

```
@implementation GameScene
{
    //..skipped..

    HUDLayer *_hud;
}
```

10. Then add the following method after the `init` method:

```
-(void)initializeHUD
{
    _hud = [[HUDLayer alloc] init];
    [self addChild:_hud z:Z_HUD];
}
```

11. Add a call to the `initializeHUD` method at the end of the `init` method:

```
-(instancetype)init
{
    if (self = [super init])
    {
        //..skipped..

        [self initializeHUD];
    }

    return self;
}
```

If you don't want to use gyroscope for aiming, make sure you change the `_useGyroToAim` to `NO` while in the `init` method. If you don't have a device and are testing on the simulator, this is your only option unfortunately.

12. Finally remove the `CCLOG(@"Pitch: %f", pitch);` line from the `getGyroTargetPoint` method, since it produces too much noise in the console.

13. Build and run the game. You should see three colored labels in the top part of the screen as shown in the following screenshot:

What just happened?

Most of the time, it is a good idea to create modular code. In our case, we've decided to separate the labels into a different layer. In the current game, there won't be much happening in the HUD layer, but we still will have some code related just to HUD labels at the end. It is nice to have it in a separate source file, and not to grow our `GameScene` into an enormous monster.

> HUD is a term often used in game development. It originated from the military aviation and means heads-up display. If you watched movies such as *Top Gun* or any other movie about military planes, you must remember those crosses, numbers, and other system information displayed directly on the windshield.

The following screenshot shows the HUD:

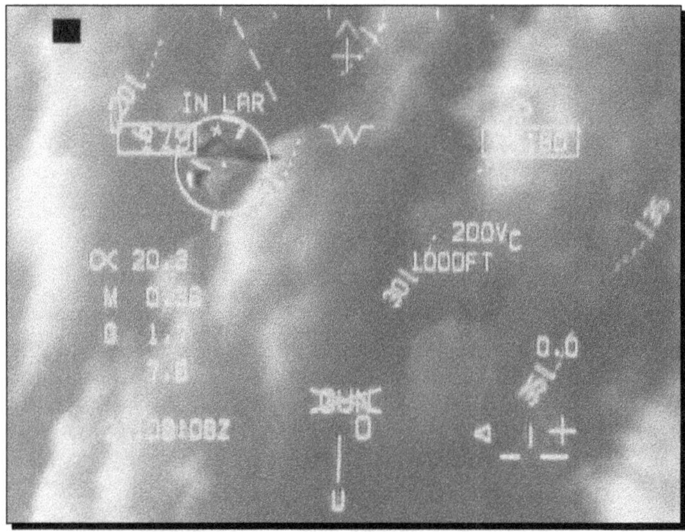

Let's start reviewing from the `HUDLayer` class. It is a descendant of the `CCNode`, and we just used this class as a container for our HUD elements. Think of it as an additional layer on top of the main game layer represented by sprite batch node. Both layers exist in the `GameScene` class.

> In addition to the obvious benefits of splitting the code, this offers a lot of flexibility. For example, we can also easily move the whole HUD layer to position it at the top or bottom of the screen, with only one line of code to hide and show all HUD elements at once, and so on.

Currently our `HUDLayer` class contains three labels, which we create in the `init` method. Let's review this method:

1. Here, we created three labels with the stub text. It will be later replaced by actual values. Since all of our labels use one font and one font size, we've created a `#define` constant for both values, to be able to quickly change it for all labels at once.

> It is a good idea to use the stub text that contains the maximum value you plan for the label. This way you will see if a label overlaps some other UI element, doesn't fit in its placeholder, and so on.

2. We set the color for each label. The `CCColor` object represents the color in Cocos2D. We've created three different colors passing different RGB components. Each color component can have values ranging from `0` to `1`.
3. We calculated variables that will help us to position our labels. We want one label to be on the left-hand side, one in the center, and one on the right-hand side. We don't want our side labels to be very close to the edge of the screen; this is why we're calculating the `labelsPaddingX` value.
4. We created the scores label. We want to place this label using its left edge; this is why we set the anchor point to the midpoint of the left edge `(0, 0.5)`. This will also make the label to extend to the right when we add more text, and the left edge will stay in its place. In other words, setting the anchor point to the left edge makes the label left-aligned.
5. We added the label with the number of birds still waiting to be spawned. In this case, we set the anchor point to the center. This way, the label will expand on both the right-hand side and the left-hand side and will be center-aligned.
6. Finally, we added the lives label. We made it right-aligned so that it expands itself to the left-hand side, making sure we don't cross the right edge of the screen.
7. We added all labels as a child of our `HUDLayer` node.

After creating the `HUDLayer` node, all we needed to do is add it as a child of the `GameScene` class. We also used this opportunity for a little housekeeping and defined z-order for all direct child nodes of the scene. This way the background will be in the back, and then there will be the batch node with the hunter, birds, and arrows inside of it. Then as a top layer, there will be the `HUDLayer` layer.

> Using enum for z-order values is quite convenient. This way it is very easy to rearrange them.

Now we have the labels on the screen, we need to update them to the actual values.

Time for action – updating labels

Let's go ahead and add the code to keep the current game stats and display them using labels:

1. Create a new group called `Common`.
2. Right-click on this group and click on **New File**; it will be **Objective-C class**. Name it `GameStats` and make it a subclass of `NSObject`. Save the file.
3. Open the `GameStats.h` file and add the following properties:

```
@property (nonatomic, assign) int score;
@property (nonatomic, assign) int birdsLeft;
@property (nonatomic, assign) int lives;
```

4. Then open the `GameStats.m` file and add the `init` method:

```
-(instancetype)init
{
    if (self = [super init])
    {
        self.score = 0;
        self.birdsLeft = 0;
        self.lives = 0;
    }

    return self;
}
```

5. Open the `HUDLayer.h` file and import the `GameStats.h` header at the top, like this:

```
#import "GameStats.h"
```

6. Then add the following method declaration:

```
-(void)updateStats:(GameStats *)stats;
```

7. Switch to the `HUDLayer.m` file and add the implementation of this method below the `init` method:

```
-(void)updateStats:(GameStats *)stats
{
    _score.string =
      [NSString stringWithFormat:@"Score: %d",
                                 stats.score];
    _birdsLeft.string =
      [NSString stringWithFormat:@"Birds Left: %d",
                                 stats.birdsLeft];
    _lives.string =
      [NSString stringWithFormat:@"Lives: %d",
                                 stats.lives];
}
```

8. Open the `Bird.h` file and change the `removeBird:` method declaration to return an integer (`int`) value:

```
-(int)removeBird:(BOOL)hitByArrow;
```

9. Switch to the `Bird.m` file and make following changes to the `removeBird:` method:

```
-(int)removeBird:(BOOL)hitByArrow
{
    [self removeFromParentAndCleanup:YES];

    int score = 0;

    if (hitByArrow)
    {
        self.birdState = BirdStateDead;
        score = (_timesToVisit + 1) * 5;
    }
    else
    {
        self.birdState = BirdStateFlewOut;
    }

    return score;
}
```

10. Open the `GameScene.m` file and add an instance variable to contain the current game stats:

```
@implementation GameScene
{
    //..skipped..

    GameStats *_gameStats;
}
```

11. Add the following `initializeStats` method below the `initializeHUD` method:

```
-(void)initializeStats
{
    _gameStats = [[GameStats alloc] init];
    _gameStats.birdsLeft = _birdsToSpawn;
    _gameStats.lives = _birdsToLose;

    [_hud updateStats:_gameStats];
}
```

12. Add a call to this `initializeStats` method at the end of the `init` method as follows:

```
[self initializeStats];
```

It is important to add a call to the `initializeStats` method after the `[self initializeHUD];` line since we need already initialized HUDLayer before we can initialize stats.

13. Find the `update:` method and search for the `if` block where we spawn the new bird. Add the following code to the end of this block:

```
if (_timeUntilNextBird <= 0 && _birdsToSpawn > 0)
{
    //..skipped..

    _gameStats.birdsLeft = _birdsToSpawn;
    [_hud updateStats:_gameStats];
}
```

14. Still in the `update:` method, scroll down and find this line:

```
_birdsToLose--;
```

15. Add the following two lines right below it:

```
_gameStats.lives = _birdsToLose;
[_hud updateStats:_gameStats];
```

16. There is one more place in the `update:` method to add to the stats update code. Scroll down and find the place where we remove the bird and the arrow after their collision (bird hit by the arrow case). Change the code inside the `if` block as follows:

```
if (CGRectIntersectsRect(arrow.boundingBox,
    bird.boundingBox))
{
      [arrow removeFromParentAndCleanup:YES];
      [_arrows removeObject:arrow];

      int score = [bird removeBird:YES];
      [_birds removeObject:bird];

       _gameStats.score += score;
       [_hud updateStats:_gameStats];

      break;
}
```

17. Build and run the game. Now you should see actual stats in labels as shown in the following screenshot:

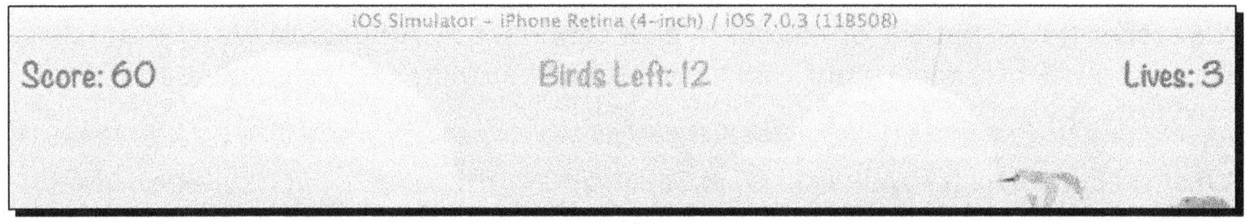

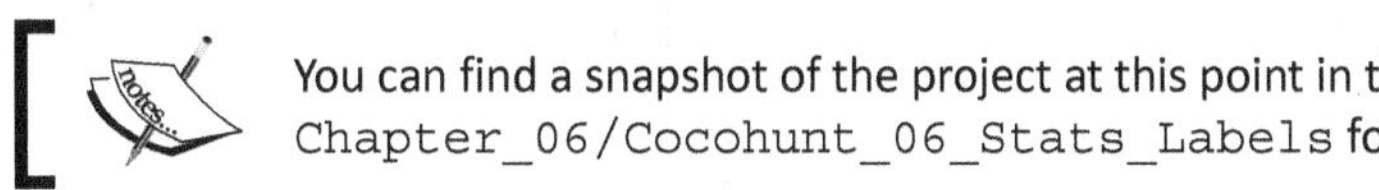

You can find a snapshot of the project at this point in the `Chapter_06/Cocohunt_06_Stats_Labels` folder.

What just happened?

First of all, we added a new class called `GameStats` to hold the current game stats. We could have created separate variables and/or partially reuse already existing ones, but we'll add more stats later and will pass this whole class instance to the other scene where we'll display the game stats after each round, so it is a good idea to have everything wrapped in one class.

Then we updated the `HUDLayer` class to take this `GameStats` class instance and update the labels using stats.

After that, we made one interesting change to the `removeBird:` method of the `Bird` class. Now it returns the number of scored points, depending on how many times the bird already visited the game field. The faster the hunter hits the bird, the more points he gets.

The rest of the changes are simply initializing stats and updating their values when something happens. We decrease the amount of birds left when we spawn one, decrease lives when we let the bird fly away from us, and increase points when we hit the bird using the amount of points returned by the `removeBird:` method. There are lots of places to add the code, but the code itself is very straightforward.

Using bitmap fonts for better performance

As we've seen before, `CCLabelTTF` is very easy to use, but we also must be aware of its drawbacks; the biggest one of which is its poor performance. Fortunately, we have an alternative way of rendering text with the help of bitmap fonts and the `CCLabelBMFont` class in Cocos2D.

What are bitmap fonts? Well, since OpenGL can't draw text natively, but it surely can draw images very well, it is obvious that we can use images to represent our text. We can simply create an image containing all letters, and then when we need to write some text, we just draw each letter in its place on the screen.

> To visualize this process, just recall some movie where an evil guy cuts letters from newspapers and magazines to create anonymous threating letters. The only difference is that we have an unlimited number of each letter because nothing is really cut.

Also, as we already know drawing images one by one is a pretty expensive operation, so it would be better to group letter images in some kind of spritesheet just as we did with normal images and draw all the text at once. This approach is much faster than what `CCLabelTTF` does behind the scenes.

Let's see how to create a bitmap font.

Choosing a bitmap font generator

As I've mentioned before, a bitmap font is very similar to a spritesheet. Each font is represented by two files:

- The first one is an image file (usually `.png`) that contains images of all the letters of this font.

> We're speaking about the letters since most of the time when we say text, we think about words and letters, but the font can contain any symbol just like a usual font does (for example, the `"`, `!` `()` symbols are often included in bitmap fonts).

- The second one is an `.fnt` file, which functions very similar to a `.plist` file in spritesheet's files pair. This `.fnt` file is usually a plain text file that contains information about each letter, such as the position in the spritesheet and spacing before and after this letter.

There are different variations (such as binary .fnt format), but most of the time the bitmap font is just a .png image and an .fnt text file. The .fnt format is quite simple. You can find information about it on the Internet, but the easiest way is just to get some .fnt file and the corresponding image and review them using your favorite text editor and image viewer apps.

Although the .fnt format is quite simple, and you can create it manually in any text editor (I've done this myself a few times), it is much easier to use a tool to generate the bitmap font.

There aren't many utilities that allow you to create bitmap fonts easily, but the **Glyph Designer** application is a definite favorite here. It is not free, but it is totally worth the money.

> If you just cannot afford Glyph Designer, you can try to use alternatives listed in the CCLabelBMFont class description at http://www.cocos2d-iphone.org/docs/api/Classes/CCLabelBMFont.html (shortened to: http://bit.ly/1iPXnfH). Search for the bitmap font generator on the Web or find already-made free bitmap fonts.

My advice is to download the trial version of Glyph Designer and work with it. It will not allow you to export the result, but I've provided the published files, so you will be able to complete this chapter and learn everything you need about bitmap fonts. Later, you will be able to decide which utility to use or even create the .fnt file manually.

Time for action – creating a bitmap font using Glyph Designer

First of all, we will need to download and install Glyph Designer. Go to http://71squared.com/glyphdesigner to download and install the Glyph Designer application.

We're going to create three different fonts:

- A font for the "You win!" label that will appear when you win the game
- A font for the "You lose!" label that will appear when you lose the game
- A font for points that will float out of the bird when we hit it with the arrow

Let's start with the font for the "You win!" label:

1. Open the Glyph Designer application and save the empty project anywhere you like. Name the project WinFont.GlyphDesigner.
2. Select the Chalkduster font from the list of fonts on the left.

> You can start typing Chalkduster in the search area at the top of the fonts list to save time searching for the font.

3. Set the size of the font at the bottom to `64`. You can use the slider or type the font size by hand, which is much faster.
4. On the right-hand side of Glyph Designer find the **Glyph Fill** section. Leave the drop-down value at **Gradient**. Change the gradient angle to `185`. Click on the left-hand side slider, set it to a light green color (**RED:0 GREEN:201 BLUE:68**), click on the right-hand side slider, and set it to an orange color (**R:254 G:98 B:0**).
5. If you have a full version of Glyph Designer, then find the **Export** button on the top-right corner and click on it. Name the file `win`. This will create the `win.png` and `win.fnt` files. If you have a trial version, just remember that we've exported the font at this point.
6. Now change the font size to `128` and export the bitmap font, but this time name it `win-hd`. This will create two files `win-hd.png` and `win-hd.fnt`.
7. Save the project file, since we're going to copy it shortly.

If you have the trial version, then you won't be able to complete steps 5 and 6 since export is disabled in the trial version. Don't worry about that, it is only important to remember the settings that we set and that we've exported the font two times with different sizes.

You can find the resulting fonts in the book's supporting files at `Chapter_06/Assets/BitmapFont` and the Glyph Designer project files at `Chapter_06/Assets/BitmapFont/GlyphDesignerProjects`.

That's it for the win font. The Glyph Designer project should look similar to the following screenshot:

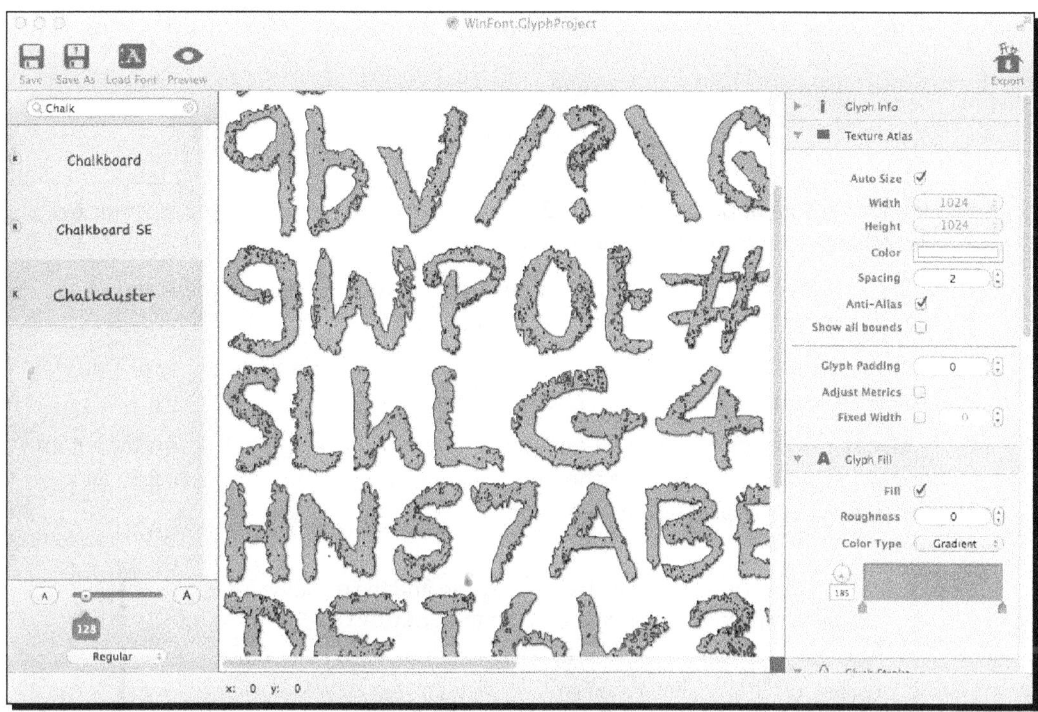

It is time to create the font for the "`You lose!`" label. It will be very similar to the win label font—only the colors will be different— so we're going to copy the project and just tweak the colors.

1. Copy `WinFont.GlyphProject` and rename it to `LostFont.GlyphProject`. Then open this new `LostFont.GlyphProject` project.
2. Find the **Glyph Fill** section on the right-hand side and change the left-hand side slider color to a deep red (**R:201 G:0 B:75**).
3. The font size should be set at `128` as we left it in the **WinFont** project that we've copied. Click on **Export** to export the font and name it `lost-hd`. This will create the `lost-hd.png` and `lost-hd.fnt` files.
4. Change the font size to `64` and export the font named `lost`. This will create the `lost.png` and `lost.fnt` files.

That's it for the losing font. We need one more font for the points. Refer to the following steps:

1. Create a new Glyph Designer project and save it as `Points.GlyphProject`.
2. Set the font to `Superclarendon` and font size to `16`.
3. Set the **Glyph Fill** options. Set the gradient angle to `185`. Then set the left-hand side slider color to a dark blue (**R:0 G:6 B:201**) and the right-hand side slider color to something close to cyan (**R:104 G:228 B:254**).
4. Below the **Glyph Fill** section, find the **Included Glyphs** section, and instead of all those symbols only enter the digits `0123456789`.
5. Make sure the font size is set to `16` and export the font. Name it `points`. This will create the `points.png` and `points.fnt` files.
6. Then change the font size to `32` and export the font once again, but this time name it `points-hd`. This will create the `points-hd.png` and `points-hd.fnt` files. That's it. We have all the fonts we need.

> As I've mentioned before, you can find the resulting fonts in the book's supporting files in the `Chapter_06/Assets/BitmapFont` folder and in the Glyph Designer project files in the `Chapter_06/Assets/BitmapFont/GlyphDesignerProjects` folder.

What just happened?

Creating the bitmap font with Glyph Designer was quite easy, especially compared to manual creation of the bitmap font. To create the bitmap font, we selected the basic font, selected its properties such as color, shadow and so on, and then we just exported the `.png` image and the `.fnt` file.

There are a few tricky parts. The first one is exporting the font two times with different sizes. This is required to have two bitmap fonts: one for non-Retina and the second one for Retina. Since the bitmap font is only an image, we need to provide two images to support both screen types.

The second trick is that we've only used the digits `0123456789` for the `points` font, while with the win and lose labels, we've included all the characters. This is because we might change our mind and instead of `"You win"`, present a label like `"Congratulations!"`, so we need to be sure that we can use any standard symbols in the labels. On the other hand, with the `points` font, we're sure that we will only display numbers. This means we don't need any other characters or symbols and can save some disk space and memory by not including them in the font image.

As you can see, the `-hd` versions of the fonts are quite heavy, for example `win-hd.png` is about 1 MB. Be sure to include only symbols that you'll use and reuse the font.

I encourage you to have a look at the images that we've generated and open the `.fnt` files in your favorite text editor. If you open any `.fnt` file (`points.fnt` or `points-hd.fnt` will be easiest to read since they don't have a lot of symbols) you will see that everything it contains is just coordinates and rectangles of each letter in the image file, and information about offset and spacing between letters.

Using the bitmap font in the game

Using the bitmap font in the game is very easy. To do this, you just need to use the `CCLabelBMFont` class instead of the `CCLabelTTF` class for all your fonts.

However, you must not forget that the bitmap font is generally an image, so you won't be able to create one font and use it for all your sizes of labels in your game because scaling the font down or up too much will make it look bad.

Time for action – adding hit points

Okay, let's add a point floating from the bird we hit with an arrow:

1. The first thing we need to do is to add the fonts to the Xcode project. We're going to add all fonts at once, not only the `points` font. There are a lot of files, so it would be better to create a group for them. Go ahead and create a subgroup called `Fonts` in the `Resources` group.
2. Add all the font files that we've created to that group. You should have a total of `12` files: two files (`.png` and `.fnt`) per font, `2` font variations (Retina and non-Retina), and total of `3` fonts. This gives us `2 * 2 * 3 = 12`.

If you have the trial version of Glyph Designer or some issues with exporting files, you can just take all the font files from the `Chapter_06/Assets/BitmapFont` folder in the book's supporting files.

3. After adding the font files, open the `Bird.m` file, and add the following method:

```
-(void)displayPoints:(int)amount
{
    //1
    NSString *ptsStr = [NSString stringWithFormat:@"%d", amount];
    CCLabelBMFont *ptsLabel =
      [CCLabelBMFont labelWithString:ptsStr
                             fntFile:@"points.fnt"];
    ptsLabel.position = self.position;

    //2
    CCNode *batchNode = self.parent;
    CCNode *scene = batchNode.parent;
    [scene addChild:ptsLabel];

    //3
    float xDelta1 = 10;
    float yDelta1 = 5;
    float yDelta2 = 10;
    float yDelta4 = 20;
    ccBezierConfig curve;
    curve.controlPoint_1 =
      ccp(ptsLabel.position.x - xDelta1,
          ptsLabel.position.y + yDelta1);
    curve.controlPoint_2 =
      ccp(ptsLabel.position.x + xDelta1,
          ptsLabel.position.y + yDelta2);
    curve.endPosition =
      ccp(ptsLabel.position.x,
          ptsLabel.position.y + yDelta4);

    //4
    float baseDuration = 1.0f;

    //5
    CCActionBezierTo *bezierMove =
     [CCActionBezierTo actionWithDuration:baseDuration
                                   bezier:curve];

    //6
    CCActionFadeOut *fadeOut =
      [CCActionFadeOut actionWithDuration:baseDuration * 0.25f];

    //7
    CCActionDelay *delay =
      [CCActionDelay actionWithDuration:baseDuration * 0.75f];

    //8
```

```
    CCActionSequence *delayAndFade =
      [CCActionSequence actions:delay, fadeOut, nil];

    //9
    CCActionSpawn *bezieAndFadeOut =
      [CCActionSpawn actions:bezierMove,
                             delayAndFade,
                                   nil];

    //10
    CCActionRemove *removeInTheEnd = [CCActionRemove action];

    //11
    CCActionSequence *actions =
      [CCActionSequence actions:bezieAndFadeOut,
                                removeInTheEnd,
                                        nil];

    //12
    [ptsLabel runAction:actions];
}
```

4. Then find the `removeBird:` method and add a call to this `displayPoints:` method in case the bird is hit by an arrow. Also, while in this method, move the call to the `removeFromParentAndCleanup:` method to the end of the `removeBird:` method since we only need to remove `self` after displaying the points label. This will be explained later:

```
-(int)removeBird:(BOOL)hitByArrow
{
    [self stopAllActions];

    //remove the removeFromParentAndCleanup: from here

    int score = 0;
    if (hitByArrow)
    {
        self.birdState = BirdStateDead;
        score = (_timesToVisit + 1) * 5;

        [self displayPoints:score];
    }
    else
    {
        self.birdState = BirdStateFlewOut;
    }

    [self removeFromParentAndCleanup:YES];
    return score;
}
```

5. Build and run the game. You should see floating labels with points when you hit a bird, as shown in the following screenshot:

Floating points in place of the bird that we've just hit by an arrow

What just happened?

Apart from adding the font files to the project, which should be an obvious thing to do since we need to add the fonts before we can use them, we've only added one huge method to display those floating points and a call to this method in case an arrow hits the bird.

The big method might look scary at first, but it won't be after we review it. However before reviewing the method, I'd like to explain what we want to achieve with this method.

What we want is to add a label using our `points` font, we then want them to float up using the curvy trajectory, and at some point, we want them to start fading out but still move until they totally fade away. The last part means that at some point two actions must be running for our label (move and fade out) simultaneously.

Now let's review each code block marked with a number. Refer to the following points:

1. We created the `CCLabelBMFont` label using the `points.fnt` file and the string with the amount of points we need to display. Set the label position to the same position as the bird that is being hit.

2. We added the label to the scene. This might be a bit tricky. Here is how we access the scene: our label is the child of the batch node, and the batch node is the child of the scene. So when we take the parent of the label, we take the batch node, and when we take the parent of the batch node, we get the scene itself.

> We cannot add the label as a child node of the bird or the child node of the bird's parent node, which is a batch node. The reason for this is that the batch node can only have children that use the sprite frame (image) from its spritesheet. Our font is not a part of the spritesheet, and this means we cannot add it as a child node to batch node. Also, since we're referencing a parent property of the bird, we moved the `removeFromParentAndCleanup:` method to the end of the `removeBird:` method.

3. This scary code block just configures the Bézier curve that the label will move along.

> Bézier curves are commonly used to define a continuous, curvy trajectory with only a few points.

4. This is the duration that the label is visible on the screen—from the moment we add and show it until it completely fades out. It is important to understand that this duration includes the interval when the label starts to fade out and disappears.
5. We created the action that will move our label along the Bézier curve. It will move the label during the whole `baseDuration` time interval.
6. Then we created the action that will fade out our label (make it invisible). We want this action to last 25 percent of the time of the label life (`baseDuration`). This means that the label will move along 75 percent of the curve line completely visible before it even starts to fade away.
7. Since we don't want our label to start fading right after appearing on the screen, we needed to delay the fading action by 75 percent of the label's lifetime.
8. We created a sequence that contains a delay action, and then delayed the fade action. This sequence just does nothing for 75 percent of `baseDuration` and then will fade out within 25 percent (`baseDuration * 0.25`) of the time.
9. Here comes the interesting part. We need to run the action that moves our label along the curve and the sequence that waits and then fades out simultaneously. If we run both actions at the same time, then the label will be moving all the time, and after 75 percent of the movement is complete, it will start to fade out, but will still be moving. The `CCActionSpawn` action allows multiple actions to fire simultaneously, so we're using it in our final sequence.

10. We want to remove our label at the end, so we created an action that will remove the label.
11. Then we formed a final sequence. This will start the label movement and the wait and fade actions simultaneously, as shown in the following diagram, and then after executing both actions, it will call the action that removes the label.
12. We ran the sequence.

Here is a diagram that will help you understand the sequence of actions:

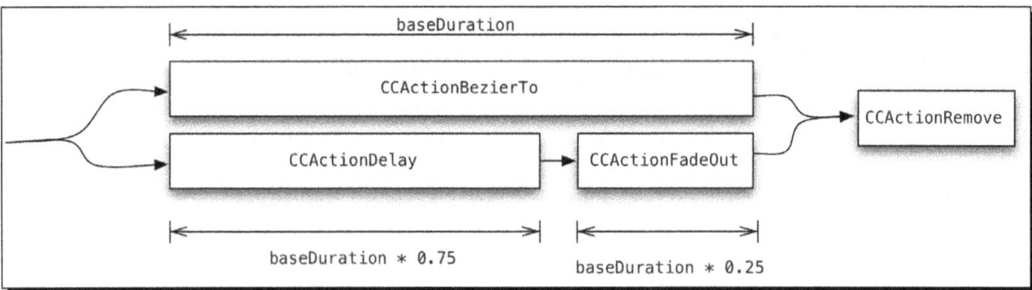

Chronology of actions applied on the points label

As you can see, we can easily create complicated scenarios using the actions.

Time for action – adding the win and lose labels

It is time to use our win and lose fonts. Perform the following steps:

1. Open the `GameScene.m` file, and add another z-order value at the top:

```
typedef NS_ENUM(NSUInteger, Z_ORDER)
{
    Z_BACKGROUND,
    Z_BATCH_NODE,
    Z_LABELS,
    Z_HUD
};
```

2. Scroll down and add the `displayWinLoseLabelWithText:` method below the `won` and `lost` methods:

```
-(void)displayWinLoseLabelWithText:(NSString *)text
                           andFont:(NSString *)fontFileName
{
    CGSize viewSize = [CCDirector sharedDirector].viewSize;
    CCLabelBMFont *label =
```

```
        [CCLabelBMFont labelWithString:text
                               fntFile:fontFileName];

    label.position = ccp(viewSize.width * 0.5f,
                         viewSize.height * 0.75f);

    [self addChild:label z:Z_LABELS];
    label.scale = 0.01f;

    CCActionScaleTo *scaleUp =
      [CCActionScaleTo actionWithDuration:1.5f
                                    scale:1.2f];
    CCActionEaseIn  *easedScaleUp =
      [CCActionEaseIn actionWithAction:scaleUp
                                  rate:5.0];
    CCActionScaleTo *scaleNormal =
      [CCActionScaleTo actionWithDuration:0.5f
                                    scale:1.0f];

    CCActionSequence *scaleUpThenNormal =
       [CCActionSequence actions:easedScaleUp, scaleNormal, nil];

    [label runAction:scaleUpThenNormal];
}
```

3. Add a call to this method inside the `lost` and `won` methods instead of the `CCLOG` macro:

```
-(void)lost
{
    self.gameState = GameStateLost;
    [self displayWinLoseLabelWithText:@"You lose!"
      andFont:@"lost.fnt"];
}

-(void)won
{
    self.gameState = GameStateWon;
    [self displayWinLoseLabelWithText:@"You win!"
      andFont:@"win.fnt"];
}
```

4. These are the main actions to display the labels themselves, but let's adjust our game speed to make testing, winning, and losing easier. Find the `update:` method and adjust the maximum and minimum intervals to spawn birds:

```
int nextBirdTimeMax = 3;
int nextBirdTimeMin = 1;
```

5. Then, inside the `spawnBird` method, adjust the minimum and maximum speeds of the bird:

```
int maxTime = 6;
int minTime = 4;
```

6. Scroll all the way up to the `init` method and change the number of birds to spawn and the number of birds we can let go before we lose:

```
_birdsToSpawn = 10;
_birdsToLose = 1;
```

7. Finally, switch to the `Bird.m` file and change the initial value of `_timesToVisit` to `1` inside the `initWithBirdType:` method. This will make it more interesting:

```
_timesToVisit = 1;
```

8. Build and run the game. It should be relatively easy to lose and win to see the corresponding labels. If you have any difficulty winning, you can adjust some of the preceding parameters.

When you develop the game, you often need to check the game's reaction in different situations that require you to make a series of actions to trigger. Instead of actually winning and losing to test how the label looks, it would be easier just to put a call to `displayWinLoseLabelWithText:` somewhere inside the `onEnter` method and check that the label is positioned correctly, actions run okay, and so on. If you will be performing the additional tasks described in the *Have a go hero* section, I encourage you to do just that instead of spending time on winning and losing, or even hitting the bird.

You can find the final project of this chapter in the `Chapter_06/Cocohunt_06_Final` folder in the book's supporting files.

What just happened?

It is much better to see the labels on the screen rather than monitoring the console output to check whether you won or lost the game; here, I am not referring to the actual players who won't even see the console output on their devices.

The code of the `displayWinLoseLabelWithText:` method should be pretty straightforward, except the part with easing actions. Easing actions help you to run your action using nonlinear functions. You can either speed up or slow down the action at the beginning or at the end.

We'll talk about easing actions later in the book. In our case, we're using easing to slow down our label's scaling at the beginning to make it pop out of the screen, instead of boringly scaling out.

Have a go hero

Since this chapter is about rendering text, I encourage you to experiment with labels and fonts:

- For example, you can change the font used for the labels in the HUD, maybe even use a different font and font size for each label.

> If you wonder what fonts are available, you can use the `UIFont` class's `familyNames` with the `fontNamesForFamilyName` method to list all the fonts available. Alternatively, you can visit the website `http://iosfonts.com/` for font availability information.

- Try repositioning labels on the screen or pick different colors.
- Add shadows to the **Score**, **Birds Left**, and **Lives** labels using the `shadowColor` property, which sets the color of the shadow and `shadowOffset`, which in turn sets offset for the shadow.
- Set the outline for the **Score**, **Birds Left**, and **Lives** labels using the `outlineColor` and `outlineWidth` properties.
- In addition to simple strings, you can create a label using an attributed string, just as you can in a usual iOS application (iOS 6 or higher). To do this, you can use the `attributedString` property of the `CCLabelTTF` class or construct labels using `labelWithAttributedString:` constructor.
- If you have a full version of Glyph Designer, you can create different fonts for win, lost, and points fonts. If you have a trial version, I still encourage you to play with different options and use the **Preview** button in Glyph Designer to see how your font looks.

> You can also search the Web for free bitmap fonts and use them for the labels. There is a list of websites with fonts you can use at the end of *Chapter 12, Standing Out – Integrating Game Center and In-App Purchases*. Alternatively, you can use some free tools listed in the `CCLabelBMFont` class description at `http://www.cocos2d-iphone.org/docs/api/Classes/CCLabelBMFont.html` (shortened: `http://bit.ly/1iPXnfH`). The only reason that I've used Glyph Designer is that it has a beginner-friendly interface and allows you to understand the main aspects of creating bitmap fonts. Also, it is the most commonly used tool as far as I know. When you understand this, you can use other tools or even create the `.fnt` file manually.

- I also think you can create a better action sequence for the `"You win!"` and `"You lose!"` labels' appearance. Why don't you rotate them while they are popping out? Maybe instead of popping out, you can make them slide from the side or the bottom edge of the screen?

Pop quiz – labels

Q1. What label class should you use if you plan to update the text of the label very frequently?

1. `CCLabelTTF`
2. `CCLabelBMFont`

Q2. Can you use attributed string with `CCLabelTTF`?

1. Yes, using the `attributedString` property
2. Yes, using the `attributedString` property, but only on iOS 6 or higher

Q3. Can you rotate and scale the `CCLabelBMFont` and `CCLabelTTF` labels?

1. Yes, but only `CCLabelTTF`
2. Yes, but only `CCLabelBMFont`
3. No, you can't rotate and scale both
4. Yes, you can rotate and scale both

Q4. Can you use actions (for example, `CCActionMoveTo`) with labels?

1. Yes, but only with `CCLabelTTF`
2. No, you can't use actions with labels
3. Yes, with both CCLabelTTF and CCLabelMBFont labels

Summary

Text is a very important component almost in any game. Especially, as you can see when we say text, we don't necessarily mean black and white strict text. Using a bitmap font, we can create cool-looking fonts while still generating generic text on the fly.

In addition to learning how to render text, we've seen that labels are not very different from sprites or other Cocos2D nodes. They have same properties, such as scale, rotation, and opacity. You can manipulate the labels using actions and create cool effects.

In the next chapter, we're going to talk about how to liven up the game using more animations and particle systems.

7
Animations and Particle Systems

We have already seen several ways to animate our game objects. We have moved the bird from one side of the screen to another, we've animated the birds' wings, and finally we've animated the hunter reloading the arrow and the arrow flying after it was shot.

These are all examples of animations. In fact, there are many ways you can animate your object and you don't always need multiple images to animate it. As an alternative, you can just change its position, scale, rotation, or other properties over time to bring the static image to life. By the way, this is exactly how animation is translated from Latin—the act of bringing to life. Your goal as a game developer is to make the player believe that the object is alive, irrespective of how you achieve this.

In this chapter, we will cover the following topics:

- Frame-based animation
- Animating objects by changing their properties over time, using Cocos2D actions
- Reviewing the skeletal animation
- Creating a particle system from scratch
- Using predefined particle systems that come with Cocos2D
- Using Particle Designer and shared particle systems

Using frame-based animation

Specifying multiple images (frames) is very common and in many cases, the most realistic way to animate your game objects. So we will start this chapter by speaking about frame-based animation.

Frame-based animation is quite simple from a developer's point of view. You just have multiple images that are called frames, where each frame depicts your game object at some point in time during the animation. For example, if you shoot an arrow, you might have the following frames:

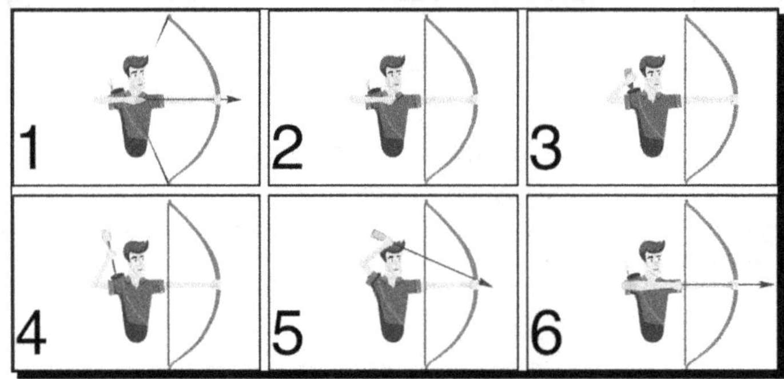

Hunter shooting and reloading the arrow

In the preceding image, frame **1** is our initial frame with the arrow still in the bow. We use this frame as a still image when aiming. In frame **2**, the arrow is shot and disappears from the hunter's game object as it is now a separate object. Frames **3** to **6** depict the hunter taking another arrow and putting it in the bow. Then we return to frame **1** and it looks like the hunter tenses the bow (when we go from frame **6** to frame **1**).

This way we get a looped animation. This is possible because the last frame depicts our game object in position, right before the first frame. It is very important to meet this condition, in case you want your animation to repeat seamlessly, just like animating the bird flying.

Time for action – exploding coconut

We are going to add one more animation that demonstrates more aspects of frame-based animation. For this, we are going to create a new scene that will appear during the start of the game. This scene is what is often called as a splash screen.

1. Open the Xcode project where we left it in the previous chapter.

As always, if you don't have the code after completing the previous chapter, you can find the code in the `Chapter_06/Chapter_06_Final` folder in the book's supporting files and use it as a starter project.

You can download book's supporting files by visiting the `www.packtpub.com/support` page and following the instructions.

2. Let's add the frames of our animation to our Xcode project. Create a new subgroup in the `Resources` group and call it `ExplodingCoconut`.
3. Open the book's supporting files available in the `Chapter_07/Assets/ExplodingCoconut/Animation` folder and select all files (*command* + *A*). Drag all the images to the `ExplodingCoconut` group in Xcode and add them to the project.
4. Then open the `Chapter_07/Assets/ExplodingCoconut/StartupScreen` directory (next to the `Animation` directory). You will see the following files:
    - `Default.png`
    - `Default@2x.png`
    - `Default-568h@2x.png`

   Before adding these files to the Xcode project, you should remove the files named in the same way that already exist in the Xcode project. They were added by default by the Cocos2D template. Find them in the Xcode project and remove them (make sure you select **Move to Trash**).
5. After removing the generated `Default*.png` files in Xcode, drag those three files listed earlier to the `Resources` group and add them to the project.
6. Now, when we have added all the required files, it is time to create the scene. Right-click on the `Scenes` group and click on **New File**. Select the **Objective-C class**, name it `IntroScene`, and make it a subclass of `CCScene`. Then save the file.
7. Open the `IntroScene.m` file and import the following three header files:

```
#import "GameScene.h"
#import "cocos2d.h"
#import "CCAnimation.h"
```

8. Then add an instance variable:

```
@implementation IntroScene
{
    CCSprite* _explodingCoconut;
}
```

9. And finally add the following methods that will set up and play the animation:

```
-(instancetype)init
{
    if (self = [super init])
    {
        CGSize viewSize =
          [CCDirector sharedDirector].viewSize;

        _explodingCoconut =
          [CCSprite spriteWithImageNamed:@"Exploding_Coconut_0.png"];
        _explodingCoconut.position = ccp(viewSize.width * 0.5f,
                                         viewSize.height * 0.5f);

        [self addChild:_explodingCoconut];
    }

    return self;
}

-(void)onEnter
{
    [super onEnter];
    [self animateCoconutExplosion];
}

-(void)animateCoconutExplosion
{
    NSMutableArray *frames = [NSMutableArray array];
    int lastFrameNumber = 34;
    for (int i =0; i <= lastFrameNumber; i++)
    {
        NSString *frameName =
          [NSString stringWithFormat:@"Exploding_Coconut_%d.png", i];
        CCSpriteFrame *frame =
          [CCSpriteFrame frameWithImageNamed:frameName];
        [frames addObject:frame];
```

```
    }

    CCAnimation *explosion =
      [CCAnimation animationWithSpriteFrames:frames delay:0.15f];
    CCActionAnimate *animateExplosion =
      [CCActionAnimate actionWithAnimation:explosion];
    CCActionEaseIn *easedExplosion =
      [CCActionEaseIn actionWithAction:animateExplosion rate:1.5f];

    CCActionCallFunc *proceedToGameScene =
      CCActionCallFunc *proceedToGameScene =
        [CCActionCallFunc actionWithTarget:self
          selector:@ selector(proceedToGameScene)];
    CCActionSequence *sequence =
     [CCActionSequence actions:easedExplosion, proceedToGameScene,
    nil];
    [_explodingCoconut runAction:sequence];
}

-(void)proceedToGameScene
{
    [[CCDirector sharedDirector]
      replaceScene:[[GameScene alloc] init]];
}
```

10. Now we need to display this scene in the beginning of the application. Open the `AppDelegate.m` file and import the `IntroScene.h` header at the top as follows:

```
#import "IntroScene.h"
```

11. Then, while still in the `AppDelegate.m` file, scroll down to the `startScene` method and make the following changes to run the `IntroScene` class as the first scene of the game:

```
-(CCScene *)startScene
{
    return [[IntroScene alloc] init];
}
```

12. Build and run the game. You should see a lonely coconut that explodes after some time. The animation starts when the debug labels appear on the bottom-left corner, since this is the time when we get control from the iOS. Refer to the following screenshot:

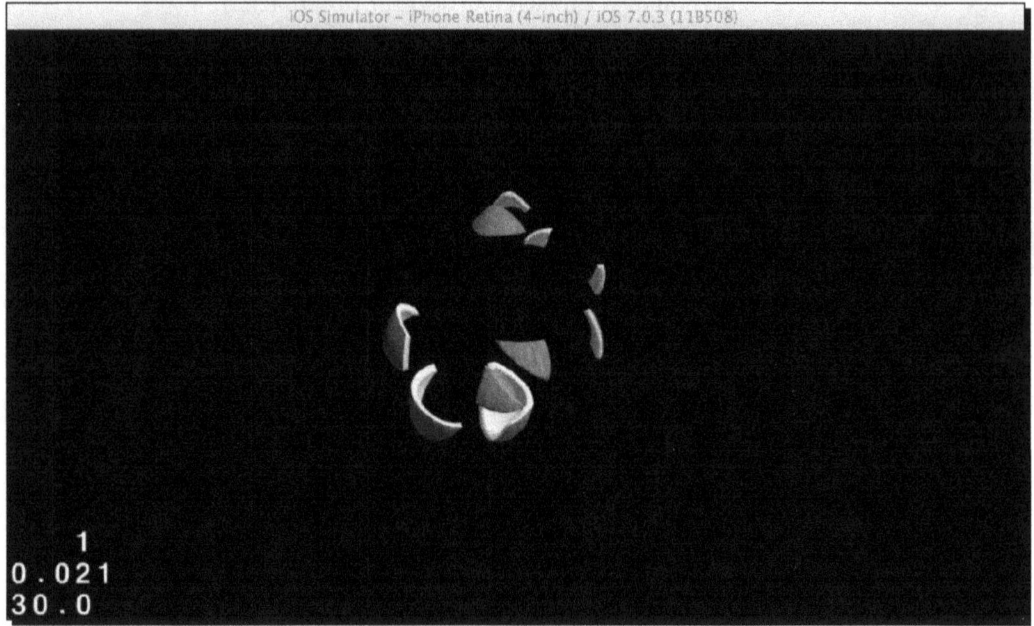

Exploding coconut as the splash screen

What just happened?

In addition to using frame-based animation that should already be pretty familiar, we have done a few new things. We have added one more scene as a splash screen and we have used `CCDirector` to replace the currently running scene.

We will review the coconut explosion and adding the splash screen process in detail. However, we are going to leave the `CCDirector` class-related code until the *Chapter 9, User Interface and Navigation*, later in the book. In fact, the only important thing we did using `CCDirector` is switched to the `GameScene` class after the explosion animation finished playing.

Coconut explosion animation

Exploding the coconut should be very familiar. We loaded the frames, set up animation, and added an easing action, which we'll discuss in a moment.

However, there are a few important things to take note of.

The first thing is that we didn't use a spritesheet to store the animation frames. Instead, we just used separate images for each animation frame. This is not the best approach, but you will see why we had to do this in a moment.

The second thing is that we have a significant amount of frames. Each frame is quite big. Every frame covers the full screen and a little more in the case of a 3.5 inch Retina display (for example, iPhone 4S), since we've used the same animation for 3.5 inch and 4 inch Retina displays.

This is the reason we didn't use a spritesheet to store all the frames, since we have a limit on a maximum texture size that I mentioned before.

As you see from this exploding coconut example, it is important to keep the right amount of frames and maintain minimum frame size when creating frame-based animation because otherwise you can easily end up wasting lots of memory and encounter performance issues.

We've seen some better examples of animation before and we'll see more of them later in the book. With this exploding coconut, I wanted to stress the features of frame-based animation by overemphasizing them.

And even with all the animation of the frames, the image still looks jerky. This is because the coconut's fragments move very fast and if we wanted to start our animation with some kind of slow-motion visual effect, we had to provide many frames in the beginning.

You might wonder why we needed to use such big images, especially in early frames when the coconut takes up only a small portion on the screen. The reason for this is that the animation frame is always at the center of the sprite, and you have to be very careful when you specify frames of different size. Here is an illustration of what can happen:

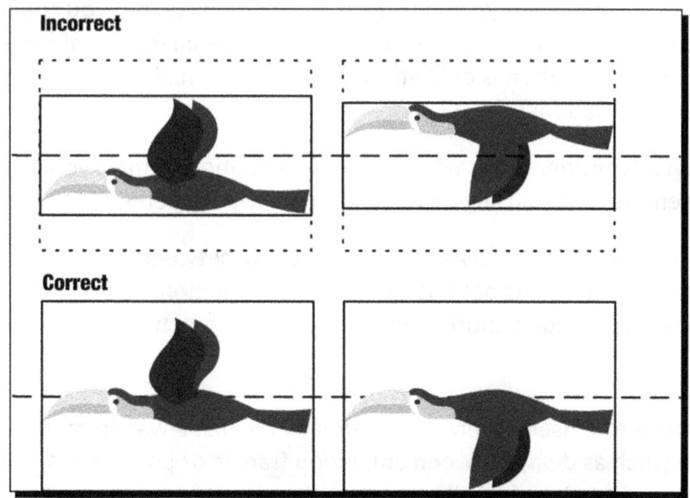

Incorrect and correct animation of frame image sizes

I've created a small project that you can find at `Chapter_07/FrameSizeIssues` that demonstrates the issue with a jumping bird sprite because I've cropped each image, and thus the center of the bird is not at the same position for each frame anymore.

In the preceding image, the dotted line shows the common bounding box of all frames of the animation. In other words, no animation frame exceeds the bounds marked by the dotted line. The bold line shows the size of the frame image. The horizontal line shows the center of the sprite.

As you can see in the first incorrect case (in the preceding image), we have tried to save some space by cropping the frames. Since every frame is placed in the center of the sprite, each frame will bounce up and down to position itself centered vertically.

If we create all frames of the same size, as it is shown in the correct case, the bird won't jump up and down and only the wings will move—even with a price of some of the unused space in each image.

Some of the tools such as TexturePacker can trim the empty space around the image in the spritesheet to get a smaller resulting image. However, they save the original size of image internally. Then, when the sprite is created from the spritesheet, its original size is restored, by simply adding all the removed whitespace at runtime. This would have worked if we had a small explosion, but since most of the coconut explosion frames are very big, we still cannot fit all of them in one spritesheet.

You can make the situation better or worse by specifying a different anchor point, compensating the position change, and using other techniques, but you should always keep in mind such behavior. Sometimes, it is just easier to create all frames of the same size. Of course, our explosion animation is only an example and normally, I would not recommend creating fullscreen animations.

Other than different considerations when creating animation frames, you can only control the delay between the frames using an animation delay parameter.

However, you don't always want to have the same delay between all frames of animation. This is where you can use easing actions to make the animation slower or faster in the end or at the start or even provide a more complicated easing function.

Easing actions

Easing actions that we've used several times already are just a way to modify the linear property change (such as delay between animation frames or position change when using the `CCActionMoveTo` action) from linear to nonlinear.

For example, when you want to add a stone falling from the point **A** in the air to the point **B** on the ground using `CCActionMoveTo`, you don't want it to move at a constant speed. Instead you want it to accelerate while falling. Refer to the following diagram:

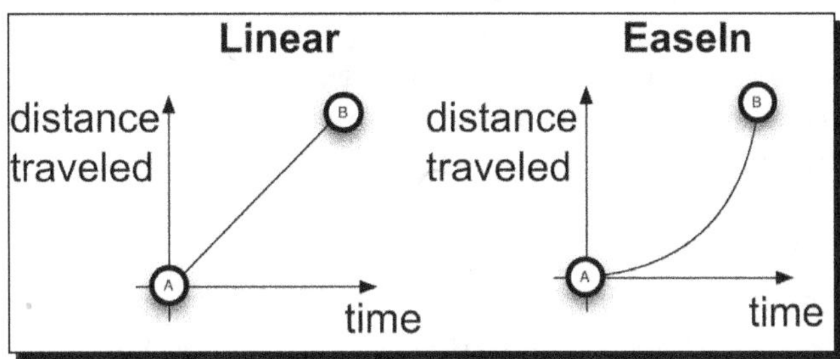

In the preceding image, it is shown how the stone would move from point **A** to point **B** using a linear function (for example, simply running `CCActionMoveTo`). In this case, this falling stone simply traveled the exact same amount each frame, but this wouldn't look like falling.

> To get more visual representation of different easing actions, please visit `http://kirillmuzykov.com/cocos2d-iphone-easing-examples/`.

However, if we wrap the `CCActionMoveTo` action in the `CCActionEaseIn` easing action, we will change the linear movement to a more realistic movement (slow at the beginning and faster in the end).

> Easing actions work with a variety of other actions, not just with `CCActionMoveTo`, since all they do is just modify the time passed to the inner action. This way we can even use some actions such as `CCActionEaseBounceOut` to bounce out from the ground after falling by making time run backwards, without adding extra actions or arguments to the simple `CCActionMoveTo` action.

There are lots of easing actions in Cocos2D; you can find all of them in the Cocos2D documentation (`http://www.cocos2d-iphone.org/docs/api/index.html`) by searching classes starting with `CCActionEase`.

Adding a splash screen

Adding a splash screen is not related to animations, but since we are playing an animation on it, let's review one trick that can make your animation on the splash screen shine.

The trick is to set the default image that is displayed by iOS to the first frame of your animation. This way while your application is loaded by iOS and even before you get the control in the code, you display a static image.

The player sees the static image that comes to life when our game is fully loaded by iOS. This is much nicer than just a flicker that changes the default image to the splash screen or even a straight to the menu scene.

Our splash screen is just an example. In real-world games, you could animate the menu appearing on the screen or something much showier. And while this animation is playing, you could preload some resources, such as the sound effects, music, or images without making the player stare some static **Loading** label.

When to use frame-based animation

As you can see, frame-based animation does not give too much room for a developer's imagination and creativity. Designer draws the animation and all you need to do is to turn it on or off, maybe switch between animations in the corresponding moment, and control its speed if required.

If you need to animate something at a very slow rate, such as a slow motion movement or simply some character slowly moving his hand, you will have to provide a lot of frames so that it doesn't look jerky.

Don't forget that animation frames take disk space and memory and we're pretty limited on memory on mobile devices. So if you use too much memory and ignore the memory warning, your game will be simply terminated by iOS.

However, even with all that said, frame-based animation is still the best way to animate your game objects in most cases. It is as close as you can get to realistic animation, if you create a sufficient amount of frames. All other animation techniques sometimes look too unnatural, although it is not always a bad thing. However, if you want most realistic animations, then frame-based animation is your choice.

Sometimes you don't even have a choice, for example, a character that is 64 x 64 pixels walking across the screen. The character is too small to apply any form of Cocos2D property animation other than position, so you simply have to resort to frame-based animation to show that it is walking.

Animating using actions

Although frame-based animation looks really cool, sometimes you don't want to use it. Maybe you want to save some memory or you just don't have a designer friend and if you are as bad at drawing as I am, then maybe it is better not to try to draw the animation by yourself.

Besides that, in some cases, using frame-based animation is complete overkill. Remember our bird flying around from one side of the screen to another? We could create an animation with each frame equal to the width of the screen and move the bird, just like we did with exploding coconut pieces.

Fortunately, instead of doing this, we can just change the bird's `position` property or use the `CCActionMoveTo` action. We will achieve the same effect with less effort and without wasting any disk or memory space.

> In game development, it is always a good idea to think about the best way to achieve the desired goal with minimum efforts. Being a good game developer is sometimes similar to being a good illusionist. You just need the player to see what you want him to see, and not necessarily do this as in real life.
>
> For example, if we'd wanted to show the bird flying, we could use real physics, simulating the air and the bird's wings movement that make the bird fly, but it would be too complicated. Instead, we have created an animation of the bird flittering its wings and moving the bird from one side of the screen to another using just the `position` property.

If you remember any really old game, you might notice that there are many places when a hero or an enemy is animated by just scaling or rotating. The reason to use such animation technique is that at that time there were heavy hardware limitations. You could not just create dozens of animations at that time, since they would not fit in device memory. However, it looked cool anyway. We are going to create similar old-school animations.

Time for action – hitting the bird animation

Currently, when the hunter hits the bird, it just disappears from the screen. This does not look very realistic. I mean the hunter does not have some kind of disintegrator blaster or something like that, and the last time I checked the arrow does not work this way.

Let's fix this by adding falling and rotation animation:

1. Open the `Bird.m` file and add the following method right below the `animateFly` method:

```
-(void)animateFall
{
    CGPoint fallDownOffScreenPoint =
      ccp(self.position.x, -self.boundingBox.size.height);

    CCActionMoveTo *fallOffScreen =
      [CCActionMoveTo actionWithDuration:2.0f
                         position:fallDownOffScreenPoint];

    CCActionRemove *removeWhenDone = [CCActionRemove action];
```

```
    CCActionSequence *fallSequence =
      [CCActionSequence actions: fallOffScreen,
                                 removeWhenDone,
                                 nil];

    [self runAction:fallSequence];

    CCActionRotateBy *rotate =
      [CCActionRotateBy actionWithDuration:0.1
                        angle:60];

    CCActionRepeatForever *rotateForever =
      [CCActionRepeatForever actionWithAction:rotate];
    [self runAction:rotateForever];
}
```

2. Then find the `removeBird:` method and update it as follows:

```
-(int)removeBird:(BOOL)hitByArrow
{
    [self stopAllActions];

    int score = 0;
    if (hitByArrow)
    {
        self.birdState = BirdStateDead;
        score = (_timesToVisit + 1) * 5;

        [self displayPoints:score];

        [self animateFall];
    }
    else
    {
        self.birdState = BirdStateFlewOut;
        [self removeFromParentAndCleanup:YES];
    }

    return score;
}
```

That's it, only two changes are required.

> Note that we've moved the `[self removeFromParentAndCleanup:YES];` call and now it is called only in case a bird flies away from the screen. If you don't do this, the bird will disappear without having the chance to fall and show this nice animation.

3. Build and run the game, and then shoot some birds. You should see them spinning while falling down off the screen.

> You can find a snapshot of the project at this point in the `Chapter_07/Cocohunt_07_Splash_and_Birds` folder.

What just happened?

Of course, this is not a Hollywood-quality video effect, but it is much better than the bird just disappearing from the screen. The code to achieve this is quite simple.

When the arrow hits the bird, the `animateFall` method is called. This method sets up two actions to run simultaneously. The first action moves the bird down the screen and removes it in the end, while the second one rotates the bird forever. Well, not forever, but until it is removed from the scene at the end of the first action sequence. However, it is convenient to use the forever-lasting action, since we don't know the amount of rotations it will take to completely fall off the screen.

This is a fast and easy way to add some animations to your game without having to draw all the frames. Of course, it is not as good as frame-based animation, especially if you need to show a lot of details and/or want to achieve a very realistic look and feel. However, you can do a lot more than just rotating the bird with this technique and sometimes it is better to prefer action-based animation to frame-based animation due to performance and simplicity considerations.

Skeletal animation

The last animation technique that we'll briefly talk about will be skeletal animation.

> There are also other techniques used for animation. However, the three that we will be reviewing in this chapter are the most commonly used ones. Also, we will be reviewing skeletal animation from the point of view of 2D games. In the 3D games world, it is a bit different.

The skeletal animation technique is a try to get both of the two worlds: controlled movement as in frame-based animation and ability to create any required amount of intermediate frames as in the action-based technique.

Using this technique, you can create pretty complicated animations without lots of frame images. Of course, you might still be able to create a better animation using frame-based animation, but in some cases, when you simply cannot create frame-based animation for every situation, skeletal animation is the only solution.

Here is how it works. Instead of one image, you split your animated game object into separate parts, like this:

Splitting a character into parts and creating different animation frames

Then, as you can see, using these body parts, you can create any frame of the animation. For example, you can see frames from walking and running animations in the preceding image.

We have already used skeletal animation to some extent for our hunter to rotate the torso when he is aiming. This is not exactly animation but the idea is the same. Of course, there are many tools that allow you to create skeletal animation, export it in some format (for example, XML), and then load it in Cocos2D, so you don't have to write a lot of code. However, we won't cover this process since it is a quite advanced topic and doesn't fit in the scope of this book.

I just hope that you have the big picture regarding skeletal animation and know that you can use it when required.

The most popular tool to create 2D skeletal animation is **Spine**. You can find more information on it, as well as some documentation and tutorials, at `http://esotericsoftware.com`.

Creating particle systems for advanced effects

A particle system is a special technique that uses many small particles (images or other graphic objects) to simulate effects that are hard to get using other render techniques. Examples are fire, rain, fog, explosion, and many others. Refer to the following image for an example:

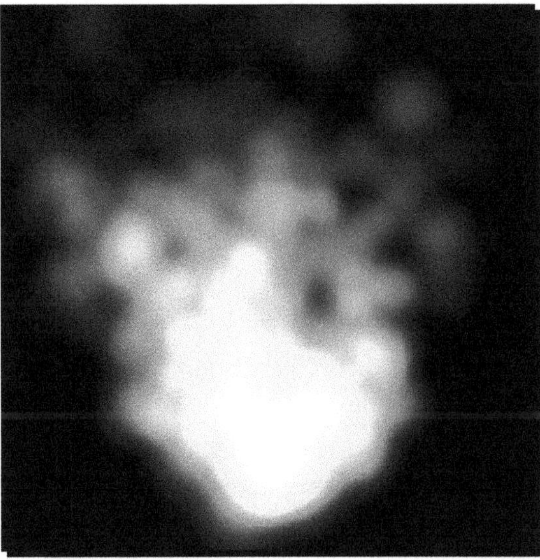

Fire particle system

Particle systems might look difficult at the first glance because of the amount of parameters you can and often have to configure to create one, but the main concept is quite simple. You have a particle, in most cases this is just a small image, and you have an emitter that emits many copies of that particle.

Of course, there is not much sense in creating every particle at the same position, with the same size and rotation, since these particles will just overlap (just like if you add the same sprite many times in the same position) and all you will see is just one particle. This does not seem like a lot of fun. However, if we set the different movement vector for each particle and the different starting position relative to the emitter, this will immediately create that fuzzy effect that we want. And if we go even further and use a different start and end color of the particles, start and end size, and so on, it will add even more randomness. In fact, there are many other configuration options for the particles that allow us to produce really cool effects.

Let's create one particle system and it will get much clearer.

Time for action – adding the feathers explosion

We are going to add an explosion of feathers when the arrow hits the bird. We will create about 100 feather particles at the bird's center point and then explode them in different directions gradually fading away.

To do this, we are going to add a few methods into the `Bird.m` file and call it when an arrow hits the bird. After that, we will just add our particle image to the project and we are done. Refer to the following steps:

1. We will start by adding the method that creates a particle system. Go ahead and open the `Bird.m` file, and add the following method right above the `removeBird:` method:

```
-(void)explodeFeathers
{
    //1
    int totalNumberOfFeathers = 100;

    //2
    CCParticleSystem *explosion =
      [CCParticleSystem
        particleWithTotalParticles:totalNumberOfFeathers];

    //3
    explosion.position = self.position;

    //4
    explosion.emitterMode = CCParticleSystemModeGravity;

    //5
    explosion.gravity = ccp(0, -200.0f);

    //6
    explosion.duration = 0.1f;

    //7
    explosion.emissionRate =
      totalNumberOfFeathers/explosion.duration;

    //8
    explosion.texture =
      [CCTexture textureWithFile:@"feather.png"];
    explosion.startColor = [CCColor whiteColor];
```

```
    explosion.endColor =
      [[CCColor whiteColor] colorWithAlphaComponent:0.0f];

    //9
    explosion.life = 0.25f;
    explosion.lifeVar = 0.75f;
    explosion.speed = 60;
    explosion.speedVar = 80;

    //10
    explosion.startSize = 16;
    explosion.startSizeVar = 4;
    explosion.endSize =
      CCParticleSystemStartSizeEqualToEndSize;
    explosion.endSizeVar = 8;

    //11
    explosion.angleVar = 360;
    explosion.startSpinVar = 360;
    explosion.endSpinVar = 360;

    //12
    explosion.autoRemoveOnFinish = YES;

    //13
    ccBlendFunc blendFunc;
    blendFunc.src = GL_SRC_ALPHA;
    blendFunc.dst = GL_ONE;
    explosion.blendFunc = blendFunc;

    //14
    CCNode *batchNode = self.parent;
    CCNode *scene = batchNode.parent;
    [scene addChild:explosion];
}
```

2. Then add a call to the preceding method in the `removeBird:` method as follows:

```
-(int)removeBird:(BOOL)hitByArrow
{
    [self stopAllActions];

    int score = 0;
    if (hitByArrow)
```

```
        {
            self.birdState = BirdStateDead;
            score = (_timesToVisit + 1) * 5;

            [self displayPoints:score];
            [self animateFall];

            [self explodeFeathers];
        }
        else
        {
            self.birdState = BirdStateFlewOut;
            [self removeFromParentAndCleanup:YES];
        }

        return score;
    }
```

3. Now we need to add the feather image to the project. To do so, create a group called `Feathers` in the `Resources` group.
4. Then add the two files contained in the `Chapter_07/Assets/Feathers` folder (`feather.png` and `feather-hd.png`) to the Xcode project in that `Feathers` group.
5. Build and run the game. Now when you hit the bird, you should see an explosion of feathers as shown in the following screenshot:

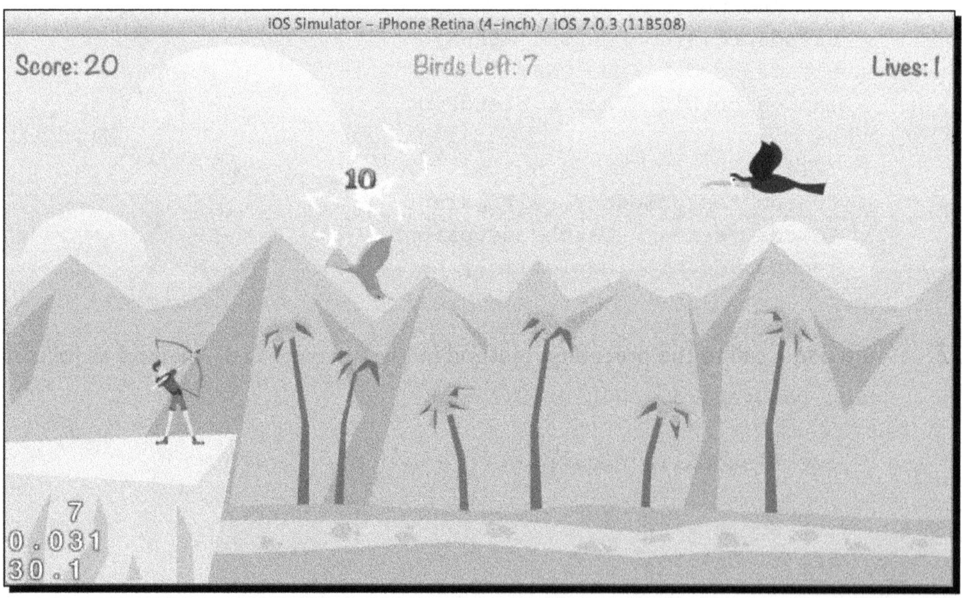

What just happened?

The `explodeFeathers` method can look quite scary with all those parameters. However, it is just because the particle system has a lot of configuration options. We will review some of them shortly but first let's discuss how the particle system works.

As I have mentioned before, each particle system has the emitter and the particles. Emitter does exactly what the name suggests; it emits particles. The particles are the tiny images, in our case, feathers. By setting all those properties, we configure how to emit our particles, their speed, rotation, color, how long they will live, and so on.

Let's review each line of the code in the `explodeFeathers` method:

1. Maximum amount of particles sets the maximum amount of feathers there can be at the same time.
2. This line of code creates a particle system with the specified amount of particles.
3. The position of the particle system is set to the bird's center position. In our case, this will be the center point of our feather explosion.
4. The emitter mode is set to `gravity`.

There are two modes, `gravity` and `radius`. In the `gravity` mode, particles move away or towards the gravity center. This is what we need for a system such as explosion. The other mode `radius` is useful when you want to rotate the particles around the emitter. The `radius` mode can be used to create spiral effects.

5. This line sets the gravity value applied to the particles. Our feathers are going to explode from the center in many directions, but we also want them to fall down since they are affected by gravity.
6. This is the amount of time in which emitter should emit new particles. In our case, we want this to be a short interval, since we are simulating explosions.

Sometimes, you want the emitter to emit new particles for a very long time, even infinitely. For example, if you create a fire, you want it to run infinitely. In this case, you can set the duration property to the `CCParticleSystemDurationInfinity` constant.

7. This line sets the emission rate of the particles. It is very useful in conjunction with infinite duration, since you can control how many particles per second you want to create.

8. This block of code sets the image to use as our particle and its start and end color. You can open the `feather.png` image (or `feather-hd.png` to see the Retina version) and see that there is a small white feather. This is the base image for our particles. We have also set the starting color (when the particle is created) and the end color (when the particle life is ended). We want our feathers to start completely white and gradually fade away. Since we want our feather to remain white, we only change the alpha of the end color using the `colorWithAlphaComponent:` method that returns the same color, with only the alpha change to the given value.

> Our feather image is white and we set the color to white. In most cases, particle images are also white but the start and end colors are not white. This works exactly as with our white arrow image used as an aiming indicator that we're coloring green if we're inside the shooting radius and red if we're outside. White color is just multiplied on the required color and we can get our particle in different colors using just one image. We will see our feathers change color in the next section, where we'll use them as flame particles.

9. The `life` property sets how long each particle is going to live for after it is emitted. The `speed` property sets how fast the particle will move. As you can see, we also set the `lifeVar` and `speedVar` properties—these are the variance properties. Since we didn't want all of our particles to live the same amount of time and to move with the same speed, we added some randomness to each particle.

> Almost every property of a particle system has a property ending with `Var`. Setting this variance property will set the range for the randomness.

10. Here we set the start and the end size of the particle. If the end size is bigger than the start size, then the particles will grow, and if the end size is smaller than the start size, the particles will shrink. In our case, we didn't want the feathers to shrink or grow too much, but we still added some variance to make the effect of feathers moving closer or farther while they move, to add some depth.
11. The starting angle variance is set to a full circle. Since we just want the particles to move in all directions, we only set angle variance (`angleVar`) to full circle. In addition, we added some start and end rotation variance, to make the feathers spin a little.
12. The `autoRemoveOnFinish` property is set to `YES`. This tells the particle system to remove itself when it is done. This is very useful since we don't need to keep a reference to the particle system and check if it is finished to remove it from the scene.

13. This sets how the particles will blend with the background. Setting this property as we did will make our feathers a little less transparent.

> Blending is the process of mixing the current image (source or `src`) pixels color with anything that was already rendered before (background or destination or `dst`). The final color is calculated using the formula `final = (src * blendFunc.src) + (dst * blendFunc.dst)`. So, by setting different blending functions, you can regulate how the particle will blend with the background.
>
> There is a great online tool by Anders Riggelsen that can help you to visualize different blending modes at `http://www.andersriggelsen.dk/glblendfunc.php`.
>
> By the way, this property is not exclusive for particle systems and can be used with many other Cocos2D nodes (sprites, labels, and so on).

Blending can be hard to understand at first but for now the important thing to remember is that if you have a problem with how a particle system looks on a particular background, you can try to tweak the blending function before changing anything else.

14. Finally, we have added the particle system to the scene.

It might seem that particle systems are very complicated, but they are not. The reason for such a long explanation is that particle systems have many configuration options. And you don't have to know every value for every configuration property in advance. In fact, creating particle systems is mostly a trial and error process when you tweak the particle system configuration and check the result until you are happy with the look.

If you don't want to spend your time creating and tweaking your particle system from scratch, you can either use one of the predefined particle systems that come with Cocos2D or use a visual tool to see the changes made in real time.

Let's start by using a predefined particle system.

Time for action – adding a fire to the scene

We are going to add a campfire to our scene. We will add an image of the campfire base and the fire burning on top of it. To do this, follow these steps:

1. Create a new group in `Resources` and call it `Campfire`.
2. Open the book's supporting files at `Chapter_07/Assets/Campfire` and add the `campfire.png` and `campfire-hd.png` images to the Xcode project in the `Campfire` group.

3. Open the `GameScene.m` file and add the following method below the `onEnter` method:

```
-(void)startFire
{
    CGSize viewSize = [CCDirector sharedDirector].viewSize;

    //1
    CCSprite *campfire =
      [CCSprite spriteWithImageNamed:@"campfire.png"];
    campfire.position = ccp(viewSize.width * 0.5,
                            viewSize.height * 0.05f);
    [self addChild:campfire];

    //2
    CGPoint campfireTop =
      ccp(campfire.position.x,
          campfire.position.y +
            campfire.boundingBox.size.height * 0.5f);

    //3
    CCParticleFire *fire =
      [CCParticleFire particleWithTotalParticles:300];
    fire.position = campfireTop;

    //4
    fire.texture =
      [CCTexture textureWithFile:@"feather.png"];

    //5
    fire.scale = 0.3f;

    //6
    [self addChild:fire];
}
```

4. Then add a call to the preceding method at the end of the `onEnter` method as follows:

```
-(void)onEnter
{
    [super onEnter];
    self.gameState = GameStatePlaying;
    [self initializeControls];
    [self startFire];
}
```

5. Build and run the game. You will see a campfire burning in the bottom part of the screen as shown in the following screenshot:

What just happened?

This time, instead of configuring all parameters of the particle system, we used the predefined `CCParticleFire` class. This class simply inherits from the `CCParticleSystem` class and sets some values that correspond to the fire particle system.

> There are more predefined particle systems that come with Cocos2D. Just start typing `CCParticle` and you will see them in the code completion pop up, or search for them in the Cocos2D documentation at `http://www.cocos2d-iphone.org/docs/api/index.html`.
>
> Also, you can find the `ParticleTest` test in the `cocos2d-tests-ios.xcodeproj` project that comes with Cocos2D distribution. We reviewed it at the end of *Chapter 2, Hello Cocos2D*.

Let's review the `startFire` method:

1. Added background image for our campfire: This is not required for particle system, but it looks nicer when the fire does not just start somewhere in the air.
2. We found the top-middle point of the campfire image: This is where we place our particle system.
3. This time we have created the particle system with the maximum of `300` particles.

4. This might look strange, but we have reused the feathers image as our particle. This is done intentionally just to show you how our white feather image becomes a fire particle with only start and end colors set by `CCParticleFire`.
5. The default `CCParticleFire` is a little too big. Instead of tweaking the particle system properties, we just scaled it down to show that you can still apply Cocos2D properties such as `scale` and `rotation` to a particle system.
6. Finally, we added the particle system to the scene.

As you can see, the fire burns infinitely. This is because `CCParticleFire` internally sets the duration to `CCParticleSystemDurationInfinity`, so it emits particles all the time using the `emissionRate` property unlike our feathers explosion, which emits for only a short period of time.

Time for action – using Particle Designer

Predefined particle systems that come with Cocos2D are a good way to start, but in many cases, you will want to create a custom particle system and tweak all the properties. This way you will have to build and run the game after each change to test the particle system. This is not very efficient.

There are a few tools that can help you to design a particle system and Particle Designer 2 is definitely one of the best. Let's use it to add a sun to our game scene:

1. First of all, you need to download and install Particle Designer. Visit `http://71squared.com/en/particledesigner` to download and then install it.
2. Open the Particle Designer app and immediately press the cloud button in the top-right corner as shown in the following screenshot:

The cloud button

3. This will open the gallery with the shared particle systems (particle systems created by other users and shared with you).

4. We are going to use one. Search for the **Red Sun**, click on it and you should immediately see the sun particle system in the preview, as shown in the following screenshot:

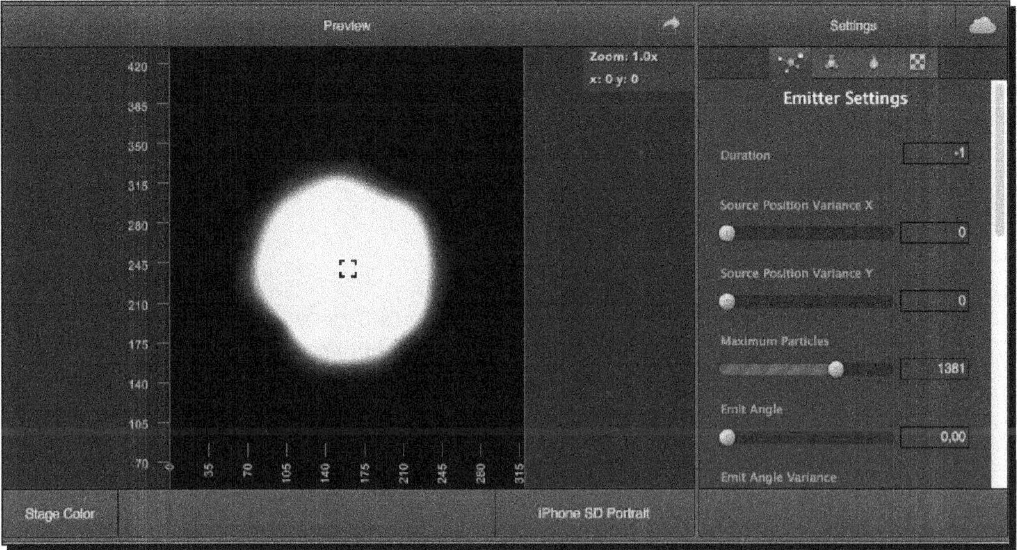

5. You can click the same button where the cloud was before (now there should be an icon with sliders) and you will see settings for this particle system. You can change them and see the changes immediately in the preview window.

6. If this was a full version of Particle Designer (not a trial), we could export this particle system in a `.plist` file. For now, let's pretend we did that and let's take the result file from the `Chapter_07/Assets/Sun` folder. Just open this folder and see the file called `sun.plist` that contains all the information about particle systems.

7. Open Xcode and create a group called `Sun` in the `Resources` group. Add the `sun.plist` file to that group.

8. Then open the `GameScene.m` file and add the following method after the `startFire` method:

```
-(void)createTheSun
{
    CGSize viewSize = [CCDirector sharedDirector].viewSize;

    CCParticleSystem *sun =
      [CCParticleSystem particleWithFile:@"sun.plist"];
```

```
        sun.position = ccp(viewSize.width  * 0.05f,
                           viewSize.height * 0.9f);
        [self addChild:sun];
    }
```

9. Then add a call to the preceding method at the end of the `onEnter` method:

```
    -(void)onEnter
    {
        [super onEnter];
        self.gameState = GameStatePlaying;
        [self initializeControls];

        [self startFire];

        [self createTheSun];
    }
```

10. Build and run the game. You should see the sun shining in the upper-left corner, below the score label as shown in the following screenshot:

Don't worry if your frame rate is low and the game is very slow. If you run the game on the actual device, it will run 60 FPS without problems. Unfortunately, a simulator does not always allow you to check how your game will actually perform on a real device due to lack of hardware acceleration.

After reading the following *What just happened?* section, if you wish to experiment with the sun a little, please wrap the call to the `createTheSun` method in the following `#if` directive that will only enable the particle system on the actual device:

```
#if !TARGET_IPHONE_SIMULATOR
[self createTheSun];
#endif
```

This is so that we can continue testing on the simulator.

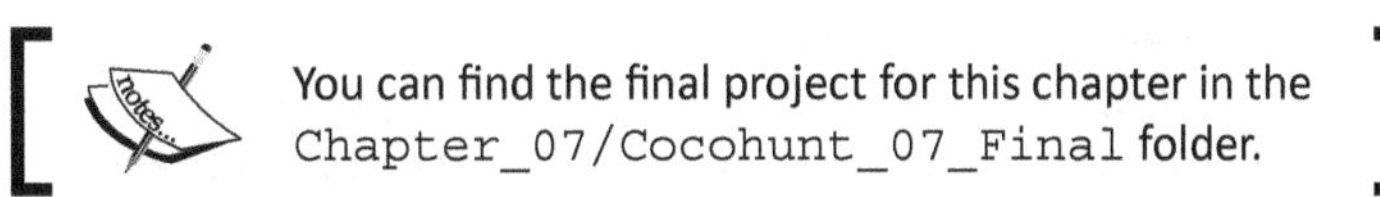

You can find the final project for this chapter in the `Chapter_07/Cocohunt_07_Final` folder.

What just happened?

We have just added a particle system with three lines of code. Of course, we didn't create it from scratch and just used a ready particle system, but it is still very impressive.

So how does this work? I am sure you have already understood that Particle Designer immediately visualizes all the particle system property changes, just like if you'd change a line of code, and then build and run the game. Of course, it is much faster to do this in Particle Designer.

Then, when you have designed the particle system, you just export it in the `.plist` file, which contains all the properties and even the embedded particle texture. After that, you only need to load this file in Cocos2D, which supports this file format.

Have a go hero

This is one of the most creativity-rewarding *Have a go hero* sections in the book. Here are a few things that you can try:

- **Change the bird falling animation**: You can make it jump a little and scale when hit. Rotate it in different directions; maybe even randomize direction and rotation speed.
- **Tweak the feather explosion animation parameters**: Change the number of feathers. Change the radius of the explosion by tweaking the life of the particle parameters.
- **Tweak the feather color depending on the bird type**: Currently all feathers are always white, but our birds are in different colors. You can use the `birdType` property to adjust the start and end colors of the feathers depending on the bird type.

- **Tweak the fire particle system**: Add some smoke. Create and use a new particle in any graphics editor and use it as a fire particle. This is a very useful experience.
- **Create a radial particle system**: You can create your own radial system.
- **Change the splash screen animation**: You can try to draw the animation yourself! Even if you absolutely cannot draw (like me), you can draw a few frames of animation. Alternatively, you can find free animation on the Web. Please refer to the end of *Chapter 12, Standing Out– Integrating Game Center and In-App Purchases*, for a list of websites where you can find free animations.
- **Create your own particle system in Particle Designer**: Try creating snowflakes, a fountain, and a ring of fire. You won't be able to export these but you will understand all the main properties and can even try to recreate it in the code.

Pop quiz – animations and particle systems

Q1. How would you animate a cannonball shot from the cannon?

1. Create frame-based animation for the whole trajectory of the ball
2. Used Cocos2D actions to move the single ball sprite along the trajectory

Q2. What parameter of the particle system using gravity mode do you need to change to get a bigger explosion?

1. `endSize`
2. `duration`
3. `life`
4. `endColor`

Summary

In this chapter, we have reviewed different animation techniques and learned when to use a certain type of animation taking into account its pros and cons.

While learning about animations, we have added a nice old-school bird fall animation, so it no longer just disappears from the screen.

In the second part of the chapter, we met particle systems, which are really cool and can add some very nice effects to your game. We created one from the ground up, used the predefined particle system provided by Cocos2D, and took a short look at some tools that allow you to create particle systems in almost no time.

Just as with animations, we had a chance to add a particle system to our game and added a feather explosion when the arrow hits the bird. This way all of our objects have corresponding reactions on different game events and our Cocohunt game scene is currently very close to a simple but complete level.

In the chapters ahead, we will add sound and a user interface and it will look even nicer. In fact, we are going to add sound and music to the game already in the next chapter. You will see that this will immediately take the game to another level.

8
Adding Sound Effects and Music

Sound effects and music are very important in modern games. I am sure you can remember some recent popular game where the "Better with headphones" sign appears on the splash screen.

Many games just would not be that good without the atmosphere created with sound effects and music. In this chapter, we will learn how to add them to our game. We will add sound effects when we shoot the arrow, hit the bird, and in other places where you would expect to hear sounds in the real world. In addition to this, we are going to make our game even cooler by adding some background music.

In this chapter, we will cover the following topics:

- Playing sound effects
- Playing music and background sounds
- Switching between music tracks
- Making use of stereo headphones
- Finding sound effects for our game
- Adding sound effects and preloading them

Creating AudioManager and playing sound effects

You can play sound effects and music on iOS without using any game engine in many different ways, but as I have mentioned before, one of the goals of the game engine such as Cocos2D is to make our lives easier.

This is why Cocos2D uses a great library called ObjectAL that provides a nice interface to the underlying OpenAL framework. A good thing about using ObjectAL is that it provides different levels of control.

For example, there is a class called `OALSimpleAudio`, which provides a very simple interface to play audio and requires absolutely no knowledge of how things work internally. This class is suitable for most games and provides all the required features to play background and foreground audio files.

On the other hand, you can always go deeper and use some lower-level class that will be more complex, but will also give you more control.

We will start with the basic `OALSimpleAudio` functionality and will build on top of it along the way.

Time for action – adding the AudioManager class

We are going to create a simple singleton class and put all the code related to the audio playback into it.

> Although we could play any sound effect with just a single line of code by using `OALSimpleAudio`, we are going to create a special class called `AudioManager`. This will allow us to keep the audio playback code separate from the rest of our code.
>
> This is a good idea as it allows you to tweak the playback in one place and even switch to some other audio framework without going through all the code and searching and replacing the code. It also decentralizes the access to the audio playback, which means the main screen, game screen, and cut scenes can all control audio.

We will start from almost an empty class, and we will fill it with code as we complete the tasks of adding sound effects and music to our game by performing the following steps:

1. Open the Cocohunt Xcode project at the point where we left it in the previous chapter.

> If you have completed the previous chapter, you can continue working with your project. Alternatively, you can take the included final project from the previous chapter and use it as a starter project. You can find the final project for the previous chapter at the `Chapter_07/Chapter_07_Final` folder in the book's supporting files, which can be downloaded from `www.packtpub.com/support` and follow the instructions.

2. Right-click on the `Common` group and create a new **Objective-C class**. Call it `AudioManager` and make it a subclass of `NSObject`.

3. Open the `AudioManager.h` file and add the following method declarations:

```
-(void)playSoundEffect:(NSString *)soundFile;

+(instancetype)sharedAudioManager;
```

4. Then, open the `AudioManager.m` file and import the `OALSimpleAudio.h` header file at the top as follows:

```
#import "OALSimpleAudio.h"
```

5. Add the following implementation of the methods we declared earlier:

```
-(void)playSoundEffect:(NSString *)soundFile
{
    [[OALSimpleAudio sharedInstance] playEffect:soundFile];
}

+(AudioManager *)sharedAudioManager
{
    static dispatch_once_t pred;
    static AudioManager * _sharedInstance;
    dispatch_once(&pred, ^{
       _sharedInstance = [[self alloc] init];
    });
    return _sharedInstance;
}
```

Don't worry about the `sharedAudioManager` method implementation. It is a standard and recommended way to create a singleton. We will discuss this in a moment.

6. That is it! Build the game and check whether there are any errors. There is no reason to run the game right now as you will see no visual changes. However, you should always build the game and check that there are no errors before continuing.

What just happened?

We have not done much yet, but we have laid out a good foundation for our future code. We have created a singleton class that we will be able to use at any point in the game and we have created a method that plays sound effects using the given sound file name.

As I've mentioned in one of the previous chapters, singletons are quite useful if you want to have a globally accessible decentralized instance. In our case, we want to be able to control audio playback from any scene in our game; this is why we need this global object.

The `sharedAudioManager` method simply creates the only singleton instance when you first access this method. This is why we used the `dispatch_once_t` predicate.

> You can find out more about using **Grand Central Dispatch** (**GCD**) from Apple's documentation at `https://developer.apple.com/library/mac/documentation/performance/reference/gcd_libdispatch_ref/Reference/reference.html` (short link: `http://bit.ly/1hISyQ0`).

Don't worry about this singleton-related code. The only thing you need to understand that a singleton will be globally accessible and as there will be only one instance, we can use instance variables to store the data shared between all scenes of the game.

> Although you will do completely fine if you simply remember how to create a singleton and when to use it, learning at least a bit more about singletons as well as about other design patterns can be quite useful.

Now, back to the audio playback-related code. The following is the declaration of the method that is used to play sound effects in the `OALSimpleAudio.h` file:

```
- (id<ALSoundSource>) playEffect:(NSString*) filePath
```

It takes the audio file path and returns the strange `id<ALSoundSource>` value as a return value. You can think of this return value as a currently played sound identifier or a reference to the sound that you have just played. This value can be used to identify the sound, for example, if you want to stop the looped playback.

You might notice that there are not many options in the `playEffect:` method shown earlier. This is because this simple method just calls the more general `playEffect:` method that has more parameters as shown in the following code:

```
- (id<ALSoundSource>) playEffect:(NSString*) filePath
                          volume:(float) volume
                           pitch:(float) pitch
                             pan:(float) pan
                            loop:(bool) loop;
```

In the preceding code, you see you can set the sound effect to loop and change other options. The following is some brief information about each parameter:

- `filePath`: This is the path to the audio file to play.
- `volume`: This is the level of the volume to play at, where 0 means no sound and 1.0 is the original volume.
- `pitch`: This is the pitch to play at, where 1.0 is the original sound. Passing a higher pitch value makes the sound play at a higher note. Passing a lower pitch will make the effect sound lower.
- `pan`: This is the pan that affects stereo playback. Passing -1.0 will play the sound at the far left (almost no sound in the right headphone), while passing +1.0 will play the sound at the far right.
- `loop`: If set to `YES`, this sound effect will be looped.

Of course, it is hard to understand all these parameters without examples. We will see how to use them later in this chapter, but first we need to find some sound effects and add them to our game.

Time for action – finding and playing our first sound effect

Now that we have the basic code to play sound effects ready, I am sure you are eager to try it. We are going to find some sound effects, add them to the game, and even play one.

There are many places on the Web where you can find some free sound effects for your game. You can find a bigger list of websites with free sound effects and music at the end of the book in *Chapter 12, Standing Out– Integrating Game Center and In-App Purchases*. This final chapter can be downloaded for free from the Packt website at `www.packtpub.com/support`, as it does not fit in the print book.

You can choose any sound effects you like. The only thing you need to take into account is the supported audio formats.

You can find detailed information about iOS supported formats at `https://developer.apple.com/library/ios/documentation/AudioVideo/Conceptual/MultimediaPG/UsingAudio/UsingAudio.html` (short link: `http://bit.ly/RLfmsx`).

Most of the files on the Web are in the `.wav` or `.mp3` formats and should work just fine. Perform the following steps:

1. Let's download some sound effects from the Web. Open the `http://freesound.org/` website and search for the sound effects that we should play in the following situations:
   - When the hunter shots the arrow from the bow
   - When the arrow hits the bird
   - When you win the game
   - When you lose the game

This is not important for this sample case, but if you are making a real project, note the license of the each audio file you download. For example, you cannot use an audio file licensed under the noncommercial license in the game you are going to sell.

2. When you find several candidates for each sound effect, save them somewhere on the disk and name the files corresponding to the situation (for example, `arrow_shot.wav`).

If you cannot find the good sound effects or don't want to spend time searching right now, you can use the files I've prepared for you. To do this, open the book's supporting files folder available at `Chapter_08/Assets/SoundEffects`, and here, you will find four files: `arrow_shot.wav`, `bird_hit.mp3`, `lose.wav`, and `win.wav`.

3. Create a new group in the `Resources` group and call it `Sound`. Add all the four audio files that you have found or have taken from the book's supporting files to this group.

It is very important to check that the **Add to targets** list has **Cocohunt** checked, as Xcode can unselect this checkbox for some audio formats that are supported, but have less common extensions, and will not include this sound file in the app bundle. Make sure you have settings as shown on the following screenshot:

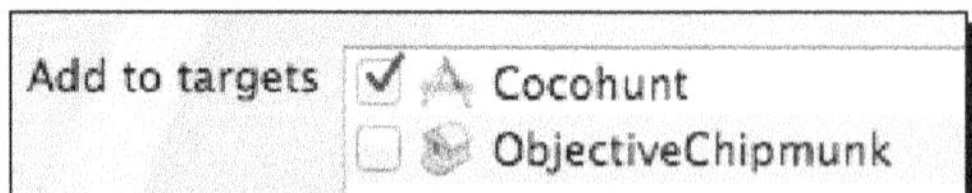

4. Now it is time to play some sound effects. We will start with the sound of shooting the arrow. Open the `Hunter.m` file and import the `AudioManager.h` header at the top as follows:

```
#import "AudioManager.h"
```

5. Then, find the `shootAtPoint:` method and add the following code at the beginning of the method:

```
-(CCSprite*)shootAtPoint:(CGPoint)point
{
    [[AudioManager sharedAudioManager]
      playSoundEffect:@"arrow_shot.wav"];

    //..skipped..
}
```

Note that my audio file is named `arrow_shot.wav`; if you have not used the files that come with the book, then you have to specify the name of your file.

6. Build and run the game. You should hear a sound every time the hunter shoots an arrow.

What just happened?

We have just played the first sound effect in our game. I hope you are happy with the sound effect that you have chosen or with the file I selected if you used the file from the book's supporting files. The player will hear this sound very often, so you have to make sure it is not annoying.

If the sound is not playing, check whether you have mistyped the file name and selected the **Add to targets** checkbox when adding the file. You can check whether the file is included in the app bundle by going to the project properties, selecting the **Cocohunt** target from the **TARGETS** list on the left of the screen, then switching to the **Build Phases** tab and checking whether your sound file is present in the **Copy Bundle Resources** list, as shown in the following screenshot:

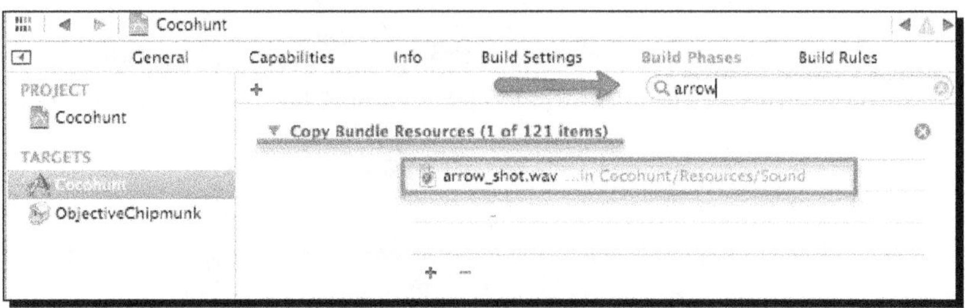

If you have spent time searching for sound effects, you must have realized that it takes a lot of time to find a good sound, while playing it using our `AudioManager` and `OALSimpleAudio` methods is less time consuming.

Let's play the rest of the sound effects.

Time for action – playing the remaining sound effects

We have added all the sound effects files to our project previously, so what we are going to do now is just add some code to play them. We need to add the code in three places: when the arrow hits the bird, when we lose, and when we win the game.

Let's start making changes by performing the following steps:

1. Open the `Bird.m` file and import the `AudioManager.h` header file at the top as follows:

```
#import "AudioManager.h"
```

2. Next, find the `removeBird:` method and add the corresponding sound effect that will be played when the bird is hit by an arrow:

```
-(int)removeBird:(BOOL)hitByArrow
{
    //..skipped
    if (hitByArrow)
    {
        //..skipped..

        [[AudioManager sharedAudioManager]
          playSoundEffect:@"bird_hit.mp3"];
    }
    //..skipped..
}
```

Note that I have used the file named `bird_hit.mp3` (which is in the `.mp3` file format); if your file is named differently, then you have to adjust that line of code.

3. The final file we need to change is the `GameScene.m` file. Open it and import the `AudioManager.h` header file at the top using the following line of code:

```
#import "AudioManager.h"
```

4. Then, scroll down and find the `lost` and `won` methods. Add the code to play the corresponding sound at the beginning of each method as follows:

```
-(void)lost
{
    [[AudioManager sharedAudioManager]
      playSoundEffect:@"lose.wav"];

    self.gameState = GameStateLost;
    [self displayWinLoseLabelWithText:@"You lose!"
                              andFont:@"lost.fnt"];
}

-(void)won
{
    [[AudioManager sharedAudioManager]
      playSoundEffect:@"win.wav"];

    self.gameState = GameStateWon;
    [self displayWinLoseLabelWithText:@"You win!"
                              andFont:@"win.fnt"];
}
```

Don't forget to change the audio file names if you aren't using the files that come with the book.

5. That's it! Build and run the game and enjoy the sounds. Win and lose the game to make sure that the corresponding sound is played.

You can find snapshot of the project at this stage in the `Chapter_08/Cocohunt_08_Sound_Effects` folder.

What just happened?

We have added the code to play three remaining sound effects that we added earlier. The code itself should be very simple, so I am not going to cover it.

The other thing that just happened is that you have probably just used several files under some license. In my case, it was the Creative Commons Attribute license, so I must give the credit to the people who created these sound effects.

I say probably because if you did not use the files that came with the book, you might have used sound files under the Creative Commons Public Domain license and don't have to attribute anyone, but I think it is always a good idea to attribute a person who helped you to make your game.

> Later, we are going to add an **About** scene to the game, and normally, I put the credits there, but as I'm writing a book, I'll put some credits right in the text.
>
> This book and the sample game use the following sounds from Freesound:
>
> `arrow_shot.wav` by EverHeat at `http://freesound.org/people/EverHeat/sounds/205563/`
>
> `bird_hit.mp3` by haydensayshi123 `http://freesound.org/people/haydensayshi123/sounds/138678/`
>
> `lose.wav` by Benboncan `http://freesound.org/people/Benboncan/sounds/73581/`
>
> `win.wav` by bone666138 `http://freesound.org/people/bone666138/sounds/198874/`
>
> Thank you!

Have a go hero

There is no limit to perfection. This is totally about picking the sound for the game. The following are some thoughts about how you can improve your skills and the game:

- If you have not searched for the sound and just used the files that came with the book, I strongly encourage you to do a search and maybe change some files. When you spend some time searching, you will learn to estimate the time required to find the corresponding sound effects.
- If you have searched but are still unhappy with any sound, try to find a better one. Searching for the exact sound effect (for example, the bird hit by an arrow) does not always work. For example, I've used a melon squash sound for a zombie head explosion effect in one of my games, so you have to think what sound can be close to what you want.
- You can add a sound of a falling bird, a sound when you lose one life or a sound when a new bird is spawned. Just don't add a sound that plays for a long duration or the game will end up as a cacophony.

Music and background sounds

I hope you agree that the game is so much better now that it has sounds. Let's add some background sounds and music to make it even better.

Time for action – adding background sounds

First, we are going to add some background sounds because it is too quiet in our tropical forest. We are going to generate some sound and then use it in the game by performing the following steps:

1. We are going to use an online sound generator website. Visit the `http://naturesoundsfor.me` and create a new sound. I've set this up by adding **Fire** by navigating to **Nature** | **Fire**, **Forest Ambient** by navigating to **Nature** | **Forest Ambient** (both at 20 percent volume), and **Grasshopper** by navigating to **Other Animals** | **Grasshopper** at 10 percent volume, but set the grasshopper track to play intermittently (there is a dropdown for that at the bottom). Refer to the following screenshot:

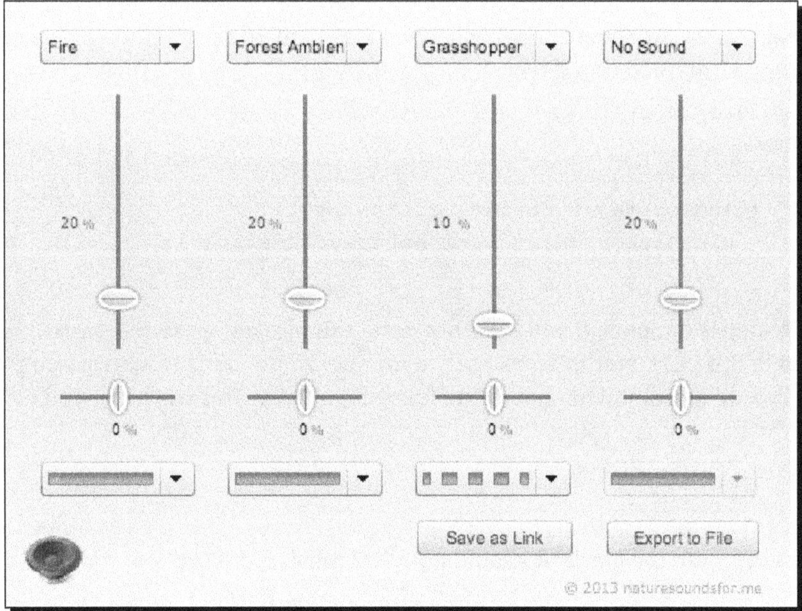

My nature sound settings

2. Then, click on the **Export to File** button in the bottom-right corner and select the length of **1 minute**. After processing the file, it will allow you to save the file in the `.ogg` format.

3. The bad news is that the `.ogg` format is not supported. So, we need to convert it. You can use your favorite audio converter to convert the file to `.mp3`. I have used the media.io online converter, which is available at `http://media.io`. Alternatively, you can just grab the `naturesounds.mp3` file from the `Chapter_08/Assets/BackgroundSound` folder. If you converted the file yourself, call the resulting file `naturesounds.mp3`.
4. Add the `naturesounds.mp3` file to the `Sound` group next to the other sound effects.
5. Switch to `AudioManager.h` and add the following method declaration above the `sharedAudioManager` class method:

```
-(void)playBackgroundSound:(NSString *)soundFile;
```

6. Then, open the `AudioManager.m` file and add the implementation of this method as follows:

```
-(void)playBackgroundSound:(NSString *)soundFile
{
    [[OALSimpleAudio sharedInstance] playBg:soundFile
    loop:YES];
}
```

7. Finally, open the `GameScene.m` file and add a call to this method in the end of the `onEnter` method as follows:

```
-(void)onEnter
{
    //..skipped..
    [[AudioManager sharedAudioManager]
      playBackgroundSound:@"naturesounds.mp3"];
}
```

8. This step is optional. If you have not done this already, go to the `GameScene.m` file, and in the `init` method, change the number of the birds to spawn and the number of lives to be somewhere near the following values. This will allow you to hear more of the background sound without losing or winning the game:

```
_birdsToSpawn = 30;
_birdsToLose = 5;
```

9. Build and run the game. It should now feel much more like a campfire in a forest.

You can find snapshot of the project at this point in the `Chapter_08/Cocohunt_08_Ambient` folder.

What just happened?

You have to be prepared that if you're a one-man studio and are creating games yourself, you will have to learn about different sound file formats and how to convert them from the initial format to the required format.

In the first part, we used one of the many online tools that allow you to generate the sounds and convert them. There are many helpful websites, so try searching one every time you need something.

Back to the code; let's review the code we have used to play the background sound as follows:

```
[[OALSimpleAudio sharedInstance] playBg:soundFile loop:YES];
```

You might have noticed that we've used the `playBg:` method instead of the `playEffect:` method. The `playBg:` method is intended for playing background audio files more efficiently, but this comes at a price that you can only play one background track at a time.

> The iPhone supports only one audio track using hardware acceleration, while all other audio tracks are played on CPU. So, the practice is to play the background song in MP3 (heavily compressed audio) and sound effects (which are smaller and less frequently used) in a lightly compressed format (for example, CAF) in CPU. You can use the **afconvert** tool in OS X to convert your audio files.

Just as with `playEffect:`, we have used a simplified method with only two parameters, as we only wanted to loop it. All the `playBg:` methods in the end just call the following method using the default parameters:

```
-(bool) playBg:(NSString*) filePath
        volume:(float) volume
           pan:(float) pan
          loop:(bool) loop
```

So, if you need more control, you can use this method.

Time for action – adding music

Background ambient sound is good, but not for our kind of game. What we really need is some music. Let's add the code to play the music, and as we don't want one song playing over and over again, we're going to implement switching between the tracks by performing the following steps:

1. First of all, we will need some music. Create the group called `Music` in the `Resources` group. Then, open the book's supporting files available at `Chapter_08/Assets/Music` and add all the music files into this group.

> You can use your favorite music instead of the music that comes with the book, just name the files the same way or make sure you adjust the code. Also, don't forget about the licenses if you're going to upload the game into the App Store.

2. Open the `AudioManager.h` file and import a module using the following `@import` directive:

```
@import AVFoundation.AVAudioPlayer;
```

> Note that we're using `@import` and not `#import`, as we are importing a module.

3. Then, make the `AudioManager` class conform to the `AVAudioPlayerDelegate` protocol by changing its declaration line as follows:

```
@interface AudioManager : NSObject<AVAudioPlayerDelegate>
```

4. The last change in the `AudioManager.h` file is to add the following two method declarations:

```
-(void)playMusic;

-(void)stopMusic;
```

5. Now, switch to the `AudioManager.m` file and add the following instance variables:

```
@implementation AudioManager
{
    NSArray* _musicFiles;

    OALAudioTrack *_currentTrack;
    OALAudioTrack *_nextTrack;
}
```

6. Then, add the `init` method as shown in the following code:

```
-(instancetype)init
{
    if (self = [super init])
    {
      _musicFiles = @[@"track_0.mp3", @"track_1.mp3",
                      @"track_2.mp3", @"track_3.mp3",
                      @"track_4.mp3", @"track_5.mp3"];

      _currentTrack = nil;
      _nextTrack = nil;
    }

    return self;
}
```

7. Add the `playMusic` method implementation below the `init` method as follows:

```
-(void)playMusic
{
    //1
    if (_currentTrack)
    {
        NSLog(@"The music is already playing");
        return;
    }

    //2
    int startTrackIndex = arc4random() % _musicFiles.count;
    int nextTrackIndex = arc4random() % _musicFiles.count;
    NSString *startTrack =
      [_musicFiles objectAtIndex:startTrackIndex];
    NSString *nextTrack  =
      [_musicFiles objectAtIndex:nextTrackIndex];

    //3
    _currentTrack = [OALAudioTrack track];
    _currentTrack.delegate = self;
    [_currentTrack preloadFile:startTrack];
    [_currentTrack play];

    //4
    _nextTrack = [OALAudioTrack track];
    [_nextTrack preloadFile:nextTrack];
}
```

8. Then, after the `playMusic` method, add the `nextTrack` method as follows:

```
-(void)nextTrack
{
    //1
    if (!_currentTrack)
        return;

    //2
    _currentTrack = _nextTrack;
    _currentTrack.delegate = self;
    [_currentTrack play];

    //3
    int nextTrackIndex = arc4random() % _musicFiles.count;
    NSString *nextTrack  =
      [_musicFiles objectAtIndex:nextTrackIndex];
    _nextTrack = [OALAudioTrack track];
    [_nextTrack preloadFile:nextTrack];
}
```

9. Now, add the following `audioPlayerDidFinishPlaying:` method, which is a part of the `AVAudioPlayerDelegate` protocol:

```
- (void)audioPlayerDidFinishPlaying:(AVAudioPlayer *)player
                       successfully:(BOOL)flag
{
    dispatch_async(dispatch_get_main_queue(), ^{
        [self nextTrack];
    });
}
```

10. Then, add the last method (for now), the `stopMusic` method, in the `AudioManager.m` file, as shown in the following code:

```
-(void)stopMusic
{
    if (!_currentTrack)
    {
        NSLog(@"The music is already stopped");
        return;
    }

    [_currentTrack stop];
    _currentTrack = nil;
    _nextTrack = nil;
}
```

11. It is time to play the music. Open the `GameScene.m` file and replace the following line in the `onEnter` method:

```
[[AudioManager sharedAudioManager]
     playBackgroundSound:@"naturesounds.mp3"];
```

12. Replace the preceding line of code with the following:

```
[[AudioManager sharedAudioManager] playMusic];
```

13. Don't forget that we also need to stop the music when the game stops. Find the `lost` and `won` methods and add the following line at the beginning of each method:

```
-(void)lost
{
    [[AudioManager sharedAudioManager] stopMusic];
    //..skipped..
}

-(void)won
{
    [[AudioManager sharedAudioManager] stopMusic];
    //..skipped..
}
```

14. Build and run the game. Now, instead of the ambient background sound, you should hear some music! I hope you like my pick or have managed to change the music to your favorite tracks and are now enjoying them.

All sound tracks are taken from the `http://www.nosoapradio.us` website. This site has old-school music that you can use in your games. Thanks DST (also known as Night Driver)!

Make sure that you play the game long enough to hear the change of the music tracks.

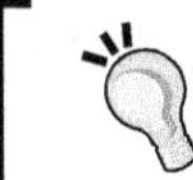

You can either again change the `_birdsToSpawn` and `_birdsToLose` settings in the `init` method or just find some shorter audio tracks.

What just happened?

That was quite a lot of code to play some music! Let's start with a bird's eye view on what we've done and why we had to write all this code instead of using the good old `playBg:` method.

The issue with using the `playBg:` method is that it can play or preload *only one* file at a time. This means that if you are playing one music track and then trying to play or even preload the next one, the first music track stops. We don't want that!

> This is only true for the background tracks and the `playBg:` method, you can still play several (up to 32) sound effects simultaneously using the `playEffect:` method. This is why there are no issues when you shoot the arrow and the previous arrow hits the bird at the same moment. Two sound effects are played at the same time without any problems.

We could just wait until the first file completes and starts preloading another one, but it takes some time to preload a file and we will experience a small period of silence when one music track has already stopped and the next one has not yet started playing.

Here is how we solve it. We have created two separate `OALAudioTrack` objects to play the `_currentTrack` music track and keep the preloaded `_nextTrack` music track ready. Then, when the `_currentTrack` music track has finished playing, we immediately start playing the `_nextTrack` track.

At this point, we don't need the `_currentTrack` music track anymore, but need to preload the next file and store it somewhere. This is why we put the `_nextTrack` music track in the `_currentTrack` variable, as it will actually play now and load the new track in the `_nextTrack` variable. Then, we keep repeating this process.

Now, after a brief review, let's review each method in detail. We'll start with the following `playMusic:` method:

1. The first thing this method checks is whether there is any music already playing. The `_currentTrack` file is used as an indicator in several places.
2. After this, the two random indexes are picked. These indexes are used to pick two random music tracks. Right now, this can be the same music track (same index), and this is not very good, but I will leave it up to you to fix this.
3. This is where the current track is created. Note that there are two important things. First, we set the `delegate` property to `self`, as we want to get a notification when this file finishes playing. This is why we have made the `AudioManager` class conform to the `AVAudioPlayerDelegate` protocol, to be able to get notifications. The second important thing is that we start to play the track immediately.

4. The next track is created. Unlike the current track, we don't set the `delegate` property and don't play the file just yet.

Okay, now there is one music track playing and another one preloaded and ready to play. The `AudioManager` class does nothing from this point and waits until the `audioPlayerDidFinishPlaying:` method of the `AVAudioPlayerDelegate` protocol is called.

If you are not familiar with the delegate concept of `Objective-C`, I suggest that you visit `https://developer.apple.com/library/ios/documentation/general/conceptual/CocoaEncyclopedia/DelegatesandDataSources/DelegatesandDataSources.html` (short link: `http://bit.ly/1spzRWT`).

In the `audioPlayerDidFinishPlaying:` method, we simply call the `nextTrack` method, but we want to call it outside the delegate thread on the main queue, as we're going to change `delegate`; this is why we use `dispatch_async`.

Now, let's review the `nextTrack` method, but very briefly, as it is quite easy and does almost the same as the second part of the `playMusic` method:

1. It checks whether there is a current track to make sure that the next track is never called when the music is stopped.
2. The next track becomes current. Note that we set `delegate` of this track, as we now want a notification from it.
3. A random number for the next track is generated and the actual next track is created and preloaded.

This is how we change tracks until we win or lose. Then, we just stop the music and free the current and preloaded next tracks.

By creating several separate `OALAudioTrack` objects, you can play several background tracks simultaneously. You can even do cross-fade and other mixing effects by gradually decreasing volume of one track while increasing the volume of another one.

Enhancing Cocohunt sound effects

Now that we know how to play sound and music, we will see how we can optimize our code and use some of the more advanced sound effect parameters.

Time for action – preloading sound effects

Sound effects are typically much smaller than music files, and using formats such as **Core Audio Format** (**CAF**) will decrease the time used to decode the on-disk file into memory and prepare it for playing.

> Remember that sound effects are decoded and played on CPU, so we should avoid using too many heavily compressed formats such as MP3 for sound effects. This is why I mention different formats such as CAF. Such formats take more space on the disk, but are easier to decode. Of course, for a simple game like ours, we don't have to worry about this.

However, if you want to make sure that there is no delay when the sound effect is played for the first time, you need to preload it. Let's perform the following steps:

1. Open the `AudioManager.h` file and add the following `#define` statements at the top, right above the `@interface` declaration as follows:

```
#define kSoundArrowShot @"arrow_shot.wav"
#define kSoundBirdHit   @"bird_hit.mp3"
#define kSoundWin       @"win.wav"
#define kSoundLose      @"lose.wav"
```

2. Then, add the following method declaration:

```
-(void)preloadSoundEffects;
```

3. After this, switch to the `AudioManager.m` file and add the `_soundEffects` instance variable as follows:

```
@implementation AudioManager
{
    NSArray* _soundEffects;
    //..skipped..
}
```

4. Initialize this variable inside the `init` method as follows:

```
-(instancetype)init
{
    if (self = [super init])
    {
      _soundEffects = @[kSoundArrowShot,
```

```
                            kSoundBirdHit,
                            kSoundLose,
                            kSoundWin];
        //..skipped..
    }

    return self;
}
```

5. Then, add the following implementation of the `preloadSoundEffects` method that we've declared in the header file:

```
-(void)preloadSoundEffects
{
    for (NSString *sound in _soundEffects)
    {
      [[OALSimpleAudio sharedInstance]
        preloadEffect:sound
        reduceToMono:NO
        completionBlock:^(ALBuffer *b)
        {
          NSLog(@"Sound %@ Preloaded", sound);
        }];
    }
}
```

6. Switch to the `IntroScene.m` file and import the `AudioManager.h` header at the top as follows:

```
#import "AudioManager.h"
```

7. Then, in the end of the `onEnter` method, add a call to the `preloadSoundEffects` method as follows:

```
-(void)onEnter
{
    [super onEnter];
    [self animateCoconutExplosion];

    [[AudioManager sharedAudioManager]
      preloadSoundEffects];
}
```

8. Finally, search for all calls to the `AudioManager` class's `playSoundEffect:` method and replace hardcoded strings with the `#define` values as follows:

   - In the `Hunter.m` file, in the `shootAtPoint:` method:

   ```
   [[AudioManager sharedAudioManager]
       playSoundEffect:kSoundArrowShot];
   ```

- In `Bird.m`, in the `removeBird:` method:

  ```
  [[AudioManager sharedAudioManager]
      playSoundEffect:kSoundBirdHit];
  ```

- In `GameScene.m`, in the `lost` method:

  ```
  [[AudioManager sharedAudioManager]
      playSoundEffect:kSoundLose];
  ```

- Again, in `GameScene.m`, in the `won` method:

  ```
  [[AudioManager sharedAudioManager]
      playSoundEffect:kSoundWin];
  ```

9. Build and run the game. It will be hard to notice any difference except for the output that appears in the console before the exploding coconut animation is even complete. Refer to the following code:

```
Cocohunt[70370:70b] Sound arrow_shot.wav Preloaded
Cocohunt[70370:70b] Sound bird_hit.mp3 Preloaded
Cocohunt[70370:70b] Sound lose.wav Preloaded
Cocohunt[70370:70b] Sound win.wav Preloaded
```

These lines mean that even before we leave the splash screen, all sound effects are preloaded and ready to be played.

What just happened?

We have just learned two things. The first is how you can preload your sound files and the second is how splash screen animation can hide the loading process.

I don't think the code needs a lot of explanation. The `preloadEffect:` method asynchronously preloads the sound effects and caches them. Putting this code in the splash or intro screen is a common technique, and you can use this approach to preload your other resource such as textures and data files.

Just don't preload everything because you can. If you have many sound effects that are played in different scenes or in different levels, you shouldn't load all of them at the beginning of the game. Don't forget that you have limited memory, especially on mobile devices.

Time for action – playing a sound at position

We are going to use the pan parameter of the playEffect: method to play the sound effect when a bird is hit at the position where the bird was actually hit. For example, when the bird is on the left-hand side of the screen and if it is hit, the sound will be louder in the left headphone, and when the bird is on the right-hand side of the screen and if it is hit, the sound will be played louder in the right headphone. The farther the bird is from the center of the screen, the higher the volume will be of the sound in the corresponding headphone. To test this, you will require headphones. Now perform the following steps:

1. Open the AudioManager.h file and add the following method declaration:

```
-(void)playSoundEffect:(NSString *)soundFile
         withPosition:(CGPoint)pos;
```

   Then, open the AudioManager.m file and import the cocos2d.h header at the top as follows:

```
#import "cocos2d.h"
```

2. After this, add the following implementation of the playSoundEffect:withPosition: method:

```
-(void)playSoundEffect:(NSString *)soundFile
         withPosition:(CGPoint)pos
{
    float pan =
      pos.x / [CCDirector sharedDirector].viewSize.width;
    pan = clampf(pan, 0.0f, 1.0f);
    pan = pan * 2.0f - 1.0f;

    [[OALSimpleAudio sharedInstance] playEffect:soundFile
                                          volume:1.0
                                           pitch:1.0
                                             pan:pan
                                            loop:NO];
}
```

3. Finally, switch to the Bird.m file and in the removeBird: method, change the code to use the new version of the playSoundEffect: method as follows:

```
[[AudioManager sharedAudioManager]
  playSoundEffect:kSoundBirdHit withPosition:self.position];
```

4. This is an optional step. To hear the changes more clearly, open the GameScene.m file and comment out the line where we start playing the music.

5. Build and run the game. If you have headphones, you can plug them into your Mac or run the game on the device and plug headphones into it. Now, if you hit the bird at the right edge of the screen, then the sound is louder in the right headphone and if you hit the bird near the left edge, the sound is louder in the left headphone.

> You can find the final project for this chapter in the `Chapter_08/Cocohunt_08_Final` folder in the book's supporting files.

What just happened?

This is what you get almost for free when you use a game engine and an audio framework. We have used the `pan` parameter to make a better use of the stereo headphones.

If you set `pan` to `-1.0`, then the sound is played only in your left headphone, and if you set `pan` to `+1.0`, then the sound is played only in the right one. What we have done is used the left-hand side of the screen as the `-1.0` value for the `pan` and the right edge of the screen as `1.0`. This way, the sound comes from the point where the bird was hit.

> What we have done is a very simplified technique to create positional audio. In positional audio, you can hear sounds from any direction in three-dimensional spaces, including behind, in front of, above, or below you. You can use positional audio if you use the lower-level `ALSource` class and its `position` and `referenceDistance` properties, but this is out of the scope of this book.

Have a go hero

As I have mentioned before, there is no limit to perfection, but we must stop and continue to the next chapters. The following is another list of improvements you can try to apply to the Cocohunt game:

- Currently, the arrow sound is a bit too quiet. Of course, we can fix this by modifying the audio file, but why don't we use the `volume` parameter of the `playEffect:` method, just as we did with `pan`?
- There is a technique that is used in many games where you collect coins. If you collect a streak of coins, each next collected coin sounds a bit different. You can do the same with the birds; just increase the `pitch` parameter for every bird hit within a time interval and reset the `pitch` parameter if the player is too slow and the streak has ended.

> You can learn more about ObjectAL and check out some more advanced demos at `http://kstenerud.github.io/ObjectAL-for-iPhone/`.

Pop quiz – playing audio

Q1. Can you play several sound effects simultaneously using the `playEffect:` of the `OALSimpleAudio` class?

1. Yes
2. No

Q2. Can you play several background tracks simultaneously using the `playBg:` method of the `OALSimpleAudio` class?

1. Yes
2. No

Q3. Can you play several background tracks simultaneously using several separate `OALAudioTrack` objects?

1. Yes
2. No

Summary

In this chapter, we learned to play sound effects and music. In addition to this, we reviewed several resources where you can find or generate the audio files. With this knowledge, you will be able to make your game much better. In the next chapter, we are going to move on from level one to a more complete game and will add some more scenes and learn how to switch between them.

9

User Interface and Navigation

Almost every game these days makes good use of different user interface elements such as buttons, sliders, and menus. And of course, most of the games consist of more than one game scene. In this chapter, we're going to review how Cocos2D can help us build a good user interface and navigate between scenes.

In this chapter, we are going to review the following topics:

- Adding buttons, and handling events when a player taps them
- Creating toggle buttons to represent on/off switches
- Animating the user interface's appearance using Cocos2D actions
- Creating more scenes and navigating between them using transitions
- Using the scroll view to fit more contents in a single scene
- Using the table view to represent table data
- Using the text field to get the user text input

Using buttons

Creating a good user interface and convenient navigation is very important! Equally important is to take into account that we want the player to stay in our game scene for most of the time and actually play the game. If the game has a bad or obscure user interface or navigation, the player might not even stay in the game for long enough to actually play it.

If the player needs to tap ten times to restart the game after each failure, then the player won't play the game for long. This will be pretty evident; if you open the App Store, you can read all the negative reviews of any game with a bad user interface.

After labels, the second most commonly used user interface controls are buttons. They are used everywhere, and it is logical that we will start our review of Cocos2D controls by adding some buttons, which are represented by the `CCButton` class.

Time for action – adding menu buttons

In this section, we are going to add a new scene with a vertical menu. This will be a typical main menu scene, which is present in many games. When we complete this scene, a player will be able to start the game, read more about the game itself, or view highscores.

First things first, we will add a scene with a basic menu to see how you can create and align buttons in Cocos2D:

1. Open the **Cocohunt** project from where we left it in the previous chapter.

> Just as always, you can continue working on the project from the place we left it at the end of the previous chapter, or take the final project from the book's supporting files at `Chapter_08/Cocohunt_08_Final` and use it as a starter project.
>
> You can download the book's supporting files by visiting `www.packtpub.com/support` and following the instructions.

2. Right-click on the `Scenes` group and create a new **Objective-C class**. Call this class `MenuScene` and make it a subclass of the `CCScene` class.
3. Open the `MenuScene.m` file and import the following headers:

```
#import "cocos2d.h"
#import "cocos2d-ui.h"
#import "GameScene.h"
```

4. Then, add the `_menu` instance variable as follows. It will contain all of the buttons of our menu:

```
@implementation MenuScene
{
    CCLayoutBox *_menu;
}
```

5. Add the `addBackground` method where we'll just set up a nice background image as follows:

```
-(void)addBackground
{
    CCSprite *bg = [CCSprite
      spriteWithImageNamed:@"menu_bg.png"];
    bg.positionType =
      CCPositionTypeMake(CCPositionUnitNormalized,
                         CCPositionUnitNormalized,
                         CCPositionReferenceCornerBottomLeft);
    bg.position = ccp(0.5f, 0.5f);
    [self addChild:bg];
}
```

6. Then, add the `addMenuButtons` method, which will actually create the menu buttons, align them, and add them to the scene:

```
-(void)addMenuButtons
{
    //1
    CCSpriteFrame *startNormalImage =
      [CCSpriteFrame frameWithImageNamed:@"btn_start.png"];

    //2
    CCSpriteFrame *startHighlightedImage =
      [CCSpriteFrame
        frameWithImageNamed:@"btn_start_pressed.png"];

    //3
    CCButton *btnStart = [CCButton buttonWithTitle:nil
                            spriteFrame:startNormalImage
                highlightedSpriteFrame:startHighlightedImage
                   disabledSpriteFrame:nil];

    //4
    [btnStart setTarget:self
              selector:@selector(btnStartTapped:)];

    CCSpriteFrame *aboutNormalImage =
      [CCSpriteFrame frameWithImageNamed:@"btn_about.png"];
    CCSpriteFrame *aboutHighlightedImage =
      [CCSpriteFrame
        frameWithImageNamed:@"btn_about_pressed.png"];
    CCButton *btnAbout =
      [CCButton buttonWithTitle:nil
                    spriteFrame:aboutNormalImage
         highlightedSpriteFrame:aboutHighlightedImage
            disabledSpriteFrame:nil];
```

```
        [btnAbout setTarget:self
                   selector:@selector(btnAboutTapped:)];

        CCSpriteFrame *highscoresNormalImage =
          [CCSpriteFrame
            frameWithImageNamed:@"btn_highscores.png"];
        CCSpriteFrame *highscoresHighlightedImage =
          [CCSpriteFrame
            frameWithImageNamed:@"btn_highscores_pressed.png"];
        CCButton *btnHighscores =
          [CCButton buttonWithTitle:nil
                        spriteFrame:highscoresNormalImage
             highlightedSpriteFrame:highscoresHighlightedImage
                disabledSpriteFrame:nil];
        [btnHighscores setTarget:self
                        selector:@selector(btnHighscoresTapped:)];

        //5
        _menu = [[CCLayoutBox alloc] init];
        _menu.direction = CCLayoutBoxDirectionVertical;
        _menu.spacing = 40.0f;

        //6
        [_menu addChild:btnHighscores];
        [_menu addChild:btnAbout];
        [_menu addChild:btnStart];

        //7
        [_menu layout];

        //8
        _menu.anchorPoint = ccp(0.5f, 0.5f);
        _menu.positionType =
          CCPositionTypeMake(CCPositionUnitNormalized,
                             CCPositionUnitNormalized,
                             CCPositionReferenceCornerBottomLeft);
        _menu.position = ccp(0.5f, 0.5f);

        [self addChild:_menu];
    }
```

7. Then, we need to call the `addBackground` and `addMenuButtons` methods from the `init` method in order to run them when the scene is created. Add the following `init` method to do this:

```
    -(instancetype)init
    {
        if (self = [super init])
        {
            [self addBackground];
```

```
        [self addMenuButtons];
    }

    return self;
}
```

8. Then, we need to add the methods that we have specified in the `@selector` parameter as the button targets. They will be called when we tap the corresponding button. Go ahead and add the following methods, which right now are just stubs for the future code (except the `btnStartTapped:` method, which opens the `GameScene` scene):

```
-(void)btnStartTapped:(id)sender
{
    CCLOG(@"Start Tapped");

    [[CCDirector sharedDirector]
        replaceScene:[[GameScene alloc] init]];
}

-(void)btnAboutTapped:(id)sender
{
    CCLOG(@"About Tapped");
}

-(void)btnHighscoresTapped:(id)sender
{
    CCLOG(@"Highscores Tapped");
}
```

9. As you can see from the previous steps, we are using some images in our code. We use images as a background scene and for normal and highlighted button's states. Of course, this means we need to add them to the Xcode project. To do this, create a subgroup in the `Resources` group and call it `Menu`. Then, open the book's supporting files in `Chapter_09/Assets/Menu` and add all images from that folder to the `Menu` group.

10. Now, when we are done with our `MenuScene` class, we need to display it. Open the `IntroScene.m` file and import the `MenuScene.h` file as follows:

```
#import "MenuScene.h"
```

11. Then, find the `proceedToGameScene` method and change the scene to run the `MenuScene` class instead of the `GameScene` class:

```
-(void)proceedToGameScene
{
    [[CCDirector sharedDirector]
      replaceScene:[[MenuScene alloc] init]];
}
```

12. In addition, while we are in the `IntroScene` class, we will disable the exploding coconut animation in the beginning since it takes a lot of time, and we don't want to wait for it at the start of every game. Find the `onEnter` method and make the following changes:

```
-(void)onEnter
{
    [super onEnter];
     //[self animateCoconutExplosion];
    [self proceedToGameScene];

    [[AudioManager sharedAudioManager] preloadSoundEffects];
}
```

13. Build and run the game. Now, you should see the menu scene with three buttons on a nice background, as shown in the following screenshot:

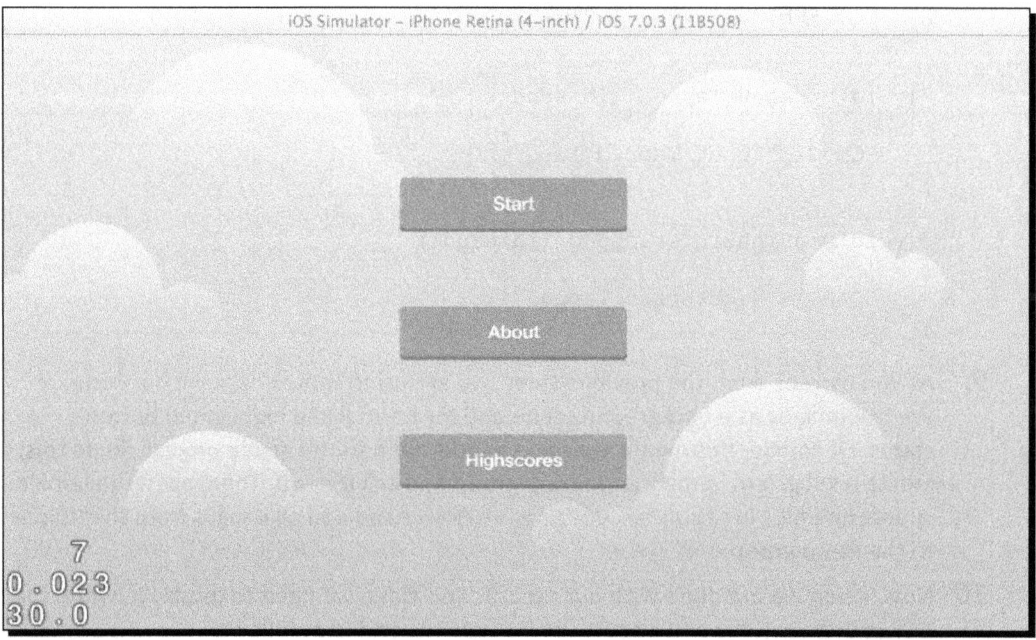

In addition, if you tap on any button, you should see the output in the console, which is similar to what is shown in the following code. Moreover, you should notice that the buttons are actually pushed down when tapped.

```
Cocohunt[37217:70b] Start Tapped
Cocohunt[37217:70b] About Tapped
Cocohunt[37217:70b] Highscores Tapped
```

What just happened?

In addition to adding buttons, we have used a few other important features of Cocos2D. Let's review all of them.

Adding buttons

We have just used some buttons to handle the user input. All of that looks nice, but wait a second, we have already handled user input when we handled touches to aim and shoot. What is the difference between that and the `CCButton` class?

The answer is that there is no big difference. The `CCButton` class is just a node that contains the title label and the image for the background. It handles the image change when the button state changes (normal, highlighted, or disabled) and notifies us when the button is tapped by calling the callback that we have passed to the `setTarget:` method.

Nothing stops you from creating your own button class. However, if you take a look at the `CCButton.m` file in Cocos2D source code, I am sure you will quickly come to the conclusion that you don't want to repeat all that code, unless you have a significant reason to do that (for example, you need a button that behaves completely differently, you want to handle some additional events, or you want to animate a button differently).

Now, when we know that there is no magic behind the still very useful `CCButton` class, let's review the code we wrote to create the menu. I think we should only review the `addMenuButtons` method since everything else (creating a scene, displaying the background, adding images, and so on) should be clear by now.

So here we go, the `addMenuButtons` method:

1. The `CCButton` object has three states: normal, highlighted, and disabled. You can specify an image for each state. In this line, we have loaded the `btn_start.png` image to be used for the background of the button as its normal state background.
2. This code simply loads another image that is to be used when the button is in its highlighted state (for example, when you tap on it).

> I encourage you to take a look at the images that we have added in order to see the difference. In fact, we are going to add a lot of images in this chapter. I believe it will help you understand if you review each image that we are using.

3. Here, we created the button using the `buttonWithTitle:` factory method with most parameters. Let's take a closer look at each parameter:
    - `title`: This parameter displays a text on the label (`CCLabelTTF`) that is over the button's background. Since we have the text on the button image itself, we're not going to use this property, and therefore we will set it to nil. We will use this property later in this chapter for a different kind of button.
    - `spriteFrame`: This parameter displays an image as the button's background when the button is in its normal state (neither pressed, nor disabled).
    - `highlighted`: This parameter displays an image when the button is in its highlighted state. The button will be in this state when you press it, until you release your finger, or when the button is used as a toggle button (can be on and off). We will see how to use the toggle buttons shortly.
    - `disabled`: This parameter displays an image when the button is disabled. It can be useful if you want to show that there is a button, but the player cannot press it just yet. For example, the player should complete an action before pressing this button.
4. After the button is created, we set its target. For the button, this specifies which method to call when the button is pressed.

All user interface controls in Cocos2D are subclasses of the `CCControl` class. By setting the target of the control, you specify the method to be called when the action is triggered by the control. Every control calls this method in its specific case. For example, the button calls this method when clicked, the slider when dragged, and so on, but you always set the target when you want to get notified by the control.

5. After two more buttons were created in a similar way, we used another interesting class of Cocos2D called `CCLayoutBox`. The `CCLayoutBox` class is an implementation of the abstract class called `CCLayout`. Layout classes are used to manage the layout of their child nodes. To use them, you add the child nodes to the layout class instance and then call the `layout` method. The `CCLayoutBox` class can lay out its children in vertical or horizontal rows.

There can be other implementations of the `CCLayout` class that lay out their children differently, for example, in a grid. You can subclass `CCLayout` and create your own implementation to lay out our nodes.

This is exactly how we want our buttons to be. In this code, we created the layout class, set its direction to vertical, and specified the spacing between the buttons.

6. Then, we added the buttons. Note that we added each button as a child node of the layout. This was not required; we could add them directly to the scene and lay them out manually, but adding them to `CCLayoutBox` and using its layout method saves us from having to calculate button positions and does everything for us.

You can use `CCLayout*` classes to lay out any nodes (for example, sprites, labels, and so on), not only the buttons.

7. Then, we called the `layout` method that created our nice menu, which we saw in the earlier screenshot.
8. As a final step, we positioned the menu at the center of the screen and added it to the scene.

Using normalized coordinates

There is one interesting thing described in the final step. We didn't use `[CCDirector sharedDirector].viewSize` this time to calculate the menu position relative to the center of the screen. Instead, we used the `positionType` property to specify that we want to use normalized units in the `position` property.

Normalized coordinates use values from `0` to `1` instead of points or pixels in a way similar to the anchor point. However, `anchorPoint` specifies the point in the node itself, while `position` specifies the point in the parent node. Since the parent for `_menu` is the scene itself, setting the normalized position to `(0.5, 0.5)` puts it right in the center of the scene.

The `positionType` property takes the `CCPositionType` structure as a value. Here is how it is defined in Cocos2D:

```
typedef struct _CCPositionType
{
    CCPositionUnit xUnit;
    CCPositionUnit yUnit;
    CCPositionReferenceCorner corner;
} CCPositionType;
```

We use a helper function called `CCPositionTypeMake` that creates this structure from three parameters, where each parameter is simply assigned to the corresponding structure field:

- `xUnit`: This parameter specifies the unit type for the *x* axis. On iOS, it can be either normalized units or points (default) that we have used many times before.
- `yUnit`: This parameter specifies the unit type for the *y* axis. Yes, you can specify different units for the *x* and *y* axes. For example, you can specify `positionType` like this:

  ```
  CCPositionTypeMake(CCPositionUnitPoints,
                     CCPositionUnitNormalized,
                     CCPositionReferenceCornerBottomLeft);
  ```

  Then, specify the *x* coordinate in points and the *y* coordinate as normalized, (like `ccp(320, 0.5)`) to align the node at `320` pixels horizontally on all devices, but also make sure it is centered vertically on all devices.
- `corner`: This parameter is a reference corner to use when calculating coordinates.

I know it is quite difficult to get this straight away, so here is an example. Let's imagine we want to position our node in the center of the *x* axis and in the middle of the lower half of the parent.

If we use normalized coordinates for both the *x* and *y* axes, and set the reference corner to the bottom-left corner (`CCPositionReferenceCornerBottomLeft`), then we need to set the position of the child node to the `(0.5, 0.25)` point, as shown in the following figure:

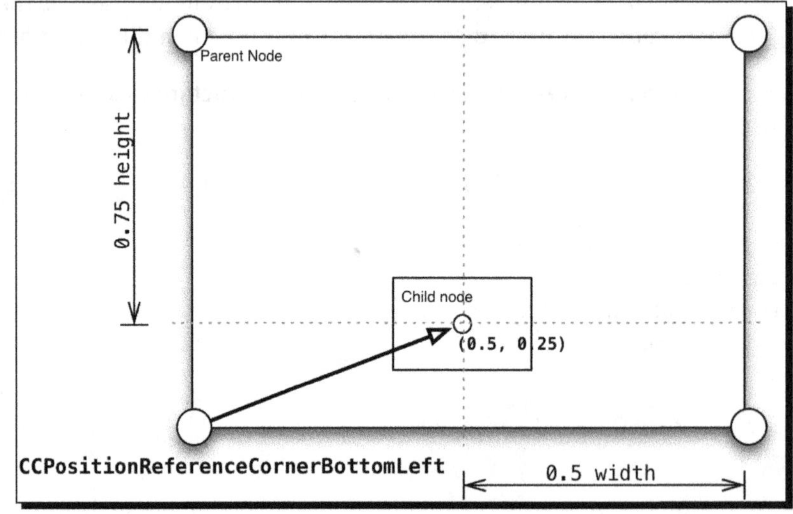

Setting the position using normalized coordinates with the bottom-left reference corner

Note that we use a small node, possibly a sprite, with an anchor point at the center of the node.

However, if we use the top-right corner as a reference corner (`CCPositionReferenceCornerTopRight`), then we need to set the position of the same node to `(0.5, 0.75)`. Note the vector displaying how we calculate the position in the following figure:

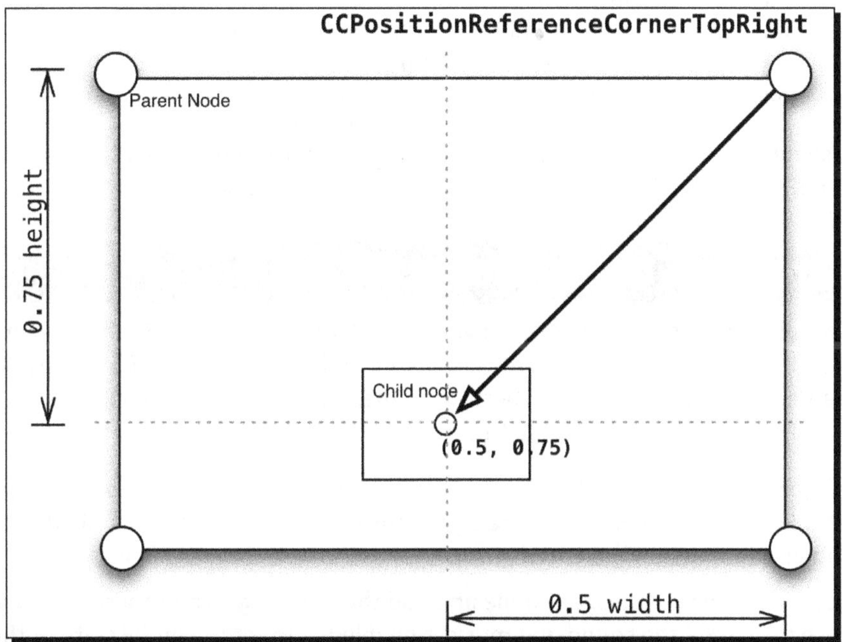

Setting the position using normalized coordinates with the top-right reference corner

Don't worry if you still don't fully understand this concept and where to use it. It will become much clearer when we use normalized coordinates to position buttons and other elements throughout this chapter. Also, you will be perfectly fine using only the bottom-left corner or not using the normalized coordinates at all and calculating the position as we did before. However, in this case, you will deprive yourself from a very convenient feature.

Replacing the currently running scene

We've already discussed different methods of `CCDirector` related to scene management in *Chapter 3, Cocos2D – Under the Hood*. It is time to use them in practice.

In fact, we've already used the `replaceScene:` method before, when we switched to the game scene after the coconut explosion. However, I promised to provide a more detailed explanation in this chapter.

When the game starts, Cocos2D automatically runs the scene returned from the `startScene` method in `AppDelegate`. However, as we discussed previously, games usually consist of several scenes.

The `replaceScene:` method is one of the methods you can use to switch to a new scene. When we call the `replaceScene:` method with a new scene, Cocos2D terminates the currently running scene and starts running the provided scene. So the function does exactly as it is says; that is, it replaces the currently running scene with a new one.

We will use more of this and other methods related to scene management through this chapter, so it will become much clearer. Now, let us return to the buttons.

Time for action – toggling sound and music

It is a common task in many games to provide the ON and OFF switch. The most common scenario that I always come across is turning sound and music on and off. We are going to use the same `CCButton` class to add buttons to the `MenuScene` class to allow a user to turn the sound and music on and off. To do this, perform the following steps:

1. Create the group named `SoundButtons` in the `Resources` group. Then, open the book supporting files at `Chapter_09/Assets/SoundButtons` and add the button images to that newly created group.

2. Open the `AudioManager.h` file and add the following two properties that we'll use to check if the sound and music is enabled, and set the initial state of the buttons as follows:

```
@property (nonatomic, readonly) BOOL isSoundEnabled;
@property (nonatomic, readonly) BOOL isMusicEnabled;
```

3. While still in the `AudioManager.h` file, add two more method declarations:

```
-(void)toggleSound;
-(void)toggleMusic;
```

4. After that, open the `AudioManager.m` file and add two instance variables that will be used internally by the properties we added before:

```
@implementation AudioManager
{
    //..skipped..

    BOOL _isSoundEnabled;
    BOOL _isMusicEnabled;
}
```

5. Initialize them at the end of the `init` method:

```
-(instancetype)init
{
    if (self = [super init])
    {
        //..skipped..

        _isSoundEnabled = YES;
        _isMusicEnabled = YES;
    }

    return self;
}
```

6. Scroll down and add the implementations of the `toggleSound` and `toggleMusic` methods that we declared in the header file:

```
-(void)toggleSound
{
    _isSoundEnabled = !_isSoundEnabled;
}

-(void)toggleMusic
{
    _isMusicEnabled = !_isMusicEnabled;
    if (!_isMusicEnabled && _currentTrack)
    {
        [self stopMusic];
    }
}
```

7. Now, we need to add checks in both variants of the `playSoundEffect:` method and in the `playMusic` method. Please find these methods and add checks as listed in the following code to the corresponding method:

```
-(void)playMusic
{
    if (!_isMusicEnabled)
        return;

    //..skipped..
}

-(void)playSoundEffect:(NSString *)soundFile
{
    if (!_isSoundEnabled)
        return;

    [[OALSimpleAudio sharedInstance] playEffect:soundFile];
}

-(void)playSoundEffect:(NSString *)soundFile
           withPosition:(CGPoint)pos
{
    if (!_isSoundEnabled)
        return;

    //..skipped..
}
```

8. Then, when we're done with `AudioManager`, open the `MenuScene.m` file and import the `AudioManager.h` header at the top:

```
#import "AudioManager.h"
```

9. Add two instance variables for the sound and music toggle buttons:

```
@implementation MenuScene
{
    CCLayoutBox *_menu;

    CCButton *_btnSoundToggle;
    CCButton *_btnMusicToggle;
}
```

10. Scroll down and add the `addAudioButtons` method, which will create the buttons, right beneath the `addMenuButtons` method:

```
-(void)addAudioButtons
{
    //1
    CCSpriteFrame *soundOnImage =
      [CCSpriteFrame frameWithImageNamed:@"btn_sound.png"];
    CCSpriteFrame *soundOffImage =
      [CCSpriteFrame
        frameWithImageNamed:@"btn_sound_pressed.png"];
    _btnSoundToggle = [CCButton buttonWithTitle:nil
                                    spriteFrame:soundOnImage
                         highlightedSpriteFrame:soundOffImage
                            disabledSpriteFrame:nil];
    //2
    _btnSoundToggle.togglesSelectedState = YES;

    //3
    _btnSoundToggle.selected =
      [AudioManager sharedAudioManager].isSoundEnabled;

    //4
    _btnSoundToggle.block = ^(id sender){
        [[AudioManager sharedAudioManager] toggleSound];
    };

    //5
    _btnSoundToggle.positionType = CCPositionTypeNormalized;
    _btnSoundToggle.position = ccp(0.95f, 0.1f);
    [self addChild:_btnSoundToggle];

    //6
    CCSpriteFrame *musicOnImage =
      [CCSpriteFrame frameWithImageNamed:@"btn_music.png"];
    CCSpriteFrame *musicOffImage =
      [CCSpriteFrame
        frameWithImageNamed:@"btn_music_pressed.png"];
    _btnMusicToggle = [CCButton buttonWithTitle:nil
                                    spriteFrame:musicOnImage
                         highlightedSpriteFrame:musicOffImage
                            disabledSpriteFrame:nil];
    _btnMusicToggle.togglesSelectedState = YES;
    _btnMusicToggle.selected =
      [AudioManager sharedAudioManager].isMusicEnabled;
```

```
        _btnMusicToggle.block = ^(id sender){
            [[AudioManager sharedAudioManager] toggleMusic];
        };

        //7
        float musicButtonOffset =
          _btnSoundToggle.boundingBox.size.width + 10;
        CGPoint soundButtonPosInPoints =
          _btnSoundToggle.positionInPoints;

        _btnMusicToggle.positionType =
          CCPositionTypeMake(CCPositionUnitPoints,
                             CCPositionUnitNormalized,
                             CCPositionReferenceCornerBottomLeft);

        _btnMusicToggle.position =
          ccp(soundButtonPosInPoints.x - musicButtonOffset, 0.1f);

        [self addChild:_btnMusicToggle];
    }
```

11. Finally, call the `addAudioButtons` method from the `init` method as follows:

```
    -(instancetype)init
    {
        if (self = [super init])
        {
            [self addBackground];
            [self addMenuButtons];
            [self addAudioButtons];
        }

        return self;
    }
```

12. Build and run the game. You should see two round buttons to enable and disable sound in the game at the bottom-right corner. You can toggle them, and then run the game and check if there is sound and music in the game. Refer to the following screenshot:

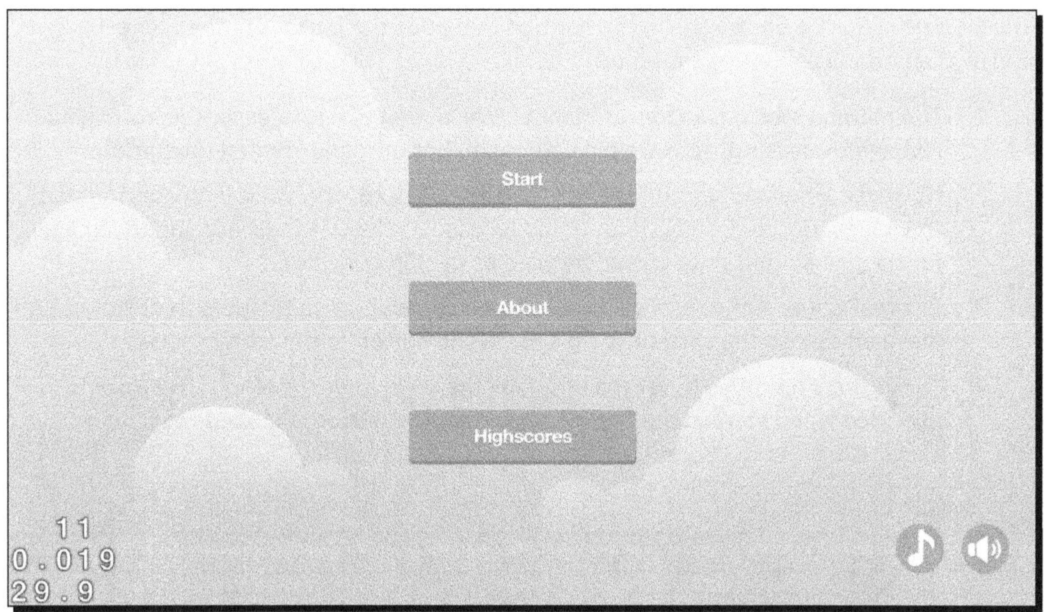

The state of the buttons and audio settings are not saved across application launches because we don't store them anywhere in the persistent storage (for example, on the disk). To fix this, we need to save and load their values in `NSUserDefaults` in `AudioManager`. We'll do this in a moment.

What just happened?

With only small changes, the buttons behaved differently. Now, you can use buttons to toggle the state in your game on and off.

Our changes in `AudioManager` were quite trivial. We just added the `isSoundEnabled` and `isMusicEnabled` properties to check if the music and sound were enabled, the `toggleSound` and `toggleMusic` methods to toggle these properties, and a few checks to ensure that the sound or music is enabled when we want to play them.

Note that the properties are `readonly`. This way, we only allow reading the value, while we set the underlying instance variables (that are used by the properties) in the toggle methods. Thereby, we can make some other actions while toggling the property. For example, we can stop the music if it is playing in the `toggleMusic` method.

The interesting part is once again in the method that adds the buttons to the scene. Let's review the `addAudioButtons` method in detail:

1. The method starts in a familiar manner. We loaded two images for the normal and highlighted states, just as we did with menu buttons, and created the button.
2. However, when we set `togglesSelectedState` to `YES`, we told the button that the image for the normal state should be used as the OFF indicator and the image for the highlighted state should be used as the ON indicator.
3. In a real game, audio settings will be stored somewhere in the persistent storage, so we need to load the current value and set the button to the correct state.
4. This is the alternative to set the target by the `setTarget` method. The block is executed when you tap the button, and when the button is tapped, we simply execute the `toggleSound` method of `AudioManager`.

> You can read more about blocks at `https://developer.apple.com/library/mac/Documentation/Cocoa/Conceptual/Blocks/Articles/00_Introduction.html` (shortened: `http://bit.ly/1jR71YZ`).

5. We set the position of the sound toggle button by using the normalized coordinates again. This time, instead of calling the `CCPositionTypeMake` function, we used a predefined value. The `CCPositionTypeNormalized` class is defined as follows:

```
#define CCPositionTypeNormalized CCPositionTypeMake(
CCPositionUnitNormalized, CCPositionUnitNormalized,
CCPositionReferenceCornerBottomLeft)
```

   So, this is just a shorter way of writing the same thing that we did before. Also, this time, we didn't use any layout classes, and added the button to the bottom-right corner of the scene directly.

6. Here, we created the music toggle button in exactly the same way as we created the sound toggle button.
7. However, we positioned the music button a bit differently. The reason to do this is that if we place the sound button at `(0.95, 0.1)` and the music button at `(0.8, 0.1)` using normalized coordinates, we will achieve almost the same result as we did here, but on different resolutions, the distance between the buttons will be different. This will happen since the distance is `0.95 - 0.8 = 0.15` of the width, so it depends on the screen width. We don't want that, so instead, we use points for the *x* axis while still using normalized coordinates for the *y* axis. We set the position of the music button at `10` points to the left, relative to the sound button. The `positionInPoints` property always returns the position in points (independent of `positionType` used), which can be quite useful sometimes.

Time for action – storing settings in NSUserDefaults

Right now, the audio settings are not saved across the game launches because we only save them in instance variables in memory. To fix this, we're going to save them in `NSUserDefaults` and load them when the game starts, as follows:

1. Open the `AudioManager.m` file and add the following `#define` statements to define the keys we'll use to save and load the corresponding audio setting:

```
#define kSoundKey @"AudioManager_Sound"
#define kMusicKey @"AudioManager_Music"
```

2. Scroll down to the `toggleSound` method and add the code to save the sound setting at the end of the method, right after it's changed:

```
-(void)toggleSound
{
    _isSoundEnabled = !_isSoundEnabled;

    [[NSUserDefaults standardUserDefaults]
      setBool:_isSoundEnabled forKey:kSoundKey];

    [[NSUserDefaults standardUserDefaults]
      synchronize];
}
```

3. Also, add the code to save the music setting at the end of the `toggleMusic` method:

```
-(void)toggleMusic
{
    //..skipped..

    [[NSUserDefaults standardUserDefaults]
      setBool:_isMusicEnabled forKey:kMusicKey];

    [[NSUserDefaults standardUserDefaults]
      synchronize];
}
```

4. Now, we need to load the saved settings in the `init` method instead of just setting them to `YES`. Find the following code inside the `init` method:

```
_isSoundEnabled = YES;
_isMusicEnabled = YES;
```

5. Replace the preceding code with the following line:

```
[self loadSettings];
```

6. And of course, add the `loadSettings` method as follows:

```
-(void)loadSettings
{
    //1
    NSUserDefaults *userDefaults =
      [NSUserDefaults standardUserDefaults];

    //2
    NSDictionary *audioDefaults = @{kSoundKey : @YES,
                                     kMusicKey : @YES};
    [userDefaults registerDefaults:audioDefaults];

    //3
    _isSoundEnabled = [userDefaults boolForKey:kSoundKey];
    _isMusicEnabled = [userDefaults boolForKey:kMusicKey];
}
```

7. Build and run the game. Toggle the sound or music (or both), and restart the game. This time, the audio setting should be saved.

You can find a snapshot of the project at this point in the `Chapter_09/Cocohunt_09_Menu_and_Audio` folder.

What just happened?

If you have some iOS development experience, then I'm afraid you haven't learned anything new and can skip to the following *Have a go hero* section.

If not, then here is what is going on.

The `NSUserDefaults` class is used to store the user settings that you want to persist between the game launches. It works really simply. There are several methods such as `setBool:forKey:`, `setInteger:forKey:`, or `setObject:forKey:`, which you can use to save the data to user defaults.

You can only store `NSData`, `NSString`, `NSNumber`, `NSDate`, `NSArray`, or `NSDictionary` using the `setObject:forKey:` method. So, if you have a custom type, you might need to serialize it to `NSData` first or save each of its fields separately. However, this might be the sign that you need to choose a different persistent storage type.

After setting the values, we've used the `synchronize` method that forces the `NSUserDefaults` to write itself to the disk.

I say "forces" because the `synchronize` method is automatically invoked at periodic intervals. So normally, you should use this method only if you cannot wait for the automatic synchronization or want to make sure the data is written to the disk without any chance of losing it.

Calling the `synchronize` method frequently may result in reduction of game performance.

Of course, in addition to saving these settings in the `toggleSound` and `toggleMusic` methods, we need to load them. This is what we did in the `loadSettings` method that is called from the `init` method.

Don't forget that `AudioManager` is a singleton, so we load the settings only once.

Let's review the `loadSettings` method in detail:

1. Here, we just saved ourselves from retyping `[NSUserDefaults standardUserDefaults]` each time.
2. When we first run the game, we have no audio settings saved since we didn't call the `toggleSound` and `toggleMusic` methods yet. However, we want to make sure our game starts with the sound and music on; after all, we spent so much time searching for all those sound effects.
3. To do this, we specified default values for our keys using the `registerDefaults:` method. This method registers the default values from a provided dictionary, and later, in case it doesn't find the saved settings, it will use defaults.

Note that the `registerDefaults:` method doesn't write anything to the disk, so you should call it every time the game starts.

You can call it from multiple classes (each class sets its own defaults that are appended) or from `AppDelegate`, and specify all defaults at once (for example, loaded from the `Plist` file stored in your game bundle or received from a web service).

4. Here, we just get either default values or values saved using `setBool:forKey:` if we toggled the sound or music at least once before.

Of course, this is only one of the ways you can store the data. There are some books completely dedicated to how to store data in iOS, so I'm not going to cover this topic in the book. After all, you might already be familiar with storing data in iOS and only want to know how to create games using Cocos2D.

> You can find out more about this topic at `https://developer.apple.com/library/ios/documentation/Cocoa/Conceptual/UserDefaults/AccessingPreferenceValues/AccessingPreferenceValues.html` (shortened: `http://bit.ly/1lDXY03`).

Have a go hero

Here is the list of things that you can try in order to consolidate your knowledge:

- Add a sound effect when you tap a button
- Change the spacing between the buttons
- Lay out the menu buttons horizontally
- Place the sound and music toggle buttons at the top-left corner using normalized coordinates

Navigating between scenes

Now, when we have all those buttons on the menu scene, we should make them work. In the early chapters of the book, we discussed the significance of the `CCDirector` class. We have already used some of its properties, and of course, we have used the `replaceScene:` method to load the game scene when you tap on the **Start** button.

With `replaceScene:`, everything should be quite clear. You create a new scene and pass it to the `replaceScene:` method, and now, this new scene is running and the old one is terminated and deallocated.

In this part of the chapter, we are going to use another method of the `CCDirector` class called `pushScene`. This method can be used to display the scene without deallocating the currently running scene. In addition, we are going to use the `CCTransition` class for a smooth transition between scenes, and of course, we are going to add more scenes to our game.

Time for action – pushing AboutScene

Imagine that you have just finished the game and are about to release it. I am sure you want to tell the world something about yourself or your game studio, give a link to your website, and so on. Even if you don't want a lot of attention, putting a link to your website with information about your other games is a good idea from the marketing point of view. In this way, players can discover your other games or applications.

You can do all of this in AboutScene, so we are going to add one:

1. First, we are going to add some images to the project. Create a new group in the Resources group and call it About. Open the book's supporting files available in Chapter_09/Assets/About and add all images to the About group in the Xcode project.
2. Create a new scene called AboutScene in the Scenes group.
3. Open the AboutScene.m file and import the following headers:

```
#import "cocos2d.h"
#import "cocos2d-ui.h"
#import "MenuScene.h"
```

4. Then, add the init method, which calls the methods that we'll add shortly:

```
-(instancetype)init
{
    if (self = [super init])
    {
        [self addBackground];
        [self addText];
        [self addBackButton];
        [self addVisitWebSiteButton];
    }

    return self;
}
```

5. Add a method to add a background image as follows:

```
-(void)addBackground
{
    CCSprite *bg =
      [CCSprite spriteWithImageNamed:@"about_bg.png"];
    bg.positionType = CCPositionTypeNormalized;
    bg.position = ccp(0.5f, 0.5f);
    [self addChild:bg];
}
```

6. Add a method that adds a label with some stub text. Set the `aboutText` variable to a long text:

```
-(void)addText
{
    CGSize viewSize = [CCDirector sharedDirector].viewSize;

    NSString *aboutText = @"Put some long text here!";
    NSString *aboutFont = @"AppleSDGothicNeo-Medium";
    float aboutFontSize = 14;
    CGSize aboutTextRect = CGSizeMake(viewSize.width * 0.8f,
                                      viewSize.height * 0.6f);

    CCLabelTTF *aboutLabel =
      [CCLabelTTF labelWithString:aboutText
                         fontName:aboutFont
                         fontSize:aboutFontSize
                       dimensions:aboutTextRect];

    aboutLabel.positionType = CCPositionTypeNormalized;
    aboutLabel.position = ccp(0.5f, 0.3f);

    aboutLabel.color = [CCColor orangeColor];
    aboutLabel.shadowColor = [CCColor grayColor];
    aboutLabel.shadowBlurRadius = 1.0f;
    aboutLabel.shadowOffset = ccp(1.0f,-1.0f);
    [self addChild:aboutLabel];
}
```

7. Now, add a method that adds a button to visit the website. Remember that all these methods are called from the `init` method:

```
-(void)addVisitWebSiteButton
{
    CCSpriteFrame *normal =
      [CCSpriteFrame frameWithImageNamed:@"btn_9slice.png"];
    CCSpriteFrame *pressed =
      [CCSpriteFrame
        frameWithImageNamed:@"btn_9slice_pressed.png"];

    CCButton *btnVisitWebsite =
      [CCButton buttonWithTitle:@"Visit Web Site"
                    spriteFrame:normal
         highlightedSpriteFrame:pressed
            disabledSpriteFrame:nil];
    btnVisitWebsite.positionType = CCPositionTypeNormalized;
    btnVisitWebsite.position = ccp(0.5f, 0.1f);

    btnVisitWebsite.horizontalPadding = 12.0f;
```

```
    btnVisitWebsite.verticalPadding = 4.0f;
    btnVisitWebsite.label.fontName = @"HelveticaNeue-Bold";
    btnVisitWebsite.label.fontSize = 10.0f;

    btnVisitWebsite.block = ^(id sender)
    {
        [[UIApplication sharedApplication]
         openURL:[NSURL URLWithString:@"http://packtpub.com"]];
    };

    [self addChild:btnVisitWebsite];
}
```

8. Finally, add a method that adds a back button, and a method that handles when the player taps on it:

```
-(void)addBackButton
{
    CCSpriteFrame *backNormalImage =
      [CCSpriteFrame frameWithImageNamed:@"btn_back.png"];
    CCSpriteFrame *backHighlightedImage =
      [CCSpriteFrame
        frameWithImageNamed:@"btn_back_pressed.png"];
    CCButton *btnBack =
      [CCButton buttonWithTitle:nil
                    spriteFrame:backNormalImage
         highlightedSpriteFrame:backHighlightedImage
            disabledSpriteFrame:nil];

    btnBack.positionType = CCPositionTypeNormalized;
    btnBack.position = ccp(0.1f, 0.9f);

    [btnBack setTarget:self selector:@selector(backTapped:)];
    [self addChild:btnBack];
}

-(void)backTapped:(id)sender
{
    CCTransition *transition =
      [CCTransition transitionCrossFadeWithDuration:1.0f];
    [[CCDirector sharedDirector]
      popSceneWithTransition:transition];
}
```

9. Then, open the `MenuScene.m` file and import the `AboutScene.h` header:

```
#import "AboutScene.h"
```

10. Find the `btnAboutTapped:` method and replace it with the following:

```
-(void)btnAboutTapped:(id)sender
{
    AboutScene *aboutScene = [[AboutScene alloc] init];
    CCTransition *aboutTransition =
      [CCTransition transitionCrossFadeWithDuration:1.0f];

    [[CCDirector sharedDirector] pushScene:aboutScene
                            withTransition:aboutTransition];
}
```

11. Build and run the game. In the main menu scene, click on the **About** button and you should see `AboutScene` appearing. Clicking on the back button at the top-left corner of the screen will take you back to the main menu. Refer to the following screenshot:

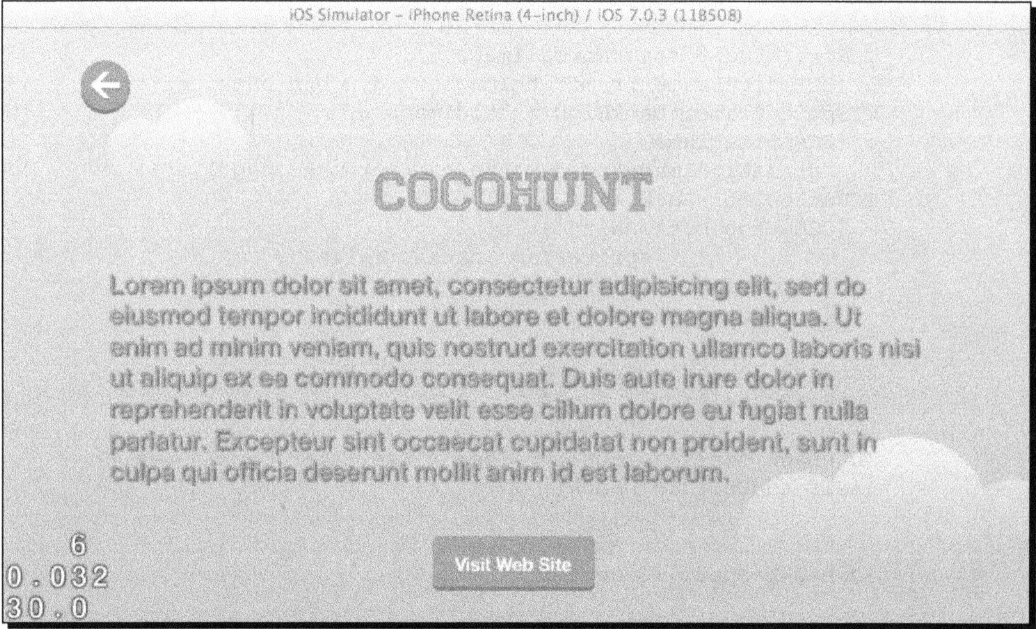

You can get dummy text from the website `http://www.lipsum.com`. The text it has is in Latin and is often used as a stub to test how the label will look with a long text, without the need to come up with some real text.

Although Latin text looks strange, don't worry, it is not summoning a demon or something like it.

What just happened?

Although `AboutScene` can hardly be the most important scene in the game, we took the chance to experiment and used several new Cocos2D features. Let's start from the final step where we made the changes to the `MenuScene` class, and then we will review each method in `AboutScene`.

Displaying AboutScene using the pushScene: method

The only change in the `MenuScene.m` file, apart from importing the `AboutScene.h` header, is in the `btnAboutTapped:` method. In this method, we made two significant changes compared to how we loaded scenes before. They are as follows:

- We used the `CCTransition` class to make a smoother transition between the scenes. If we don't use a transition, a new scene just appears on the screen. Although this works, it doesn't look very nice. With `CCTransition`, we can animate the transition between two scenes while switching between them. We will use more transitions in the next section and will discuss them in more detail.
- We used the `pushScene:` method of the `CCDirector` class for the first time in the book. We have discussed the `pushScene:` method in *Chapter 3, Cocos2D – Under the Hood*, but let me briefly refresh the difference between the `pushScene:` and `replaceScene:` methods:
    - The `replaceScene:` method deallocates the currently running scene and runs the specified scene, so you have one scene running at a time, while `pushScene:` only suspends (but not destroys) the currently running scene and pushes it back on the stack. Then, when you use the `popScene:` method, the pushed scene is removed and the original scene is restored with all of its state preserved.
    - Although `pushScene:` can be quite useful, you have to remember that the price is the memory taken up by all suspended scenes on the stack. You can use transitions with both the `replaceScene:` and `pushScene:` methods. There is also the `popSceneWithTransition:` method.

The `pushScene:` method can be useful if you only want to show some other scene for a short time but then return to the original scene right where you left it. For example, a player can play a game for some time, score some points, travel some distance, and so on. You might want to display another scene, but you don't want to restart the game and lose the player progress. To achieve this, you just suspend the current game scene and push another scene using the `pushScene:` method instead of the `replaceScene:` method.

Okay, so the only thing we did in the `MainScene` class is used a nice transition and pushed `AboutScene` for display, while suspending `MainScene`. We did not have any significant reasons to use `pushScene:` for `AboutScene`, so this is just to demonstrate how you can use this method.

Using 9-slice scaling on AboutScene

Now that we've reviewed the code in the `MenuScene` class, let's take a look at all of the code that we've added to `AboutScene`.

As you can see, we have added four methods in the `init` method:

- `addBackground`: This simply adds a background sprite. There should be nothing new here, so we are not going to review this method.
- `addBackButton`: This adds a button that uses the `popSceneWithTransition:` method to pop `AboutScene` and return to the `MenuScene` class. Again, there is nothing interesting to review.
- `addVisitWebSiteButton`: This method adds the **Visit Web Site** button at the bottom of `AboutScene`. The interesting part about this method is that it uses the `CCSprite9Slice` image and a label instead of the text that is hardcoded right in the image. We're going to review this method.
- `addText`: This adds a rectangular text area. We're going to briefly review this method right after the `addVisitWebSiteButton` method.

So let's start with the `addVisitWebSiteButton` method. As I have already mentioned, this code is interesting because it does not use the button image with the text already on it. Instead, it uses a label of the `CCButton` and an image that is scaled using the 9-slice scaling technique. This technique allows us to have one single image at design time and then stretch it as we need to at runtime without losing the appearance quality.

First of all, why do we need it? Well, it allows you to have one background image for all buttons and save a lot of disk and memory space. Don't forget that you might want to localize your game on several languages, and having a separate image for each button can waste a lot of space.

Now you might wonder why we need some kind of technique to stretch the image. Why can't we just create a simple background and stretch it the way we want? The answer is that we want the buttons to look good, and it is hard to design a good-looking button that will stretch without looking awful. Here is a demonstration of what happens when you simply stretch the button:

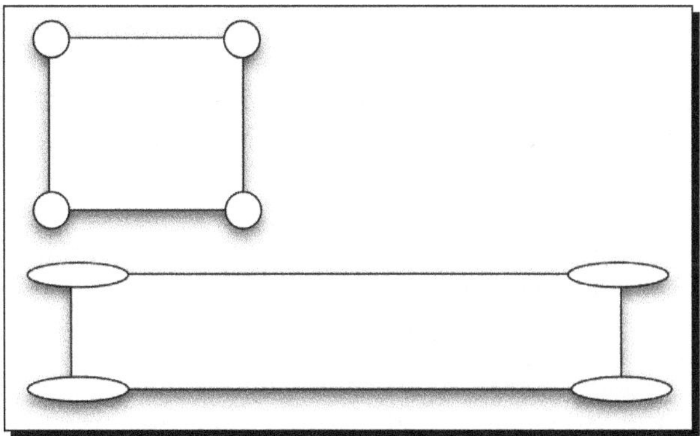

Stretching the button without using 9-slice

As you can see, the button only has four circles on the corners, and after stretching, it does not look nice. So how can we avoid this? Instead of stretching the whole image, we can stretch only some portions of it and only in some directions. The following diagram shows the same example using the 9-slice technique:

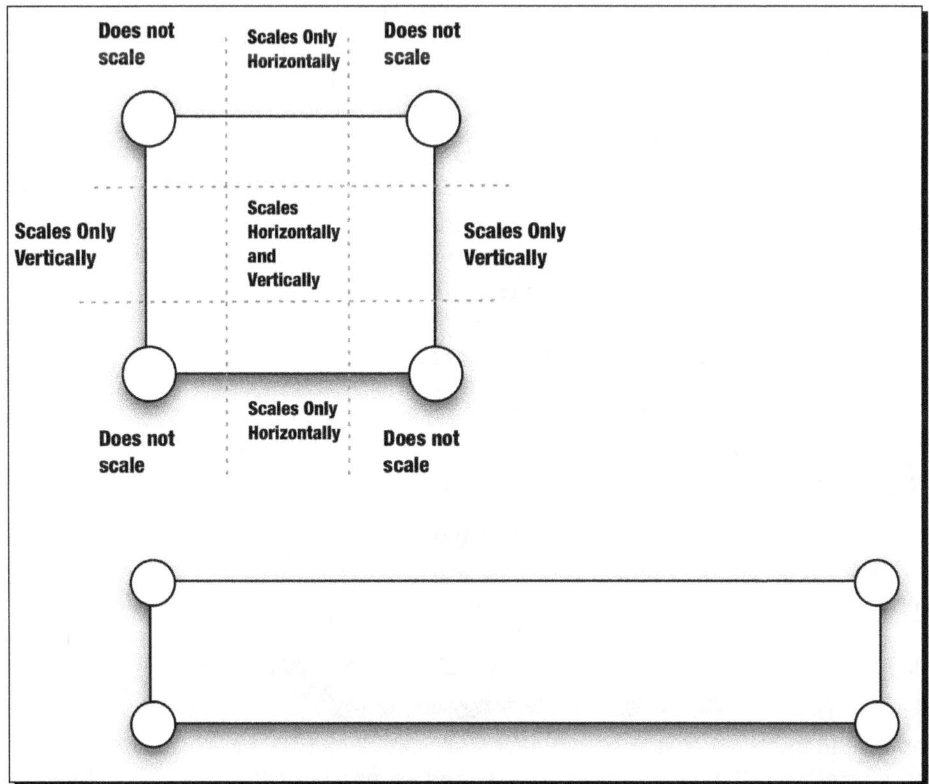

Scaling using the 9-slice technique

Now, the stretched image looks much better. Of course, this does not work with all images, but it works very well for buttons and other user-interface elements. The good thing is that you don't have to write any additional code to use it with the `CCButton` class. Just pass it as a normal image and the button will stretch it automatically to fit the label.

> You might want to add some padding just as we did, so that the label has some space around it.

This happens because the `CCButton` class uses the `CCSprite9Slice` class to draw the button's background. You can also use `CCSprite9Slice` in your code to create sprites that will stretch nicely.

Creating rectangular multiline labels

The final thing we will review in `AboutScene` is the `addText` method. There are some instances when you need to create multiline labels to display long text. Sometimes, you don't even have the text to display at that moment, but just have a rectangular area where it should be displayed later. In this case, you can use the `CCLabelTTF dimensions` parameter (or the `dimensions` property).

Let's review this code in the `addText` method:

```
CGSize aboutTextRect = CGSizeMake(viewSize.width * 0.8f,
                                   viewSize.height * 0.6f);
CCLabelTTF *aboutLabel = [CCLabelTTF
  labelWithString:aboutText
         fontName:aboutFont
         fontSize:aboutFontSize
       dimensions:aboutTextRect];
```

As you can see, this time, we passed an additional parameter called `dimensions`. This is the size of the rectangle that the label should fit in. If the label is too big, it will be clipped. You can test this by entering a long text or increasing the font size.

Sometimes, it might be useful to know that you don't need to specify the dimensions of both the width and height. You can create `CGSize` with the height as zero (`CGSizeMake(width, 0)`) and this will only limit the width of the label area.

Time for action – using more transitions

The cross-fade transition that we used for the `AboutScene` to appear looks nice, but there are more transitions that come with Cocos2D, and we need to add more scenes to our game. In this section, we are going to add the scene for highscores and for level selection.

Both scenes will be empty for now, but in the next few sections, we are going to fill them with different controls. The `HighscoresScene` class will display the table with the highest scored points, and the `LevelSelectScene` class will display a scrollable view where you can select a level to play. Currently, we only have one level, but that is going to change in the next chapter, so we must be prepared. Refer to the following steps:

1. Open the Xcode project and create two new scenes in the `Scenes` group. Name the scenes `HighscoresScene` and `LevelSelectScene`.
2. Create two new groups in the `Resources` group: `Highscores` and `LevelSelect`.
3. Open the book supporting files and add all the images from `Chapter_09/Assets/Highscores` to the `Highscores` group. Then, add all the images from `Chapter_09/Assets/LevelSelect` to the `LevelSelect` group.

As I have mentioned before, it is better to review all the images that we add every time. For example, in this case, we added background images for `HighscoresScene` and `LevelSelectScene`. We are going to use them straight away, but in addition, we added few more images that we are going to use later in the same scenes. We did it just for the sake of keeping things in one place and because I'm sure you already know very well how to add images to the project and are probably already tired of me explaining this step in detail every time.

4. Open the `HighscoresScene.m` file and replace its contents with the following code:

```
#import "HighscoresScene.h"

#import "cocos2d.h"
#import "cocos2d-ui.h"
#import "MenuScene.h"

@implementation HighscoresScene

-(instancetype)init
{
    if (self = [super init])
    {
        [self addBackground];
        [self addBackButton];
    }

    return self;
```

```
}

-(void)addBackground
{
    CCSprite *bg =
      [CCSprite spriteWithImageNamed:@"highscores_bg.png"];
    bg.positionType = CCPositionTypeNormalized;
    bg.position = ccp(0.5f,0.5f);
    [self addChild:bg];
}

-(void)addBackButton
{
    CCSpriteFrame *backNormalImage =
      [CCSpriteFrame frameWithImageNamed:@"btn_back.png"];
    CCSpriteFrame *backHighlightedImage =
      [CCSpriteFrame
        frameWithImageNamed:@"btn_back_pressed.png"];
    CCButton *btnBack =
      [CCButton buttonWithTitle:nil
                    spriteFrame:backNormalImage
         highlightedSpriteFrame:backHighlightedImage
            disabledSpriteFrame:nil];

    btnBack.positionType = CCPositionTypeNormalized;
    btnBack.position = ccp(0.1f, 0.9f);

    [btnBack setTarget:self selector:@selector(backTapped:)];
    [self addChild:btnBack];
}

-(void)backTapped:(id)sender
{
    CCTransition *transition =
      [CCTransition
        transitionPushWithDirection:CCTransitionDirectionUp
                           duration:1.0f];
    MenuScene *scene = [[MenuScene alloc] init];
    [[CCDirector sharedDirector] replaceScene:scene
                               withTransition:transition];
}

@end
```

5. Open the `LevelSelectScene.m` file and replace its contents with the following code:

```
#import "LevelSelectScene.h"

#import "cocos2d.h"
```

```
#import "cocos2d-ui.h"
#import "MenuScene.h"

@implementation LevelSelectScene

-(instancetype)init
{
    if (self = [super init])
    {
        [self addBackground];
        [self addBackButton];
    }

    return self;
}

-(void)addBackground
{
    CCSprite *bg =
      [CCSprite spriteWithImageNamed:@"level_select_bg.png"];
    bg.positionType = CCPositionTypeNormalized;
    bg.position = ccp(0.5f,0.5f);
    [self addChild:bg];
}

-(void)addBackButton
{
    CCSpriteFrame *backNormalImage =
      [CCSpriteFrame frameWithImageNamed:@"btn_back.png"];
    CCSpriteFrame *backHighlightedImage =
      [CCSpriteFrame
        frameWithImageNamed:@"btn_back_pressed.png"];
    CCButton *btnBack =
      [CCButton buttonWithTitle:nil
                    spriteFrame:backNormalImage
         highlightedSpriteFrame:backHighlightedImage
            disabledSpriteFrame:nil];

    btnBack.positionType = CCPositionTypeNormalized;
    btnBack.position = ccp(0.1f, 0.9f);

    [btnBack setTarget:self selector:@selector(backTapped:)];
    [self addChild:btnBack];
}

-(void)backTapped:(id)sender
```

```
{
    CCTransition *transition =
      [CCTransition
         transitionPushWithDirection:CCTransitionDirectionDown
                           duration:1.0f];

    MenuScene *scene = [[MenuScene alloc] init];
    [[CCDirector sharedDirector] replaceScene:scene
                               withTransition:transition];
}

@end
```

6. Open the `MenuScene.m` file and import the headers of the scenes that we've just created:

```
#import "LevelSelectScene.h"
#import "HighscoresScene.h"
```

7. Scroll down and find the `btnStartTapped:` method, and replace it with the following code:

```
-(void)btnStartTapped:(id)sender
{
    LevelSelectScene *levelSelectScene =
      [[LevelSelectScene alloc] init];
    CCTransition *transition =
      [CCTransition
        transitionPushWithDirection:CCTransitionDirectionUp
                           duration:1.0f];
    [[CCDirector sharedDirector] replaceScene:levelSelectScene
                               withTransition:transition];
}
```

8. Then, find the `btnHighscoresTapped:` method and also replace its contents with the following code:

```
-(void)btnHighscoresTapped:(id)sender
{
    HighscoresScene *hsScene = [[HighscoresScene alloc] init];
    CCTransition *hsTransition =
      [CCTransition
        transitionPushWithDirection:CCTransitionDirectionDown
                           duration:1.0f];

    [[CCDirector sharedDirector] replaceScene:hsScene
                               withTransition:hsTransition];
}
```

9. Build and run the game. Now, when you press the **Start** and **Highscores** buttons, you should see our new scenes appearing.

What just happened?

Although there is a significant amount of code required to add these two scenes, almost everything should be clear. In each scene, we added the background image and the back button, just as we did in `AboutScene`. However, this time, we used another kind of transition between the scenes.

Here is a screenshot to demonstrate our intentions:

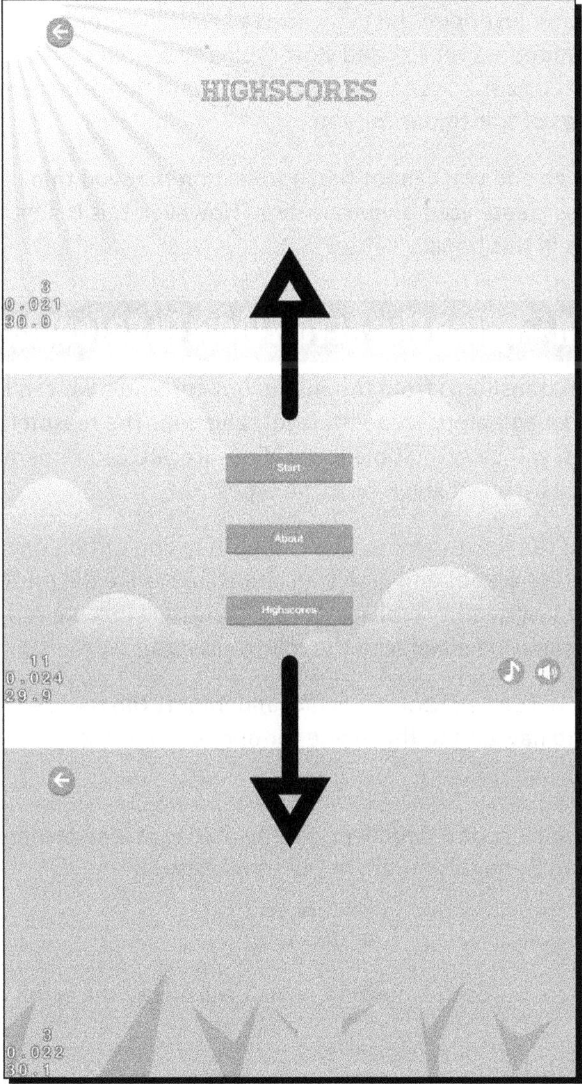

Navigation between the scenes

As you can see, we have three separate scenes, but for the player, it looks like a seamless world. When the player taps the **Highscores** button, he just looks up to the sky, and when the player taps the **Start** button, he looks down and prepares to get back on earth and start hunting.

This is just one of the examples on how you can improve your game navigation with transitions. And this is only a basic one. I am sure you can come up with even better ideas using other transitions.

To find other transitions, just open the `CCTransition.h` header from Cocos2D sources (you can just hit *command* + *Shift* + *O* and start typing to search within the project), or you can just start typing `[CCTransition transition`... and the autocomplete feature will suggest different types of transitions for you.

If this is still not enough and you cannot find a transition that you think will fit your game; ideally, you can always create your own transition. However, this is a bit more advanced and we won't cover it in this book.

Time for action – using the scroll view to select levels

It is nice to have good transitions from the menu, but currently, we can't even start the game since we display almost an empty scene for level selection. The reason for this whole scene is that in some games, you have multiple levels. I'm sure you can remember some popular game where you scroll between levels or game types.

Sometimes, the game can have so many levels that they don't fit on one screen. Of course, we could create different scenes and plan transitions just as we did on the menu scene, but in most cases, we just need a scroll view. This is exactly what we're going to do now; we're going to add a scroll view. Refer to the following steps:

1. Open the `LevelSelectScene.m` file, and import the `GameScene.h` header since we're going to navigate to this scene for one of our levels:

   ```
   #import "GameScene.h"
   ```

2. Right after the `#import` directives, add two `#define` statements. These will be our level names to distinguish them in the scroll view later:

   ```
   #define kLevelHunting    @"hunting"
   #define kLevelDodging    @"dodging"
   ```

3. Then, add the `addScroll` method, which will create the scroll view, and add it to the scene:

   ```
   -(void)addScroll
   {
       //1
   ```

```
int levels = 10;

//2
CCNode *scrollViewContents = [CCNode node];
scrollViewContents.contentSizeType = CCSizeTypeNormalized;
scrollViewContents.contentSize = CGSizeMake(levels, 1);

for (int i =0; i < levels; i++)
{
    //3
    CCButton *level = nil;
    if (i % 2 == 0)
    {
        CCSpriteFrame *levelImage =
          [CCSpriteFrame
            frameWithImageNamed:@"hunting_level.png"];
        level = [CCButton buttonWithTitle:nil
                                  spriteFrame:levelImage];
        level.name = kLevelHunting;
    }
    else
    {
        CCSpriteFrame *levelImage =
         [CCSpriteFrame
            frameWithImageNamed:@"dodging_level.png"];
        level = [CCButton buttonWithTitle:nil
                                  spriteFrame:levelImage];
        level.name = kLevelDodging;
    }

    level.positionType = CCPositionTypeNormalized;
    level.position = ccp((i + 0.5f)/levels, 0.5f);

    //4
    [level setTarget:self
            selector:@selector(levelTapped:)];

    //5
    [scrollViewContents addChild:level];
}

//6
CCScrollView *scrollView =
  [[CCScrollView alloc]
    initWithContentNode:scrollViewContents];

//7
scrollView.pagingEnabled = YES;

//8
```

```
        scrollView.horizontalScrollEnabled = YES;
        scrollView.verticalScrollEnabled = NO;

        [self addChild:scrollView];
    }
```

4. Then, add the `levelTapped:` method, which will be called when any level button is tapped:

```
-(void)levelTapped:(id)sender
{
    NSString *levelName = ((CCButton*)sender).name;
    if ([levelName isEqualToString:kLevelHunting])
    {
        GameScene *scene = [[GameScene alloc] init];
        CCTransition *transition =
          [CCTransition transitionCrossFadeWithDuration:1.0f];

        [[CCDirector sharedDirector] replaceScene:scene
                                   withTransition:transition];
    }
    else
    {
        CCLOG(@"Level not implemented: %@", levelName);
    }
}
```

5. Finally, add the call to the `addScroll` method in `init`:

```
-(instancetype)init
{
    if (self = [super init])
    {
        [self addBackground];
        [self addBackButton];
        [self addScroll];
    }

    return self;
}
```

6. Build and run the game. Press the **Start** button and scroll the screen with your finger or mouse to see different levels (only two for now). Refer to the following screenshot:

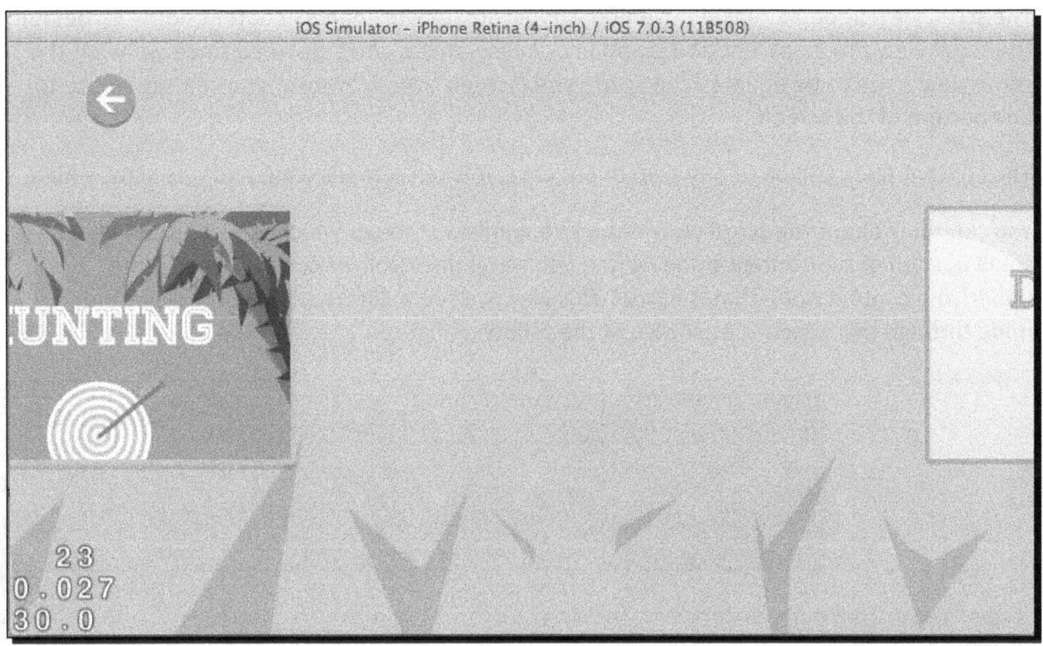

Scrolling levels

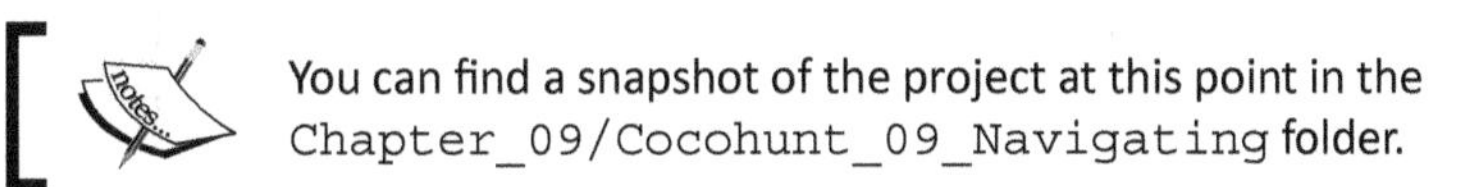

You can find a snapshot of the project at this point in the `Chapter_09/Cocohunt_09_Navigating` folder.

What just happened?

We don't have a lot of different levels in our game. Soon, we are going to add a second one, but for now, we only have one.

Scrolling between two levels is not fun. This is why we have generated ten identical buttons, where even buttons lead to hunting levels that we have already created, and odd buttons are reserved for the new level that we will add shortly.

We could not fit all the buttons on the screen at once, especially with the spacing that we intentionally made between them. This was done to make each level centered on its own page, and even more importantly, to demonstrate the paging.

Since we need more space, we used `CCScrollView` to add a scroll view. The scroll view consists of two nodes: the scroll view node itself and the content node.

The scroll view node has a fixed size and is typically smaller than its content node. By default, the scroll view fills its parent node, and in our case, this is what we need since we want the scroll view's size to be equal to the scene size (screen size). However, you can set its size to any portion of the screen.

The content node can be of any size. In our case, it is ten screens wide and one screen high.

You can think about the scroll view node as a window through which you can see only a small portion of the content node. When you scroll the scroll view, it just moves the underlying content node that is inside. This way, we see a different part of the content node through this window, as shown in the following figure:

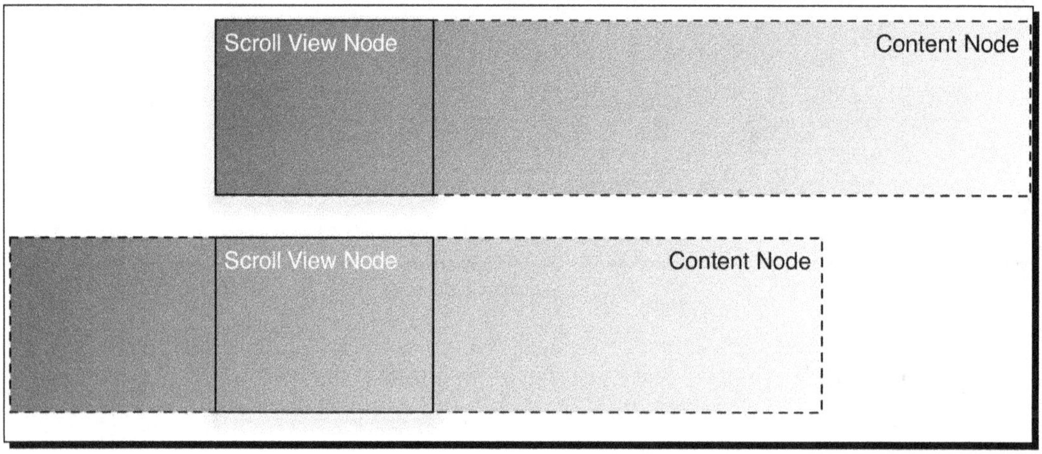

Moving the content node under the scroll view window

In the case displayed in the top half of the image, we see the leftmost part of the content node. Then, we scroll with our finger to the left and move the underlying content node. The result is shown at the bottom part of the figure. We see a different part of the content node.

After understanding the main concept of the scroll view, let's review the `addScroll` method in detail:

1. We set the amount of levels to 10. In a real game, this will be the actual number of levels or pages with levels if you have several levels on the same page.
2. Here, we created the content node and set its size using normalized size units. Normalized size units work in a very similar way to normalized coordinates that we have reviewed before. This means the content node size will be 10 times the width (number of levels) and one time the height of its parent, which will be the scroll view. The scroll view size will be equal to the screen size, as I've mentioned before, so if our content node size is `10` screens wide and `1` screen high, its size will be `(viewSize.width * 10.0f, viewSize.height * 1).`

3. This code block creates the button with the `hunting_level.png` image for even buttons and the button with the `dodging_level.png` image for odd buttons. In addition, we set different names for different button types to distinguish them later using the `name` property. Then, we set the position of the button in the content node.
4. Here, we set the target for all buttons. As you can see, we use the same method to handle all button types. This is why we needed to set the name of the buttons, so that we could distinguish them in the handler method.
5. The button is added to the content node of the scroll view.
6. Then, after all buttons are added to the content node, the scroll view itself is created using this content node.
7. The paging is then enabled, and we can scroll exactly one page in any direction. If we scroll enough, then the scroll view will do the rest of the job, and if we do not scroll enough, the scroll view will reset its position to the original page.

It is very easy to understand the difference by turning the paging on and off.

8. Since we only want horizontal scrolling, we enable it and disable the vertical scrolling.

That's it. The scroll view does the rest of the job.

When we tap on the button, a `levelTapped:` method is called, and a button that was tapped is passed as a `sender` argument. The code in the `levelTapped:` method uses the `name` property of the button to check what level should be loaded. For now, it works only for the buttons with the **Hunting** level.

Now, we can start the game again. This is good since we are going to add some dialogs to the game scene itself.

Have a go hero

Here is a list of things to try:

- Try all different transitions
- Write the code with the `pushScene:` method to push scenes until the game crashes and count how many scenes you have managed to push until it crashed
- Change the label's font size, position, and displayed text in `AboutScene`

- Change the back button arrow to point down in `HighscoresScene` (using the `rotation` property) and point up in `LevelSelectScene`
- Use Cocos2D actions (for example, `CCMoveBy`) to set up a button floating around the screen

Don't forget to back up your project in case you break something. Also, changes from this list might not be compatible with the code that we add later.

Creating modal dialogs and using text input

Often, there are moments in the game when you need to display a dialog and require the user to choose an option before continuing. For example, you might want to prompt for the player's name when they achieve a highscore.

Of course, you can just use the `pushScene:` method and display the whole new scene. However, sometimes, these dialogs are so small and you want them to cover only a small portion of the underlying scene.

Also, sometimes, you don't want to suspend the running scene while showing the dialog. There are tons of other cases when you might want to show a modal dialog without a separate scene.

In this chapter, we are going to create several custom dialogs and use the built-in `UIAlertView` class. We are going to create a pause dialog, a dialog to enter the highscore, and a dialog that is displayed after you win or lose the game.

Time for action – pausing the game with a pause dialog

We will start with adding a pause dialog to allow the player to pause the game:

1. Create a new group in `Resources` and call it `Dialogs`. Then, open the book's supporting files in `Chapter_09/Assets/Dialogs` and add all the images to that group.
2. Create a new **Objective-C class** in the `Scenes` group. Name the class `PauseDialog` and make it a subclass of `CCNode`.

Note that it is a subclass of `CCNode` not `CCScene`. We have used a similar approach when we created the `HUDLayer` class. You can read *Chapter 6, Rendering Text*, to refresh your memory. We are going to use `CCNode` as a base class for all dialogs.

3. Open the `PauseDialog.h` file and add the following property. It will allow the object, which creates the dialog to be notified when the dialog is closed.

```
@property (nonatomic, copy) void(^onCloseBlock)(void);
```

If you are unfamiliar with blocks, I suggest that you read Apple's documentation at `https://developer.apple.com/library/ios/documentation/cocoa/Conceptual/Blocks/Articles/00_Introduction.html`. I am sure you will love them.

4. Switch to the `PauseDialog.m` file and import the following headers:

```
#import "cocos2d.h"
#import "cocos2d-ui.h"
```

5. Then, add the `init` method, which calls the methods to set up the modal dialog and lay out all the user interface elements, that we'll add shortly:

```
-(instancetype)init
{
    if (self = [super init])
    {
        [self setupModalDialog];
        [self createDialogLayout];
    }

    return self;
}
```

6. Add a method that will set up the required node properties in order to make it work as a modal dialog:

```
-(void)setupModalDialog
{
    self.contentSizeType = CCSizeTypeNormalized;
    self.contentSize = CGSizeMake(1, 1);
    self.userInteractionEnabled = YES;
}
```

7. Add the `createDialogLayout` method, which creates and positions all the user interface elements:

```
-(void)createDialogLayout
{
    CCSprite *bg =
      [CCSprite spriteWithImageNamed:@"pause_dialog_bg.png"];
    bg.positionType = CCPositionTypeNormalized;
```

```
bg.position = ccp(0.5f, 0.5f);
[self addChild:bg];

CCSpriteFrame *closeNormalImage =
  [CCSpriteFrame frameWithImageNamed:@"btn_close.png"];
CCSpriteFrame *closeHighlighgtedImage =
  [CCSpriteFrame
    frameWithImageNamed:@"btn_close_pressed.png"];
CCButton *btnClose =
  [CCButton buttonWithTitle:nil
                spriteFrame:closeNormalImage
     highlightedSpriteFrame:closeHighlighgtedImage
        disabledSpriteFrame:nil];
btnClose.positionType = CCPositionTypeNormalized;
btnClose.position = ccp(1,1);
[btnClose setTarget:self
           selector:@selector(btnCloseTapped:)];
[bg addChild:btnClose];


CCSpriteFrame *restartNormalImage =
  [CCSpriteFrame frameWithImageNamed:@"btn_restart.png"];
CCSpriteFrame *restartHighLightedImage =
  [CCSpriteFrame
   frameWithImageNamed:@"btn_restart_pressed.png"];
CCButton *btnRestart =
  [CCButton buttonWithTitle:nil
                spriteFrame:restartNormalImage
     highlightedSpriteFrame:restartHighLightedImage
        disabledSpriteFrame:nil];
btnRestart.positionType = CCPositionTypeNormalized;
btnRestart.position = ccp(0.25f, 0.2f);
[btnRestart setTarget:self
             selector:@selector(btnRestartTapped:)];
[bg addChild:btnRestart];

CCSpriteFrame *exitNormalImage =
  [CCSpriteFrame frameWithImageNamed:@"btn_exit.png"];
CCSpriteFrame *exitHighLightedImage =
  [CCSpriteFrame
    frameWithImageNamed:@"btn_exit_pressed.png"];
CCButton *btnExit =
  [CCButton buttonWithTitle:nil
                spriteFrame:exitNormalImage
     highlightedSpriteFrame:exitHighLightedImage
        disabledSpriteFrame:nil];
btnExit.positionType = CCPositionTypeNormalized;
```

```
    btnExit.position = ccp(0.75f, 0.2f);
    [btnExit setTarget:self
             selector:@selector(btnExitTapped:)];
    [bg addChild:btnExit];
}
```

8. Add the following methods to handle buttons:

```
-(void)btnCloseTapped:(id)sender
{
    if (self.onCloseBlock)
        self.onCloseBlock();

    [self removeFromParentAndCleanup:YES];
}

-(void)btnRestartTapped:(id)sender
{
    CCLOG(@"Restart");
}

-(void)btnExitTapped:(id)sender
{
    CCLOG(@"Exit");
}
```

9. Add the `touchBegan:` method to swallow all touches outside the dialog window to make it modal:

```
-(void)touchBegan:(UITouch *)touch withEvent:(UIEvent *)event
{
    CCLOG(@"Touch swallowed by the pause dialog");
}
```

10. Now, open the `GameScene.m` file and import the `PauseDialog.h` and `cocos2d-ui.h` headers:

```
#import "PauseDialog.h"
#import "cocos2d-ui.h"
```

11. Then, add two more z-order values for the pause button and the dialogs:

```
typedef NS_ENUM(NSUInteger, Z_ORDER)
{
    Z_BACKGROUND,
    Z_BATCH_NODE,
    Z_LABELS,
    Z_HUD,
    Z_PAUSE_BUTTON,
    Z_DIALOGS
};
```

12. Scroll down and add the following two methods:

```
-(void)addPauseButton
{
    CCSpriteFrame *pauseNormalImage =
      [CCSpriteFrame frameWithImageNamed:@"btn_pause.png"];
    CCSpriteFrame *pauseHighlightedImage  =
      [CCSpriteFrame
         frameWithImageNamed:@"btn_pause_pressed.png"];

    CCButton *btnPause =
      [CCButton buttonWithTitle:nil
                    spriteFrame:pauseNormalImage
         highlightedSpriteFrame:pauseHighlightedImage
            disabledSpriteFrame:nil];
    btnPause.positionType = CCPositionTypeNormalized;
    btnPause.position = ccp(0.95f, 0.05f);
    [btnPause setTarget:self
               selector:@selector(btnPauseTapped:)];

    [self addChild:btnPause z:Z_PAUSE_BUTTON];
}

-(void)btnPauseTapped:(id)sender
{
    if (_gameState != GameStatePlaying)
        return;

    _gameState = GameStatePaused;

    for (Bird *bird in _birds)
        bird.paused = YES;

    for (CCSprite *arrow in _arrows)
        arrow.paused = YES;

    PauseDialog *dlg = [[PauseDialog alloc] init];
    dlg.onCloseBlock = ^{

        _gameState = GameStatePlaying;

        for (Bird *bird in _birds)
            bird.paused = NO;

        for (CCSprite *arrow in _arrows)
            arrow.paused = NO;

    };
    [self addChild:dlg z:Z_DIALOGS];
}
```

13. Finally, add a call to the `addPauseButton` button method to the end of the `init` method:

```
-(instancetype)init
{
    if (self = [super init])
    {
        //..skipped..

        [self addPauseButton];
    }

    return self;
}
```

14. Build and run the game. Start the game and then click on the **Pause** button. Close the pause dialog using the close (*X*) button. The **Exit** and **Restart** buttons should currently only output their names to the console.

What just happened?

Our pause dialog works pretty simply. The dialog itself is just a node that is displayed in the game scene. This works in a very similar way as our `HUDLayer`. However, there are a few interesting techniques that we used when creating this dialog.

Using a background image as a container for UI elements

Since we don't want to cover the whole screen, we added a small image to the `PauseDialog` node that works as a pause dialog background, as shown in the following screenshot:

The pause_dialog_bg.png image is used as a pause dialog background

Since all the buttons of the pause dialog are inside this small image, we added them as child nodes of this background sprite instead of the node itself.

In *Chapter 3, Cocos2D – Under the Hood*, we discussed that every `CCNode` descendant can have child nodes. We're using this right now to position all elements relative to the background image.

Let's review the piece of code in the `createDialogLayout` method:

```
btnClose.positionType = CCPositionTypeNormalized;
btnClose.position = ccp(1,1);
```

This piece of code creates the close button. As you can see, we used normalized coordinates with the bottom-left reference corner (this is how `CCPositionTypeNormalized` is defined) and set the position of the close button to `(1,1)`. This is the top-right corner of the parent node.

Since we add the button to the background and the button's anchor point is `(0.5, 0.5)`, we set the button's center to the top-right corner of the pause dialog, exactly where we wanted.

The rest of the `createDialogLayout` method creates other buttons and sets the methods that will be called when the buttons are pressed.

Swallowing touches

Even though our game is on pause, since we change `_gameState` to `GameStatePaused` in the `btnPauseTapped:` method, we don't want to think what happens if the player touches the game scene outside the small pause dialog. There can be some other buttons or controls in your game, and it is much easier to know that the player just cannot do anything until they resume or exit the game.

Fortunately, there is an easy way to solve this. In the `setupModalDialog` method, we set the size of our node to cover the whole game scene, and by setting the `userInteractionEnabled` property to `YES`, we are letting Cocos2D know that our node wants to handle touches.

As we know by now, touches are handled in a reverse render order. In other words, the nodes on the top (high z-order) will get a chance to handle, and more importantly, cancel the touch before the underlying nodes.

Our `PauseDialog` is the topmost node right now because we added it to the scene with the following line (where `Z_DIALOGS` is the highest z-order we have):

```
[self addChild:dlg z:Z_DIALOGS];
```

This way, when the player touches the screen anywhere outside the button's rectangles of the pause dialog, the `touchBegan:` method of the `PauseDialog` class is called before all other nodes even have a chance to know that the player touched the screen.

The buttons in the pause dialog still work because they are children of the `PauseDialog` node and are thus rendered on top of it. Even though we didn't set their z-order, they have the `zOrder` property set to `0` by default. The node renders everything in three steps: renders children with `zOrder < 0`, renders itself in case it is a render node, and finally renders children with `zOrder >= 0`.

Our implementation of the `touchBegan:` method in the `PauseDialog` class simply swallows the touch by not processing it and not calling the `touchBegan:` method on `super` class to pass the touch to the underlying nodes.

Pausing and resuming the game

The pausing and resuming of the game both happen in the `btnPauseTapped:` method in the `GameScene.m` file.

When the pause button is tapped, we check that we are in a valid state to pause the game. If we already won, lost, or the game has not yet started, we don't want the player to pause the game.

If the game is in the correct game state, then we set `_gameState` to `GameStatePaused`. This will disable shooting, bird spawning, and so on, everything except the objects that are moved using Cocos2D actions (for example, `CCActionMoveTo`). To pause the birds and the arrows, we need to iterate through arrays that contain them and set their `pause` property to `YES`.

Instead of iterating through the `_birds` and `_arrows` arrays and pausing all objects, we could just use the scene's `pause` property and this would stop all of its child nodes too.

However, this would also stop the fire from burning, and could stop some other actions that you may still want to run. For example, you might want the pause dialog to not simply appear on the screen immediately but appear using some animation. Setting the `pause` property of the scene would stop this animation from running too because the pause dialog is the child node of the scene.

Another elegant solution is to keep all the game objects in a separate node and not in the scene directly. This way, you can simply pause this node.

After pausing everything, we display `PauseDialog` and assign its `onCloseBlock` property to the block that will resume the game. This block is executed from the `btnCloseTapped:` method in the `PauseDialog.m` file at the moment we tap the close button. This is done right before the dialog is removed from the game scene.

Time for action – restarting and exiting the game

There are still two buttons in the pause dialog that currently simply output to the console instead of actually doing something. Let's add the code for the **Exit** and **Restart** buttons. In addition, we are going to create a `LoadingScene` class, which will help us to avoid memory errors and will use `UIAlertView` to confirm the exit from the game.

Looks like a lot of work, so let's start:

1. Open the Xcode project and create a new scene named `LoadingScene` in the `Scenes` group.
2. Then, open the `PauseDialog.m` file and import the `LoadingScene.h` and `MenuScene.h` headers:

```
#import "LoadingScene.h"
#import "MenuScene.h"
```

3. Find the `btnRestartTapped:` method and replace its contents with the following code:

```
-(void)btnRestartTapped:(id)sender
{
    LoadingScene *loadingScene = [[LoadingScene alloc] init];
    CCTransition *transition =
      [CCTransition transitionCrossFadeWithDuration:1.0f];

    [[CCDirector sharedDirector] replaceScene:loadingScene
                                withTransition:transition];
}
```

4. Then, find the `btnExitTapped:` method and replace its contents with the following code:

```
-(void)btnExitTapped:(id)sender
{
    UIAlertView *alert = [[UIAlertView alloc]
                           initWithTitle:@"Exit confirmation"
                                 message:@"Are you sure?"
                                delegate:self
                       cancelButtonTitle:@"No"
                       otherButtonTitles:@"Yes", nil];
    [alert show];
}
```

5. Right below the `btnExitTapped:` method, add the `alertView:clickedButtonAtIndex:` method, as shown in the following code. It will be called automatically when the player taps any button in the alert dialog.

```
- (void)alertView:(UIAlertView *)alertView
clickedButtonAtIndex:(NSInteger)buttonIndex
{
    if (buttonIndex == 1)
    {
        MenuScene *menuScene = [[MenuScene alloc] init];
        CCTransition *transition =
          [CCTransition transitionCrossFadeWithDuration:1.0f];
        [[CCDirector sharedDirector] replaceScene:menuScene
                                   withTransition:transition];
    }
}
```

6. Then, switch to the `PauseDialog.h` header and make the `PauseDialog` class conform to the `UIAlertViewDelegate` protocol since this is required to use `UIAlertView`:

```
@interface PauseDialog : CCNode<UIAlertViewDelegate>
```

7. Open the `GameScene.m` file and add the `onExit` method right after the `onEnter` method:

```
-(void)onExit
{
    [super onExit];
    [[AudioManager sharedAudioManager] stopMusic];
}
```

8. Finally, switch to the `LoadingScene.m` file and replace its contents with the following code:

```
#import "LoadingScene.h"

#import "cocos2d.h"
#import "GameScene.h"

@implementation LoadingScene

-(instancetype)init
{
    if (self = [super init])
    {
        CCLabelTTF *loading =
          [CCLabelTTF labelWithString:@"Loading..."
                             fontName:@"Georgia-BoldItalic"
                             fontSize:24];
        loading.anchorPoint = ccp(0.5f, 0.5f);
```

```
            loading.positionType = CCPositionTypeNormalized;
            loading.position = ccp(0.5f, 0.5f);
            [self addChild:loading];
        }

        return self;
    }

    -(void)onEnterTransitionDidFinish
    {
        [super onEnterTransitionDidFinish];

        CCTransition *transition =
          [CCTransition
            transitionRevealWithDirection:CCTransitionDirectionDown
                                 duration:1.0f];
        GameScene *scene = [[GameScene alloc] init];
        [[CCDirector sharedDirector] replaceScene:scene
                                   withTransition:transition];
    }

    @end
```

9. Build and run the game. Now, you should be able to restart and exit the game from the pause dialog.

What just happened?

Most of the code we added should be clear. We added the code to navigate to the `MenuScene` class in case the player taps the **Exit** button. But before that, we displayed `UIAlertView` to make sure the player didn't accidentally tap the **Exit** button.

We also added the code to restart the game. To restart the game, we simply create a new `GameScene` class (via `LoadingScene`) when the player taps the **Restart** button. Of course, we could add a `restart` method to the `GameScene` class, which will reset the state to the initial one, but sometimes, the simpler way is just to recreate the `GameScene` class.

The reason for using `LoadingScene` and not creating a new `GameScene` right in the `btnRestartTapped:` method is pretty simple. We need to do this to avoid memory errors.

When the `btnRestartTapped:` method is executed, we have one instance of `GameScene` running, since `PauseDialog` is just a node in it. If we create one more `GameScene` instance, we'll have two `GameScene` instances in memory at the same time.

Typically, the `GameScene` class is the heaviest scene in the game. This means it loads a lot of resources and consumes a lot of memory. So, instead of having two instances of it simultaneously, we first switch to the lightweight `LoadingScene` and let the current `GameScene` class be deallocated. Then, we create a new `GameScene` class in `onEnterTransitionDidFinish` and switch to it.

> Currently, nothing bad will happen if we don't use the `LoadingScene` technique since our `GameScene` is not that heavy. However, I wanted to show you this trick so that you could use it in case you need it in a real-life game.

One last change we made is that we added the `onExit` method to the `GameScene` class. This method is declared in `CCNode` and is thus present in all of its descendant nodes, such as our scene.

This method is called when the node leaves the stage. In our case, we use it to stop the music when the current `GameScene` is replaced with `MenuScene` on exit or another instance of the `GameScene` on restart.

There are four methods that can be used to execute the code at some point of the node lifecycle. They are as follows:

- `onEnter`: This is called when the node enters the stage, for example, when you display a scene using the `replaceScene:` or `pushScene:` method. Also, if you use transition, then `onEnter` is called when the transition starts.
- `onEnterTransitionDidFinish`: This is the same as `onEnter`, but it is called when the enter transition is completed. Add a code in this method if you want to wait while the transition completes, before starting some action.

> For example, it is a good idea to start the game timer when the transition completes, so that the players don't think it is unfair to count time when they can't play the game. By the way, it is also a good idea to let the player start playing after the transition completes.

- `onExit`: This is called when the node leaves the stage. If you use the transition, then this method is called when the transition finishes.
- `onExitTransitionDidStart`: This is called when the exit transition starts.

> The loose term "enters the stage" or "leaves the stage" is used because there are several scenarios when this happens, and this term describes all of them very well. For example, the scene enters the stage when it is displayed using `CCDirector`, while other `CCNode` descendants, such as `CCSprite`, enter the stage when they are added to the scene and leave the stage each time they are removed from the scene. Since we can remove the node without destroying it and add it again to the scene, the node's `onEnter` and `onExit` methods can be called multiple times for the same node.

The `onEnter` method is also a good candidate to place the initialization code, the one that we have right now in the `init` method. The reason for this is that the `onEnter` method is called when the current scene starts running and the previous scene is deallocated (if you use `replaceScene:` not `pushScene:` of course). This way, you won't get two heavy scenes in memory at the same time.

Here's how we could avoid using the extra loading scene. If we placed all the code of the `GameScene` class in the `onEnter` method, we could easily create one more instance of `GameScene` right in the `btnRestartTapped:` method instead of creating the intermediate `LoadingScene`.

This would have just created an empty scene, since no initialization code (loading sprites, creating labels, and so on) would run because it is not in the `init` method. Then, when we call the `replaceScene:` method, Cocos2D will remove the current scene and only after that call the `onEnter` method on the second instance. This way, we would not get two scenes with all the sprites, labels, and other resources in memory at the same time.

> A very important thing to remember when using any of those methods is to call its `super` (for example, `[super onEnter]`); otherwise, you most likely will get hard-detectable bugs.

Time for action – displaying stats when losing and winning

There are a few more dialogs that we need to add quickly. The first one is the dialog that is displayed when we win or lose the game. In this dialog, we will display the gathered statistics and again the same buttons to restart or exit the game. Otherwise, you cannot do anything when you win or lose.

1. Open an Xcode project and create a new `CCNode` subclass called `WinLoseDialog`. It is better to place this too in the `Scenes` group in order to keep things more organized.

2. Open the `GameStats.h` file and add the `timeSpent` property; we will use it to count the time that the player spent to beat or lose the level:

```
@property (nonatomic, assign) float timeSpent;
```

3. Open the `GameStats.m` file and initialize this property to `0` inside the `init` method:

```
self.timeSpent = 0;
```

4. Open the `GameScene.m` file and find the `update:` method. Add the following line, right after the line where we check that the game state is `GameStatePlaying`:

```
-(void)update:(CCTime)dt
{
    if (self.gameState != GameStatePlaying)
        return;

    _gameStats.timeSpent += dt;

    //..skipped..
}
```

This will add time to the `timeSpent` property when the player is actually playing the game.

5. Open the `WinLoseDialog.h` file and import the `GameStats.h` header:

```
#import "GameStats.h"
```

6. Then, add the `initWithGameStats:` method declaration:

```
-(instancetype)initWithGameStats:(GameStats *)stats;
```

7. After that, open the `WinLoseDialog.m` file and add the following headers:

```
#import "cocos2d.h"
#import "cocos2d-ui.h"

#import "MenuScene.h"
#import "LoadingScene.h"
```

8. Then, add the following `#define` statements to define common font properties for the stats labels:

```
#define kKeyFont          @"HelveticaNeue"
#define kKeyFontSize      12
#define kKeyX             0.2f

#define kValueFont        @"HelveticaNeue-Bold"
#define kValueFontSize    12
#define kValueX           0.8f

#define kLine1Y                   0.7f
#define kMarginBetweenLines       0.08f
```

9. Add the following instance variable:

```
@implementation WinLoseDialog
{
    GameStats *_currenStats;
}
```

10. Then, add the `init` method as follows:

```
-(instancetype)initWithGameStats:(GameStats *)stats;
{
    if (self = [super init])
    {
        _currenStats = stats;

        [self setupModalDialog];

        [self createDialogLayout];
    }

    return self;
}
```

11. Add the following methods to set up a modal dialog and add the user interface elements:

```
-(void)setupModalDialog
{
    self.contentSizeType = CCSizeTypeNormalized;
    self.contentSize = CGSizeMake(1, 1);
    self.userInteractionEnabled = YES;
}

-(void)createDialogLayout
{

    CCSprite *bg =
      [CCSprite spriteWithImageNamed:
        @"win_lose_dialog_bg.png"];
    bg.positionType = CCPositionTypeNormalized;
    bg.position = ccp(0.5f, 0.5f);
    [self addChild:bg];

    NSDictionary *stats =
      @{ @"Score" :
        [NSString stringWithFormat:@"%d", _currenStats.score],
      @"Lives Left" :
        [NSString stringWithFormat:@"%d", _currenStats.lives],
      @"Time Spent" :
        [NSString stringWithFormat:@"%.1f s",
```

```
        _currenStats.timeSpent] };

    float margin = 0;
    CCColor *fontColor = [CCColor orangeColor];

    for (NSString *key in stats.allKeys)
    {
        CCLabelTTF *lblKey =
          [CCLabelTTF labelWithString:key
                             fontName:kKeyFont
                             fontSize:kKeyFontSize];
        lblKey.color = fontColor;
        lblKey.anchorPoint = ccp(0.0f, 0.5f);
        lblKey.positionType = CCPositionTypeNormalized;
        lblKey.position = ccp(kKeyX, kLine1Y - margin);
        [bg addChild:lblKey];

        CCLabelTTF *lblValue =
          [CCLabelTTF labelWithString:[stats objectForKey:key]
                             fontName:kValueFont
                             fontSize:kValueFontSize];
        lblValue.color = fontColor;
        lblValue.anchorPoint = ccp(1.0f, 0.5f);
        lblValue.positionType = CCPositionTypeNormalized;
        lblValue.position = ccp(kValueX, kLine1Y - margin);
        [bg addChild:lblValue];

        margin += kMarginBetweenLines;
    }

    CCSpriteFrame *restartNormalImage =
      [CCSpriteFrame frameWithImageNamed:@"btn_restart.png"];
    CCSpriteFrame *restartHighLightedImage =
      [CCSpriteFrame
        frameWithImageNamed:@"btn_restart_pressed.png"];
    CCButton *btnRestart =
     [CCButton buttonWithTitle:nil
                   spriteFrame:restartNormalImage
       highlightedSpriteFrame:restartHighLightedImage
          disabledSpriteFrame:nil];
    btnRestart.positionType = CCPositionTypeNormalized;
    btnRestart.position = ccp(0.25f, 0.2f);
    [btnRestart setTarget:self
      selector:@selector(btnRestartTapped:)];
    [bg addChild:btnRestart];

    CCSpriteFrame *exitNormalImage =
     [CCSpriteFrame frameWithImageNamed:@"btn_exit.png"];
```

```
        CCSpriteFrame *exitHighLightedImage =
          [CCSpriteFrame
            frameWithImageNamed:@"btn_exit_pressed.png"];
        CCButton *btnExit =
          [CCButton buttonWithTitle:nil
                        spriteFrame:exitNormalImage
             highlightedSpriteFrame:exitHighLightedImage
                disabledSpriteFrame:nil];
        btnExit.positionType = CCPositionTypeNormalized;
        btnExit.position = ccp(0.75f, 0.2f);
        [btnExit setTarget:self
                  selector:@selector(btnExitTapped:)];
        [bg addChild:btnExit];
    }
```

12. Add methods to handle the tapped buttons and swallow touches as follows:

```
-(void)btnRestartTapped:(id)sender
{
    LoadingScene *loadingScene = [[LoadingScene alloc] init];
    CCTransition *transition =
      [CCTransition transitionCrossFadeWithDuration:1.0f];

    [[CCDirector sharedDirector]
      replaceScene:loadingScene withTransition:transition];
}

-(void)btnExitTapped:(id)sender
{
    MenuScene *menuScene = [[MenuScene alloc] init];
    CCTransition *transition =
     [CCTransition transitionCrossFadeWithDuration:1.0f];

    [[CCDirector sharedDirector]
      replaceScene:menuScene withTransition:transition];
}

-(void)touchBegan:(UITouch *)touch withEvent:(UIEvent *)event
{
    //do nothing, swallow touch
}
```

13. Then, open the `GameScene.m` file and import the `WinLoseDialog.h` header:

```
#import "WinLoseDialog.h"
```

14. After that, update the `won` and `lost` methods and add the following lines at the end of each method:

```
-(void)lost
{
    //..skipped..

    WinLoseDialog *wlDialog =
      [[WinLoseDialog alloc]
          initWithGameStats:_gameStats];
    [self addChild:wlDialog];
}

-(void)won
{
    //..skipped..

    WinLoseDialog *wlDialog =
      [[WinLoseDialog alloc]
        initWithGameStats:_gameStats];
    [self addChild:wlDialog];
}
```

15. Now, find the `displayWinLoseLabelWithText:` method and adjust the height at which the label appears, or it will appear on top of the dialog:

```
label.position = ccp(viewSize.width * 0.5f,
                     viewSize.height * 0.85f);
```

16. Finally, for easier testing, find the place where you set the number of birds to spawn and number of birds to lose, and set both the values to `1`:

```
_birdsToSpawn = 1;
_birdsToLose = 1;
```

17. Build and run the game. Win and lose the game by hitting the only bird or letting it fly away and you should see the new dialog. Refer to the following screenshot:

You can find a snapshot of the project at this point in the `Chapter_09/Cocohunt_09_Dialogs` folder.

What just happened?

Now, we can start the game, play it until we win or lose, get some statistics, and finally exit or restart the game instead of staring at the screen forever.

Currently, the statistics only show how much time we spent by completing the level or how long we lasted. However, I'm sure you've got the idea of gathering statistics.

What we did is we just created a class where we can keep all the different variables that the user might be interested in. In fact, we already created this `GameStats` class quite some time ago, keeping in mind how we will use it later.

After that, we found a place where we can update the stats. In our particular case, this was the `update:` method in the `GameScene` class. Finally, we displayed everything we gathered in the final dialog.

It might seem strange, but players love different stats. They love it even more if it is linked to some kind of achievement. For example, there can be an achievement if you beat the level for five seconds, or hit three birds within one second, and so on.

In the final chapter of this book, we are going to learn how to integrate Game Center and will add several achievements based on different stats.

The final thing we are left with in this chapter is to complete our highscores scene.

Entering and displaying highscores

I have a feeling you are already tired of creating all those dialogs and buttons. Unfortunately, creating games is not only the fun of creating a great gameplay prototype. When you are about to release your game, you suddenly remember that it would be nice if users could compete using a highscores table, and if they could pause and restart the game since they don't have a **Stop** button in Xcode.

We will take a small break and will complete our `HighscoresScene` class, and then we will create the final dialog for this chapter and for the whole book.

Time for action – displaying highscores with CCTableView

Tables are great for displaying data. We are going to use a table control provided by Cocos2D to display a list of the highest scored points by our players. The table will contain a list of player names and their scores.

Since we are not prompting for the player's name just yet, we are going to display dummy data, and in the next section, we are going to replace it with real highscores.

Let's start:

1. Open the `HighscoresScene.h` file and import the `cocos2d-ui.h` header:

```
#import "cocos2d-ui.h"
```

2. Then, make the `HighscoresScene` class conform to `CCTableViewDataSource`:

```
@interface HighscoresScene: CCScene<CCTableViewDataSource>
```

3. After that, switch to the `HighscoresScene.m` file and define the constants of the row height and font properties:

```
#define kHighscoreRowHeight 32
#define kHighscoreFontName @"Helvetica"
#define kHighscoreFontSize 12
```

4. Scroll down and add the `addHighscoresTable` method as follows:

```
-(void)addHighscoresTable
{
    //1
    CCTableView *highscoresTable = [[CCTableView alloc] init];

    //2
    highscoresTable.rowHeight = kHighscoreRowHeight;

    //3
    highscoresTable.anchorPoint = ccp(0.5, 1.0f);

    //4
    highscoresTable.positionType = CCPositionTypeNormalized;
    highscoresTable.position = ccp(0.5f, 0.65f);
    highscoresTable.contentSizeType = CCSizeTypeNormalized;
    highscoresTable.contentSize = CGSizeMake(1, 0.4f);

    //5
    highscoresTable.userInteractionEnabled = NO;

    //6
    [self addChild:highscoresTable];

    //7
    highscoresTable.dataSource = self;
}
```

5. Then, add the call to the `addHighscoresTable` method in the `init` method:

```
-(instancetype)init
{
    if (self = [super init])
    {
        [self addBackground];
        [self addBackButton];
        [self addHighscoresTable];
    }

    return self;
}
```

6. Now, we need to implement the `CCTableViewDataSource` protocol methods to fill the table. To do this, add the following two methods:

```
- (CCTableViewCell*) tableView:(CCTableView*)tableView
nodeForRowAtIndex:(NSUInteger) index
{
    //1
```

```
    NSString *playerName =
      [NSString stringWithFormat:@"Player #%d", index];
    int score = 100 - index;

    //2
    CCTableViewCell * cell = [[CCTableViewCell alloc] init];
    cell.contentSizeType =
      CCSizeTypeMake(CCSizeUnitNormalized, CCSizeUnitPoints);
    cell.contentSize = CGSizeMake(1, kHighscoreRowHeight);

    //3
    CCSprite *bg =
     [CCSprite spriteWithImageNamed:@"table_cell_bg.png"];
    bg.positionType = CCPositionTypeNormalized;
    bg.position = ccp(0.5f, 0.5f);
    [cell addChild:bg];

    //4
    CCLabelTTF *lblPlayerName =
     [CCLabelTTF labelWithString:playerName
                        fontName:kHighscoreFontName
                        fontSize:kHighscoreFontSize];
    lblPlayerName.positionType = CCPositionTypeNormalized;
    lblPlayerName.position = ccp(0.05, 0.5f);
    lblPlayerName.anchorPoint = ccp(0, 0.5f);
    [bg addChild:lblPlayerName];

    //5
    NSString *scoreString =
      [NSString stringWithFormat:@"%d pts.", score];
    CCLabelTTF *lblScore =
      [CCLabelTTF labelWithString:scoreString
                         fontName:kHighscoreFontName
                         fontSize:kHighscoreFontSize];
    lblScore.positionType = CCPositionTypeNormalized;
    lblScore.position = ccp(0.95f, 0.5f);
    lblScore.anchorPoint = ccp(1, 0.5f);
    [bg addChild:lblScore];

    //6
    return cell;
}

- (NSUInteger) tableViewNumberOfRows:(CCTableView*) tableView
{
    return 5;
}
```

7. Build and run the game. Tap the **Highscores** button in the main menu, and you should see the test data displayed in our highscores table, as shown in the following screenshot:

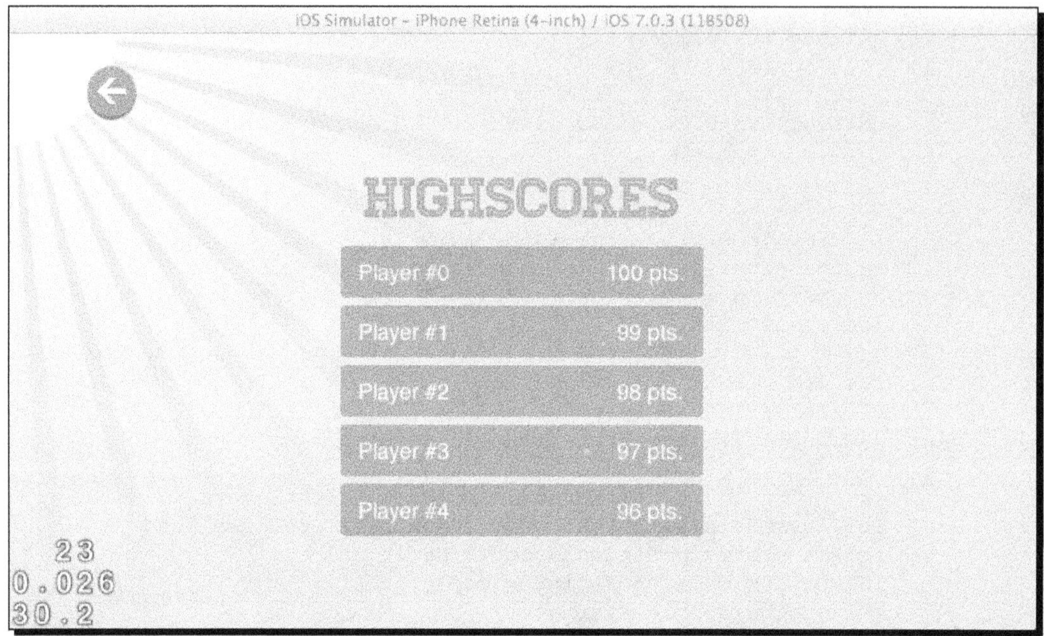

The highscores table

What just happened?

The scene in the preceding screenshot is looking much better than the empty background with a back button. Let's start our review from the `addHighscoresTable` method. Please follow the numbered comments in the method:

1. First of all, we created a `CCTableView` instance, which we are going to add to our scene and fill with highscores.
2. After the table was created, we set the properties to display our table as we want. We used the `table_cell_bg.png` image as a cell background. This image is 28 points high, so setting the row height to `32` will add a margin of two points on the top and at the bottom. Of course, we will need to center the image in the cell.
3. It is easier to position our table using its top edge. So we changed the anchor point to be in the middle of the top edge.
4. Then, we set the position and size using normalized units.

5. We disabled the user interaction since we don't want the table to scroll. The table is based on the scroll view, but we won't show more than five elements in it, so we don't need the scrolling.

> You can easily check how the table is scrolled by setting the `userInteractionEnabled` property to `YES` and adjusting the number of elements in the table by returning a larger number of rows from the `tableViewNumberOfRows:` method.

6. We then added the table to the scene.
7. Remember we made the `HighscoresScene` to conform to the `CCTableViewDataSource` protocol. This is the line that explains why we did it. We are going to use the `HighscoresScene` class as `dataSource` for the table view. This means that the table view will call the methods on the `HighscoresScene` scene to get the data for the table. Hold on a second and I will explain this further.

The `CCTableView` protocol works in a similar way to `UITableView`.

> If you are unfamiliar with `UITableView`, then think of it this way. You tell the table view which object has the data by setting the `dataSource` property. Since this can be any object, the table view needs to know how to get data from this object. The simplest way to do this is to guarantee that there are some methods with known names that can be called by the table view to get the data. This is exactly what conforming to the `CCTableViewDataSource` protocol guarantees.

Here is how the `CCTableViewDataSource` protocol is declared:

```
@protocol CCTableViewDataSource <NSObject>

(CCTableViewCell*) tableView:(CCTableView*)tableView
        nodeForRowAtIndex:(NSUInteger) index;
- (NSUInteger) tableViewNumberOfRows:(CCTableView*) tableView;

@optional

(float) tableView:(CCTableView*)tableView
  heightForRowAtIndex:(NSUInteger) index;

@end
```

As you can see, there are two methods that are required, `tableView:nodeForRowAtIndex:` and `tableViewNumberOfRows:`. The `tableViewNumberOfRows:` method simply returns the number of rows present in the table, and the `tableView:nodeForRowAtIndex:` method returns a table cell for the specified row index.

For now, we have hardcoded the number of rows to `5`, so let's review the `tableView:nodeForRowAtIndex:` method as follows:

1. Here, we generated the test data that we will change to the actual player name and score in the next section.
2. The table cell that we need to return from this method is created. This time, we mix the unit points and normalized units to set the width and height of the cell.
3. The `table_cell_bg.png` image is used as the background for the cell and is added as a child of the cell. The text label is much more visible on a background. Also, the whole table will look better with the cell background rather than just text hanging in the air.
4. The player-name label is positioned on the left side of the cell. The text in the label is left aligned using `anchorPoint`.
5. The score is placed on the right-side and is right-aligned. Both labels are added as a child of the background in order to position them vertically at the center of the background image.
6. The cell is returned and added to the table with all of its contents.

This is everything that is required to add a table to your game and fill it with data.

Time for action – using the text field

What's the purpose of the highscores table if you can't beat any of the highscores? Let's change that and replace the test data with the actual highscores. To do this, we're going to need the player to enter their name when they beat a highscore:

1. Create a new **Objective-C class** in the `Common` group. Name the class `HighscoreManager` and make it a subclass of `NSObject`.
2. Open the `HighscoreManager.h` file and replace its contents with the following code:

```
#import "GameStats.h"

#define kMaxHighscores 5

@interface HighscoreManager: NSObject

-(NSArray *)getHighScores;
```

```
-(BOOL)isHighscore:(int)score;

-(void)addHighScore:(GameStats *)newHighscore;

+(HighscoreManager *)sharedHighscoreManager;

@end
```

3. Then, open the `HighscoreManager.h` file and replace its contents with the following code:

```
#import "HighscoreManager.h"

@implementation HighscoreManager
{
    NSMutableArray *_highScores;
}

-(instancetype)init
{
    if (self = [super init])
    {
        _highScores = [NSMutableArray
                           arrayWithCapacity:kMaxHighscores];
    }

    return self;
}

-(BOOL)isHighscore:(int)score
{
    return (score > 0) && ((_highScores.count < kMaxHighscores)
            || (score > [_highScores.lastObject score]));
}

-(void)addHighScore:(GameStats *)newHighscore
{
NSAssert([newHighscore.playerName length] > 0,
  @"You must specify player name for the highscore!");

    for (int i=0; i < _highScores.count; i++)
    {
        GameStats *gs = [_highScores objectAtIndex:i];
        if (newHighscore.score > gs.score)
        {
            [_highScores insertObject:newHighscore atIndex:i];

            if (_highScores.count > kMaxHighscores)
```

```
                [_highScores removeLastObject];

            return;
        }
    }

    if (_highScores.count < kMaxHighscores)
    {
        [_highScores addObject:newHighscore];
        return;
    }
}

-(NSArray *)getHighScores
{
    return _highScores;
}

+(HighscoreManager *)sharedHighscoreManager
{
    static dispatch_once_t pred;
    static HighscoreManager * _sharedInstance;
    dispatch_once(&pred, ^{ _sharedInstance = [[self alloc] init];
    });
    return _sharedInstance;
}

@end
```

4. Open the `GameStats.h` file and add a new property called `playerName` to store the player name in addition to the score in the game stats:

```
@property (nonatomic, copy)   NSString *playerName;
```

5. Now, it is time to create a dialog that will ask the player to enter their name if they get a highscore. Create a new `CCNode` subclass in the `Scenes` group and call it `HighscoreDialog`.

6. Open the `HighscoreDialog.h` file and replace its contents with the following code:

```
#import "CCNode.h"
#import "GameStats.h"

@interface HighscoreDialog : CCNode

@property (nonatomic, copy) void(^onCloseBlock)(void);

-(instancetype)initWithGameStats:(GameStats *)stats;

@end
```

7. Then, open the `HighscoreDialog.m` file and import the following headers:

```
#import "cocos2d.h"
#import "cocos2d-ui.h"
#import "HighscoreManager.h"
```

8. Then, add the following instance variables:

```
@implementation HighscoreDialog
{
    GameStats *_currentStats;

    CCTextField *_playerNameInput;
    CCLabelTTF  *_validateResult;
}
```

9. Add the `initWithGameStats:` method:

```
-(instancetype)initWithGameStats:(GameStats *)stats
{
    if (self = [super init])
    {
        _currentStats = stats;
        [self createDialogLayout];
    }

    return self;
}
```

10. Add the `createDialogLayout` method to add and position all the user interface elements:

```
-(void)createDialogLayout
{
    CGSize viewSize = [CCDirector sharedDirector].viewSize;

    CCSprite *background =
      [CCSprite spriteWithImageNamed:@"highscore_dialog_bg.png"];
    background.position = ccp(viewSize.width * 0.5f,
                              viewSize.height * 0.5f);
    [self addChild:background];

    CCSpriteFrame *textFieldFrame =
     [CCSpriteFrame
       frameWithImageNamed:@"highscore_dialog_textfield.png"];
    _playerNameInput =
      [CCTextField textFieldWithSpriteFrame:textFieldFrame];
    _playerNameInput.string = @"Player1";

    _playerNameInput.preferredSize = textFieldFrame.rect.size;
    _playerNameInput.padding = 4.0f;
```

```
        _playerNameInput.fontSize = 10.0f;

        _playerNameInput.positionType = CCPositionTypeNormalized;
        _playerNameInput.anchorPoint = ccp(0.5f, 0.5f);
        _playerNameInput.position = ccp(0.5f, 0.7f);
        [background addChild:_playerNameInput];

        _validateResult = [CCLabelTTF labelWithString:@""
                                             fontName:@"Helvetica"
                                             fontSize:8];
        _validateResult.color = [CCColor redColor];
        _validateResult.positionType = CCPositionTypeNormalized;
        _validateResult.position = ccp(0.5f, 0.6f);
        [background addChild:_validateResult];


        CCSpriteFrame *okNormalImage =
          [CCSpriteFrame frameWithImageNamed:@"btn_ok.png"];
        CCSpriteFrame *okHighlightedImage =
          [CCSpriteFrame frameWithImageNamed:@"btn_ok_pressed.png"];

        CCButton *btnOk = [CCButton buttonWithTitle:nil
                                        spriteFrame:okNormalImage
                             highlightedSpriteFrame:okHighlightedImage
                                disabledSpriteFrame:nil];
        btnOk.positionType = CCPositionTypeNormalized;
        btnOk.position = ccp(0.5f, 0.2f);
        [btnOk setTarget:self selector:@selector(btnOkPressed:)];
        [background addChild:btnOk];
    }
```

11. Add the `btnOkPressed` method to handle the **OK** button tap:

```
    -(void)btnOkPressed:(id)sender
    {
        NSString *playerName = _playerNameInput.string;
        if ([self validatePlayerName:playerName])
        {
            _currentStats.playerName = playerName;
            [[HighscoreManager sharedHighscoreManager]
              addHighScore:_currentStats];

            if (self.onCloseBlock)
                self.onCloseBlock();

            [self removeFromParentAndCleanup:YES];
        }
    }
```

12. Add a method used to validate the player name as follows:

```
-(BOOL)validatePlayerName:(NSString *)playerName
{
    BOOL isEmpty = ([playerName length] != 0);

    if (!isEmpty)
    {
        _validateResult.visible = YES;
        _validateResult.string = @"Player name cannot be empty!";
    }
    else
    {
        _validateResult.visible = NO;
    }

    return isEmpty;
}
```

13. Finally, add a method to swallow touches:

```
-(void)touchBegan:(UITouch *)touch withEvent:(UIEvent *)event
{
    //swallow touch
}
```

14. Now, open the `WinLoseDialog.m` file and import the `HighscoreDialog.h` and `HighscoreManager.h` headers:

```
#import "HighscoreDialog.h"
#import "HighscoreManager.h"
```

15. After that, add the code to display the highscore dialog, in case the player beats someone's score. To do this, update the `initWithGameStats:` method as follows:

```
-(instancetype)initWithGameStats:(GameStats *)stats;
{
    if (self = [super init])
    {
        _currenStats = stats;

        [self setupModalDialog];

        if ([[HighscoreManager sharedHighscoreManager]
             isHighscore:_currenStats.score])
        {
            HighscoreDialog *hsDialog =
              [[HighscoreDialog alloc]
```

```
                initWithGameStats:_currenStats];

            hsDialog.onCloseBlock = ^{
                [self createDialogLayout];
            };
            [self addChild:hsDialog];
        }
        else
        {
            [self createDialogLayout];
        }
    }

    return self;
}
```

16. As a final change, we need to display highscores from `HighscoreManager` rather than test data in the `HighscoresScene` class. First of all, open the `HighscoresScene.m` file and import the `HighscoreManager.h` header:

```
#import "HighscoreManager.h"
```

17. Then, make the following changes in the `tableView:nodeForRowAtIndex:` and `tableViewNumberOfRows:` methods:

```
- (CCTableViewCell*)tableView:(CCTableView*)tableView
nodeForRowAtIndex:(NSUInteger) index
{
    //1
    GameStats *highscore =
     [[[HighscoreManager sharedHighscoreManager]
        getHighScores] objectAtIndex:index];
    NSString *playerName = highscore.playerName;
    int score = highscore.score;

     //..skipped..
}

- (NSUInteger) tableViewNumberOfRows:(CCTableView*) tableView
{
    return [[HighscoreManager sharedHighscoreManager]
              getHighScores].count;
}
```

18. Build and run the game. Play several times and make some highscores. Then, check the highscores table and try to beat them!

Of course, it is hard to score different amount of points if you adjusted `_birdsToSpawn` in the `GameScene` class to spawn only one bird for `WinLoseDialog` testing. You can adjust this value to a different number as well as other parameters such as the time between the birds spawned and their speed, until you are pleased with the game difficulty.

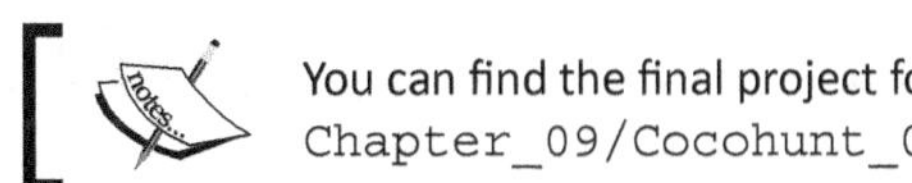

You can find the final project for this chapter in the `Chapter_09/Cocohunt_09_Final` folder.

What just happened?

We have just added everything that is required to create a local highscores table. Later in the book, in *Chapter 12, Standing Out – Integrating Game Center and In-App Purchases*, we will see how to use Game Center to share your highscores online, but for now, let's review the changes we've made to each file.

We added the `HighscoreManager` class to store and manage the highscores. It is a common practice to create a singleton to manage some specific data of the game. The methods in the `HighscoreManager` class should be very self-explanatory, but let's view a short description of what each method does:

- `getHighScores`: This method returns all highscores that are currently on record. Currently, we store a maximum of five highscores, but this can be easily changed. Also, right now, all highscores are removed when the game is restarted, but we're not going to fix this since we'll switch to Game Center anyway.
- `isHighscore`: This method checks if the current score is the highscore. We used this method to check if we should display the dialog to enter a new highscore.
- `addHighScore`: This method adds a new highscore while keeping the highscores table ordered and limiting the highscore's count.

After we created a class to manage the highscores, we needed to create a dialog to enter the new highscores. This is why we have created the `HighscoreDialog` dialog.

In this dialog, we only have a text field and an **OK** button. To display the text field, we have used the `CCTextField` class. I am sure you are already more than familiar with how we created the button, so let's concentrate on the `CCTextField` class.

This control creates a text field, which you can use to ask a player to enter some text information. Since, by default, a text field has no background design, we used the `highscore_dialog_textfield.png` image as a background. We also used the size of the image to set the size of the text field.

Adding some padding is required to make the text look better. Don't interfere with the edges of the background image.

To get or set the text field's value, we used the `string` property. Since we require the player to enter a name, we set it to the `Player1` value initially and also validate that the player does not try to submit an empty string as a player name. In this case, we show an error label.

The final change was made in `WinLoseDialog`. We simply checked if the current score is a highscore, and then, before displaying `WinLoseDialog` itself, we displayed `HighscoreDialog` to add the player's name. This time, we also used the `onCloseBlock` block to be notified when `HighscoreDialog` is closed, and we then continued and displayed the `WinLoseDialog` dialog.

Have a go hero

There are lots of things you can try to improve in the current look and feel of the game. Here is a list of some of them that come to mind:

- Currently, dialogs just pop up immediately on the screen. Make them appear by animating their movement with Cocos2D actions. For example, make them scale up, such as the win and lose labels, or slide from the left- or right-side of the screen.

To make the dialog slide from the top, just create it offscreen and run `CCActionMoveTo` to move it to the desired position. To make it pop out, create the initial dialog with `scale` set to `0.01f` and use `CCActionScaleTo` just as we did with the **You Win!** label. In both cases, using an easing action can make the animation much more realistic.

- Display the **No Highscores** label instead of the table view when there are no highscores to display.

To do this, simply add a label with the **No Highscores** text and check the highscores count inside the `init` method. If there are no highscores, display the label and hide the table view, and if there are some highscores, hide the label and display the table view.

- Save the name that the player entered somewhere in the `HighscoreManager` class. Next time, set the text field in `HighscoreDialog` to it, instead of the `Player1` name always appearing.

> You can save the name in an instance variable in `HighscoreDialog` or even save it in user defaults to persist the player name between the game restarts.

- Gather some additional statistics about the player. For example, you can gather how many consecutive birds the player hits before missing (hot streak!).

Pop quiz

Q1. Which properties can be set using normalized units?

1. `position`
2. `contentSize`
3. `position` and `contentSize`
4. None, you can only specify `position` and `contentSize` in points

Q2. What is the best method of the scene to start spawning enemies, make the player character run, and so on, if you are using a transition to display the scene?

1. `onEnter`
2. `onExitTransitionDidStart`
3. `onEnterTransitionDidFinish`
4. `init`

Q3. How many states with different background images can have `CCButton`?

1. 0
2. 1
3. 2
4. 3

Summary

In this chapter, we spent a lot of time reviewing Cocos2D classes that can help your game make a two-way dialog with the player. After completing all sections of this chapter, you should be more than familiar with the main Cocos2D user interface controls and know how to combine them to create a convenient user interface.

You should never underestimate the significance of creating convenient user interfaces in your game. Just as I mentioned earlier, it is almost as important as your game's mechanics. Of course, we didn't spend too much time polishing things and working on the user interface in this chapter since we already spent a lot of time on it in the previous chapters.

However, I would say that the reward is that after all the changes we have made in this chapter, this looks like a completed game! It may be a simple one; nonetheless, it has all the basic components in place. Of course, it requires some polishing, and there are lots of things to improve, but after completing the game so far, you can say that you can create Cocos2D games.

In the next chapter, we are going to review physics engine integration in order to make more complicated games. However, many popular games in App Store don't use anything outside of the scope that we have already covered.

10
Physics

There are many games that are great without any physics or with some basic or completely unrealistic physics. However, there is something attractive in games that have realistic physics. In this chapter, we're going to review how to integrate a physics engine in our game and get some nice physics almost effortlessly, well, at least when compared to implementing the physics simulation yourself.

In this chapter, we're going to review following topics:

- Creating a physics node and physics bodies
- Using physics bodies properties
- Handling and filtering collisions
- Using joints to connect physics objects
- Applying forces and impulses

Creating a physics world

In this part of the chapter, we're going to create a new level where the hunter will regret that he made the birds angry for shooting some arrows at them. In this level, the birds will drop stones and the hunter will need to dodge them.

We will use a Cocos2D-integrated physics engine called **Chipmunk** to simulate the physics, handle collisions, and so on. However, first things first. To create physics objects and simulate physics, we need to create a physics world, or a physics node as it is called in Cocos2D.

The previous versions of Cocos2D supported two physics engines: Box2D and Chipmunk. In the third version (v3), the choice was made in favor of Chipmunk. This allowed making a tighter integration, and now it is much easier to start using physics in your Cocos2D game. However, the main concepts covered in this chapter are similar to all physics engines, so don't worry, you can decide later which physics engine to use in your games.

You can find out more about the Chipmunk physics engine at `https://chipmunk-physics.net`.

Time for action – creating a game level with physics

Let's start by creating a new level in our game. To do this, we'll need to add one more scene to the project and add some resources that we're going to use in this scene. Perform the following steps:

1. Open the **Cocohunt** Xcode project and create a new group in `Resources` group called `PhysicsLevel`.

You can continue adding code to the project you have after completing the previous chapter or take the final project of the previous chapter from the book's supporting files in the `Chapter_09/Cocohunt_09_Final` folder and use it as a starter project.

You can download book's supporting files from `www.packtpub.com/support`.

2. Then, open the book's supporting files from the `Chapter_10/Assets/PhysicsSpritesheet/result` folder and add the `.png` and `.plist` files in the `PhysicsLevel` group. These are the two spritesheets (Retina and non-Retina) that contain all the sprites we're going to use in this chapter.

The `.tps` files are the `TexturePacker` project files and are provided only for reference, so you can ignore them. If you want, you can create spritesheets yourself; just use the files from the `hd` folder to create the `physics_level-hd` spritesheet and the files from the `sd` folder to create the `physics_level` spritesheet.

3. Create a new scene in the `Scenes` group and call it `PhysicsScene`.
4. Open the `PhysicsScene.h` file and import the `cocos2d.h` header file:

```
#import "cocos2d.h"
```

5. After this, open the `PhysicsScene.m` file and add the following instance variables:

```
@implementation PhysicsScene
{
    CCPhysicsNode *_physicsNode;
    CCSpriteBatchNode *_batchNodeMain;
}
```

6. Add the `createPhysicsNode` method using the following code:

```
-(void)createPhysicsNode
{
    //1
    _physicsNode = [CCPhysicsNode node];

    //2
    _physicsNode.gravity = ccp(0,-250);

    //3
    _physicsNode.debugDraw = YES;

    //4
    [self addChild:_physicsNode];
}
```

7. We need to create a sprite batch node to be able to use spritesheets. To do this, add the `createBatchNodes` method using the following code:

```
-(void)createBatchNodes
{
    [[CCSpriteFrameCache sharedSpriteFrameCache]
      addSpriteFramesWithFile:@"physics_level.plist"];

    _batchNodeMain = [CCSpriteBatchNode
      batchNodeWithFile:@"physics_level.png"];

    [_physicsNode addChild:_batchNodeMain];
}
```

8. Now, let's add a few sprites, but before this, let's define the z-order for them to ensure that everything is displayed correctly. To do so, add the following `#define` statements right before the `@implementation` line:

```
#define kBackgroundZ     10
#define kObjectsZ        20
```

In this chapter, we're going to use the `#define` statement for the z-order values as they are also used sometimes, so you should be aware of this if you read other people's code.

9. Scroll down and add a method that adds a background image called `addBackground`, as shown in the following code:

```
- (void) addBackground
{
    CGSize viewSize = [CCDirector sharedDirector].viewSize;

    CCSprite *bg =
      [CCSprite spriteWithImageNamed:@"physics_level_bg.png"];
    bg.position = ccp(viewSize.width * 0.5f,
                      viewSize.height * 0.5f);
    [_batchNodeMain addChild:bg z:kBackgroundZ];
}
```

10. Then, we will add a method that will spawn a stone. Add a method called `spawnStone`, as shown in the following code:

```
- (void) spawnStone
{
    //1
    CCSprite *stone =
      [CCSprite spriteWithImageNamed:@"stone.png"];

    //2
    float radius = stone.contentSizeInPoints.width * 0.5f;

    //3
    CCPhysicsBody *stoneBody = [CCPhysicsBody
                                bodyWithCircleOfRadius:radius
                         andCenter:stone.anchorPointInPoints];

    //4
    stoneBody.mass = 10.0f;

    //5
    stoneBody.type = CCPhysicsBodyTypeDynamic;

    //6
    stone.physicsBody = stoneBody;

    //7
    [_batchNodeMain addChild:stone z:kObjectsZ];

    //8
    CGSize viewSize = [CCDirector sharedDirector].viewSize;
    stone.position = ccp(viewSize.width * 0.5f,
                         viewSize.height * 0.9f);
}
```

11. Of course, we need to call all the methods that we've just added. To do this, add the `onEnter` and `onEnterTransitionDidFinish` methods at the top, before all the other methods, as shown in the following code:

```
-(void)onEnter
{
    [super onEnter];

    [self createPhysicsNode];
    [self createBatchNodes];
    [self addBackground];
}

-(void)onEnterTransitionDidFinish
{
    [super onEnterTransitionDidFinish];

    [self spawnStone];
}
```

12. To see our scene, we need to add the code to load the scene from the level selection screen. Open the `LevelSelectScene.m` file and import the `PhysicsScene.h` header using the following line of code:

```
#import "PhysicsScene.h"
```

13. Then, make the following changes to the `levelTapped:` method:

```
-(void)levelTapped:(id)sender
{
    NSString *levelName = ((CCButton*)sender).name;
    if ([levelName isEqualToString:kLevelHunting])
    {
        //..skipped..
    }
    else if ([levelName isEqualToString:kLevelDodging])
    {
        PhysicsScene *scene =
          [[PhysicsScene alloc] init];
        CCTransition *transition =
          [CCTransition
            transitionCrossFadeWithDuration:1.0f];
        [[CCDirector sharedDirector] replaceScene:scene
                                   withTransition:transition];
    }
```

```
        else
        {
            CCLOG(@"Level not implemented: %@", levelName);
        }
    }
```

14. Build and run the game. Press **Start** and then select the **Dodging** level. You should see a stone falling from the top of the screen, as shown in the following screenshot:

The falling stone

I encourage you to check the spritesheet image that we've added into the `PhysicsLevel` group in `Resources` and see that there is no red circle around the stone here. What is shown in the preceding screenshot is the result of the debug draw that we've activated. We will discuss this in a moment.

What just happened?

We've just added one more level to our game. In this level, we're going to use some physics, and have already seen some of it in action. As you can see, we didn't write the code that changes the position of the stone, but it falls down due to gravity.

Let's start with a simplified explanation on how physics engines are integrated with Cocos2D.

Understanding physics bodies

The most important thing to understand at the beginning is that a physics engine works separately from a rendering engine. This means that while Cocos2D works with nodes, sprites, and so on, a physics engine such as Chipmunk works with shapes, bodies, forces, and collisions.

Think of a physics world as an alternate reality where each object is linked with its visual representation (for example, a sprite).

This makes much more sense if you remember that all sprites are just rectangles with transparent areas in them. This means that even if you have some complicated object displayed on the screen, it is not easy to automatically understand the shape of the actual object. The following is a figure from *Chapter 5, Starting the Action*:

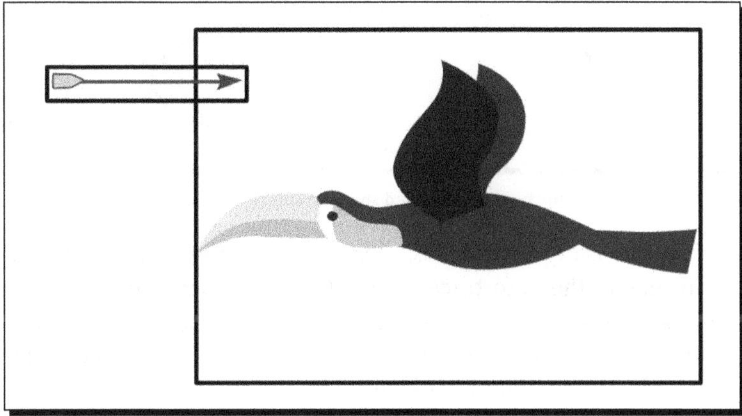

It is easy for us humans to see the actual shape of the bird, but it is quite hard to detect the correct shape of the bird automatically. Even if we create the actual pixel-perfect shape, it will be very complicated and will be hard to detect collisions with.

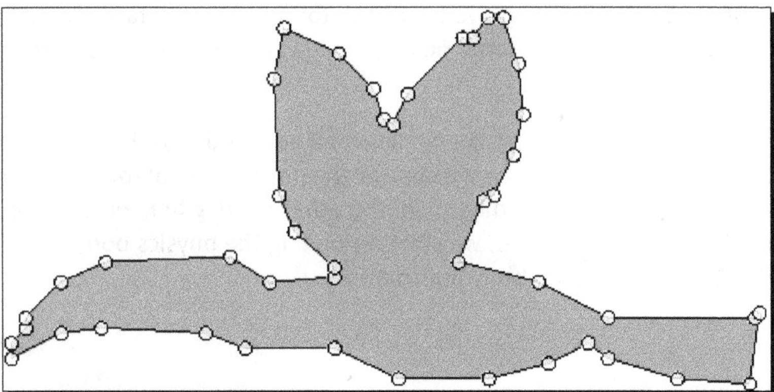

An auto-traced bird shape in the PhysicsEditor application

This is why, instead of detecting shapes from images, we simply leave Cocos2D to work with rectangles and specify physics bodies using simplified shapes. For example, we can use an oval shape to represent the bird, as shown in the following figure:

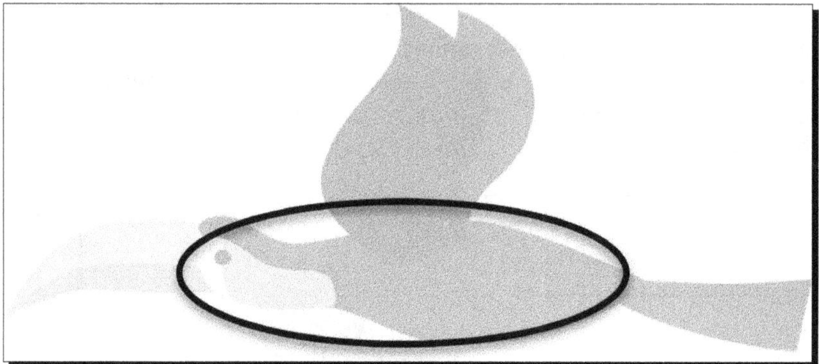

A much more simplified shape to simulate the bird

Just imagine how much easier it is to check whether two birds collide (intersect) using the simplified shape instead of the auto-traced one. Also, the arrow won't hit the bird's wings, beak, or tail, and that's okay in most cases. If we need a more accurate physics body, we can create it using a polygon shape (still not pixel perfect, but closer to the image) or even create a body that consists of several different shapes.

Linking physics bodies with Cocos2D nodes

So, we have physics bodies represented by shapes and Cocos2D sprites (or other nodes). However, we want changes that are applied to physics bodies to be applied to sprites and vice versa. For example, when the physics body is falling, we want the stone sprite to fall too; when the stone body is rotating, we want the stone sprite to rotate too. In addition, when we move the stone sprite to some position, we want the physics body to move to that position too.

To do this, we created the `CCPhysicsBody` class and assigned it to the `physicsBody` property of the sprite. This way, when we change the position or rotation of the sprite, it will update its `physicsBody` correspondingly. On the other hand, when we add the sprite to the special node called `CCPhysicsNode`, we start simulating the physics body and the sprite will also be updated using the physics body information.

The following is a diagram that illustrates this point:

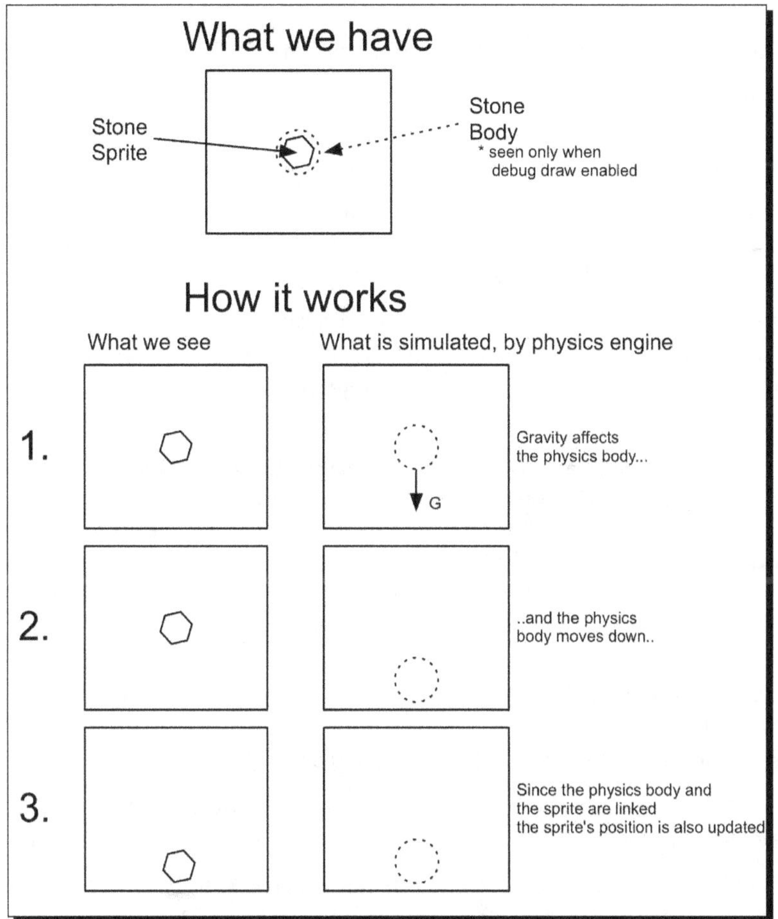

Note that steps **2** and **3** occur almost simultaneously, so normally the physics body and the node have the same transform (position and rotation). I just wanted to show the order of things.

Of course, if you change the sprite position using its `position` property, then things work the other way around, and the position of the physics body is updated.

As you can see, a physics engine works with its own objects, and in fact, they are not visualized in any way and are simply results of calculations, matrices, vectors, and so on. Unless you don't enable debug drawing, which will simply draw everything, the physics engine normally just stores in variables.

I hope this makes things at least a bit clearer and we can return to our code.

Let's review the `spawnStone` method, where we created the stone sprite and the stone physics body:

1. Here, we created the sprite as we did many times before.
2. To simulate the stone, we used the circle shape, as it is very close to the actual stone shape. Here, we've calculated the radius. The radius will be half the width of the stone sprite. This will create a circle inscribed within the bounding box of a sprite.
3. We used the `bodyWithCircleOfRadius:` method to construct a physics body using the radius and the center of the circle. Note that the center point we specified is in node space and uses points.
4. We set the body of the stone to `10` units. Physics in Cocos2D doesn't use an international system of units (SI), units such as meters or kilograms. Instead, you only set values relative to another objects.

What this means is that instead of calculating everything in some absolute units, you just set things relative to some other objects. For example, if you have a car with a mass of 100 units, then you should set the human weight to something around 5.5 units (if a car is around 1500 kg, then a typical man is around 80 kg). In most cases, you just play with these values until it feels realistic.

5. We set the body type to the `CCPhysicsBodyTypeDynamic` type. This means that our body is affected by forces such as gravity and collisions with other objects. We will discuss body types in the *Detecting and filtering collisions* section.
6. We assigned a physics body to the sprite. This way, we've attached the sprite and the physics body.
7. We added the sprite to the batch node, as the stone sprite is contained in the spritesheet. However, if we check the `createBatchNodes` method, we will see that the batch node was added to `_physicsNode`, as follows:

   ```
   [_physicsNode addChild:_batchNodeMain];
   ```

   This makes the stone sprite an indirect descendant of the physics node, which is totally okay.

As we can see, the node with the physics body doesn't have to be a direct child of `CCPhysicsNode`. However, if we try to add the node that has the physics body to the node without the physics node as ancestor, we'll get an error: **A CCNode with an attached CCPhysicsBody must be added as a descendant of a CCPhysicsNode.**

At this point, we should have a stone with the physics body added to the batch node, which in turn is added to the physics node.

It is time to review the createPhysicsNode method, which created the physics node itself. The method is very small and should be pretty straightforward. This is why we left it for the end:

1. We created the physics node using the node factory method. You probably remember that this is same as if we'd used alloc and init, but is just a little shorter.
2. We set the gravity vector to point down and have a magnitude of 250 units. The value of 250 was just picked after some experimenting. I assume it is clear why the gravity vector is pointing down.
3. Set the debug draw. Setting the debugDraw to YES enables drawing of the physics bodies and other physics objects. The red circle that you see above the stone in the earlier screenshot which shows that the stone falling is the circle body that we created using the bodyWithCircleOfRadius: method and is attached to the stone sprite.
4. We then added the physics node to the scene. This will be the only direct child of the scene. We're going to add batch nodes to the physic node and sprites to batch nodes, but no other nodes will be added to the scene itself.

Don't worry if something is unclear. The only thing important to understand right now is that there is a special node called CCPhysicsNode. If you want physics simulation, you have to create this node, add it to the scene, and add all the sprites that you want to have physics in to this node. To enable physics for the sprite, you have to create a physics body and attach it to the sprite before adding the sprite to the physics node.

Time for action – adding ground to the scene

Most of the times you'll want your object to stay on the screen instead of falling into the abyss. So, let's add some ground that will stop the stone from falling further. Refer to the following steps:

1. Open the PhysicsScene.m file and add the _ground instance variable:

```
@implementation PhysicsScene
{
    //..skipped..

    CCSprite *_ground;
}
```

2. Then, before adding the ground sprite, add one more z-order `#define` statement, between `kBackgroundZ` and `kObjectsZ` as shown in the following code:

```
#define kBackgroundZ     10
#define kGroundZ         15
#define kObjectsZ        20
```

3. Now, add the `addGround` method as follows:

```
-(void)addGround
{
    //1
    _ground = [CCSprite spriteWithImageNamed:@"ground.png"];

    //2
    CGRect groundRect;
    groundRect.origin = CGPointZero;
    groundRect.size = _ground.contentSize;

    //3
    CCPhysicsBody *groundBody =
      [CCPhysicsBody bodyWithRect:groundRect cornerRadius:0];

    //4
    groundBody.type = CCPhysicsBodyTypeStatic;

    //5
    groundBody.elasticity = 1.5f;

    //6
    _ground.physicsBody = groundBody;

    //7
    CGSize viewSize = [CCDirector sharedDirector].viewSize;
    _ground.anchorPoint = ccp(0.5f, 0);
    _ground.position = ccp(viewSize.width * 0.5f, 0);

    //8
    [_batchNodeMain addChild:_ground z:kGroundZ];
}
```

4. Add a call to the `addGround` method at the end of the `onEnter` method as shown in the following code:

```
-(void)onEnter
{
    //..skipped..

    [self addGround];
}
```

5. Open the `AppDelegate.m` file and import the `PhysicsScene.h` header using the following line of code:

```
#import "PhysicsScene.h"
```

6. Replace the `startScene` method with the following code:

```
-(CCScene *)startScene
{
    return [[PhysicsScene alloc] init];
}
```

This last step is optional, but it will save us a few seconds at each game launch by displaying the `PhysicsScene` class without the need to start and select it. You often want to make the scene you're currently working on as the start scene so that you don't have to navigate through the menu and level selection scenes at each launch. Of course, before releasing, you need to set your real start scene.

7. Build and run the game. This time, the ground stops the stone from falling into the abyss.

You can set the `_physicsNode.debugDraw` property to `NO` in the `PhysicsScene.m` file to see the stone and the ground without the red circle and rectangle over them. However, you should turn it on after each new object is added to see whether the physics body is added and positioned correctly.

What just happened?

Okay, we've created the stone and the ground, and it took us less than seven days. Pretty good!

The only interesting part is the `addGround` method, so let's review it:

1. Once again, we started by creating a sprite.
2. This time we wanted the physics body shape to be exactly as the ground image rectangle, so we created a rectangle using `contentSize` of the ground sprite.
3. We created the physics body using the `bodyWithRect:` method, which can be used to create rectangle-shaped bodies. You can also set the corner radius if you want a rounder rectangle.

The `bodyWithRect:` method takes the `CGRect` parameter, which not only has the size of the rectangle but also the origin point. This is why we had to create the `groundRect` variable in the previous step.

4. We then set the body type to the `CCPhysicsBodyTypeStatic` type. This means that a force or collision with other object does not affect the body. In other words, it is immovable unless you change its position manually.
5. We set the ground to `elasticity` to make the stone bounce when it hits the ground.
6. We attached the physics body to the ground sprite.
7. We positioned the ground at the bottom of the screen.
8. Finally, we added the ground to the batch node.

This was very similar to adding the stone, except that we used a rectangular shape and set a few properties to other values.

As `CCPhysicsBody` is used to represent all physics bodies; it has many properties to configure the body and make it different from other bodies. By modifying the properties (for example, `mass`, `density`, `friction`, and so on), you can modify the body's behavior during the simulation. All properties are described really well in the Cocos2D documentation, so I'm not going to repeat them here, except a few important ones such as the `type` property.

You can access the Cocos2D documentation right from the Xcode project by selecting **Documentation and API Reference** in the **Help** panel right within Xcode. Then, you can search for the `CCPhysicsBody` class reference. Alternatively you can visit the link: `http://www.cocos2d-iphone.org/docs/api/Classes/CCPhysicsBody.html`.

The `type` property can be either static (`CCPhysicsBodyTypeStatic`) or dynamic (`CCPhysicsBodyTypeDynamic`). The static body is immovable. Static bodies are often used to represent ground, walls, platforms, and so on. The dynamic body is affected by forces, gravity, and collisions. A good example of dynamic bodies is bowling pins, falling stones, and so on.

In some physics engines, there is a third type called kinematic. Kinematic bodies are not affected by forces, gravity, or collisions, but are moved using the code (for example, you change their position in the `update:` method). In other words, if you take the static body and make it move from the code, you can call it a kinematic body.

In our case, we have the dynamic stone, which falls down due to the gravity, and the static ground, which is not affected by the gravity and doesn't move an inch when it is hit by the stone.

Have a go hero

It might seem that there can be no fun playing with only stone and ground, but the following is a list of things that you can do with only these two objects:

- You can repeat Galileo's experiments and throw stones with different mass from the same height and see if they really fall at the same speed.
- Change the elasticity property of the ground and the stone. Create several stones with different elasticity.
- Increase the radius of the stone physics body three times. This will help you see that a physics body can be completely different from the sprite it's attached to.
- Add the code to spawn the stone at the point where you touch the screen. Build a pile of stones.
- Add a second ground at the top and set both grounds' elasticity to some high values so that the stone bounces between the two grounds.

Time for action – adding the hunter

It is time to add the hunter back to the game. However, this time the birds will have fun. So, instead of shooting the birds, the hunter will be running around and dodging the stones that they throw at him.

There will be quite a lot of code to add, so here is a brief explanation of what we want to do. We want to create a new class for our hunter, as we cannot reuse the old `Hunter` class. Our new hunter class, `PhysicsHunter`, will have two animations: idle and running. We will control the hunter by touching the screen. When we touch the screen on the left-hand side, the hunter will run to the left, and when we touch the right-hand side of the screen, the hunter will run to the right. When we don't touch the screen, the idle animation should be played. Let's start:

1. Create a new **Objective-C class** in the `GameObjects` group. Name the class `PhysicsHunter` and make it a subclass of `CCSprite`.
2. Open the `PhysicsHunter.h` file and replace its contents with following code:

```
#import "cocos2d.h"

typedef NS_ENUM(NSUInteger, PhysicsHunterState)
{
```

```
    PhysicsHunterStateIdle,
    PhysicsHunterStateRunning,
    PhysicsHunterStateDead
};

typedef NS_ENUM(NSInteger, PhysicsHunterRunDirection)
{
    PhysicsHunterRunDirectionLeft,
    PhysicsHunterRunDirectionRight
};

@interface PhysicsHunter : CCSprite

@property (nonatomic, readonly) PhysicsHunterState state;

-(void)runAtDirection:(PhysicsHunterRunDirection)direction;

-(void)stop;

@end
```

3. Then, open the `PhysicsHunter.m` file and replace its contents with the following code:

```
#import "PhysicsHunter.h"
#import "CCAnimation.h"

#define kHunterMovementSpeed    90.0f

@implementation PhysicsHunter
{
    CCAnimation *_runAnimation;
    CCAnimation *_idleAnimation;

    PhysicsHunterState _state;
    PhysicsHunterRunDirection _runningDirection;
}

-(instancetype)init
{
    if (self =
         [super initWithImageNamed:@"physics_hunter_idle_00.png"])
    {
        _state = PhysicsHunterStateIdle;

        [self createAnimations];
        [self createPhysicsBody];
    }
```

```
    return self;
}

-(void)onEnter
{
    [super onEnter];
    [self playIdleAnimation];
}

-(void)createAnimations
{
    NSMutableArray *runFrames = [NSMutableArray array];
    for (int i = 0; i < 10; i++)
    {
        CCSpriteFrame *frame =
          [CCSpriteFrame frameWithImageNamed:
            [NSString
            stringWithFormat:@"physics_hunter_run_%.2d.png",i
        ]];
        [runFrames addObject:frame];
    }
    _runAnimation = [CCAnimation
                     animationWithSpriteFrames:runFrames
                                         delay:0.075f];

    NSMutableArray *idleFrames = [NSMutableArray array];
    for (int i = 0; i < 3; i++)
    {
        CCSpriteFrame *frame =
        [CCSpriteFrame frameWithImageNamed:
          [NSString
            stringWithFormat:@"physics_hunter_idle_%.2d.png",i
        ]];
        [idleFrames addObject:frame];
    }
    _idleAnimation = [CCAnimation
                      animationWithSpriteFrames:idleFrames
                                          delay:0.2f];
}

-(void)createPhysicsBody
{
    CGPoint from = ccp(self.contentSizeInPoints.width * 0.5f,
                    self.contentSizeInPoints.height * 0.15f);
```

```
    CGPoint to = ccp(self.contentSizeInPoints.width * 0.5f,
                     self.contentSizeInPoints.height * 0.85f);
    CCPhysicsBody *body = [CCPhysicsBody
                           bodyWithPillFrom:from
                                         to:to
                               cornerRadius:8.0f];
    body.allowsRotation = NO;

    self.physicsBody = body;
}

-(void)runAtDirection:(PhysicsHunterRunDirection)direction;
{
    if (_state != PhysicsHunterStateIdle)
        return;

    _runningDirection = direction;
    _state = PhysicsHunterStateRunning;

    [self playRunAnimation];
}

-(void)stop
{
    if (_state != PhysicsHunterStateRunning)
        return;

    _state = PhysicsHunterStateIdle;
    [self playIdleAnimation];
}

-(void)playRunAnimation
{
    [self stopAllActions];

    if (_runningDirection == PhysicsHunterRunDirectionRight)
        self.flipX = NO;
    else
        self.flipX = YES;

    CCActionAnimate *animateRun =
      [CCActionAnimate actionWithAnimation:_runAnimation];
    CCActionRepeatForever *runForever =
      [CCActionRepeatForever actionWithAction:animateRun];
```

```
    [self runAction:runForever];
}

-(void)playIdleAnimation
{
    [self stopAllActions];

    CCActionAnimate *animateIdle =
      [CCActionAnimate actionWithAnimation:_idleAnimation];
    CCActionRepeatForever *idleForever =
      [CCActionRepeatForever actionWithAction:animateIdle];
    [self runAction:idleForever];
}

-(void)fixedUpdate:(CCTime)dt
{
    if (_state == PhysicsHunterStateRunning)
    {
        CGPoint newVelocity = self.physicsBody.velocity;

        if (_runningDirection ==
                PhysicsHunterRunDirectionRight)
            newVelocity.x = kHunterMovementSpeed;
        else
            newVelocity.x = -1 * kHunterMovementSpeed;

        self.physicsBody.velocity = newVelocity;
    }
}
@end
```

4. Now, open the `PhysicsScene.m` file and import the `PhysicsHunter.h` header using the following line of code:

```
#import "PhysicsHunter.h"
```

5. Then, add the `_hunter` instance variable:

```
@implementation PhysicsScene
{
    //..skipped..
    PhysicsHunter *_hunter;
}
```

6. Add the `createHunter` method as follows. Note that we enable the user interaction here to handle touches:

```
-(void)createHunter
{
    _hunter = [[PhysicsHunter alloc] init];

    CGSize viewSize = [CCDirector sharedDirector].viewSize;
    _hunter.anchorPoint = ccp(0.5f, 0);
    _hunter.position = ccp(viewSize.width * 0.5f,
                     _ground.contentSizeInPoints.height + 10);

    [_batchNodeMain addChild:_hunter z:kObjectsZ];

    self.userInteractionEnabled = YES;
}
```

7. Then, add a call to the `createHunter` method in the `onEnterTransitionDidFinish` method, as shown in the following code:

```
-(void)onEnterTransitionDidFinish
{
    //..skipped..
    [self createHunter];
}
```

8. Finally, add the `touchBegan` and `touchEnded` methods, as shown in the following code:

```
-(void)touchBegan:(UITouch *)touch withEvent:(UIEvent *)event
{
    CGPoint touchLocation = [touch locationInNode:self];
    CGSize viewSize = [CCDirector sharedDirector].viewSize;

    if (touchLocation.x >= viewSize.width * 0.5f)
        [_hunter
          runAtDirection:PhysicsHunterRunDirectionRight];
    else
        [_hunter runAtDirection:PhysicsHunterRunDirectionLeft];
}

-(void)touchEnded:(UITouch *)touch withEvent:(UIEvent *)event
{
    [_hunter stop];
}
```

9. Build and run the game. Control the hunter by touching the left- or right-hand side of the screen to run in the corresponding direction.

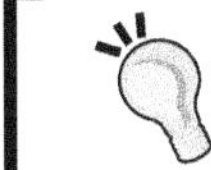

If you set `_physicsNode.debugDraw` to `NO` in the past, it will be better if you set it to `YES` now to see the pill shape of the hunter.

What just happened?

Phew, that was a lot of code. Don't worry, we're going to review it in detail. Let's start from the `PhysicsHunter` class.

This class has four instance variables. The `_runAnimation` and `_idleAnimation` variables will just store the animation data so that we don't have to load it each time.

The `_state` variable holds the current state of the hunter. The hunter can run, standstill, or be dead. The `_runningDirection` variable simply contains the direction in which the hunter is running—to the left or to the right.

In the `init` method, we used the `super` class's `initWithImageNamed:` method, as `PhysicsHunter` is a subclass of `CCSprite`. We used one of the frames of animation to initialize the hunter. In addition to this, we loaded the animations and created the physics body.

In `onEnter`, we simply started playing the idle animation, which was already loaded using the `createAnimations` method. The `createAnimations` method should be very familiar, so we won't review it.

The `createPhysicsBody` method should be also very similar to what we've done before, but in this case we used the pill shape, which works better for the player's character. Also, we set the `allowsRotation` property to `NO` as we don't want our hunter to fall during the physics simulation. This is a very useful property when you don't want your object rotated due to some forces or after colliding with other objects.

Here is the reason why the pill form works better to move characters. Refer to the following screenshot:

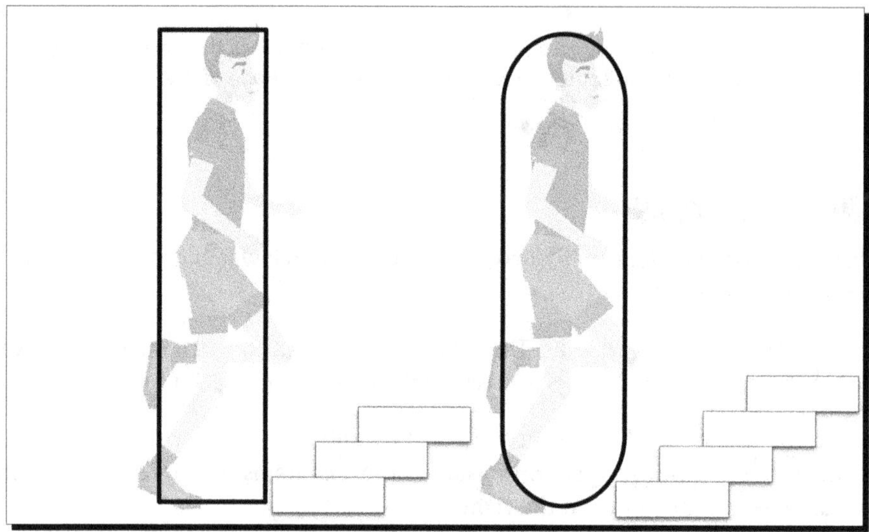

In the case of a rectangular body, the character will just stop pushing into the lower staircase rectangle because he can't rotate and fall, as he would normally do. While with a pill-shaped body, the character will move up along the stairs. Okay, let's get back to our code.

The `runAtDirection:` method is called when we touch the screen. In this method, we check whether we're in the correct state to switch to the running state. The only valid state is `PhysicsHunterStateIdle`, as we can't switch to the running state from the `PhysicsHunterStateDead` state. We're not filming the Running Dead, are we?

The only thing the `runAtDirection:` method does after checking the state is that it remembers the direction in which to run and starts playing the running animation.

The `stop` method is opposite to the `runAtDirection:` method. It is called when we lift the finger and simply changes the state to idle and starts playing the idle animation.

The `playRunAnimation` and `playIdleAnimation` methods simply stop all the running actions (the other animation) and start playing the corresponding animation. The only thing that `playRunAnimation` does in addition to this is flip the sprite horizontally to face the direction the hunter is running.

We're going to review the `fixedUpdate:` method later, so let's switch to the `PhysicsScene.m` file. There is not much to review.

In the `PhysicsScene.m` file, we added the code to create the `PhysicsHunter` class instance and add it to the scene. I doubt whether there is something that we didn't do before.

In the `touchBegin:` method, we check which side of the screen the player touches and call the `runAtDirection:` method to run in the corresponding direction, while in the `touchEnded:` method, we make the hunter stop.

Understanding the fixedUpdate: method

The `fixedUpdate:` method looks very familiar to the `update:` method, which we've used several times before. In fact, they are pretty similar. So, what is the difference?

The difference between them is that the `update:` method is called once per frame and the `fixedUpdate:` method is called at a constant rate. Don't see the difference? Let me explain.

The time passed between the `update:` method calls is variable, as it depends on the current frame rate. In other words, it can be 1 millisecond after the last `update:` call or 5 seconds in the case of a really bad frame rate.

The variable time step is okay if you're simply drawing something on the screen, but generally doesn't work well if you perform a physics simulation.

Imagine that in your game, you're shooting a bullet at a wall and you simulate physics using a variable time step. Each bullet is fired absolutely the same way (for example, the same starting speed, same angle, and so on; I mean that they are completely identical).

You fire your first bullet and it hits the wall. Then, you fire your second bullet, but this time, your frame rate drops for some reason (for example, a system process or even another thread in your game eats up some of your CPU time).

This leads to a big delay between the `update:` calls. Your second bullet just flies through the wall without hitting it because in the previous `update:` call, the bullet wasn't hitting the wall, and in the next `update:` call, the bullet has already passed the wall. Refer to the following diagram:

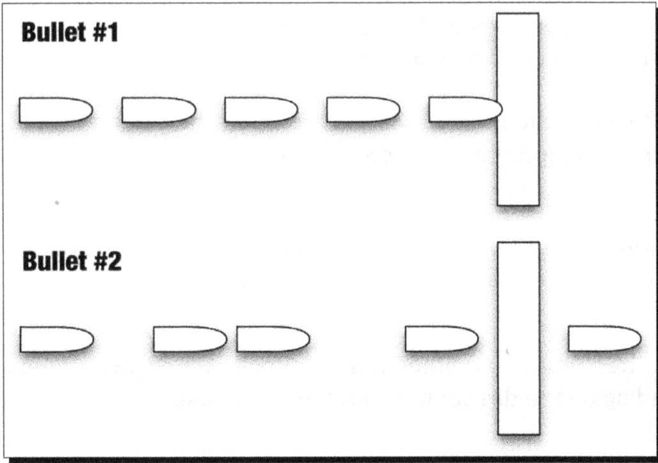

This is not what you expected. You expected that the two identically shot bullets will hit the wall at the same time and in the same place, but instead, the second bullet didn't even hit the wall.

Imagine this happening in a network game, where each instance of the game on different devices has its own simulation, and **Bullet #1** is simply simulated on your device, while **Bullet #2** is the same bullet simulated on your opponent's device.

Using the fixed time step makes your game much more reliable. Of course, it doesn't solve all the problems, but your physics simulation becomes much more consistent and repeatable (that is, if you record your actions when you win the level, you can play back them and will always win it).

Using a bullet as an example might not be the best idea. Your fixed time step might be still too big if your bullet is moving really fast. This is why for things such as bullets and lasers, it is often better to use the raytracing technique (that is, calculate the vector at the time of shooting the bullet to detect collision).

This is why there is a `fixedUpdate:` method. The `fixedUpdate:` method is called at a constant rate, and you should use this method to manipulate the physics object instead of the `update:` method.

The `dt` parameter of the `fixedUpdate:` method will have the same value at each call, even if your game freezes for a time longer than the fixed update interval. However, the exact value depends on the `CCSetupFixedUpdateInterval` configuration parameter that you can adjust in `AppDelegate`.

In other words, unless you change the `CCSetupFixedUpdateInterval` configuration option, the `dt` parameter will always be `0.016667` (1/60 of a second, which is the default value of `CCSetupFixedUpdateInterval`), and if your game freezes for a longer time, the `fixedUpdate:` method will be called multiple times to catch up.

Now that the existence of the `fixedUpdate:` method is a bit clearer, let's review what we're doing in our `fixedUpdate:` method in the `PhysicsHunter` class.

There is a great article about fixed time step at `http://gafferongames.com/game-physics/fix-your-timestep/`.

The code of the `fixedUpdate:` method is quite simple. We're just setting a new velocity for the hunter depending on the direction the hunter is running.

Setting the velocity is visually almost the same as updating the position of the hunter over time (for example, `newPosition += speed * dt`). After all, we've moved a bird by incrementing its position in one of the earlier chapters.

However, changing positions doesn't impact the properties of the physics body, and therefore, the physics engine doesn't understand that the body is in motion. For example, this means that the body won't move by inertia when you stop changing its position property, while we can clearly see that right now, the hunter moved using his `velocity` property and slides for some time due to inertia even after we lift our finger.

> When dealing with physics bodies, you should always try to manipulate them using physics properties (for example, set the velocity, apply forces and impulses, and so on).

I'm sure you've noticed a couple of problems with our hunter. If you run to the edge of the edge, he simply runs off the ground and falls into the abyss. Also, when you lift your finger (or release your mouse button), the hunter slides for some time due to inertia, as we've just discussed. Let's fix this.

Time for action – fixing the hunter movement

The good thing that comes from the fact that physics simulation and rendering are independent is that we can create physics bodies with just a few lines of code without any images, using just the `CCNode` class.

In this section, we're going to add the `addBoundaries` method, which will add two invisible physics bodies to the sides of the screen so that the hunter doesn't fall off the screen. In addition to this, we're going to adjust the friction of the hunter's physics body so that he doesn't slide too much.

1. Open the `PhysicsScene.m` file and add the `addBoundaries` method, as shown in the following code:

```
-(void)addBoundaries
{
    CGSize viewSize = [CCDirector sharedDirector].viewSize;
    CGRect boundRect =
      CGRectMake(0, 0, 20, viewSize.height * 0.25f);

    CCNode *leftBound = [CCNode node];
    leftBound.position =
      ccp(0, _ground.contentSize.height + 30);
    leftBound.contentSize = boundRect.size;
```

```
        CCPhysicsBody *leftBody =
          [CCPhysicsBody bodyWithRect:boundRect cornerRadius:0];
        leftBody.type = CCPhysicsBodyTypeStatic;
        leftBound.physicsBody = leftBody;

        [_physicsNode addChild:leftBound];

        CCNode *rightBound = [CCNode node];
        rightBound.contentSize = boundRect.size;
        rightBound.anchorPoint = ccp(1.0f, 0);
        rightBound.position = ccp(viewSize.width,
                                  leftBound.position.y);

        CCPhysicsBody *rightBody =
          [CCPhysicsBody bodyWithRect:boundRect cornerRadius:0];
        rightBody.type = CCPhysicsBodyTypeStatic;
        rightBound.physicsBody = rightBody;

        [_physicsNode addChild:rightBound];
    }
```

2. Then, add a call to the `addBoundaries` method at the end of the `onEnterTransitionDidFinish` method, as shown in the following code:

```
-(void)onEnterTransitionDidFinish
{
    //..skipped..
    [self addBoundaries];
}
```

3. Now, let's fix the hunter sliding. Open the `PhysicsHunter.m` file and find the `createPhysicsBody` method. Set the body friction as shown in the following line of code:

```
body.friction = 3.0f;
```

4. That's it. Build and run the game. Note that the hunter no longer slides too much when he stops running. Also, note the red rectangles on the sides of the level. Remember to enable `_physicsNode.debugDraw` to see them. As there are no images drawn, we only see physics bodies.

You can find a snapshot of the project at the this point in the `Chapter_10/Cocohunt_10_Physics_Scene` folder.

What just happened?

We've just added two physics bodies without any visible part. Note that the hunter's physics body penetrates the boundaries if you don't stop running. If we had made the boundaries too thin, the hunter would have overrun them at some point.

[You can check this yourself by decreasing the width of `boundRect`.]

Setting the `friction` property to a higher value decreased the slide time of the hunter. I think that's pretty obvious, and this is exactly what you would expect in the real world.

[The friction between two colliding bodies is calculated by multiplying their frictions. This way, setting `0` as the friction for a body will mean zero friction with any other bodies.]

For now, I think we've reviewed enough information about adding physics bodies, so let's continue to the fun part—collisions!

Detecting and filtering collisions

If we start the game right now and don't move the hunter, the stone will fall straight on his head. As we're not creating a game about some superhero, this should lead to some bad consequences for the hunter.

To be able to react to the stone falling on the hunter's head, we need to detect the collision between the hunter and the stone. Fortunately, it is quite easy to do so.

Time for action – detecting and ignoring collisions

It is time to detect when the stone hits the hunter. When the stone collides with the hunter, the player will lose.

In addition to this, we're going to detect when the stone hits the ground. In this case, we're going to ignore the collision and let the stone fall through the ground. We need to do this to avoid a lot of stones lying on the ground and hurting the hunter's legs. Just joking, he has shoes, right? The real reason is that the large number of stones on the level will simply block our hunter at some point. Refer to the following steps:

1. Open the `PhysicsHunter.m` file and in the `createPhysicsBody` method, set the `body.collisionType` property to `@"hunter"`, as shown in the following code:

```
-(void)createPhysicsBody
{
```

```
    //..skipped..

    body.collisionType = @"hunter";

    self.physicsBody = body;
}
```

2. Then, add the `die` method, which will be called when the stone hits the hunter, as shown in the following code:

```
-(void)die
{
    if (_state != PhysicsHunterStateDead)
    {
        CCParticleExplosion *explode =
          [CCParticleExplosion node];

        explode.texture =
          [CCTexture textureWithFile:@"feather.png"];
        explode.positionType = self.positionType;
        explode.position = self.position;
        [[CCDirector sharedDirector].runningScene
           addChild:explode];


        [self removeFromParentAndCleanup:YES];
    }

    _state = PhysicsHunterStateDead;
}
```

3. Switch to the `PhysicsHunter.h` header file and add the `die` method declaration so that we can call it from `PhysicsScene`, using the following line of code:

```
-(void)die;
```

4. After this, open the `PhysicsScene.h` file and make the `PhysicsScene` class conform to the `CCPhysicsCollisionDelegate` protocol, using the following line of code:

```
@interface PhysicsScene : CCScene<CCPhysicsCollisionDelegate>
```

5. Switch to the `PhysicsScene.m` file and add the following line to the `createPhysicsNode` method:

```
-(void)createPhysicsNode
{
    _physicsNode = [CCPhysicsNode node];
```

```
    _physicsNode.gravity = ccp(0,-250);

    _physicsNode.collisionDelegate = self;

    _physicsNode.debugDraw = YES;

    [self addChild:_physicsNode];
}
```

6. After this, find the `addGround` method. Set the `collisionType` property of `groundBody` to the `@"ground"` value, as shown in the following code:

```
-(void)addGround
{
    //..skipped..

    CCPhysicsBody *groundBody =
      [CCPhysicsBody bodyWithRect:groundRect cornerRadius:0];

    groundBody.collisionType = @"ground";

    groundBody.type = CCPhysicsBodyTypeStatic;

    //..skipped..
}
```

7. Then, in the `spawnStone` method, set the `stoneBody.collisionType` property to `@"stone"`, as shown in the following code:

```
-(void)spawnStone
{
    //..skipped..

    CCPhysicsBody *stoneBody = [CCPhysicsBody
                                   bodyWithCircleOfRadius:radius
                             andCenter:stone.anchorPointInPoints];

    stoneBody.collisionType = @"stone";

    stoneBody.mass = 10.0f;

    //..skipped..
}
```

8. Add the following two methods, which will be called when collisions occur:

```
-(BOOL)ccPhysicsCollisionBegin:(CCPhysicsCollisionPair *)pair
                         stone:(CCNode *)stone
                        ground:(CCNode *)ground
{
    return NO;
}

-(BOOL)ccPhysicsCollisionBegin:(CCPhysicsCollisionPair *)pair
                        hunter:(CCNode *)hunter
                         stone:(CCNode *)stone
{
    [_hunter die];
    return YES;
}
```

9. The final step is to add the ability to restart the scene after the hunter dies so that we can experiment without the need to relaunch the game. Find the `touchBegan:` method and add the following code right at the start of the method:

```
-(void)touchBegan:(UITouch *)touch withEvent:(UIEvent *)event
{
    if (_hunter.state ==  PhysicsHunterStateDead)
    {
        [[CCDirector sharedDirector]
          replaceScene:[PhysicsScene node]];
        return;
    }

    //..skipped..
}
```

10. Build and run the game. Stand still and let the stone hit the hunter. After this, restart the game by tapping anywhere on the screen and run away from the falling stone to see it falling through the ground.

You can find a snapshot of the project at this point in the `Chapter_10/Cocohunt_10_Collisions` folder.

What just happened?

Don't pay too much attention to the explosion particle system. We could have created some sort of animation or made the hunter blink and disappear, but as we already know how to do this, I have decided not to waste time on this and just use something to show that the hunter was hit.

Let's concentrate on the collision detection. Here's what we've done:

- We assigned different collision types to all of our objects using the `collisionType` property.
- We made `PhysicsScene` to conform to the `CCPhysicsCollisionDelegate` protocol and added two methods, one to handle the collisions between the hunter and the stone and the other for the collisions between the stone and the ground.
- We set `_physicsNode.collisionDelegate` to `self` (`PhysicsScene`) in order to get notified about collisions. This is also the reason to conform to `CCPhysicsCollisionDelegate` protocol.

All the three steps are required to be able to detect collisions. Let's start reviewing from the part where we set the `_physicsNode.collisionDelegate` to `self`.

```
_physicsNode.collisionDelegate = self;
```

The previous line of code tells the physics node that it should call the `PhysicsScene` method to notify it about collisions. To ensure that `PhysicsScene` can respond to the following methods, we made it conform to the `CCPhysicsCollisionDelegate` protocol.

This protocol has four optional methods, which are as follows:

- The `ccPhysicsCollisionBegin:` method that is called once when two bodies begin colliding. Here is its signature:

  ```
  (BOOL)ccPhysicsCollisionBegin:(CCPhysicsCollisionPair *)pair
                             typeA:(CCNode *)nodeA
                             typeB:(CCNode *)nodeB;
  ```

  If you return `NO` from this method, the collision will be ignored. We've done this in the case of the stone and ground collision, as we don't want the stone to collide with the ground.

- The `ccPhysicsCollisionPreSolve:` method that is called at every fixed step while two bodies are in contact. This method runs before the physics solver. If you return `NO` from this method, the collision is ignored for current time step. Refer to the following code:

  ```
  -(BOOL)
  ccPhysicsCollisionPreSolve:(CCPhysicsCollisionPair *)pair
  ```

```
                             typeA:(CCNode *)nodeA
                             typeB:(CCNode *)nodeB;
```

- The `ccPhysicsCollisionPostSolve:` method also runs at every fixed step while bodies are in contact. The only difference is that it runs after the physics solver. Refer to the following code:

```
-(void)
ccPhysicsCollisionPostSolve:(CCPhysicsCollisionPair *)pair
                            typeA:(CCNode *)nodeA
                            typeB:(CCNode *)nodeB;
```

- The `ccPhysicsCollisionSeparate:` method is called when two bodies stop colliding. Refer to the following code:

```
-(void)
ccPhysicsCollisionSeparate:(CCPhysicsCollisionPair *)pair
                           typeA:(CCNode *)nodeA
                           typeB:(CCNode *)nodeB;
```

Imagine the ball is thrown at the wall. When the ball touches the wall for the first time, the `ccPhysicsCollisionBegin:` method is called. This method is called only once.

Then, for the entire time the ball touches the wall, and this can last a few moments, the `ccPhysicsCollisionPreSolve:` and the `ccPhysicsCollisionPostSolve:` methods are called. These methods can be called multiple times during the time the ball collides with the wall.

Finally, when the ball bounces back off the wall, the `ccPhysicsCollisionSeparate:` method is called. This completes the life cycle of the collision.

It might seem strange that there are two different methods called while two bodies are colliding, the pre-solve and the post-solve methods. The pre-solve method is called before the physics solver runs, in other words, before the collision outcome is calculated. In the pre-solve method, you can influence the collision outcome by adjusting properties such as `density` and `friction`. As you probably guessed, the post-solve method is called after the physics solver runs. You cannot adjust the collision outcome anymore, but instead, you can get some of the calculated values such as the `totalKineticEnergy` and `totalImpulse` properties of `CCPhysicsCollisionPair`. For more information, you can take a look at the `CCPhysicsNode.h` header file in the Cocos2D sources or in the Cocos2D documentation.

If you were very attentive, you might have noticed two strange things: we have two `ccPhysicsCollisionBegin:` methods and both have a slightly different signature. The following are our methods (notice the highlighted parameter names):

```
-(BOOL)ccPhysicsCollisionBegin:(CCPhysicsCollisionPair *)pair
                          stone:(CCNode *)stone
                         ground:(CCNode *)ground
{
    return NO;
}

-(BOOL)ccPhysicsCollisionBegin:(CCPhysicsCollisionPair *)pair
                         hunter:(CCNode *)hunter
                          stone:(CCNode *)stone
{
    [_hunter die];
    return YES;
}
```

The following is the signature of the original `ccPhysicsCollisionBegin:` method:

```
-(BOOL)ccPhysicsCollisionBegin:(CCPhysicsCollisionPair *)pair
                          typeA:(CCNode *)nodeA
                          typeB:(CCNode *)nodeB;
```

Do you see the difference? Both of our methods have different parameter names. Instead of `typeA` and `typeB`, one method has the `stone` and the `ground` parameters and the other has the `hunter` and the `stone` parameters.

If you set a breakpoint in each method, you will see that one method is only called when the stone and the ground collide, and the other one only when the hunter and the stone collide. How does Cocos2D know about the stone, ground, and hunter collision types?

The answer is in the question itself. If you remember, we set the collision types of our objects, which are as follows (each line in its own method):

```
body.collisionType = @"hunter";        //in PhysicsHunter.m
stoneBody.collisionType = @"stone";  //in spawnStone (PhysicsScene)
groundBody.collisionType = @"ground";//in addGround (PhysicsScene)
```

This is where we set which body has which collision type and which method should be called when they collide. This might look tricky, especially if you haven't seen this technique before, but it is quite convenient.

If you have one object that collides with anything and you don't want to create a special method for each pair of possible collisions, you can use a `wildcard` parameter name as the last parameter (for example, `…stone:(CCNode*)stone wildcard:(CCNode*)wildcard`). This method will be called every time the stone collides with something.

Let's summarize. If you want to detect collisions between two objects, you must set the `collisionType` properties of their physics bodies to some string values. Then, you need to create a method with parameters named in the same way as the values you set the `collisionType` properties. Finally, you need to set the physics node `collisionDelegate` property so that that the method is called when the collision occurs (don't forget to make your scene conform to the `CCPhysicsCollisionDelegate` protocol).

Sensors

Sometimes, you still need to detect collision, but don't want the collision to affect your object. A good example is when your character is collecting coins. You want to know when the character is colliding with coin, to collect it, but you don't want your character to bounce back if he runs into the coin.

To achieve this, you can use the `sensor` property of the `CCPhysicsBody` class. If you set the `sensor` property to `YES`, you will still be notified about collisions, but physics bodies will pass through the sensor just as if the collision was ignored.

Time for action – filtering collisions using a collision mask

In the previous section, we learned how to detect and ignore collisions. However, creating a special method for each collision pair and returning `NO` to ignore each collision is not the best way, especially if you want to completely ignore the collision between two object types.

The approach shown previously works much better if you only need to filter some of the collisions. Then, you can have some kind of an `if` statement and return `NO` only for some object pairs.

So, let's see how we can filter collisions in a different way. We're going to set the `collisionCategories` property for the ground and the hunter and the `collisionMask` property for the stone physics bodies. Perform the following steps:

1. Open the `PhysicsScene.m` file and remove the following `ccPhysicsCollisionBegin:` method for the stone and the ground pair, the one where we return `NO`:

```
-(BOOL)ccPhysicsCollisionBegin:(CCPhysicsCollisionPair *)pair
                         stone:(CCNode *)stone
                        ground:(CCNode *)ground
```

Make sure that you leave a method that calls `[_hunter die];`.

2. Find the `addGround` method and set the `groundBody.collisionCategories` property as follows, right after where we set the collision type:

```
groundBody.collisionType = @"ground";
groundBody.collisionCategories = @[@"obstacles"];
```

3. Then, in the `spawnStone` method, set the `stoneBody.collisionMask` as follows:

```
stoneBody.collisionType = @"stone";
stoneBody.collisionMask = @[@"hunters"];
```

4. Finally, open the `PhysicsHunter.m` file and in the `createPhysicsBody` method, add the `collisionCategories` property, right after the line where we set the collision type:

```
body.collisionType = @"hunter";
body.collisionCategories = @[@"hunters"];
```

5. Build and run the game. Everything should work the same way; the stone should hit the hunter, but it should fall through the ground. The hunter should still not fall through the ground.

You can find a snapshot of the project at this point in the `Chapter_10/Cocohunt_10_CollisionMasks` folder.

What just happened?

We've used one more way to filter collisions. This time, instead of ignoring the collision in collision handler, we've set up a filter using `collisionMask` and `collisionCategories`.

Here's how it works. The `collisionCategories` property takes an array of categories (max 32) and makes the physics body a member of these categories. When you set the `collisionMask` property, you set the categories that you want to collide with.

In our case, we've put the hunter in the `hunters` category and the ground in the `obstacles` category. We also set the collision mask of the stone only to the `hunters` category. This way, the stone will collide with the hunter, but not with the ground.

An important thing to note is that by default, `collisionCategories` is set to `nil`, which means that the physics body is the member of all possible categories. So, if you remove the following line of code, the stone will start colliding with the ground because the ground will be a member of all categories, including the `hunters` category:

```
groundBody.collisionCategories = @[@"obstacles"];
```

This might not be what you expected, so keep this in mind.

Time for action – filtering collisions using collision groups

Sometimes, setting up collision categories and collision masks can be a little bit more than you need, especially when you only need to filter the collision between two object types; just like in our case!

Let's quickly review one more method to filter collisions using the `collisionGroup` property:

1. First of all, we need to remove the code that sets collision categories and the collision mask. In the `PhysicsHunter.m` file, find the `createPhysicsBody` method and remove the following line:

   ```
   body.collisionCategories = @[@"hunters"];
   ```

2. Then, open the `PhysicsScene.m` file and remove the following line from the `addGround` method:

   ```
   groundBody.collisionCategories = @[@"obstacles"];
   ```

   Also, remove the following line of code from the `spawnStone` method:

   ```
   stoneBody.collisionMask = @[@"hunters"];
   ```

   This will remove the collision filtering that we've added in the previous *Time for action* section.

3. Now, it is time to implement collision filtering using the collision group. In the `PhysicsScene.m` file, add following instance variable:

   ```
   @implementation PhysicsScene
   {
       //..skipped..
       NSObject *_stoneGroundCollisionGroup;
   }
   ```

4. Then, add the following code at the beginning of the `onEnter` method, right after the call to `super onEnter`:

   ```
   -(void)onEnter
   {
       [super onEnter];

       _stoneGroundCollisionGroup =
        [[NSObject alloc] init];

       //..skipped..
   }
   ```

5. Then, set the `collisionGroup` property of `groundBody` in the `addGround` method to `_stoneGroundCollisionGroup`:

   ```
   groundBody.collisionGroup = _stoneGroundCollisionGroup;
   ```

6. Set the `collisionGroup` property of `stoneBody` in the `spawnStone` method of `_stoneGroundCollisionGroup`:

   ```
   stoneBody.collisionGroup = _stoneGroundCollisionGroup;
   ```

7. Build and run the game. Once again, everything works just as before. The stone hits the hunter but falls through the ground. The hunter is still standing on the ground and not falling through.

[You can find a snapshot of the project at this point in the `Chapter_10/Cocohunt_10_CollisionGroup` folder.]

What just happened?

This is the simplest way to filter a collision between two object types. The rule here is that the two bodies don't collide if they share the same `collisionGroup`. This is why we just set the `collisionGroup` property of the stone and the ground bodies to the same object.

It might seem strange that we needed to create this `NSObject` instead of using strings just as we did before. Well, we can do without creating the `_stoneGroundCollisionGroup` object and just write the following:

```
groundBody.collisionGroup = @"someString";
```

We have to further write this:

```
stoneBody.collisionGroup = @"someString";
```

However, you must be careful and completely understand why you can do this. The preceding code works because `@"someString"` is the same object in both cases. This happens because the compiler creates one instance of that string literal to save some memory and just puts a reference to that one instance everywhere you type `@"someString"`.

So, although the preceding code with the string literals is working, it won't work if you set the `collisionGroup` like the following:

```
groundBody.collisionGroup = [NSString stringWithFormat:@"%d",1];
stoneBody.collisionGroup  = [NSString stringWithFormat:@"%d",1];
```

Note that in both cases, `collisionGroup` will contain the `@"1"` string, but it will be different objects and collision filtering won't work. Also, note that you're responsible for retaining the collision group object.

> To better understand this, you can have a look at how the `collisionGroup` property is declared: `@property(nonatomic, assign) id collisionGroup;`. Note that this is the `assign` property. This means that it doesn't retain its value. So, you need to make sure that the object you use as `collisionGroup` lives after you assign it.

Applying forces and impulses and using joints

Currently, we know how to create bodies and set their different parameters. We know how to detect or ignore collisions. However, all we can do right now is place everything in the physics node and let gravity do the work. Let's change this and take more control.

Time for action – launching stones

It doesn't take too much time to win our game right now. Just take one step to the left or right and the stone will fall without hitting the hunter. If this is the punishment for shooting birds, then our hunter isn't going to learn anything.

It is time to throw more stones and make them fall at different places to make the hunter run around the level to avoid being hit by stones. Perform the following steps:

1. Open the `PhysicsScene.m` file, add `_timeUntilNextStone`, and add the `_stones` array instance variables, as shown in the following code:

   ```
   @implementation PhysicsScene
   {
       //..skipped..
       float _timeUntilNextStone;
       NSMutableArray *_stones;
   }
   ```

2. Add the following code to initialize the array and the time counter in the `onEnter` method, right below the `[super onEnter];` line:

   ```
   -(void)onEnter
   {
       [super onEnter];

       _stones = [NSMutableArray array];
   ```

```
        _timeUntilNextStone = 2.0f;

        //..skipped..
    }
```

3. Then, add the `fixedUpdate:` method with the following code to spawn and remove stones:

```
-(void)fixedUpdate:(CCTime)dt
{
    for (CCSprite *stone in [_stones copy])
    {
        if (stone.position.y < -10)
        {
            [_stones removeObject:stone];
            [stone removeFromParentAndCleanup:YES];
        }
    }

    if (_hunter.state != PhysicsHunterStateDead)
    {
        _timeUntilNextStone -= dt;
        if (_timeUntilNextStone <= 0)
        {
            _timeUntilNextStone = 0.5f +
                                  arc4random_uniform(1.0f);
            [self spawnStone];
        }
    }
}
```

4. Remove the code where we set the stone position at the end of the `spawnStone` method and replace it with following code:

```
-(void)spawnStone
{
    //..skipped..
    [_batchNodeMain addChild:stone z:kObjectsZ];

    [_stones addObject:stone];
    [self launchStone:stone];
}
```

5. Finally, add the `launchStone:` method right below the `spawnStone` method, as shown in the following code:

```
-(void)launchStone:(CCSprite *)stone
{
    //1
    CGSize viewSize = [CCDirector sharedDirector].viewSize;
    stone.position = ccp (viewSize.width * 0.5f,
                          viewSize.height * 0.9f);

    //2
    float xImpulseMin = -1200.0f;
    float xImpulseMax = 1200.0f;
    float yImpulse = 2000.0f;
    float xImpulse = xImpulseMin +
                   2.0f * arc4random_uniform(xImpulseMax);

    //3
    [stone.physicsBody applyImpulse:ccp(xImpulse, yImpulse)];
}
```

6. Build and run the game that looks much closer to the apocalypse, as you can see in the following screenshot:

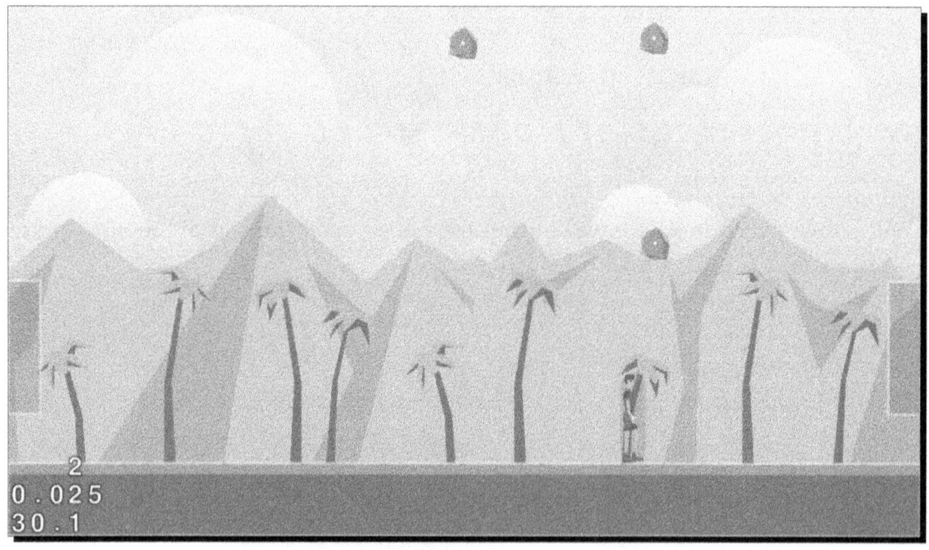

You can find a snapshot of the project at this point in the `Chapter_10/Cocohunt_10_Impulses` folder.

What just happened?

To make the game more interesting, we're spawning not one stone but an infinite number of stones at some interval. In addition to this, we applied some impulse to the stone so that it didn't just fall down due to gravity, but was launched instead.

The code in the `fixedUpdate:` method related to spawning, and removing stones is very similar to what we did when we spawned birds, so we're not going to discuss it here.

> Note that we stop spawning stones when the hunter dies. For the sake of simplicity, we don't have the game state and we just use the hunter state. Sometimes, this is enough and you don't have to overload your game objects with states.

The interesting part is that instead of just placing the stone and letting it fall, we use the `launchStone:` method to launch the stone. Let's review the `launchStone:` method in detail:

1. We set the stone at its starting point. All stones will be launched from here and their end position (point where they intersect with ground) will depend on the impulse we apply to them.
2. Here, we calculated the random value for the *x* component of the impulse. Take a look at the next diagram to get a better understanding.
3. Finally, after all the calculations are done, we apply the calculated impulse to the stone using the `applyImpulse:` method. This method simply takes a vector that contains the direction and magnitude of the impulse. Refer to the following diagram:

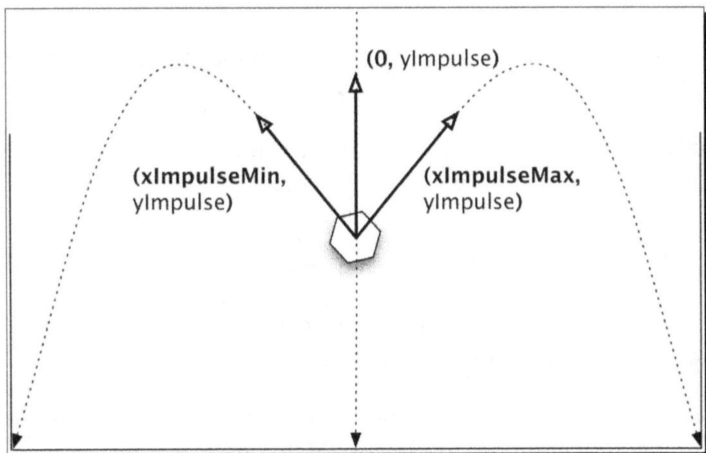

As you can see in the preceding diagram, we've picked the `xImpulseMin` and `xImpulseMax` values in a way that picking any random value in between will cause the stone to fall between the left and right edges of the screen.

All the three values, `xImpulseMin`, `xImpulseMax`, and `yImpulse`, are simply picked using the trial and error method for this sample. The drawback of this method is that it won't work for different screen sizes. You can solve this by adding the code to calculate the values depending on the screen size.

Impulses versus forces

There are several ways to make the physics body move. Of course, the most straightforward one is just to change its position, but this will be more like teleporting the physics body. Another way is to set the velocity of the physics body, but the body rarely moves with a constant velocity and manually calculating the velocity doesn't seem too fun.

So, the most common way to make the physics engine do your work is applying forces and impulses to the bodies. This way, the physics engine will take care of acceleration, slowdown, and other properties.

You might wonder what the difference between applying forces and impulses is. The forces act gradually over time, while impulses act instantly. In other words, you need to apply a force for some time to move something, and applying an impulse will change the velocity of the body immediately.

Imagine a railroad car standing on the rails. You can slowly drive a locomotive next to it and start pushing. The railroad car will slowly accelerate. This is force applied.

Now, imagine a locomotive driving at the full speed into the railroad car, making it move instantly. This is impulse applied.

You can see what happens if you change the code in the `launchStone:` method to use the `applyForce:` method instead of the `applyImpulse:` method, as shown in the following line of code:

```
[stone.physicsBody applyForce:ccp(xImpulse, yImpulse)];
```

The stone will simply fall down because you applied a force for a short time interval. Don't forget to change this line back.

Both methods have their purpose and you don't need to rule out either of them.

Have a go hero

The following are few things that you can try:

1. Right now, stones are colliding with the left and right boundaries (the invisible physics bodies), but you know enough about filtering collisions to stop this because it is strange when the stones collide with some invisible objects.

   To fix this, you can use any of the techniques to filter or ignore collisions that we've discussed before. The simplest way will be to set the collision group of the boundaries created in the `addBoundaries` method to `_stoneGroundCollisionGroup`. This way, the stones will fall through them just as they fall through the ground.

2. You can also move the starting point at which the stones are launched to the left, to the right, lower and higher, and see how this affects the point where they intersect with the ground line.
3. Change the rate of stones spawned by adjusting the `_timeUntilNextStone` variable in the `fixedUpdate:` method. You can count how many stones were already spawned or the time passed since the start of the level and decrease the interval, making it harder to play as time goes by.

Time for action – adding angry birds

At the moment, the stones are just launched from the air. Of course, if we move the stone's spawning point above the screen, we can imagine that there are some birds flying high and dropping the stones.

[In fact, we placed the launch point below the screen edge so that you can see them being launched.]

However, wouldn't it be cooler to see your enemy, to look them in the eyes? Let's do this and add some birds that are dropping stones.

What we're going to do is to spawn a bird off the screen. The bird will carry a stone using a joint.

[Joints are constraints that used to simulate interaction between objects. For example, you can simulate one object tied with a rope to another one. It will become clear in a moment.]

This bird will fly into the level and will drop the stone at the target point.

1. To keep things organized, create a new **Objective-C class** in the `GameObjects` group. Name the class `PhysicsBird` and make it a subclass of our `Bird` class, as we're going to reuse some of the code.

2. Open the `PhysicsBird.h` file and replace its contents with following code:

```
#import "Bird.h"

@interface PhysicsBird : Bird

@property (nonatomic, weak)   CCSprite *stoneToDrop;

-(void)flyAndDropStoneAt:(CGPoint)point
                   stone:(CCSprite*)stone;

@end
```

3. Then, switch to the `PhysicsBird.m` file and replace its contents with following code:

```
#import "PhysicsBird.h"
#import "cocos2d.h"

typedef NS_ENUM(NSUInteger, PhysicsBirdState)
{
    PhysicsBirdStateIdle,
    PhysicsBirdStateFlyingIn,
    PhysicsBirdStateFlyingOut
};

@implementation PhysicsBird
{
    PhysicsBirdState _state;
    CGPoint _targetPoint;

    CCPhysicsJoint *_stoneJoint;
}

-(instancetype)initWithBirdType:(BirdType)typeOfBird
{
```

```
    //1
    if (self = [super initWithBirdType:typeOfBird])
    {
        //2
        _state = PhysicsBirdStateIdle;

        //3
        CCPhysicsBody *body =
          [CCPhysicsBody
            bodyWithCircleOfRadius:self.contentSize.height*0.3f
                         andCenter:self.anchorPointInPoints];
        body.collisionType = @"bird";
        body.type = CCPhysicsBodyTypeDynamic;
        body.mass = 30.0f;
        self.physicsBody = body;
    }

    return self;
}

-(void)flyAndDropStoneAt:(CGPoint)point stone:(CCSprite*)stone
{
    //1
    _state = PhysicsBirdStateFlyingIn;
    _targetPoint = point;
    self.stoneToDrop = stone;

    //2
    self.stoneToDrop.physicsBody.collisionMask = @[];
    self.physicsBody.collisionMask = @[];

    //3
    float distanceToHoldTheStone =
      self.contentSize.height * 0.5f;
    self.stoneToDrop.position =
      ccpSub(self.position, ccp(0, distanceToHoldTheStone));

    //4
    _stoneJoint =
      [CCPhysicsJoint
        connectedDistanceJointWithBodyA:self.physicsBody
                                  bodyB:stone.physicsBody
                                anchorA:self.anchorPointInPoints
                              anchorB:stone.anchorPointInPoints];
```

```
}

-(void)fixedUpdate:(CCTime)dt
{
    //1
    float forceToHoldBird =
      -1 * self.physicsBody.mass * self.physicsNode.gravity.y;

    //2
    if (_state == PhysicsBirdStateFlyingIn)
    {
        //3
        float forceToHoldStone =
          -1 * self.stoneToDrop.physicsBody.mass *
             self.physicsNode.gravity.y;

        //4
        float forceUp = forceToHoldBird + forceToHoldStone;

        //5
        [self.physicsBody applyForce:ccp(-1500, forceUp)];

        //6
        if (self.position.x <= _targetPoint.x)
        {
            _state = PhysicsBirdStateFlyingOut;
            [self dropStone];
        }
    }
    else if (_state == PhysicsBirdStateFlyingOut)
    {
        //7
        float forceUp = forceToHoldBird * 1.5f;

        //8
        [self.physicsBody applyForce:ccp(0, forceUp)];

        //9
        CGSize viewSize = [CCDirector sharedDirector].viewSize;
        if (self.position.y > viewSize.height)
        {
            [self removeFromParentAndCleanup:YES];
        }
    }
```

```
}

-(void)dropStone
{
    self.stoneToDrop.physicsBody.collisionMask = nil;
    [_stoneJoint invalidate];
}

@end
```

4. After we have the bird, we need to launch it. However, before we can use the bird images in this scene, we need to add another sprite batch node, as the bird frames are in another spritesheet. Open the `PhysicsScene.m` file and add the `_batchNodeBirds` instance variable, as shown in the following code:

```
@implementation PhysicsScene
{
    //..skipped..

    CCSpriteBatchNode *_batchNodeBirds;
}
```

5. Then, in the end of the `createBatchNodes` method, add the code to initialize and add a new batch node to the physics node. It is important to add the code at the end of the method, as we're not going to use z-orders for simplicity and will simply add a new batch node after the existing one to make sure it is on top of it. Add the following code:

```
-(void)createBatchNodes
{
    //..skipped.. _batchNodeMain created and added here

    [[CCSpriteFrameCache sharedSpriteFrameCache]
      addSpriteFramesWithFile:@"Cocohunt.plist"];

    _batchNodeBirds =
      [CCSpriteBatchNode
        batchNodeWithFile:@"Cocohunt.png"];

    [_physicsNode addChild:_batchNodeBirds];
}
```

6. The final step before we can launch the bird is import the `PhysicsBird.h` header using the following line of code:

```
#import "PhysicsBird.h"
```

7. Now, when we have everything prepared to launch the bird, add the `launchBirdWithStone:` method right below the `launchStone:` method, as shown in the following code:

```
-(void)launchBirdWithStone:(CCSprite *)stone
{
    //1
    CGSize viewSize = [CCDirector sharedDirector].viewSize;
    PhysicsBird *bird = [[PhysicsBird alloc]
                         initWithBirdType:BirdTypeBig];
    bird.position = ccp(viewSize.width * 1.1f,
                        viewSize.height * 0.9f);
    [_batchNodeBirds addChild:bird];

    //2
    CGPoint targetPosition = _hunter.position;

    //3
    [bird flyAndDropStoneAt:targetPosition stone:stone];
}
```

8. To use another method to launch stones, find the `spawnStone` method and find the following line of code in it:

```
[self launchStone:stone];
```

Replace the previous line of code with the following:

```
[self launchBirdWithStone:stone];
```

9. There are a few more steps. Remove the call to `spawnStone` from the `onEnterTransitionDidFinish` method, or at least place it after the hunter is created. Otherwise, the first bird won't have a target. This is shown in the following code:

```
-(void)onEnterTransitionDidFinish
{
    [super onEnterTransitionDidFinish];

    [self createHunter];
    [self spawnStone];

    [self addBoundaries];
}
```

10. The final step we need to perform in the `fixedUpdate:` method is to adjust the minimum time interval between two birds; otherwise there will be too many birds on the screen. Find the following line in the `fixedUpdate:` method:

```
_timeUntilNextStone = 0.5f + arc4random_uniform(1.0f);
```

Adjust the minimum time interval; for example set it to be `1` second, as shown in the following line of code:

```
_timeUntilNextStone = 1.0f + arc4random_uniform(1.0f);
```

11. Build and run the game. You should see a pack of birds carrying stones and trying to drop them on the hunter, as shown in the following screenshot:

If you have `_physicsNode.debugDraw` enabled, you can safely disable it here (set to `NO`). As this is the last change to the level, you can now sit back and watch everything without the debug information drawn on screen.

> You can find code of the final project for this chapter in the `Chapter_10/Cocohunt_10_Final` folder.

What just happened?

Once again, it takes some code to add a new fully functional class to the game. However, most of the code is only to glue everything together. We're going to review everything and it will then become much clearer.

Creating the PhysicsBird class and giving it the stone

Let's start from the end and review the changes in the `PhysicsScene` class first.

The bird images are contained in the `Cocohunt` spritesheet. To use them, we needed to create another `CCSpriteBatchNode` and add it to the scene. Only after this could we create sprites or animations that use the sprite frames from this spritesheet.

This way, we have two batch nodes in our scene at the same time. The `_batchNodeMain` batch node draws all sprites from the `physics_level` spritesheet. The `_batchNodeBirds` batch draws all the sprites from the `Cocohunt` spritesheet, although we need only the bird's animation from it. Each sprite is added as a child to the corresponding batch node, and both batch nodes are added to the physics node.

> We take this approach because we want to reuse the bird's images that were contained in another spritesheet. In a real game, you can also have multiple batch nodes if all your sprites don't fit on one spritesheet. Remember that there is a limit on the maximum texture size, which we discussed in *Chapter 4, Rendering Sprites*.

The second change that we've made to the `PhysicsScene.m` file is that we used the `launchBirdWithStone:` method instead of the `launchStone:` method. This method spawns a bird off the screen and tells it to drop the stone at `targetPosition`.

Let's review the code of the `launchBirdWithStone:` method:

1. We created an instance of the `PhysicsBird` class. We set its position offscreen and added to the `_batchNodeBirds` batch node, as the `PhysicsBird` class uses birds images.
2. We then set the target to the hunter position.
3. We commanded the bird to fly to the target point and drop the stone. Note that we passed the stone, which we created earlier to the bird.

All changes made in the `PhysicsScene.m` file can be described in one sentence. We created and positioned a bird and commanded it to take the stone and drop it at the target point.

The rest is done in the `PhysicsBird` class, which we're going to review now.

The PhysicsBird class – using joints and applying force

The `PhysicsBird` class was created to contain the code to manage both the bird and the stone when they are together and when the bird is flying away. We could have created the bird sprite in the `PhysicsScene` class and written the code to manage both the bird and the stone in the `PhysicsScene` class, but this would lead to less maintainable and reusable code.

So, what do we want from the bird? We want it to display the flying bird animation, take the stone, fly to some point, drop this stone, and fly away. Let's review how each of the methods in `PhysicBird` class solve its task.

We'll start with the `initWithBirdType:` method. The code in this method sets the animation, sets the initial state of the bird to the `PhysicsBirdStateIdle` state, and creates the physics body. Refer to the following points:

1. The task of displaying the flying bird is fully solved by inheriting our class from the `Bird` class and reusing its `initWithBirdType:` method, which starts the animation.

   You can go back to *Chapter 4, Rendering Sprites*, to see where we created this method.

2. We need the `_state` variable to control our bird's state. There are three states that the bird can be in. The bird can only move to the next state (for example, it can't go from `PhysicsBirdStateFlyingOut` to `PhysicsBirdStateFlyingIn`). The three states are as follows:

   - The `PhysicsBirdStateIdle` state means that the bird is just created. This is the state we set in the `initWithBirdType:` method.
   - The `PhysicsBirdStateFlyingIn` state means that the bird is flying towards the target point. After changing to this state, the bird starts moving.
   - The `PhysicsBirdStateFlyingOut` state means that the bird dropped the stone and is flying out. When we switch to this state, the bird should drop the stone and fly away.

3. The final part of the `initWithBirdType:` method is a creation of the physics body. The physics body is required as we're going to apply forces to the bird to move it. Also, we will attach a stone to the bird's body using a joint.

Now, let's review the `flyAndDropStoneAt:` method where we give the stone to the bird and tell the bird where to drop this stone:

1. Here, we set the current state of the bird to `PhysicsBirdStateFlyingIn`. This will cause the bird to start moving in the direction of the target point. We also saved the target point and the reference to the stone the bird is carrying.
2. The `collisionMask` properties of both the bird and the stone are set to an empty array. This means that we don't want them to collide with anything. As the bird is carrying a stone, it shouldn't collide with other birds or stones falling from the sky.

> By default, `collisionMask` is set to `nil`, which means that the body wants to collide with *everything*. Setting it to an empty array has a different meaning. We provide an empty list of categories that we want to collide with; thus, it won't collide with anything.

3. Here, we positioned the stone to be under the bird. In the `distanceToHoldTheStone` variable, we calculated the distance at which we want the bird to hold the stone. Then, we used the `ccpSub` function to subtract this distance from the bird's position, and as a result, we got the initial position for the stone.
4. We created the distance joint that will connect the stone and the bird.

If you haven't used a physics engine before, the word "joint" might be completely new and unclear. Let's spend some time reviewing what joints are.

Joints are used to connect the bodies together. However, just as in the real world, two bodies can be connected in several ways.

Think of how glue sticks two objects together and they almost become one object. No matter how you manipulate one of the objects, the distance between them stays constant. You cannot rotate one of the objects without rotating the other and so on.

Now, think about tying two objects together with a rope at some distance, such as a dog on a leash. The dog can move freely around the human, who holds the leash; it can rotate without rotating the human. However, the dog has a maximum distance it can move away from the human.

This and other examples show how you can use joints to connect your bodies. In our case, we're using a distance joint to connect the stone to the bird. A distance joint simply maintains the distance between two objects. This is exactly what we want as we want to simulate the bird carrying the stone on some kind of a non-stretchable rope.

> Launch the game and watch how the stone is swinging a little while the bird carries it. If you increase the value of `distanceToHoldTheStone`, it will swing even more. An example of this would be a helicopter transporting something using the long cable.

To create a joint, you first need to add both bodies to the physics node, and only after this can you create the joint using the `CCPhysicsJoint` class, which is used to create different joint types.

The final method to review is the `fixedUpdate:` method:

1. First, we calculated what force is required to hold the bird in the air. Our bird is affected by gravity force, which is calculated as `F = m * g`. To keep our bird in the air, we need to apply the same force in the opposite direction (that is, up), which is why we multiply by `-1`.
2. Then, we determined the state of the bird as the bird has different behavior when carrying a stone and when flying away.
3. If the bird is in the `PhysicsBirdStateFlyingIn` state, it means that the bird is carrying a stone. This means that we also need to add force to hold the stone.
4. The `forceUp` holds the total force required to hold the bird and the stone in the air. The joint doesn't have any weight.
5. Here, we applied the force to the bird, and there are a few things to note about this:
   - We applied force to the bird, but as the stone is attached to the bird via the joint, it will not fall.
   - Applying a force of `-1500` in the *x* axis all the time will make the bird accelerate more and more. You can already see this. If the bird flew a little longer, the value of its velocity would be high as there are no forces to resist it.
6. If the bird passed its target point, it should drop the stone and switch to the `PhysicsBirdStateFlyingOut` state.
7. If the bird is in the `PhysicsBirdStateFlyingOut` state, then the bird is not carrying a stone anymore. This means that no additional force is required, but as we want the bird to fly upwards on its way out, we multiplied the force by 1.5 to overcome gravity and fly up.
8. Note that zero force is applied in the *x* axis, but the bird still moves forward due to inertia.
9. If the bird has left the screen, it is removed. This is important because if we don't remove unused objects, it will reduce our game's performance over time.

The final method to review is the `dropStone` method. In this method, we reset the stone `collisionMask`, as the stone has to collide with the hunter.

The second thing that we did is invalidate the joint using the `invalidate` method. When you invalidate the joint, it is disabled and removed. In our case, we can think of it as the rope breaking and the stone falling down.

After you invalidate the joint, you cannot reuse it.

That's it. These are all the methods that make our peaceful bird from the first part of the book into a bloodthirsty monster.

Have a go hero

The following is a list of things that can make this level much more interesting:

- Call the `launchStone:` and `launchBirdWithStone:` methods randomly or even spawn two stones each time and use both methods simultaneously.
- Make the bird target the hunter more precisely. To do this, the bird must release the stone at some distance before the target point, as the stone is moving forward due to inertia.
- Make the bird fly to the level from the left-hand side of the screen as well.
- Apply force to the hunter instead of setting the hunter's velocity.

Pop quiz – physics

Q1. How will you shoot the arrow from a bow?

1. By calling the `applyForce:` method on the arrow body once
2. By calling the `applyImpulse:` method on the arrow body once
3. By setting the arrow body's `velocity` property once
4. By setting the arrow body's `velocity` property in the `fixedUpdate:` method each time step

Q2. How will you implement the acceleration of a car using the gas pedal?

1. By applying force using the `applyForce:` method all the time while the gas pedal is pressed
2. By applying impulse using the `applyImpulse:` method all the time while the gas pedal is pressed
3. By setting the `velocity` property to a constant value when the gas pedal is pressed
4. By setting the `velocity` to a constant value when the gas pedal is pressed and changing the value of `velocity` to `0` when the gas pedal is released

Q3. Which method should you use to update your physics objects?

1. `update:`
2. `fixedUpdate:`
3. `constantUpdate:`
4. `physicsUpdate:`

Summary

In this chapter, we've learned the basics of using a physics engine in your game. Although we learned how to create and manipulate physics bodies, detect collisions, and apply forces and impulses, we barely scratched the surface of what you can do with a physics engine.

We haven't created more complicated physics bodies using polygon shapes or even multi-shape bodies. We didn't use sensors and haven't created complicated mechanisms using joints.

However, I think that information presented in this chapter might be already too overwhelming, especially if you have only just begun to learn how to use physics in your games. Nonetheless, I'm sure this chapter has everything you need to know to start creating physics-enabled games and continue learning advanced topics. I can assure you that the result of learning will be totally worth it!

In the next chapter, we will see how to create larger worlds using tile maps.

11
Working with Tile Maps

Some of the games require really large worlds. Just imagine an RPG where the whole dungeon should fit in one screen. This will be a very small dungeon, not larger than a dressing room of some celebrity. Alternatively, you will have to scale everything down so that your game will be pixels fighting other pixels.

The solution is pretty obvious: create a larger world and follow the player, just as the camera follows the actor during the movie shooting. However, creating and managing a large world manually can be quite a task. This is where tile maps come to the rescue and make creation and usage of large levels much easier.

In this chapter, we are going to create a new bigger level using a tile map and will demonstrate some techniques to move your character through this world.

In this chapter, we will cover the following topics:

- Creating the tileset from a set of separate images
- Creating a tile map that contains several layers
- Making the tile map support both the Retina and non-Retina displays
- Scrolling the level
- Using parallax scrolling for more realistic scrolling

Creating tile maps

When we use tile maps, we create a large world using a set of reusable small tiles. A set of such tiles is called a tileset. Here is a tileset that we are going to create and use in our new level:

Here is a part of the level created using the tiles from this tileset:

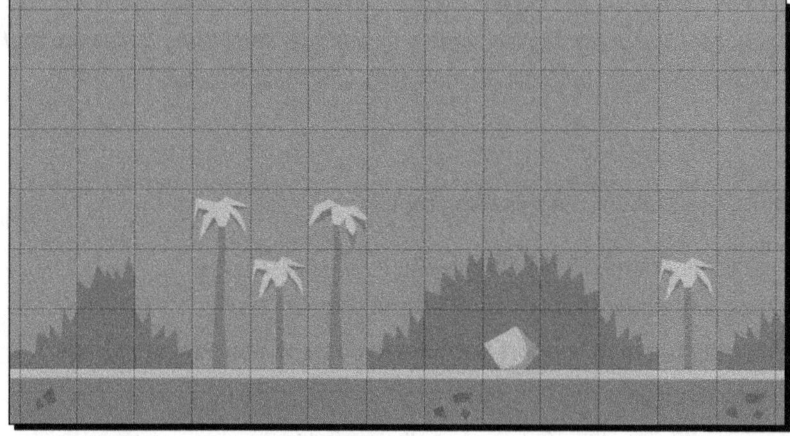

As you have probably guessed, each tile from the set is placed on a grid that forms a tile map. The tile map can be very big, while still not consuming all of your memory since only the visible part is displayed.

Creating a tile map usually takes two steps. First, you create a tileset image and then you arrange tiles to form a tile map. Let's start by creating a tileset.

Time for action – creating a tileset

Before we can create a tile map, we need to create a tileset. This is quite easy to do using the **TexturePacker** app that we have used before. Once again, the free version will be enough for our tasks.

We will create a special spritesheet that we are going to use as a tileset. Perform the following steps:

1. Open the **TexturePacker** application. You should have installed it during *Chapter 4, Rendering Sprites*. A new project is created by default, but create one if required.
2. Open the book's supporting files in the `Chapter_11/Assets/Tilemap/Images/sd` folder and select all images. Drag those images to the **TexturePacker** app.

[To download the book's supporting files, please visit `www.packtpub.com/support` and follow the instructions.]

3. Set the **TextureSettings** option in the left-hand side pane of **TexturePacker** as follows:
    - **Algorithm**: Select **Basic**
    - **Sort by**: Select **Name**
    - **Border padding**: Enter `2`
    - **Shape padding**: Enter `2`
    - **Allow rotation**: Select **Uncheck**
    - **Trim mode**: Select **None**

[It is very important to set paddings and remember those values, since you'll need to specify them later. Otherwise, your tileset image won't be split into tiles correctly and/or you will get gaps or overlapping tiles.]

After adjusting the settings, you should see an image in the preview pane identical to the sample tileset image shown at the beginning of this chapter.

4. Save the **TexturePacker** project as `tilemap.tps` in some folder. We will put all the files in this folder, so please create a special folder.
5. Publish the spritesheet to this folder by selecting **Publish** in the **File** menu or using the *command* + *P* shortcut. Name the spritesheet `tilemap.plist`.

What just happened?

At this point, you should have the following three files:

- `tilemap.tps`: This is just a **TexturePacker** project. We saved it just in case and won't use it in the future.
- `tilemap.png`: This is the tileset image. This is the only file we need and we've done all the previous actions only to create it.
- `tilemap.plist`: This is the `.plist` part of the spritesheet. As you remember, it contains the information about the individual sprite positions within the spritesheet image. However, we won't need it to create a tile map, so you can simply ignore this file.

So the only file we need is the `tilemap.png` image, since tile maps don't use a `.plist` file and instead just require images in the tileset to be positioned using the grid. This is why we've set so many options in the **TexturePacker** project.

Instead of using **TexturePacker**, you could create a tileset image in your favorite graphics editor, such as Photoshop or GIMP. Each tile image is 32 x 32 pixels so you could just create a grid of the tiles, adding some constant padding value between the tiles. Using the **TexturePacker** project does this automatically, even though it is not designed to create tilesets and produces the unneeded `.plist` file.

Now, when we have the tileset image, it is time to create a tile map.

If you have any issues creating a tileset image or for some reason you cannot create it right now, you can use the `tilemap.png` image in the `Chapter_11/Assets/Tilemap/Result` folder. You can also compare this file with the one that you have created to check whether they are identical.

Time for action – creating a tile map

One of the best applications to create a tile map is a free app called **Tiled** created by Thorbjørn Lindeijer. We are going to use the app to create a simple level using the tileset that we have just created. Perform the following steps:

1. Open the `http://www.mapeditor.org/` website and download the Tiled application. You will need **Tiled for OS X**. When the download completes, open the `.dmg` file and copy the `Tiled.app` into the `Applications` folder on your Mac.

2. Run the `Tiled.app` and create a new project by selecting the **New** option in the **File** menu. Set the new project options as follows:

    - **Orientation**: Select **Orthogonal**
    - **Layer format**: Select **Base64 (zlib compressed)**
    - **Tile size**: Set both **Width** and **Height** to `32 px`
    - **Map size**: Set **Width** to `64 tiles` and **Height** to `10 tiles`

    The resulting **Map Size** should be **2048 x 320** pixels.

3. Select the **New Tileset** option from the **Map** menu. Name the tileset anyway you like, as it is irrelevant (I have named it `Jungle`). Click on the **Browse** button and select the `tilemap.png` image that we have just created. Don't click on the **OK** button just yet.

4. In the **Tiles** group, set **Tile width** and **Tile height** to `32 px`. Set the **Margin** and **Spacing** to `2 px`. Leave the **Drawing Offset** at `X:0` and `Y:0`. Now, you can click on the **OK** button.

    Here is how your **New Tileset** dialog should look:

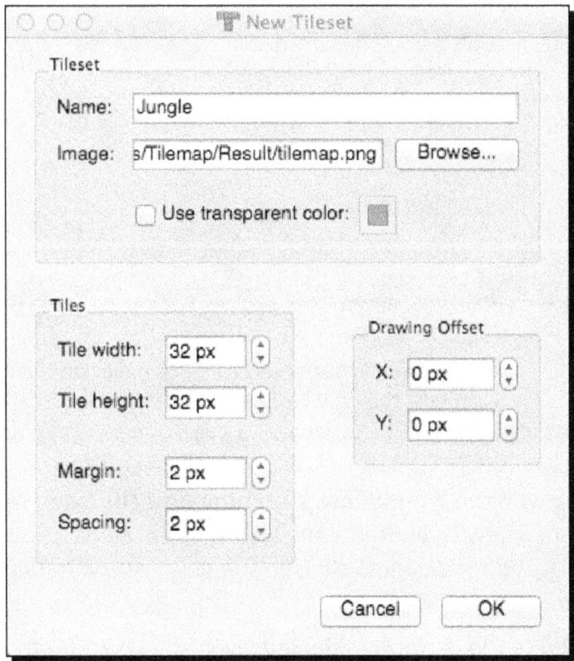

5. Save the tiled map file to the same folder where the `tilemap.png` image is placed. Name it `tilemap.tmx`.

6. In the **Layers** pane on the right-hand side, rename **Tile Layer 1** (by double-clicking on it) to `Ground`.

7. Use different ground tiles from the tileset to fill the bottom row of the tile map, like this:

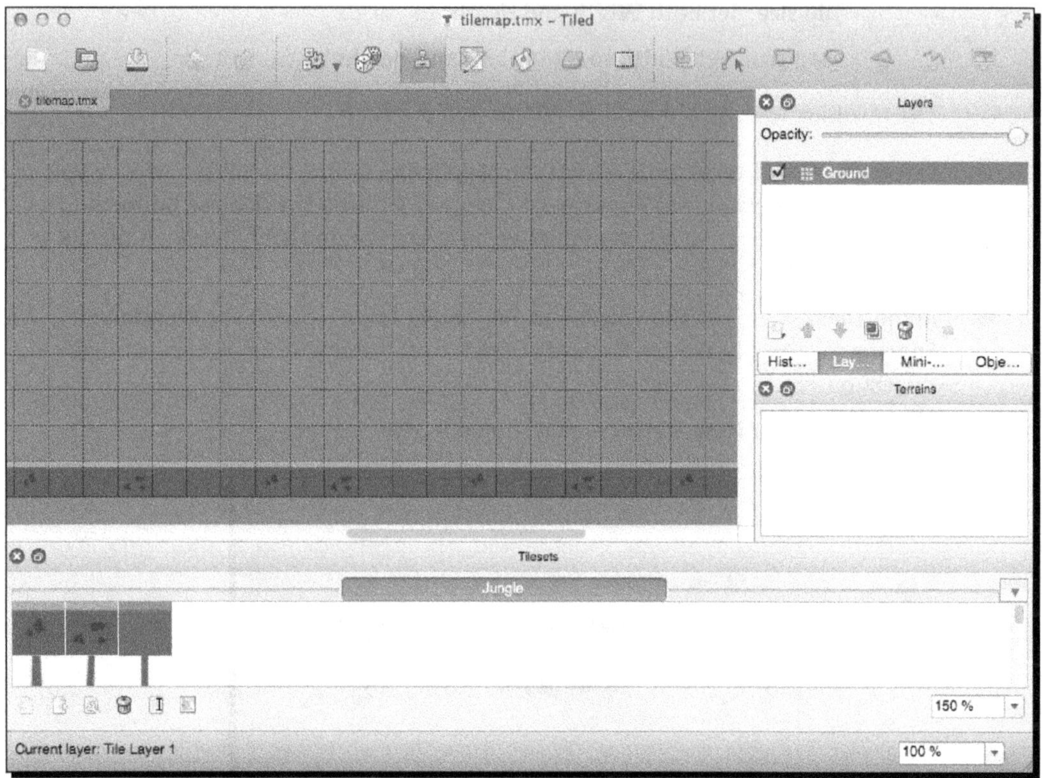

If you don't want to spend time placing tiles on the map, you can take the final `tilemap.tmx` file from the `Chapter_11/Assets/Tilemap/Result` folder.

8. After finishing with the ground row, select the **Add Tile Layer** option in the **Layer** menu to create a new layer. Name the layer `Trees`. Select this layer in the **Layers** pane on the right-hand side and click on the down arrow to move it below the **Ground** layer.

9. Tiles are added to the currently selected layer, so make sure the **Trees** layer is selected and then add trees to the level. To create a tree, you should place several tiles on top of each other. There are total three parts of the trunk and two different treetops. You can make shorter trees by skipping the lower parts of the trunk. Here is an example:

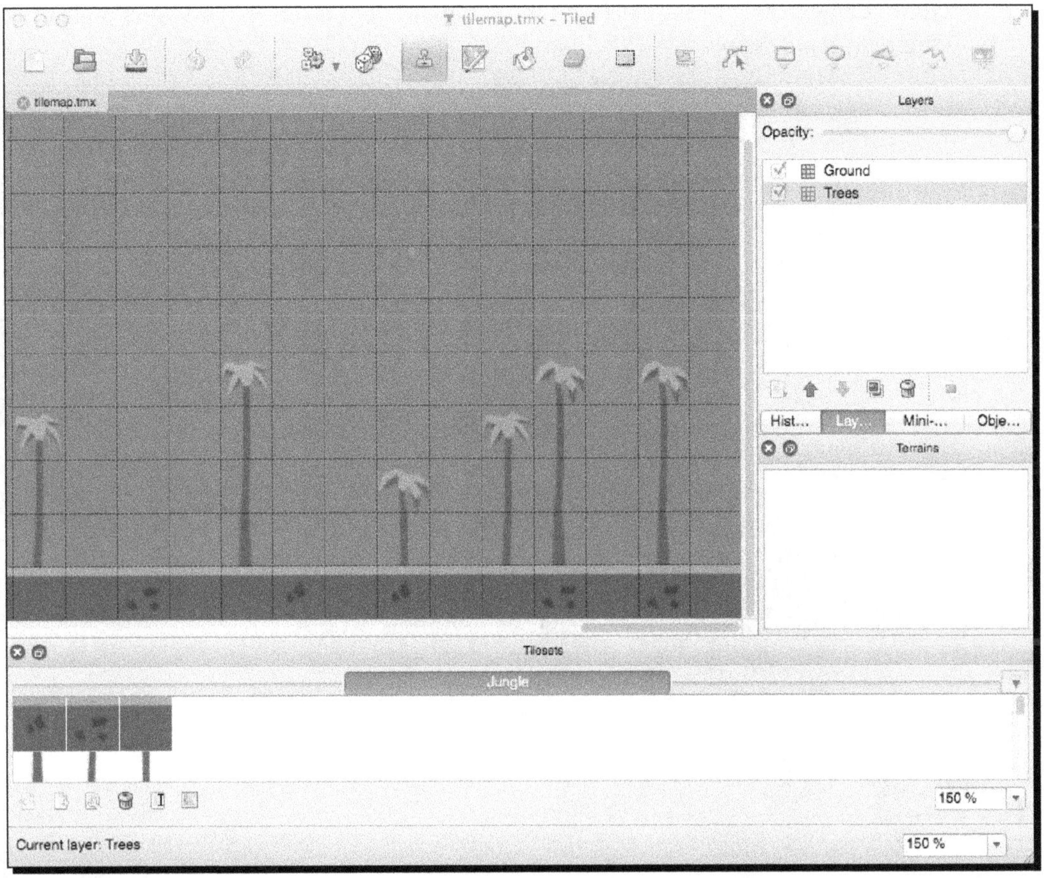

10. Now let's add some bushes. Create new tile layer and call it **Bushes**. Use the down arrow to move it below both the **Ground** and the **Trees** layers.

11. Use the green bushes tiles to add some bushes to the level. The bushes also consists of several parts that you can combine differently to create different bushes. Make sure you select the **Bushes** layer before adding any bushes.

> Don't be afraid to overwrite the tree tile if you want to place the bush behind the tree. Since they are on different levels, the bush tile will be added behind the tree tile in the same grid cell. In other words, all the bushes (or any other objects in the **Bushes** layer) will end up behind trees.

Here is an example of bushes (note the three different layers in the **Layers** pane on the right-hand side):

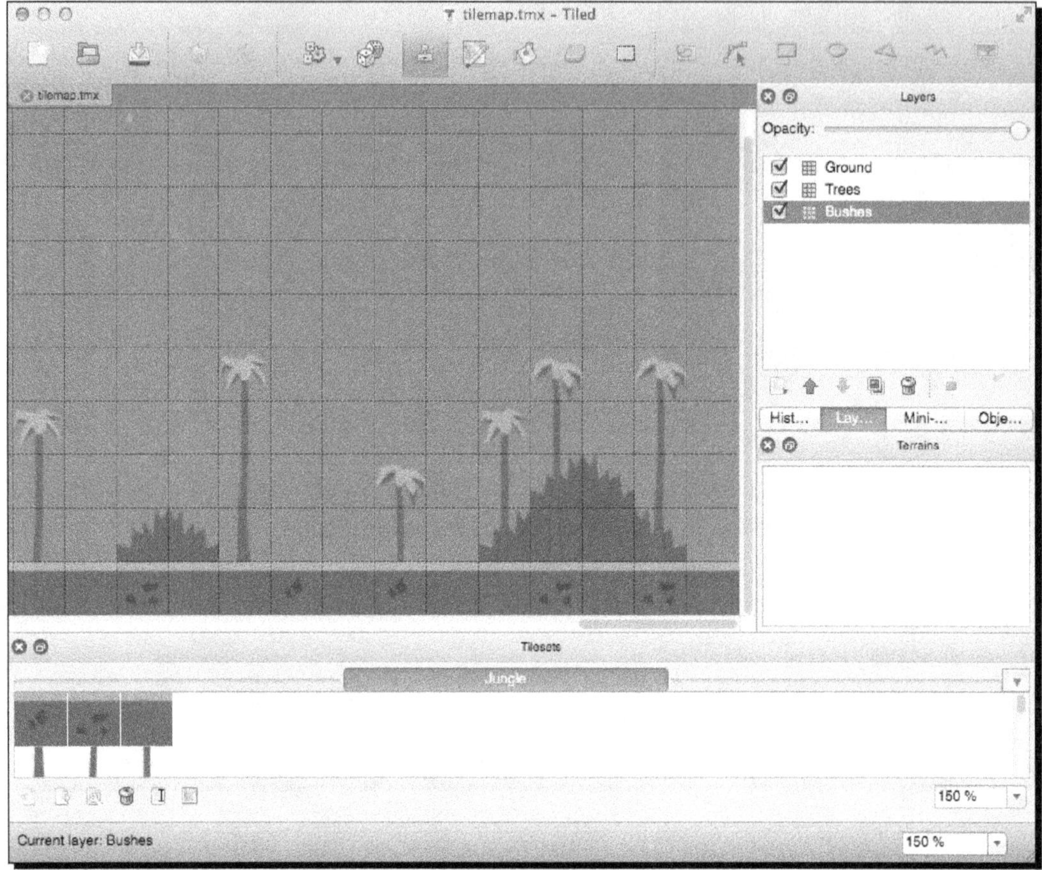

12. Save the `tilemap.tmx` file once again to save the latest changes and close the **Tiled** application, since we have finished working with it.

What just happened?

With only a few tiles, we have created a much bigger world. In fact, we only limited ourselves by 64 tiles width so that it didn't take too much time filling this sample tile map. We could have easily created a much larger tile map.

Let's discuss some of the tile map creation process. First of all, let's review some of the options that we've set while creating the tile map:

- **Orientation**: We have set this to orthogonal. The orthogonal tile maps are the most often used tile maps in two-dimensional games. We have just seen them in action, and they just represent a grid that consists of rectangular tiles. Another type of the map is an isometric tile map. The isometric tile maps are used to create games with an isometric view, but still staying in a two-dimensional world. When you use an isometric tile map, you use diamond tiles instead of rectangular, and thus you create an illusion of a three-dimensional view. Here is an example of a isometric tile map (note that tile map is still two-dimensional grid, it is just a visual illusion of 3D):

You can find the tile map project file and images used to create this sample in the `Chapter_11/IsometricSample` folder. The tileset images were created by Indie Squid (`http://indiesquid.com`).

We won't cover creating isometric tile maps in this book, but the main idea behind them is same as with orthogonal tile maps—use many small tiles to generate a large world.

- **Layer format**: The **Base64 (zlib compressed)** option means that the information about each layer will be compressed to save some disk space.
- **Tile size**: This is the size of the single tile in pixels. We use the 32 x 32 px square tiles, but in some cases, you might want to use rectangular tiles (for example, 64 x 32 px). This mostly depends on the size of the images used to create a tileset.
- **Map size**: This is the size of the tile map in tiles. It is important to note that this size is in tiles, not in pixels or points.

The values that we set when we added the tileset are pretty much the same as earlier. There are few things to note:

- The **Tile width** and **Tile height** value can be different from the **Tile size** value of the tile map.
- The **Margin** option is the **Border padding** setting that we set in the **TexturePacker** project. The **Spacing** option is the **Shape padding** setting in the **TexturePacker** project. These settings are very important, since if you set them wrong, your tileset will be imported incorrectly. Here is an example of what will happen if we set the **Margin** option and the **Spacing** option to `0` instead of the `2px` that we've actually used. Refer to the following screenshot:

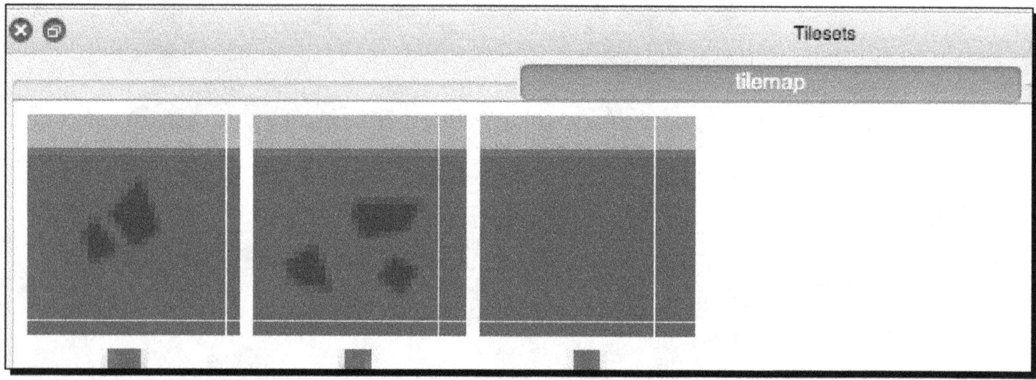

As you can see, the grid is calculated incorrectly. White lines over the ground tiles show how the tileset was sliced by the Tiled application because of the incorrect **Margin** and **Spacing** values.

Time for action – creating the Retina version of the tile map

Just as with many other resources used in Cocos2D games, you need to have several versions to support non-Retina and Retina displays. Luckily, we don't have to create a separate tile map for 3.5-inch Retina and 4-inch Retina displays. Also, we won't have to repeat all the steps and recreate a tile map using a different tileset.

> You need to understand that tile maps for Retina and non-Retina displays will only differ by size of images used in them, and the layout of the tiles should be the same; of course, if you don't want to display different levels for Retina and non-Retina displays.
>
> However, normally, you'd have to create two versions by simply repeating all your work and placing all tiles in the same places.
>
> Just as if you had an image and you needed a 2x image and instead of scaling it in graphics editor, you redraw it from scratch. The following technique allows you to get a Retina version of the same tile map without re-working.

What we need to do is to create a different tileset image and adjust some settings in the tile map file. Perform the following steps:

1. Let's start by creating a tileset. Open the **TexturePacker** project and create new spritesheet. This time use images from the `Chapter_11/Assets/Tilemap/Images/hd` folder.
2. Before publishing, set **TextureSettings** in **TexturePacker** to the same values as previously, consider the following aspects:
   - **Algorithm**: Select **Basic**
   - **Sort by**: Select **Name**
   - **Border padding**: Enter `2`
   - **Shape padding**: Enter `2`
   - **Allow rotation**: Select **Uncheck**
   - **Trim mode**: Select **None**

   You can save the **TexturePacker** project in the same folder where the previous **TexturePacker** project and `tilemap.tmx` files are present. Name it `tilemap-hd.tps`. We won't need it, but just in case, it is better to save it.
3. Now publish the `TexturePacker` project by navigating to the **Publish** option in the **File** menu or by using *command* + *P*. Name the spritesheet `tilemap-hd.plist`. This will create the `tilemap-hd.png` image. Once again, this is the only file we need.
4. Fortunately, we won't have to create a new tile map and place all tiles once again. Instead, we're going to copy the existing tile map and adjust some values. Before we continue, make sure these three files `tilemap.png`, `tilemap.tmx`, and `tilemap-hd.png` are in the same folder. Then copy the `tilemap.tmx` file and rename it to `tilemap-hd.tmx`.

5. Open the `tilemap-hd.tmx` file in your favorite text editor and make highlighted changes in the top part of the file. Refer to the following code:

```
<?xml version="1.0" encoding="UTF-8"?>
<map version="1.0" orientation="orthogonal" width="64"
 height="10" tilewidth="64" tileheight="64">
   <tileset firstgid="1" name="Jungle" tilewidth="64"
    tileheight="64" spacing="2" margin="2">
       <image source="tilemap.png" width="256"
       height="512"/>
 </tileset>
```

When the rest of the file is skipped, don't delete the rest of the file!

The changes you've made have simply doubled `tilewidth` and `tileheight` in two places and doubled the size of the tileset image.

It is not an error that we didn't change the `source` property of the `image` tag to `<image source="tilemap-hd.png"... />`. Cocos2D will automatically load the `-hd` version just as with a normal image.

6. Save and close the `tilemap-hd.tmx` file. At this point, you should have four files, `tilemap.png`, `tilemap.tmx`, `tilemap-hd.png`, and `tilemap-hd.tmx` in the same folder that we've just created.

It is important to work within one folder so that tile map file doesn't have a relative path to the tileset image (for example, `<image source="../src/tilemap.png"`) because Cocos2D won't be able to load the tileset image in this case.

You can have additional files in the folder such as the `.tps` and `.plist` files, but the four files mentioned earlier are all we need to add the tile map to our game.

> You can find all four files in the `Chapter_11/Assets/Tilemap/Result` folder to compare with your files or use them if for some reason you didn't create those files.

What just happened?

Fortunately, we didn't have to repeat all the steps to create a tile map duplicate for the Retina display.

> It might seem that we didn't save ourselves from a lot of work. After all, recreating such small tile map once again is not a problem. However, imagine a really huge tile map that you've designed for several days. You placed obstacles, enemies, and so on. Now, you need to create an identical one, but just chose a different setting at the time when you created it. Also, think about maintaining two versions of tile map after that.

All we had to do is create another tileset image using the **TexturePacker** project and create another `.tmx` file with a few changes. The `tileset-hd.png` file is the same tileset as we created before but just double-sized.

> To make two tileset images identical, we set the same properties in the **TexturePacker** project, including the **Sort by** property to make sure tiles are placed in the same places within the tileset. This means that you need to have the same names for the Retina and non-Retina images used to create a tileset; otherwise, they will be placed in a different order and you will have to recreate the tile map manually instead of changing a few parameters.

Since the tileset is double-sized, we also needed to double the size of the tiles in the `tileset-hd.tmx` file.

Now, we have all the files we need to add the tileset to the game.

Using the tile maps

It is a good thing to know that adding tileset to the game is much simpler than creating it. To demonstrate how to use tile maps in the Cocos2D game, we're going to create a new scene where the bird will fly through the tile map level.

Time for action – creating TilemapScene

Let's start by creating the new scene and loading our tile map. Perform the following steps:

1. Open the **Cocohunt** project and create new group in the `Resources` group called `Tilemap`.

   You can continue working on the project you have after completing the previous chapter or take the final code from the previous chapter in the book's supporting files and use it as a starter project. You can find the final code for the previous chapter in the `Chapter_10/Cocohunt_10_Final` folder.

2. Add the `tilemap.png`, `tilemap.tmx`, `tilemap-hd.png`, and `tilemap-hd.tmx` files to that group. You can use the files that you created or take the files from the `Chapter_11/Assets/Tilemap/Result` folder.
3. In addition to the tile map files, add two background image files from the `Chapter_11/Assets/Background` folder. We will use them as the background image for the scene.
4. After adding all resources, create a new scene called `TilemapScene`.
5. Open the `TilemapScene.m` file and import the `cocos2d.h` file and the `Bird.h` headers as follows:

```
#import "cocos2d.h"
#import "Bird.h"
```

6. After all the `#import` directives, but before the `@implementation` line, add the following `enum` to specify z-order values that we'll use:

```
typedef NS_ENUM(NSUInteger, zOrder)
{
    zOrderBackground,
    zOrderTilemap,
    zOrderObjects
};
```

7. Add the following instance variables:

```
@implementation TilemapScene
{
    float        _worldSize;
    CCTiledMap *_tileMap;
    Bird        *_bird;
    CCSpriteBatchNode *_batchNode;
}
```

8. Then add the following methods to add everything to the scene:

```
-(void)onEnter
{
    [super onEnter];

    [self createBatchNode];

    [self addBackground];
    [self addTilemap];
    [self addBird];
}

-(void)createBatchNode
{
    [[CCSpriteFrameCache sharedSpriteFrameCache]
      addSpriteFramesWithFile:@"Cocohunt.plist"];
    _batchNode = [CCSpriteBatchNode
      batchNodeWithFile:@"Cocohunt.png"];
    [self addChild:_batchNode z:zOrderObjects];
}

-(void)addBackground
{
    CCSprite *bg =
      [CCSprite spriteWithImageNamed:@"tile_level_bg.png"];
    bg.positionType = CCPositionTypeNormalized;
    bg.position = ccp(0.5f, 0.5f);
    [self addChild:bg z:zOrderBackground];
}

-(void)addTilemap
{
    _tileMap = [CCTiledMap tiledMapWithFile:@"tilemap.tmx"];
    _worldSize = _tileMap.contentSizeInPoints.width;
    [self addChild:_tileMap z:zOrderTilemap];
}

-(void)addBird
{
```

```
        CGSize viewSize = [CCDirector sharedDirector].viewSize;

        _bird = [[Bird alloc] initWithBirdType:BirdTypeSmall];
        _bird.flipX = YES;
        _bird.position = ccp(viewSize.width * 0.2f,
                             viewSize.height * 0.2f);
        [_batchNode addChild:_bird];
    }
```

9. Now, we need to run this scene. Open the `AppDelegate.m` file and import the `TilemapScene.h` header as follows:

```
#import "TilemapScene.h"
```

10. Then find the `startScene` method and change it to return the `TilemapScene` instance:

```
-(CCScene *)startScene
{
   return [[TilemapScene alloc] init];
}
```

11. Build and run the game. You should see a part of our tile map level and a bird flying but not moving, as shown in the following screenshot:

What just happened?

We created a scene that contains a background image, a tile map, and a bird.

The background image represents some mountains far away. When the bird moves, they will remain still; this is why we only need the image to be of the screen size.

To display the bird, we needed to create a batch node, since we are reusing the bird from our initial `GameScene` class. This is also why we needed to set `flipX` to `YES` in the `addBird` method, since the bird is facing left by default and we need it to face right.

The only new thing is the code in the `addTilemap` method. Just as I told you earlier, adding a tile map to the game is much easier than creating it.

To display the tile map, we used the `CCTiledMap` class, which is a `CCNode` subclass. In other words, this is just a usual node, just as sprite, label, and so on are. The only difference is that it loads the tile map `.tmx` file and displays tiles on the screen.

Tiles are simple sprites and are loaded on demand. If required, you can move, rotate, scale, and change other properties of the individual tile.

It will become clear in a moment why we save the size of the tile map in the `_worldSize` variable.

Time for action – moving and following the bird

What is the purpose of the big world if we can see only a small portion of it? Let's make the bird fly forward and see the whole tile map. Perform the following steps:

1. Open the `TilemapScene.m` file and add the `update:` method to move the tile map as follows:

```
-(void)update:(CCTime)dt
{
    float distance = 150.0f * dt;

    CGPoint newTilemapPos = _tileMap.position;
    newTilemapPos.x = newTilemapPos.x - distance;
    _tileMap.position = newTilemapPos;
}
```

2. You can build and run the game right now, but you will see that the bird isn't stopping when we reach the end of the tile map. So let's change the `update:` method to the following code:

```
-(void)update:(CCTime)dt
{
    float distance = 150.0f * dt;

    CGPoint newTilemapPos = _tileMap.position;
    newTilemapPos.x = newTilemapPos.x - distance;

    CGSize viewSize = [CCDirector sharedDirector].viewSize;
    float endX = -1 * _worldSize + viewSize.width;

    if (newTilemapPos.x > endX)
        _tileMap.position = newTilemapPos;
}
```

3. Build and run the game. Now the bird should fly through the tile map.

You can find a project snapshot at this point in the `Chapter_11/Cocohunt_11_Tilemap` folder.

What just happened?

It might seem strange that we're moving the tile map and not the bird. However, if we would move the bird, we would also need to move the background image, since it should seem that it is not moving.

This is another example to demonstrate that sometimes it is more convenient to make the player believe that something happened instead of actually making it happen.

Right now the bird simply stops at the end. In the real game, you can add obstacles or enemies and if the bird reaches the end of the level, then you can consider that the player completed this level.

So what we're doing is moving the tile map to the left by decreasing its position's *x* component. However, since we don't want the bird to fly when it reaches the end of the tile map, we're using `endX` to check whether the bird can still fly forward.

We need to add `viewSize.width` to `-1 * _worldSize`, since the tile map anchor point is in the bottom-left corner `(0, 0)` and we need to stop when the tile map's bottom-right corner reaches the bottom- right corner of the view.

You can remove + `viewSize.width` to see what happens and understand why we need it.

It is nice to see the bird flying or to be more precise, the tile map moving, but we can make it look much more realistic using the parallax scrolling technique.

Time for action – using parallax scrolling

The parallax scrolling technique adds depth to your game by moving different layers placed one above each other at different speed. Let's use it in our `TilemapScene` class and you'll see what I'm talking about. Perform the following steps:

1. Open the `TilemapScene.m` file and add the following instance variable:

```
@implementation TilemapScene
{
    //..skipped..

    CCParallaxNode *_parallaxNode;
}
```

2. Then find the `addTilemap` method and replace it with the following code:

```
-(void)addTilemap
{
    _tileMap = [CCTiledMap tiledMapWithFile:@"tilemap.tmx"];
    _worldSize = _tileMap.contentSizeInPoints.width;

    //1
    CCTiledMapLayer *bushes = [_tileMap layerNamed:@"Bushes"];
    CCTiledMapLayer *trees = [_tileMap layerNamed:@"Trees"];
    CCTiledMapLayer *ground = [_tileMap layerNamed:@"Ground"];

    //2
    _parallaxNode = [CCParallaxNode node];

    //3
    [bushes removeFromParentAndCleanup:NO];
    [trees removeFromParentAndCleanup:NO];
    [ground removeFromParentAndCleanup:NO];

    //4
    [_parallaxNode addChild:bushes z:0
              parallaxRatio:ccp(0.2, 0)
             positionOffset:ccp(0,0)];
```

```
        [_parallaxNode addChild:trees z:1
                 parallaxRatio:ccp(0.5, 0)
                positionOffset:ccp(0,0)];
        [_parallaxNode addChild:ground z:2
                 parallaxRatio:ccp(1,0)
                positionOffset:ccp(0,0)];

        //5
        [self addChild:_parallaxNode z:zOrderTilemap];
    }
```

3. Finally, find the `update:` method and change the code to move `_parallaxNode` instead of `_tileMap`, as follows:

```
-(void)update:(CCTime)dt
{
    float distance = 150.0f * dt;

    CGPoint newPos = _parallaxNode.position;
    newPos.x = newPos.x - distance;

    CGSize viewSize = [CCDirector sharedDirector].viewSize;
    float endX = -1 * _worldSize + viewSize.width;

    if (newPos.x > endX )
        _parallaxNode.position = newPos;
}
```

4. Build and run the game. You should see that the ground is moving fast, the trees are a bit slower, and the bushes are moving even slower than the trees. This should look much more realistic.

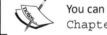

> You can find the final code for this chapter in the `Chapter_11/Cocohunt_11_Final` folder.

What just happened?

We just used one more class from the Cocos2D collection: the `CCParallaxNode` class. The `CCParallaxNode` class is a special node that moves its child nodes at a different speed, depending on the `parallaxRatio` parameter passed when you add the child node.

Let's see the code in the `addTilemap` method to see how we created `CCParallaxNode` and added the child nodes:

1. On this line, we got the reference for each separate layer we created in the tile map. You must remember that we created three different layers when we created the tile map: **Bushes**, **Trees**, and **Ground** layers. When we loaded the tile map using the `CCTiledMap` class, it created a separate `CCTiledMapLayer` node for each tile map layer. The `CCTiledMapLayer` node is a subclass of the `CCSpriteBatchNode` class and has a very similar function. It displays the tiles in one layer in one draw call. After the tile map is loaded, we can get a reference to the `CCTiledMapLayer` node directly, and further, we can use it outside and without the tile map.

> To use the `CCParallaxNode`, you don't necessarily have to use tile maps, you can add different child nodes, such as sprites, labels, and so on, and it will work with them. However, since we have a tile map with three different layers, it is much easier to use them.

2. At this point, we created the parallax node. The parallax node will manage the layers, so we needed the tile map just to load the layers; once loaded, we do not need the tile map. We could have loaded the tile map in the local variable, got the layers, added the layers to the parallax node, and let the tile map local variable be deallocated.
3. At this point, the layers are still children of the `CCTiledMap` instance. To be able to add them to `_parallaxNode`, we should remove them from `_tileMap` first, since the node can be a child of only one node at a time. However, it is important to remember that we don't want them to be deallocated. This is why we passed the `NO` parameter to the `removeFromParentAndCleanup:` method.
4. After the layers were removed from the tile map, we add them to the parallax node. Note that we specify different `parallaxRatio` and z-order. The `parallaxRatio` parameter will specify how fast the layer is moved compared to the parallax node movement. Also, note that this parameter takes a `CGPoint` since you might want to move up and down in addition (or instead) of moving left and right. We specified that the ground should move as fast as the parallax node, the trees should move at 50 percent speed and the bushes should move at 20 percent speed.

> The `parallaxRatio` values that we used are just sample values. You should pick actual values for your game depending on how deep the layer is. The deeper the layer, the less is its movement speed.

5. Finally, we added the parallax node to the scene. As I mentioned earlier, the tile map becomes unneeded at this point, so as you can see, we don't add it to the scene.

The code in the `update:` method didn't change much; we are simply moving `_parallaxNode` instead of `_tileMap`. However, we definitely can see the difference. Moving the parallax node doesn't move all the layers at the same speed, thus making it more realistic.

Have a go hero

To really see the tile map in action, you can create a much bigger tile map (for example, 200 – 300 tiles in width). A good idea is to add a few more layers with trees and bushes and assign them a different `parallaxRatio`. This will definitely help you to understand how the parallax node works.

Pop quiz – tile maps

Q1. What tile size should you use when creating a tile map if the images used to create tileset have a size of 128 x 128 pixels?

1. 64 x 64 px
2. 32 x 32 px
3. 128 x 128 px
4. 256 x 256 px

Q2. What units are used to specify map size when creating the tile map in the Tiled application?

1. Points
2. Pixels
3. Tiles
4. Inches

Q3. Can you rotate a single tile of the tile map (`CCTiledMap`) at runtime?

1. Yes
2. No

Summary

This chapter demonstrated the basics of creating and using tile maps in your games. Using tile maps is good, and in many cases, is the only way to create really large worlds for your game. Using techniques such as parallax scrolling will make your games much more realistic.

You will discover that tile maps come in different types and flavors. There are different tile sizes, orthogonal and isometric tile maps, and many ways to use layers. However, I'm sure that knowing the process from creating a tileset from separate images to the moment you load and use a completed tile map in your game will help you better understand the difference and even more importantly, the similarities between the different ways of creating and using tile maps.

In the final chapter of the book, we will review the additional features such as Game Center integration or In-App purchases you can add to your game. Also, we will review a list of tools and resources that will help you develop games.

Note that *Chapter 12, Standing Out – Integrating Game Center and In-App Purchases*, is a downloadable chapter that can be downloaded for free by visiting `http://www.packtpub.com/support` and following the instructions.

Pop Quiz Answers

Chapter 2, Hello Cocos2D

Pop quiz – hello quiz

Q1	2
Q2	1

Chapter 3, Cocos2D – Under the Hood

Pop quiz – under the hood

Q1	2
Q2	1
Q3	4

Chapter 4, Rendering Sprites

Pop quiz – sprites

Q1	3
Q2	3
Q3	4

Chapter 5, Starting the Action

Pop quiz – geometry and actions

Q1	2
Q2	2
Q3	4

Chapter 6, Rendering Text

Pop quiz – labels

Q1	2
Q2	2
Q3	4
Q4	3

Chapter 7, Animations and Particle Systems

Pop quiz – animations and particle systems

Q1	2
Q2	3

Chapter 8, Adding Sound Effects and Music

Pop quiz – playing audio

Q1	1
Q2	2
Q3	1

Chapter 9, User Interface and Navigation

Pop quiz

Q1	3
Q2	3
Q3	4

Chapter 10, Physics

Pop quiz – physics

Q1	2
Q2	1
Q3	2

Chapter 11, Working with Tile Maps

Pop quiz – tile maps

Q1	3
Q2	3
Q3	1

Index

D

E

F

G

H

I

J

K

L

M

N

O

P

R

U

X

Z

Thank you for buying
Learning iPhone Game Development with Cocos2D 3.0

About Packt Publishing

Packt, pronounced 'packed', published its first book "*Mastering phpMyAdmin for Effective MySQL Management*" in April 2004 and subsequently continued to specialize in publishing highly focused books on specific technologies and solutions.

Our books and publications share the experiences of your fellow IT professionals in adapting and customizing today's systems, applications, and frameworks. Our solution based books give you the knowledge and power to customize the software and technologies you're using to get the job done. Packt books are more specific and less general than the IT books you have seen in the past. Our unique business model allows us to bring you more focused information, giving you more of what you need to know, and less of what you don't.

Packt is a modern, yet unique publishing company, which focuses on producing quality, cutting-edge books for communities of developers, administrators, and newbies alike. For more information, please visit our website: `www.packtpub.com`.

About Packt Open Source

In 2010, Packt launched two new brands, Packt Open Source and Packt Enterprise, in order to continue its focus on specialization. This book is part of the Packt Open Source brand, home to books published on software built around Open Source licenses, and offering information to anybody from advanced developers to budding web designers. The Open Source brand also runs Packt's Open Source Royalty Scheme, by which Packt gives a royalty to each Open Source project about whose software a book is sold.

Writing for Packt

We welcome all inquiries from people who are interested in authoring. Book proposals should be sent to `author@packtpub.com`. If your book idea is still at an early stage and you would like to discuss it first before writing a formal book proposal, contact us; one of our commissioning editors will get in touch with you.

We're not just looking for published authors; if you have strong technical skills but no writing experience, our experienced editors can help you develop a writing career, or simply get some additional reward for your expertise.

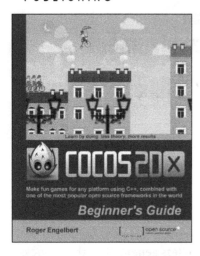

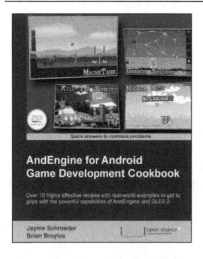

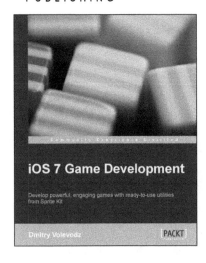

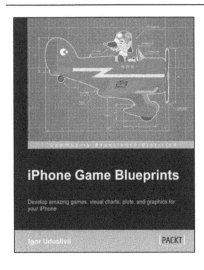

www.ingramcontent.com/pod-product-compliance
Lightning Source LLC
Chambersburg PA
CBHW081501050326
40690CB00015B/2874

* 9 7 8 1 7 8 2 1 6 0 1 4 4 *